AWS Certified Database – Specialty (DBS-C01) Certification Guide

A comprehensive guide to becoming an AWS Certified Database specialist

Kate Gawron

BIRMINGHAM—MUMBAI

AWS Certified Database – Specialty (DBS-C01) Certification Guide

Publishing Product Manager: Heramb Bhavsar

Senior Editor: Nazia Shaikh

Content Development Editor: Sean Lobo

Technical Editor: Rahul Limbachiya

Copy Editor: Safis Editing

Project Coordinator: Aparna Ravikumar Nair

Proofreader: Safis Editing

Indexer: Tejal Daruwale Soni

Production Designer: Nilesh Mohite

Marketing Coordinator: Nivedita Singh

First published: May 2022

Production reference: 1220422

Published by Packt Publishing Ltd.

Livery Place

35 Livery Street

Birmingham

B3 2PB, UK.

ISBN 978-1-80324-310-8

www.packt.com

Contributors

About the author

Kate Gawron is a full-time senior database consultant and part-time future racing driver. She was a competitor in Formula Woman, and she aspires to become a professional Gran Turismo (GT) racing driver. Away from the racetrack, Kate has worked with Oracle databases for 18 years and AWS for five years. She holds four AWS certifications, including the AWS Certified Database – Specialty certification as well as two professional Oracle qualifications. Kate currently works as a senior database architect, where she works with customers to migrate and refactor their databases to work optimally within the AWS cloud.

About the reviewers

Divaker Goel started his career in Bengaluru, India, a city that he loves. He has 18+ years' experience in various roles, including database administrator, team leader, and database manager. He has six AWS certificates and experience in multiple relational and NoSQL databases. Currently based out of Austin, Texas, he works for AWS as a database consultant. His role at AWS includes working with customers to identify their data store requirements and suggest one that best fits their use case, using his vast experience and knowledge. He also helps customers to deploy and configure databases on the cloud, migrate their on-premises data, set up monitoring, and optimize cloud usage. In his free time, he enjoys reading technical books and watching movies.

Amit Upadhyay is a certified AWS database specialist and database modernization consultant at Amazon Web Services, Inc. He received a Master's degree and PhD in computer science. He is focusing on developing a cost-effective cloud modernization framework program for industry leaders to make important financial decisions during their digital transformation journey. Amit has delivered strategies, solutions, designs, proof of concepts, and best practices for AWS high-tech, financial, and insurance customers, to refactor and modernize on a large scale commercial, complex, and mission-critical databases as AWS cloud databases, such as Amazon RDS, Aurora, Redshift, DynamoDB, ElastiCache, MemoryDB for Redis, DocumentDB, and Keyspace.

Shirin Ali Kanchwala is a database consultant for AWS who lives in Katy, Texas, with her family. Originally Canadian, Shirin brings unique experiences and approaches to every problem and solution. She works as a database migration specialist to help Amazon customers migrate their on-premises database workloads to the AWS cloud.

"To my daughter Zahabia. You are my rock. Thank you."

Table of Contents

3

Understanding AWS Infrastructure

Part 2: Workload-Specific Database Design

4

Relational Database Service

5

Amazon Aurora

6

Amazon DynamoDB

9

Amazon ElastiCache

Part 3: Deployment and Migration and Database Security

10

The AWS Schema Conversion Tool and AWS Database Migration Service

11
Database Task Automation

12
AWS Database Security

Part 4: Monitoring and Optimization

13
CloudWatch and Logging

14
Backup and Restore

15
Troubleshooting Tools and Techniques

Preface

Since 2009, when Amazon Web Services launched the first fully-managed cloud database solution (**Relational Database Service** (**RDS**), the desire for **Database Administrators** (**DBAs**) with a cloud skillset has grown rapidly. Today, the AWS Certified Database Specialty certification is one of the most sought after.

Many DBAs and other IT professionals are looking to expand their skills in cloud computing and cloud databases in particular. The differences between on-premises databases and the cloud are vast, and as such, many DBAs can find they have many barriers to overcome to adapt. This book is designed to help fill that gap. I have written this book in a practical style that will allow you the opportunity to understand both the theory of the subject and to experiment using cloud technology through hands-on workshops and labs.

By the end of this book, you will be able to comfortably explain the major concepts in cloud databases, from the basics to advanced performance tuning and troubleshooting. You will also be equipped with the practical skills to continue your learning beyond this book to develop additional skills to help progress your career. Ultimately, this book will provide you with the knowledge and skills to pass the AWS DBS-C01 exam confidently.

Who this book is for

This book is for anyone with a background working with databases who is looking to expand into the cloud or to develop their existing skills. However, this book assumes that you have a low base level of knowledge in databases or in AWS in general, and so dedicates the opening chapters to fundamental skills.

What this book covers

Chapter 1, AWS Certified Database – Specialty Exam Overview, introduces the exam topics and format and offers hints and tips to help you excel in the exam.

Chapter 2, Understanding Database Fundamentals, helps to give an overview of database technologies and explains the different types of databases, for readers not proficient in database technologies.

Chapter 3, Understanding AWS Infrastructure, offers a high-level view of AWS as a whole as well as a deeper dive into some of the AWS services you need to know.

Chapter 4, Relational Database Service, introduces the first of the AWS fully-managed database offerings.

Chapter 5, Amazon Aurora, explores a custom database service developed by AWS.

Chapter 6, Amazon DynamoDB, introduces our first NoSQL database offered by AWS.

Chapter 7, Redshift and DocumentDB, looks at two specialized database solutions, one for analytics and the other for storing data held within documents.

Chapter 8, Neptune, Quantum Ledger Database, and Timestream, explores three different database technologies: graphs, ledges, and time series.

Chapter 9, Amazon ElastiCache, looks at using a caching database to improve database and application performance.

Chapter 10, The AWS Schema Conversion Tool and AWS Database Migration Service, introduces knowledge around database migrations to AWS and changing the database engine.

Chapter 11, Database Task Automation, covers how to use automation skills and services to reduce manual work and enforce standards.

Chapter 12, AWS Database Security, dives deep into database security processes and procedures.

Chapter 13, CloudWatch and Logging, looks into how to monitor your databases and how to use CloudWatch to find anomalies and errors.

Chapter 14, Backup and Restore, offers a comprehensive explanation of AWS backup and restore techniques as well as theory on RTO and RPO.

Chapter 15, Troubleshooting Tools and Techniques, introduces troubleshooting techniques to help find and resolve common database errors.

Chapter 16, Exam Practice, provides an opportunity to test your new skills in a practice exam with questions very similar to the ones you will see in the exam.

Chapter 17, Answers, provides you with all the answers to the questions at the end of every chapter and their explanations.

To get the most out of this book

To complete the hands-on sections of this book, you will need an AWS account complete with root access. *Chapter 1, AWS Certified Database – Specialty Exam Overview*, contains instructions on how to set up your account in the best way. You will also need some software to allow you to connect to databases such as SQL Developer or MySQL Workbench.

Software/hardware covered in the book	Operating system requirements
SQL Developer	Windows, macOS, or Linux
MySQL Workbench	Windows, macOS, or Linux
AWS CLI	Windows, macOS, or Linux

If you are using the digital version of this book, we advise you to type the code yourself or access the code from the book's GitHub repository (a link is available in the next section). Doing so will help you avoid any potential errors related to the copying and pasting of code.

Each chapter may have different requirements so please review the *Technical requirements* section at the start of each chapter.

Download the example code files

You can download the example code files for this book from GitHub at `https://github.com/PacktPublishing/AWS-Certified-Database---Specialty-DBS-C01-Certification`. If there's an update to the code, it will be updated in the GitHub repository.

We also have other code bundles from our rich catalog of books and videos available at `https://github.com/PacktPublishing/`. Check them out!

Download the color images

We also provide a PDF file that has color images of the screenshots and diagrams used in this book. You can download it here: `https://static.packt-cdn.com/downloads/9781803243108_ColorImages.pdf`.

Conventions used

There are a number of text conventions used throughout this book.

`Code in text`: Indicates code words in text, database table names, folder names, filenames, file extensions, pathnames, dummy URLs, user input, and Twitter handles. Here is an example: "Mount the downloaded `WebStorm-10*.dmg` disk image file as another disk in your system."

A block of code is set as follows:

```
html, body, #map {
  height: 100%;
  margin: 0;
  padding: 0
}
```

When we wish to draw your attention to a particular part of a code block, the relevant lines or items are set in bold:

```
[default]
exten => s,1,Dial(Zap/1|30)
exten => s,2,Voicemail(u100)
exten => s,102,Voicemail(b100)
exten => i,1,Voicemail(s0)
```

Any command-line input or output is written as follows:

```
$ mkdir css
$ cd css
```

Bold: Indicates a new term, an important word, or words that you see onscreen. For instance, words in menus or dialog boxes appear in **bold**. Here is an example: "Select **System info** from the **Administration** panel."

> **Tips or Important notes**
> Appear like this.

Get in touch

Feedback from our readers is always welcome.

General feedback: If you have questions about any aspect of this book, email us at `customercare@packtpub.com` and mention the book title in the subject of your message.

Errata: Although we have taken every care to ensure the accuracy of our content, mistakes do happen. If you have found a mistake in this book, we would be grateful if you would report this to us. Please visit `www.packtpub.com/support/errata` and fill in the form.

Piracy: If you come across any illegal copies of our works in any form on the internet, we would be grateful if you would provide us with the location address or website name. Please contact us at `copyright@packt.com` with a link to the material.

If you are interested in becoming an author: If there is a topic that you have expertise in and you are interested in either writing or contributing to a book, please visit `authors.packtpub.com`.

Share Your Thoughts

Once you've read *AWS Certified Database - Specialty (DBS-C01) Certification Guide*, we'd love to hear your thoughts! Scan the QR code below to go straight to the Amazon review page for this book and share your feedback.

`https://packt.link/r/1-803-24310-4`

Your review is important to us and the tech community and will help us make sure we're delivering excellent quality content.

Part 1: Introduction to Databases on AWS

This section provides an overview of the AWS Database Specialty exam. It also introduces database fundamentals and ensures you have a good base level of database knowledge before delving deeper into AWS-specific concepts.

This section includes the following chapters:

- *Chapter 1, AWS Certified Database – Specialty Exam Overview*
- *Chapter 2, Understanding Database Fundamentals*
- *Chapter 3, Understanding AWS Infrastructure*

1
AWS Certified Database – Specialty Overview

The AWS certifications are some of the most prized in the IT industry. The specialty level exams demonstrate a high level of knowledge about the chosen subject, and obtaining such as certification can lead to increased salaries, better career options, and recognition. The first step on this path is to begin learning all the skills and techniques that will be covered in the exam and this book aims to be a comprehensive guide that will aid you greatly during your preparation.

Before we start studying the technical areas covered in the exam, it is worthwhile discussing the exam format and what types of questions will be asked. You can use this information to aid your learning as you progress through this book. You will learn how the exam works, how long you have to complete it, and how many questions there will be. You'll then learn the specific domains in the exam and the likely number of questions on each domain before learning some useful exam tips to guide you in your approach during the exam to maximize your marks.

In this chapter, we are going to cover the following topics:

- Exam format
- Exam domains
- Database security
- Exam tips

First, let's look at the exam format itself so you know what to expect when you book the AWS Certified Database – Specialty exam to when you earn that pass!

Exam format

All AWS exams are taken electronically either at a test center or remotely via an online proctoring session.

The exam lasts 180 minutes and there will be 65 questions.

The pass mark will vary slightly between each exam, but the minimum will always be 750 out of 1000. This variation is due to some questions being rated as more or less difficult than the default, so they are weighted for fairness. As a rough guide, a pass would be obtained by answering 50 questions correctly.

You are *not* penalized for incorrect answers, so you should attempt to answer all questions even if you do not know the answer.

The exam starts with a short opening section where you need to confirm your details, the exam you are taking, and the copyright that you may not share the exam questions. Once this is done, you will be given a brief overview of the exam and how to navigate through the screens.

The majority of the questions are situational style, requiring you to be able to interpret the question to work out the correct answer.

The questions are all multiple choice with two different styles:

- **Multiple choice**: Has one correct answer and three incorrect answers.
- **Multiple answer**: Has two or more correct answers out of five or more options. The question will state how many answers are expected.

You can mark each question for review at the end.

At the end of the exam, there is a survey about the exam and your preparation for it. You must complete this before receiving your exam result.

You will receive your pass or fail result immediately once you complete the survey, but you will not receive your full results and the score achieved until it has been verified. This verification normally takes 3 working days. Once the verification has been completed, you will receive an email to your registered address and you will be able to obtain your full score report, showing how well you performed on each domain. This is especially useful if you do not meet the passing grade as you will be given areas to focus your studies on for the next attempt.

Now that you understand what happens after you book and take the exam, let's look at what you'll need to know to obtain a passing grade. In the next section, we are going to look at the exam domains or areas that will need to be covered.

Exam domains

The **AWS Certified Database – Specialty (DBS-C01)** exam is split into five high-level topics covering a wide range of subjects. These are broken down as follows:

Domain	Percentage
Workload-Specific Database Design	26%
Deployment and Migration	20%
Management and Operations	18%
Monitoring and Troubleshooting	18%
Database Security	18%
TOTAL	100%

Figure 1.1 – Table showing the percentage weighting for the five domains in the exam

The percentage refers to the most likely number of questions that will be asked in the exam. You can expect a breakdown similar to the following:

Domain	Questions
Workload-Specific Database Design	17
Deployment and Migration	13
Management and Operations	12
Monitoring and Troubleshooting	12
Database Security	11
TOTAL	65

Figure 1.2 – Table showing the approximate number of questions for each domain in the exam

AWS offers a high-level description of each domain, but it doesn't fully explain all the technologies, solutions, and services you'll need to know in order to pass the exam. In the next few sections, we are going to look in more depth at what each domain really means and the key topics within it. This can be used to help guide you while you study and prepare for the exam. Let's now look at each domain in detail.

Workload-specific database design

Workload-specific database design can also sometimes be referred to as **purpose-built databases**. It means that before choosing which database to use, you look closely at the type of data that will be stored and how the application or users access it.

To succeed in this domain, you will need to know how to build a **scalable** and **resilient** database using the right database engine for the use case and to understand how to use AWS infrastructure to protect it from failures.

In order to succeed in this domain, you will need to:

- Know how to build a *scalable* and *resilient* database using the right database engine for the use case and to understand how to use AWS infrastructure to protect it from failures.
- Know the features that can be used to increase the *performance* of your databases, and which work for each different database type and use case.
- Understand and calculate the *costs* of different database solutions and how you can help to optimize costs while meeting the *performance* and *resilience* requirements of the use case.

Under this domain, the following topics will be covered:

- Selecting appropriate database services for specific types of data and workloads
- Determining strategies for disaster recovery and high availability
- Designing database solutions for performance, compliance, and scalability
- Comparing the costs of database solutions

In the following sections we will cover every topic in detail.

Selecting appropriate database services for specific types of data and workloads

This area focuses on the different database engines AWS supports and the options available for them.

You will need to know about all of the database engines that AWS offers and versions, what features are available for each, and how to apply those to a specific use case. We will spend time studying these in depth later in this book as knowing these thoroughly will be the best way to pass the exam.

Determining strategies for disaster recovery and high availability

Disaster recovery and high availability are critical topics in the exam. You will need to understand terms such as **Multi-AZ, read replicas, cross-region, and backup and restore techniques**, all of which will be covered in depth throughout this book.

You will need to know how to use these tools correctly for different database engines to meet the use case.

Designing database solutions for performance, compliance, and scalability

Each different database offers different ways to scale. You will need to understand **horizontal versus vertical scaling** and how that affects database design.

You will need to know different **compliance standards** and how AWS uses tools and services to meet them.

Comparing the costs of database solutions

For this domain, you will need to understand the different **pricing models** AWS uses for each database type, and you will learn the types of instances available as well as how pricing plans work for **serverless databases**.

You will need to be able to work out which database type is most **cost-effective** for your given use case.

Deployment and migration

The second domain you will be tested on is **deployment and migration**. This will cover creating different databases both via the **console** and the **command line** and the options available, such as cloning. For the migration, you will need to know AWS best practices on moving data to AWS and how to use the tools offered for migrations.

Under this domain, the following topics will be covered:

- Automating database solution deployments
- Determining data preparation and migration strategies
- Executing and validating data migration

We will begin by looking more closely at each topic.

Automating database solution deployments

Automation is the key to this area, and you will need to know the **AWS automation tools** and how to use them.

You will also need to know the common commands to create databases **programmatically**.

Determining data preparation and migration strategies

For this area, you will need to understand and explain the different methods of **migrating data** to AWS and the options available. This section focuses on understanding and assessing the current database and producing a strategy for the migration.

You will need to understand and explain the different methods of migrating data to AWS and the options available.

Executing and validating data migration

This area covers the migration steps and tools available to use on AWS. You will be tested on your understanding of **data validation** techniques and how AWS manages this.

You will need to understand how to monitor data migration and how to tune and optimize it.

Management and operations

Once you have migrated your data to AWS, you now need to know how to manage and operate the databases. You will need to understand **backup and restore** technologies, **maintenance tasks** and **windows**, and how to work with **database options**.

The topics covered in this domain are the following:

- Determining maintenance tasks and processes
- Determining backup and restore strategies
- Managing the operational environment of a database solution

Next, we will study these topics in detail.

Determining maintenance tasks and processes

AWS uses **maintenance windows** to allow their teams to carry out work in the background. You will need to understand how this works, what can happen during them, and how to use them for your own maintenance strategies.

Determining backup and restore strategies

This area focuses on **backup strategies** rather than the underlying technology. You will need to understand and describe terms such as **RTO** and **RPO** and know how to utilize different AWS services to meet the needs of the use case. You will need to know the fastest and most efficient options for recovering from the failure of different databases.

Managing the operational environment of a database solution

The **operational environment** includes areas such as **parameters** and **options** that can be enabled.

You will need to understand how to use these as well as best practices for consistency for large database estates.

Monitoring and troubleshooting

If your database starts to underperform or to give errors, you need to be able to identify the problem and understand **common troubleshooting techniques**. This domain focuses on database **metrics**, diagnosing faults, and how to resolve them quickly, as well as configuring **alerting**.

The topics covered in this domain are the following:

- Determining monitoring and alerting strategies
- Troubleshooting and resolving common database issues
- Optimizing database performance

Next, we will study these topics in detail.

Determining monitoring and alerting strategies

Working with AWS tools to create an **alerting strategy** that meets the needs of the use case is critical for all database deployments.

You will need to know the standard **metrics** that AWS uses and how to configure these for alerting purposes.

Troubleshooting and resolving common database issues

AWS databases have multiple **logs** to write data. You will need to know the different logs and which one to use for each problem.

You will need to understand to use the information in the logs to resolve common database problems such as **space issues** or **error messages**.

Optimizing database performance

In this area, you will need to learn how to read AWS graphs showing **database metrics** and what actions to take if there are issues.

You will need to understand how the different tools can offer deeper *insights* into the performance of the database to help analyze the problem.

Database security

The final domain will test your understanding of database security covering all aspects, from **access** and **audit controls** to **patching** for security fixes. This domain also covers **encryption** techniques, both of the stored data and in transit.

The topics covered in this domain are the following:

- Encrypting data at rest and in transit
- Evaluating auditing solutions
- Determining access control and authentication mechanisms
- Recognizing potential security vulnerabilities within database solutions

Now, let's begin to study these topics.

Encrypting data at rest and in transit

Encryption is used to make it harder for anyone unauthorized to see the data stored or in transit. You will need to know how to work with encryption at the database layer and how to encrypt connections between the application and the database.

Evaluating auditing solutions

Auditing is used to keep a record of actions made within a database, but it can cause performance issues if not configured correctly.

You will need to understand different **auditing techniques** and the tools AWS provides to assist.

Determining access control and authentication mechanisms

Databases in AWS have multiple methods for access that differ depending on the database. AWS also has its own built-in **identity management service** that can be used to restrict or grant database access.

You will need to know which methods work with which databases and how to configure and *administrate logins* using different methods.

Recognizing potential security vulnerabilities within database solutions

This area focuses on patching and why this is done. It also expects you to understand what your responsibilities are in terms of securing your own databases and what areas are the responsibility of AWS.

You will need to understand the **AWS shared responsibility model** as well as understand the patching strategies offered by AWS.

Exam tips

We've covered the format of the exam (the duration of the exam, how many questions there are) and we've looked in depth at the domains and topics you will be tested on, so you should be confident in what you need to study to be able to pass the exam.

However, knowing some tips around how to tackle the exam can make a difference in terms of a pass or fail, so it's worth taking some time to think about a strategy for the exam so that you can maximize your chances of earning that pass.

Let's take a look at a sample question:

A company's online application stores order transactions in an Amazon RDS for a MySQL database. The database has run out of available storage and the application is currently unable to take orders.

Which action should a database specialist take to resolve the issue in the shortest amount of time?

1. Configure a read replica in a different AZ with more storage space.
2. Create a new DB instance with more storage space from the latest backup.
3. Change the DB instance status from `STORAGE_FULL` to `AVAILABLE`.
4. Add additional storage space to the DB instance using the `ModifyDBInstance` action.

Follow this approach to answer the question:

To begin, you should seek to understand what the question is really asking you, and what tools and services are in scope? For this question, these are the topics you need to consider:

- **Amazon RDS for MySQL**
- **Storage**

Now, you can clearly see the database technology in use that will help work out the correct answers, but first, let's eliminate the wrong ones.

For a large number of questions, at least one of the answers is obviously incorrect. If you can quickly identify the ones that cannot be correct and then make an educated guess between the remaining ones, you are likely to get a few more questions right, which could make the difference between a pass and a fail.

Once you've worked through this book, hopefully, you should quickly be able to discount answers *1* and *3*. *3* is wrong because you cannot modify an instance status in that way, and *1* because adding a read replica does not solve the full storage problem.

That now leaves us with just two possible correct answers. If, at this point, you are not certain of the answer, you have still *doubled* your odds of guessing correctly.

In general, once you have removed the obviously incorrect answers, the ones you are left with would both work, but one meets the use case of the question more closely than the other.

The final step is to search the question for important keywords such as:

- **Shortest time**
- **Fastest**
- **Most cost-efficient**
- **Simplest**

Our question uses the phrase **'shortest amount of time'**. We can use this additional information to help us decide on the correct answer. Creating a new database instance will take a lot longer than adding more storage to our existing one, and therefore the correct answer is *4*.

You may find many questions you can simply answer without using this technique, but following this strategy on the questions you do not know will really make a difference to your final score.

To summarize the steps you should take for answering questions during the exam:

1. Identify the technologies and solutions being referred to in the question.
2. Remove answers that cannot be correct based on those technologies.

Identify the keywords in the question to help you work out the best answer from among the ones remaining. Now that you've learned the best techniques and tips to take into the exam, you should have a lot more confidence and a greater chance of success.

Summary

In this chapter, you have learned about the format the exam will take, including how many questions there will be and how long you have to answer them. We've also looked at how the exam is graded and what you need to do to earn a pass grade.

You should now know all the different topics that will be covered in the exam, which will be used to help guide your learning through this book.

And finally, we took some time to go over exam tips and techniques to help you maximize your success when you take the exam.

This information is critical for the exam, both in terms of knowing what areas to study, and knowing how best to tackle the exam. When you are unsure of an answer, the exam tips given in this chapter will be very valuable in helping you work out the most likely options.

The next chapter will start looking at the AWS infrastructure in which you will incorporate and develop databases, and the exam will include questions that will expect you to know the fundamentals of AWS beyond databases.

2
Understanding Database Fundamentals

Before we start looking at specific AWS database technologies and services, it's important to understand the different types of databases that are available and what type of **workloads** you should consider putting into each database. We are doing this so that when we start learning about the various AWS services, you will understand how and why there are so many different types and options.

We will be studying how databases differ between running them on-premises and in the cloud in terms of **access**, **administration**, and **maintenance**. These topics will appear in the exam, so being able to define the differences is important.

If you already have a database background and are comfortable with the different database types and how they work, please feel free to skip this chapter and go straight to *Chapter 3, Understanding AWS Infrastructure*. But if you want to go ahead and learn about the differences, then stick around until the end of this chapter. In this chapter, you will learn how to describe the key differences between on-premises and cloud databases and describe the different types of databases and when to use them. You will also learn how to define the benefits of a cloud database compared to an on-premises database and understand the compromises cloud databases entail.

In particular, we will be covering the following main topics:

- On-premises versus cloud databases
- SQL databases versus NoSQL
- Relational database management systems
- Key-value and document databases
- Graph and ledger databases

Now, let's begin by comparing on-premises databases to cloud databases and learn about some of the key differences that we will need to know for the **AWS Certified Database – Specialty (DBS-C01)** exam.

On-premises versus cloud databases

An **on-premises database** could be defined as follows:

> *"A database that is owned, operated, and maintained by the customer within a location that they control and have full autonomy over the database and underlying servers and networking components. This can be a server room in their office or a rented cabinet within a shared data center that the customer has full and direct access to."*

With an on-premises database, everything is done internally, from installation and implementation to running the database every day. Maintenance, security, and updates also need to be taken care of in-house. You will need to arrange for when the software will be purchased before it is installed on your servers. The customer will assume complete ownership and control, even if this is via a management company or service provider.

A **cloud database** could be defined as follows:

> *"A database that is owned, operated, and maintained by the customer within a location that they do not control and do not have full autonomy over the database and the underlying servers and networking components. This will often be a virtual machine running on a group of shared servers that the customer will have no direct access to."*

Cloud computing is the ability to provision, run, and maintain an on-demand computer system, including its servers, infrastructure, databases, and other applications. These usually require no or minimal day-to-day management of the underlying servers or network and allow the customer to focus on their applications. You can create a new database from scratch in minutes with no previous database knowledge. There are options available for utilizing a subscription model so that, in exchange for a monthly or yearly fee, the chosen **cloud provider** maintains servers, networks, and software for you. There are options for a dedicated private cloud that allows customers to use the platform completely, with no shared resources, and allows for additional customization, backup controls, and upgrades. With a shared cloud, multiple tenants share the underlying servers, but with strict controls over security and the privacy of data. As such, far fewer customizations can be made, but the costs are typically lower.

There are five main areas you will need to be aware of for the exam:

- **Scalability**: How can a database grow and shrink to handle the load expected of it?
- **Costs**: How do the costs of running a database in the cloud differ from an on-premises database?
- **Security and Access**: What security considerations need to be made when you're using a cloud database and how do you access it?
- **Compliance**: How can you stay compliant with any legal obligations when you're using a cloud database? Is this different for an on-premises database?
- **Performance and Reliability**: How does a cloud database maintain reliability compared to an on-premises database?

In this section, you will learn how to do the following:

- Describe the key differences between an on-premises database and the cloud.
- Explain the terms scalability, security, reliability, and compliance from a database perspective.
- Describe the key benefits of a cloud database and the key benefits of an on-premises database.

Let's begin by looking at our first topic – scalability – and learning how to describe the different methods that are used by cloud databases compared to on-premises databases.

Scalability

The ability to scale up and add resources quickly and easily as your requirements change is one of the biggest advantages of a cloud-based solution.

A cloud-based database would be able to add and remove resources such as CPU or memory rapidly, even programmatically to react to the changing requirements of the databases. On-premises, this would be extremely difficult, if not impossible, to achieve. The cloud also offers much faster addition of storage, so there is less of a requirement to plan growth patterns over long periods as you can simply attach further disk space as required. Again, this can even be set to grow automatically at certain usage thresholds. In contrast, on-premises, you often need to provide growth metrics for several years to ensure the database has sufficient disk space to allow it to operate for a long time, which can be inefficient as well as expensive.

The key differences between cloud databases and on-premises for *scalability* are as follows:

- Cloud databases can scale both up and down rapidly, allowing for changing requirements.
- Cloud databases do not need to be equipped with any greater storage than is required at the current time as more can easily be added.
- On-premises databases can share a server more easily to optimize resources.

Next, we will learn about how the costs differ between the cloud and on-premises.

Costs

One of the main differences between cloud databases is **cost management**. The cloud is not always a cheaper option, but the costs are easier to recognize and account for compared to on-premises. For example, when you're running a database on an on-premises server, the true cost of that system includes things such as the running costs for the data center, which can be hard to evaluate. On the cloud, all of those costs are included in the price that's paid. Costs are also often lower on the cloud as a result of the scalability provided. As we mentioned previously, on-premises databases are often over-resourced at the start of their life cycle as it can be difficult and time-consuming to change them later on. On the cloud, you would more accurately resource the database for its current workload and performance requirements with the knowledge you can easily change this later on, thereby saving money on both resources and, potentially, database licensing. The cloud also offers a **pay-as-you-go model**, where you can provision resources only when you need them.

The key differences between cloud databases and on-premises for *costs* are as follows:

- Cloud databases have clearly defined costs, including day-to-day running costs, which can be hidden when you're using on-premises databases.
- On-premises databases have typically fixed costs, which can make financial planning easier and more predictable as opposed to cloud databases, which can change from month to month.

Now, let's look at the differences between on-premises and the cloud in terms of security and access.

Security and access

One of the biggest areas of concern around migrating to the cloud is **security**. When moving to a cloud-based database, you need to consider whether the security and data separation you are being offered meets the needs of the data you will be storing. Cloud systems are made up of a mesh of servers and as a result, you will be sharing an underlying server with other databases. There are strict controls in place to ensure that your section of the server cannot be affected or accessed by another party, but for some, this concern is too high. Security in AWS follows a shared responsibility model where AWS takes responsibility for the cloud but the customer takes responsibility for the data in the cloud.

Given that you are using shared resources, the access you have to the server itself is also restricted. For example, you cannot have full root access to any of the managed services offered and you cannot have access to any virtual machine management tools within the cloud. This lack of control and inability to change certain settings on your servers or databases can cause compatibility issues, as well as further security concerns. For fully managed databases, you have no access to the servers running the database; all access must be through the database itself. This can cause significant changes to how you maintain and run the databases.

To date, there have been no breaches on any of the major cloud providers where a customer's data has been exposed due to a cloud provider's setup; in other words, *there have been no data security breaches where the cloud provider was at fault*, but there have been many breaches where the customer was. One of the largest breaches to date was *Capital One* (a large credit card company). who had a database containing the financial data of over 106 million customers fraudulently accessed by hackers. The root cause of the hack was a misconfigured firewall running in the cloud.

The key differences between cloud databases and on-premises for *security and access* are as follows:

- On-premises databases give you full control over the servers and network, allowing you to ensure your security standards are met.
- Cloud databases rely on the cloud provider maintaining their security standards on the servers and network, which can free the customer to focus on the database security solely and can simplify deployments.
- Cloud databases can be encrypted by default and can use a password and key management service to store database credentials securely without exposing them in plain text.

Now that we've learned about security and access, let's look at the next key area where there are big differences between on-premises and the cloud: compliance.

Compliance

There are regulatory controls that most companies need to abide by, whether they are legal requirements such as **General Data Protection Regulations** (**GDPR**) or industry-specific requirements such as **Health Insurance Portability and Accountability Act** (**HIPAA**) and **Provisional FedRAMP**. To meet these government and industry regulations, it is imperative that companies remain **compliant** and can demonstrate to an auditor that all their databases meet these rules. This can easily be achieved if all the data is maintained in-house, where you have full control over the data, servers, and network. However, with a cloud database, where you cannot show complete control of all the servers and networks, this can be more challenging.

If you decide to deploy a cloud-based solution, you must ensure that the cloud provider meets the requirements of the regulatory body. This information is publicly available for all the major cloud providers so that you can check and ensure the solution meets the requirements. Given the growth of cloud-based applications and databases, the majority of recognized compliance regulations now accept cloud-based solutions as compliant, so long as specific rules on deployment and configuration are followed. So, the issue of compliance for cloud-based databases is diminishing.

The key differences between cloud databases and on-premises for *compliance* are as follows:

- On-premises databases are fully under the customer's control, so you, as the customer, can ensure they meet all the required compliance standards.
- Cloud databases now meet most common regulation and compliance standards by default, allowing the customer to focus on their database rather than the compliance of the server and the network.

Now, let's learn about how performance and reliability compare between on-premises databases and cloud databases.

Performance and reliability

The **reliability** and **availability** of your data are critical. With on-premises, while you have full control over the servers and the storage, you are likely going to be limited when it comes to how many copies of the data you can keep or how many spare servers you have available in case one stops working. Cloud providers will offer an almost unlimited number of servers for your application and database, so if one were to fail, it would be moved automatically, almost immediately reducing any downtime. You can also ensure your data is saved in multiple locations within the cloud, again reducing the likelihood of a catastrophic data loss occurring to almost zero, even if a cloud data center were to go offline.

With on-premises systems, you can decide what maintenance windows you have. You can also decide if you patch or upgrade your systems and when that is done. On the cloud, these are determined for you, and you cannot always opt out of upgrades once your system version is no longer supported.

So, on the cloud, you will find that you have greater reliability in terms of your database and likely faster recovery times if you do suffer an outage, but that you have less control over patching or maintenance windows as a consequence.

The key differences between cloud databases and on-premises for *performance and reliability* are as follows:

- On-premises databases give you full control over maintenance windows and patching so that you can fully control any planned outages.
- Cloud databases can recover very quickly from any failures, thus reducing any unplanned downtime.

- Cloud databases offer multiple locations to save your data, minimizing the risk of any data loss, which, in turn, can reduce RPO and RTO and improve your business continuity planning.

With that, we've learned about the key differences between on-premises databases and cloud databases, which means you can now explain the benefits between them in terms of the following:

- Scalability
- Costs
- Security and access
- Compliance
- Performance and reliability

Now, let's look at the different types of databases that cloud providers typically support, starting with SQL databases versus NoSQL.

SQL databases versus NoSQL

One of the largest decisions to make when planning a new database deployment is whether to use a **Structured Query Language** (**SQL**) or **Not only SQL** (**NoSQL**) database. These two types of databases differ greatly and making the wrong choice can compromise the performance and the ability of your application to function.

First, let's discuss the key features of both database types before doing a deep comparison of both so that you can decide between them.

SQL databases

SQL databases are designed to excel in storing structured data. They can carry out complex querying and they commonly store the minimum data possible by reducing any duplication of the data in a table in a process known as **normalization**. Normalized data means that accessing it often requires complex joins of different tables.

Normalized data would look similar to this:

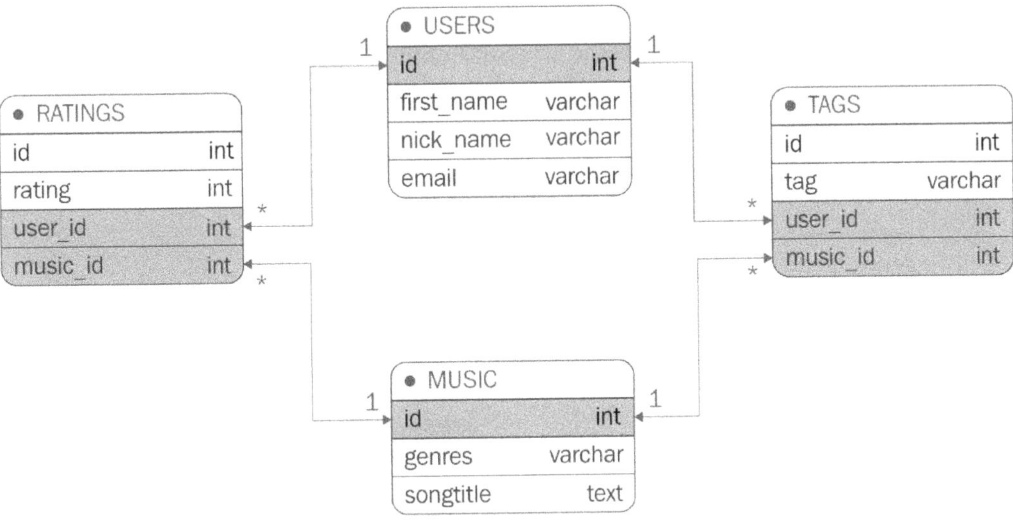

Figure 2.1 – RDBMS table structure

These tables only contain the specific columns that apply to them, so `users` only contains columns about the user and nothing about movies or ratings. The `movies` table is similar and only contains data about movies. The other two tables (`tags` and `ratings`) contain pointers back to the `users` and `movies` tables. If you wanted to get the `first_name` parameter of a user who gave a 5-star rating to a specific movie, you would have to join the three tables to retrieve this information as it is not stored in one place. For large datasets, you can see that the performance would be poor as the database has to not only obtain the data from three different locations but also combine that data before passing the results back to the user. This technique optimizes storage at the cost of performance on larger databases.

SQL databases comply with **atmoicity**, **consistency**, **isolation**, and **durability** (**ACID**) guarantees and are a good choice for *transactional data*, where data loss must be minimized and accuracy must be maintained. SQL databases are typically based on a single-node design, where adding additional nodes to scale horizontally is complex and expensive.

SQL databases sacrifice the speed and performance of large datasets in favor of consistency and durability. As a result, it is common to see performance issues and slowdowns when you're working with data in the range of millions of records.

There are two main types of SQL database that we will learn about in more detail later in this chapter:

- **Row-oriented** (relational or **online transaction processing (OLTP)**)
- **Column-orientated** (analytical or **online analytic processing (OLAP)**)

These two types of SQL databases are shown in the following diagram:

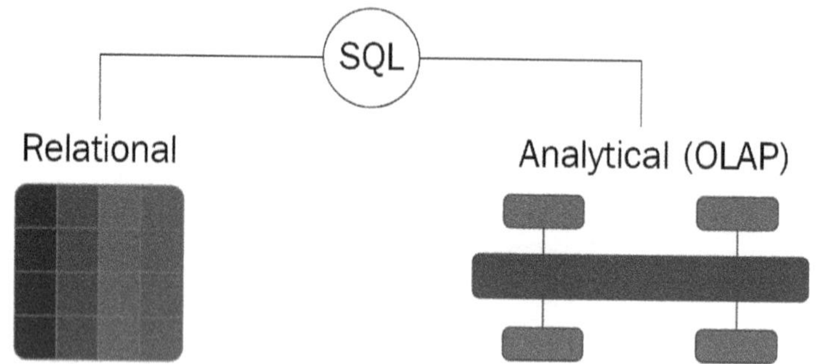

Figure 2.2 – Relational database versus an analytical or columnar database

Now, let's look at NoSQL databases to see how they differ from SQL databases.

NoSQL databases

NoSQL databases are designed for storing semi-structured or non-structured data as they don't enforce a concrete schema for tables. You can add data attributes when needed without changing the structure of the entire table. Since no particular structure is enforced by the database, they are not good at join queries. NoSQL databases support data to be stored in a similar format in which it will be most commonly accessed. The database structure is often defined by looking at the application code that will be used to access it and mimicking the same structure.

NoSQL databases can scale horizontally with ease, and they are designed to handle **partitioning** and **sharding**. NoSQL databases are commonly used when you need extremely fast response times for large amounts of data. NoSQL databases achieve this speed by compromising consistency and referential integrity with most NoSQL databases using an eventual consistency model. What this means is that there is a greater risk of data loss or inconsistent results being returned using a NoSQL database.

There are multiple types of NoSQL databases, each of which is designed for a different use case:

- **Key-value databases**
- **Document databases**
- **Column-oriented and analytics databases**
- **Graph databases**

The following diagram provides an overview of the different types of NoSQL databases:

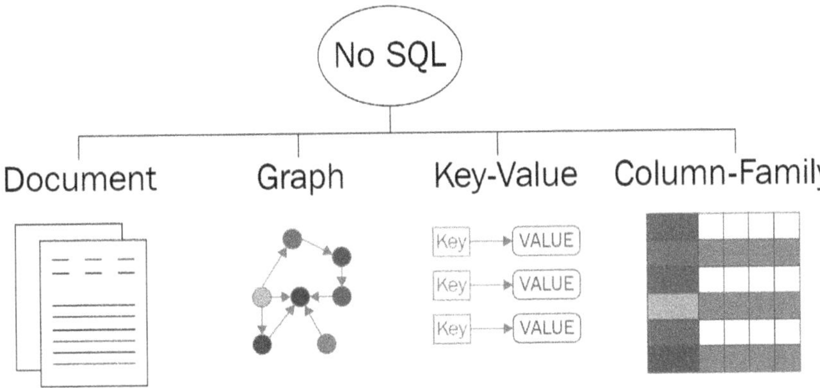

Figure 2.3 – The four main NoSQL database types

Now that we've learned about the two main database models – NoSQL and SQL – let's take a closer look at the different types within those categories, starting with relational database management systems.

Relational database management systems

SQL or RDBMS databases have two main types, which describe the way data is stored on disk:

- **Row-orientated**
- **Column-orientated**

The different methods of storing the data and how it is arranged will offer very different performance patterns (that is, fast at some things but slow at others), and knowing about the right type to use can greatly improve the performance of your application. While both database types may appear very similar on the surface, they are quite different under the hood.

In the exam, there may be a question around a customer use case and asking which database would be the best fit.

First, let's look at row-orientated, which is the more common database system.

Row-orientated databases

In a row-orientated database, the data is stored in tables in normalized form (we discussed this in the *SQL databases* section) with links or keys between them.

Row-orientated databases store the data in continuous blocks, with each row following on from the next. Let's look at an example table:

users		
first_name	last_name	age
John	Smith	36
Alex	Scott	32
Sam	Thomas	29

Figure 2.4 – A table for storing user data

Now, let's look at how this would be stored on disk:

John	Smith	36	Alex	Scott	32	Sam	Thomas	29

Figure 2.5 – Table rows stored in a line

As you can see, the data is stored in complete rows, one after another. If we were to add a new row to this table, it would be very fast for the database to do so as it simply finds the last row on the disk and adds the new data. Similarly, for reads, where you want to return the majority of the columns from each row, this will be returned efficiently. However, problems could occur if you wanted to only return one column from a table but for a large number of rows. For example, let's say you wanted to calculate the average age of all users. Here, you'd need to read a large number of blocks of data as the information you need is stored scattered across many areas of the disk. The following diagram shows that you would need to read from three different areas of the disk for just one query:

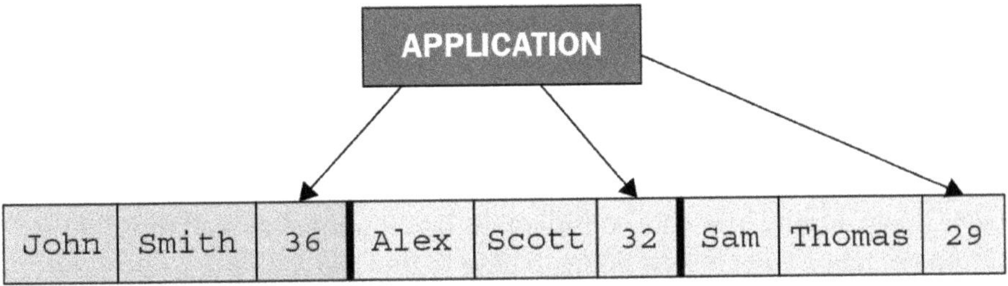

Figure 2.6 – Disk reads for a single column query

So, to summarize, we know the following about row-orientated databases:

- They are quick at writing data.
- They are efficient at retrieving data when you need the majority of the row data to be returned.
- They are inefficient when you want single columns.

Due to this behavior, a row-orientated database is commonly used for applications where there is a similar number of reads and writes and where you will use a lot of the data in each row rather than just a single column. These databases are often called **online transactional processing** databases or **OLTP** databases.

For a use case where you will be working with mostly single columns of data, you can look at column orientated or **online analytic processing** (**OLAP**) systems.

Column-orientated databases

Just like the row-orientated databases, these databases use tables that are often normalized and have links or keys between them. The difference is how the data is stored on disk.

Let's consider the same table that was shown in the preceding section – that is, *Figure 2.4*. Here, we can see the same data being stored on disk but in a column-oriented database:

Figure 2.7 – Table rows stored in a line

As you can see, this time, the data is in column groups, with each entry from each column being placed together rather than each row. If we were to add a new row to our table, it would become much more complex. Now, instead of finding the end of the last row and adding the new data there, our database needs to either find a gap on the disk in the same area as the other columns, or it needs to move everything around to make it fit. This is going to slow down adding new data considerably. If you wanted to read most of the columns from the table, you are now going to have to jump to multiple areas of the disk – a different one for each column – which, again, can cause performance problems.

However, column-orientated databases are very efficient at returning aggregate data from one or two columns, such as getting the average age of our users. Now, it just needs to go to one area of the disk and retrieve that. The following diagram shows how quick and efficient a column-orientated database is at retrieving single columns:

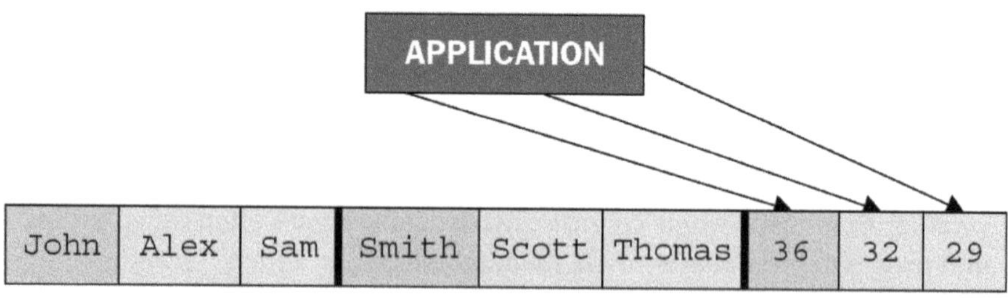

Figure 2.8 – Disk reads for a single column query

To summarize, we know the following about column-orientated databases:

- They are slow at writing data.
- They are inefficient at retrieving data when you need the majority of the row data to be returned.
- They are efficient when you want single columns.

Now, let's look at a different type of database engine – key-value databases.

Key-value and document databases

We are now going to look at key-value and document databases. These are both NoSQL databases, but they have different use cases:

- **Key-value databases** have a unique key (such as a primary key) and then values stored next to the key. Key-value databases are useful when you have large amounts of data that needs to be queried quickly and when you have data that doesn't have clearly defined columns or data structures. Key-value databases let you store almost any data in the value component without the need to strictly define it, as you would with an RDBMS, where you would specify a string or integer, for example.
- **Document databases** store data in formats such as **JavaScript Object Notation (JSON)**. JSON is used widely in programming languages, so having a database that uses the same format makes it an efficient choice for many developers. We will discuss JSON in more detail later.

First, let's look at key-value databases more closely.

Key-value databases

Key-value databases have just two main components – a *value*, which can be almost any piece of data or information, and a *key*, which stores its location. The same idea is used in many programming languages with arrays or maps. You could also consider it to be similar to the index of a book, with a list of pointers to where to find the information. Here, the same technique is used to build a persistent data store. The following is an example of their structure:

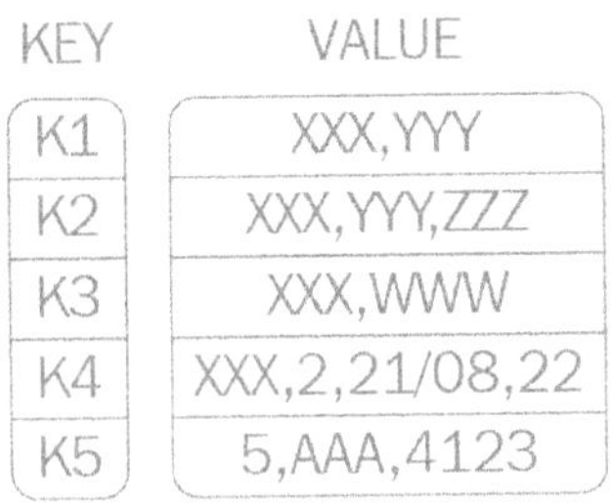

KEY
VALUE
K1
XXX,YYY
K2
XXX,YYY,ZZZ
K3
XXX,WWW
K4
XXX,2,21/08,22
K5
5,AAA,4123

Figure 2.9 – A key-value database structure

As you can see, the values do *NOT* have to be consistent, even in the same table. This can offer a lot of flexibility in table design as you can add extra information or omit it without having to redesign the table.

Key-value databases excel in the following cases:

- When your application contains a large number of small reads
- When your application contains data that is volatile and changes frequently
- When your application doesn't require complex querying, such as joins

Some typical use cases for key-value databases are as follows:

- A website shopping cart containing `user_id` as the key and cart contents as values, such as `item_id`, `quantity`, and `amount`
- A gaming scoreboard for millions of users containing `user_id` as the key and `score` as the value
- A website's login session information containing a `session_id` for the key and the session information as values, such as `pages_accessed`, `login_time`, and `session_expiry_time`

One of the main benefits a key-value database has over an RDBMS is that because the data has a key to point to the values, the data can be stored in multiple locations, even on different servers. This allows you to run multiple nodes to support horizontal scaling (where you add more servers to spread your load horizontally, as opposed to vertical scaling, where you add more resources to a single server). Given one of the main limitations of an RDBMS is performance bottlenecks due to the maximum number of resources you can give to a single server, it becomes clear how a key-value database could outperform an RDBMS for large datasets.

However, the compromise with a key-value database is around *querying*. Key-value databases are designed to be queried against the key and not around the values. While you can filter data being returned on the values, it will be considerably slower than using the key. You are also restricted in using complex SQL statements or pulling data from more than one table at a time, so joins and aggregate type queries cannot be down via the database and must be handled by the application. For an application moving from an RDBMS, this would result in a full rewrite of the code, so this must be carefully considered before you commit to the change.

To summarize, the following are the main benefits and compromises of key-value databases:

- Very fast reads on large datasets.
- Ability to scale horizontally to support huge amounts of simultaneous reads and writes.

- Values can hold almost any data without needing to be predefined, so they offer flexibility for changing application needs without redesigning the database tables.
- Slower reads on data if you need to filter against values.
- Inability to use complex SQL statements such as aggregates.
- Inability to return data from more than one table at a time.

Now that we have learned how key-value databases work, we will look at a specific type of database called a document database. While this is still a key-value database, it has a different requirement for data that's stored and a different use case.

Document databases

A *document database* is a special type of key-value database. It still holds data in the same pattern that we mentioned previously – key for the pointer and a value containing some data or information – but these databases require the data to be stored in a **document format**. What does that mean? What is a document format?

A document format for a key-value database does not mean a Word or Excel document, but rather JSON format. The following is an example of what JSON syntax looks like:

```
{
    "name":"Paul",
    "username":"pauls56",
    "books":[
        { "title":"War and Peace", "price":15 },
        { "title":"Of Mice and Men", "price":12 }
    ]
}
```

In the preceding example, you can see how the JSON structure works with values when it's given an ID (`name, username, books, title, price`) and values (`"Paul","pauls56"`). You can also see that the books section has multiple entries. This is known as **nesting** and allows for a lot of flexibility in the way information is stored and how data is retrieved. In this example, the type of data that would commonly be returned would likely be the `books` objects owned by a certain `username`. Storing the data in this way would allow all those books to be returned in one go.

With that, we have learned how a document database is a special type of key-value database and that while it follows similar rules, it has a special type of value that can be stored that must be in JSON. We also learned what JSON looks like and how it can contain nested values to add to querying.

Next, we will look at the final two types of NoSQL databases we need to know about for the exam:

- Graph databases
- Ledger databases

First, we will learn about graph databases and how to identify their use cases.

Graph and ledger databases

For the final section of this chapter, we are going to study two more database types, one NoSQL and one a special type of database that can be made both with a SQL and NoSQL database, as we will see:

- **Graph databases** are used when you want to show the connections between items in your database. For example, consider Facebook and how they use friends of friends to help identify people you are likely to know and might want to connect with. This would be a good example of when a graph database could be a good option.
- **Ledger databases** are databases that keep track of every change that has ever been made. The database will never change any existing data but will add a new version next to the original. This can be very useful for systems such as bank transactions, where it is critical to have exceptional auditing controls.

Let's start by looking at graph databases.

Graph databases

Graph databases specialize in storing data in a manner that highlights the connections between them. They don't have tables in a traditional sense but have nodes to represent the data items and edges to represent the links between them. To return to our Facebook example, the nodes would be the users and the things they like, while the edges would be the connections between the users and the things they can like. Let's see an example of what that would look like:

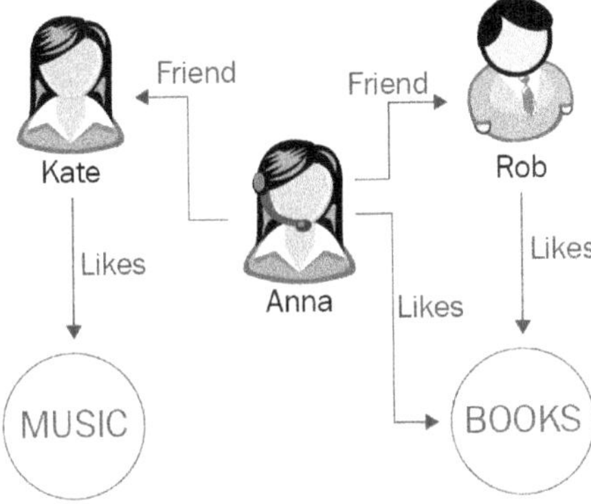

Figure 2.10 – A graph database topology

Using this model, it would be easy to find all the people who like books or, even more complicated, find everyone who has a friend who is a friend of Justin who also likes books.

Graph databases can seem very complicated to someone who is used to RDBMSes and even other NoSQL databases. In the exam, there may only be one or even no questions about graph databases, but that one question might be the difference between a passing and failing grade, so it's useful to know what they are and some typical use cases for them, even if you don't fully understand how they work as thoroughly as other database engines.

Some of the benefits and compromises of graph databases are as follows:

- They're very fast at querying, no matter how much data is loaded. Query times are dependent on the number of connections (edges) rather than the number of nodes.
- There is a clear representation of connections between data points.
- There's no unified querying language. Each graph database has a language, which can make it difficult to move applications across.
- They're less flexible than other NoSQL engines as it's difficult to change the data model once you have loaded data.

Some use cases where graph databases might be suitable are as follows:

- Mapping user buying behavior in online shops to offer good recommendations for other products
- Social media connections and links between users, interactions, and pages

In summary, graph databases are used when there is a requirement to map connections between data items. There may not be any questions on graph databases in the exam, but it's important to know about them, even if you don't fully understand the technical aspects thoroughly.

Finally, we'll look at ledger databases to finish learning about different database types.

Ledger databases

While not strictly a database engine in its own right, ledger databases are important to understand for the exam. A *ledger database* is simply one in which no existing data can ever be removed or changed; it is **immutable**. All changes or new data are appended to the record, like a version. These versions can be queried so that you can see what the data looked like at any point in time to verify its consistency.

They have three components – a current *state table* (**C**), which you would query for all normal transactions, a *history table* (**H**), which shows all the previous versions of the rows, and a *journal* (**J**), which logs all the commands that have been run. The following simple example shows a car table being updated:

C - cars

ID	Make	Model	Colour	Reg	Value
1	Ford	Mustang	Red	BG12 YHG	50000

UPDATE cars SET value = 20000 WHERE make = 'Ford'

C - cars

ID	Make	Model	Colour	Reg	Value
1	Ford	Mustang	Red	BG12 YHG	20000

H - cars

ID	Make	Model	Colour	Reg	Value
1	Ford	Mustang	Red	BG12 YHG	50000
2	Ford	Mustang	Red	BG12 YHG	20000

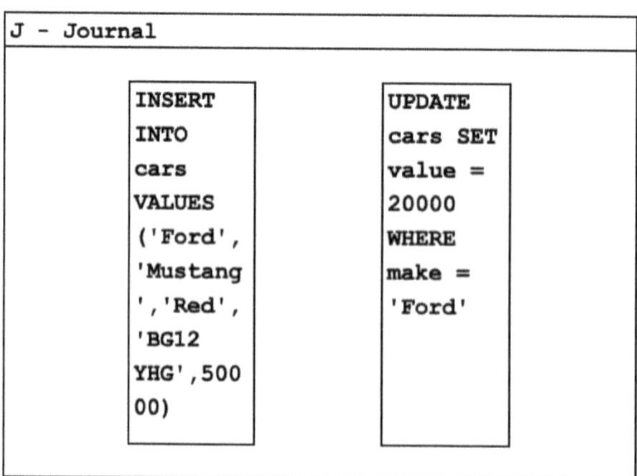

Figure 2.11 – A ledger database being updated

Let's explain what is happening here:

1. The first table, **C - cars**, holds the original state of the table after the row is inserted.
2. The bottom table, **J - Journal**, shows the `INSERT` statement that was run to populate the table.
3. Then, we update the value of all the cars where the make is **Ford** to **20000**.
4. The **C – cars** table is updated to reflect that change.
5. The **H – cars** table has a row appended to it, showing the change that was made.
6. **J – Journal** is updated to show the `UPDATE` command that we ran.

By storing the data in this way, we maintain the query speed of the current data state in the **C** tables while recording all the changes in two other locations. We are also able to query the history, **H**, table to quickly find what changes have been made. The journal also holds a long string called a *hash*. This hash is updated every time a table is changed and can be used to guarantee that the data that's stored in the tables has not been changed outside of the database queries. If you generated a hash of the history table and compared it to the journal, they must match; otherwise, this means that the data has been tampered with. This is what makes it immutable and verifiable.

Some of the use cases for databases like this are as follows:

- Any place where people need to build a circle of trust is a good place to deploy a ledger database.
- Highly critical transaction databases such as those of banks, where the data owner must be able to prove that the data is correct and has not been changed.
- An alternative to blockchain technologies. While outside the scope of this book, blockchains use a similar hash technology to guarantee data. However, over time, these chains can grow long and become too difficult to work with. Ledger databases can overcome this problem.

In the exam, you will likely only be asked one or even zero questions on ledger databases, but as with graph databases, it is useful to obtain a high-level understanding so that you can answer that additional question correctly to increase your chances of getting a pass.

Summary

In this first technical chapter, we have covered a lot of different databases, all of which will likely feature in your exam.

You should now know how to explain the benefits and compromises of cloud databases versus on-premises databases and understand the key motivations for moving to the cloud in terms of scalability, cost, security, compliance, and performance. You have also learned how all the database engines that will be covered in the exam work and how to identify key use cases for each based on their key features.

So far, we have looked at technologies that work both on-premises and in the cloud. Now, it's time to focus on the specific AWS technologies that you will need to know about for the exam. The next chapter will teach you the basics of **AWS infrastructure**, where you will deploy and maintain your databases. Without this knowledge, you will struggle in the exam as there will likely be questions on how to set up the infrastructure for your databases.

Further reading

Earlier, we briefly mentioned blockchain technology. For further information on this topic and how it can be used, please consider the following Packt book:

Blockchain by Example - `https://www.packtpub.com/free-ebook/blockchain-by-example/9781788475686`.

3
Understanding AWS Infrastructure

After learning about the different types of database engines you need to know for the AWS Certified Database – Specialty exam, it's time to start learning AWS specifics, starting with AWS infrastructure. It's important you know the basics of how AWS works, and the key components involved as they do come up in the AWS Certified Database – Specialty exam both as direct questions specifically about how to configure the cloud infrastructure ready to host a database, and also indirectly in terms of troubleshooting or access issues, which can be infrastructure-related.

Infrastructure refers to underlying services that support your database. Even the simplest of database deployments require servers, networking, firewalls, security controls, and storage. In this chapter, we are going to explore how AWS implements these components and how you can configure and build your own. We will have a mixture of theory, explaining all the different services, and hands-on practice so you can start to build your own AWS infrastructure in a secure and efficient manner ready to deploy databases in later chapters.

If you have taken other AWS exams such as AWS Solutions Architect – Associate or Professional, or you feel confident in these topics, it is still recommended to work through this chapter as revision. In later chapters and labs, we will be deploying databases into AWS so if you are unsure how to deploy the right infrastructure to do that, then it is worthwhile to complete at least the technical steps to get a working AWS environment.

In this chapter, we're going to cover the following main topics:

- **Virtual Private Cloud** (**VPC**) overview
- VPC networking
- Introducing AWS identity and access management
- Building a VPC

Let's start by looking at VPCs and their components and why they are so important. We'll end the chapter with two labs building VPCs using the console and the command line, which you'll set up in the following *Technical requirements* section.

Technical requirements

You will require an AWS Account with root access. Everything we will do in this chapter will be available as Free Tier, which means you can run all the example code without spending any money as long as your account has only been opened within the last 12 months. You will also require AWS **command-line interface** (**CLI**) access. The AWS guide (`https://docs.aws.amazon.com/cli/latest/userguide/cli-chap-configure.html`) explains the steps required but we will summarize them here:

1. Open an AWS account if you have not already done so.
2. Download the latest version of the AWS CLI from here: `https://docs.aws.amazon.com/cli/latest/userguide/welcome-versions.html#welcome-versions-v2`.
3. Create an admin user: `https://docs.aws.amazon.com/IAM/latest/UserGuide/id_credentials_access-keys.html`.
4. Create an access key for your administration user: `https://docs.aws.amazon.com/IAM/latest/UserGuide/getting-started_create-admin-group.html#getting-started_create-admin-group-cli`.
5. Run the `aws configure` command to set up a profile for your user: `https://docs.aws.amazon.com/cli/latest/userguide/cli-configure-quickstart.html#cli-configure-quickstart-creds`.

Once you have managed to set up the AWS CLI, you can start to build your AWS infrastructure, starting with the VPC.

Virtual private cloud overview

A **VPC** is a part of the AWS cloud infrastructure that is *logically isolated* for your sole use. You can think of it as your own virtual data center running in AWS.

Logically means that the underlying servers and networking components that you use may be shared with other customers, similar to how you can run virtual machines on-premises. For example, you will not have your own network connections or physical servers, but you will have complete control over your virtual network configuration and server deployments.

Isolated means a VPC is fully controlled by you, and only you and others to whom you grant access. Within the VPC, the only objects that exist are ones that you deploy.

Before we get hands-on with the AWS Console, it's important to understand some of the terms AWS uses to describe its infrastructure. The highest level of AWS infrastructure is called a **Region**. A region is a collection of data centers that are located geographically close to one another and operate together. Each individual data center (or small group of data centers located very close to each other) is called an **Availability Zone or AZ**. The following diagram gives an overview of how the regions and AZs are connected:

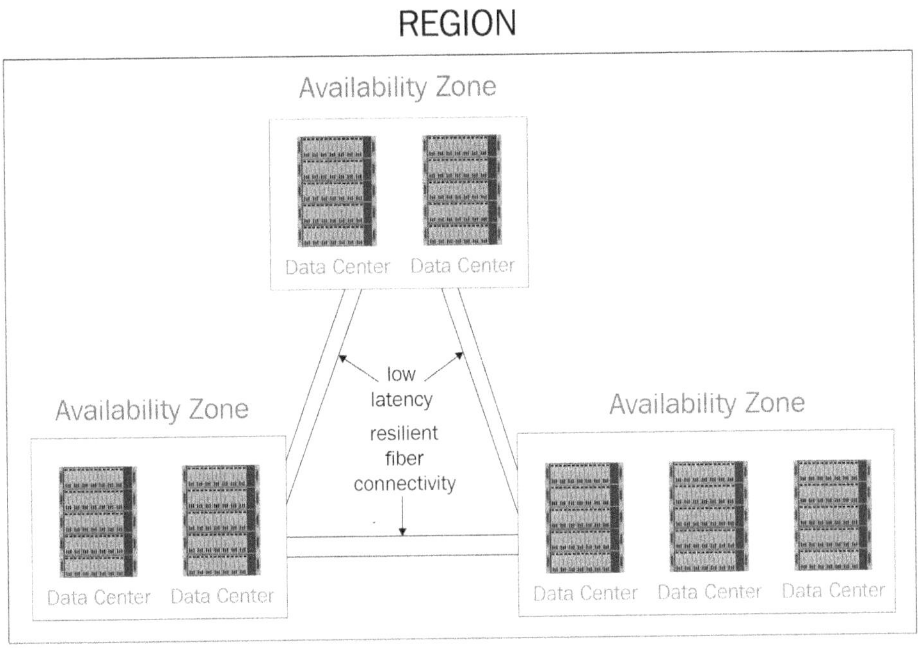

Figure 3.1 – AWS region and availability zones

When you start to deploy databases and applications and configure your networking within a VPC, the first decision is which region you want to deploy in. You will want to consider the following factors:

- *Geographical proximity to users*: Even with the fastest internet speeds, network latency is still a major performance area, and being close to your users may improve the performance of your applications.
- *Compliance and legal regulations*: For some systems, you are required to store the data in the same country as it was produced. This may force you to use only a specific region.
- *Functionality and options*: Not all regions support all AWS services and functions. If you want to use a new feature or version of a tool, you may be restricted to which region you can deploy to.

During the AWS Certified Database – Specialty exam, you will see questions specifically referring to users reporting slow speeds and what you could do to improve performance for them. Remember that the right answer might be to move your database to a region nearer the customers to reduce network latency times.

VPCs in AWS are restricted to a single region, but they can and should, for resilience reasons, span multiple AZs. If a single AWS data center was to fail for any reason, having multiple AZs in use would minimize any outages and allow for fast or even automated failover to a different data center. We'll cover multi-AZ deployments of databases in more depth in later chapters but it's important to understand the following about VPCs:

- They only operate in a single region.
- They can and should operate across multiple AZs.

To summarize, a VPC is an isolated area of the AWS cloud located in a single region where you can deploy your servers, databases, and applications across multiple AZs.

We are now going to look at the main networking and security components within a VPC. The same way an on-premises data center has networking and firewalls to control access and connectivity, a VPC contains subnets, route tables, gateways, and security groups.

VPC networking

One of the most critical areas within a VPC is networking. The network settings control which systems can talk to others, whether a server can connect to the internet or not, and greatly enhance the security of your systems by limiting access to only the parts that a user requires. The first area of a VPC network we will learn about is subnets.

Subnets

Subnets are used to logically divide your VPC network into smaller chunks that you can then control separately. When you first create a VPC, you are required to give it a network IP range (called **classless inter-domain routing** (**CIDR**)), such as `192.168.0.1/16` (this would give you 65,634 IP addresses). You can then create subnets to split this very large IP range into different segments. Subnets are typically split into **private** and **public** subnets. A private subnet will not allow traffic from the internet to reach it so is a useful place to put things such as a database that will only talk to the application and not the wider internet. A public subnet allows for internet traffic to reach it and would be a useful place to put a web-facing application.

Why would you want to create multiple subnets when you could put everything in one place? The main reasons are as follows:

- *Availability*: We learned about AZs in the previous section and how your VPC should span multiple AZs for resilience purposes. However, unlike a VPC, a subnet can only operate in a single AZ. To benefit from a multi-AZ resilient setup, you would need a subnet for each AZ as a minimum.
- *Security*: Most applications will have some parts that should be public-facing, for example, a web page would need to be accessible from the internet, and other parts that should only be accessed by internal tools and users such as the databases supporting the website. Subnets can be defined as public, which allows connections from the internet, or private, which allows you to protect your internal-only databases and applications from the outside world.
- *Segregation*: Different applications often do not need to communicate with one another. Putting them in their own subnets allows access between them to be controlled. This can help reduce the area that is exposed. If a hacker was able to gain access, they would only be able to access the systems in that one subnet. By default, all subnets in a VPC can talk to one another whether they are public or private, but this can be overridden.

The following diagram shows a typical VPC and subnet configuration that we will be building in a hands-on lab later on in this chapter. You can see how the VPC has subnets in two different AZs and also includes public and private subnets to segregate secure databases and applications from the publicly accessible web applications:

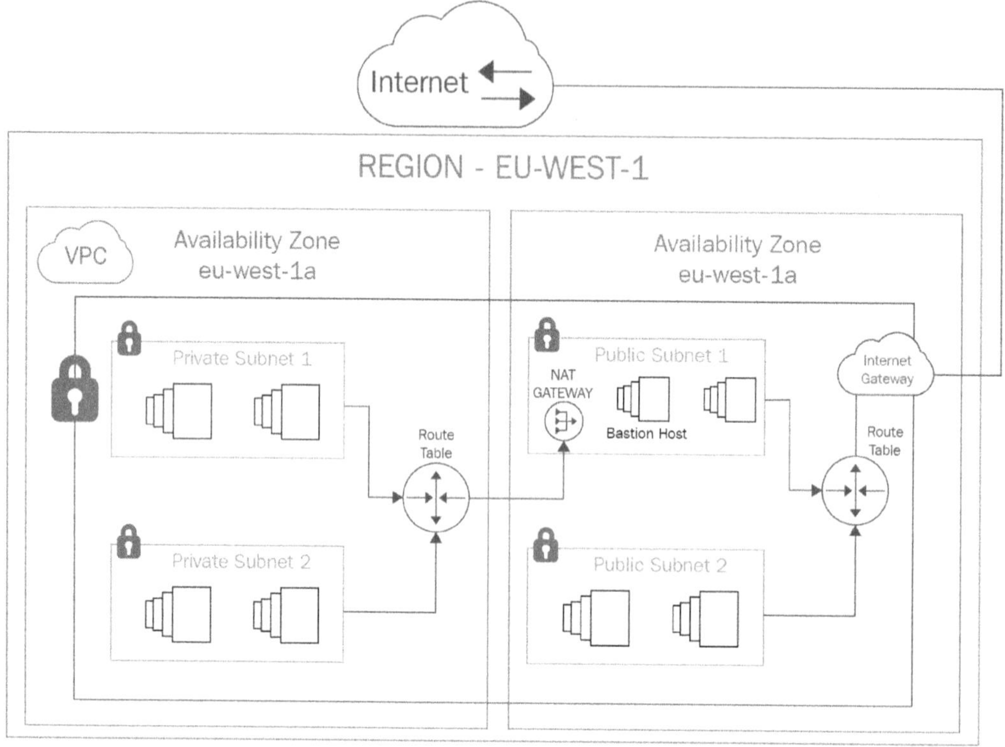

Figure 3.2 – Typical VPC setup with multi-AZ and private/public subnets

You can see three other components in the previous diagram:

- Route table
- NAT gateway
- Internet gateway

The three components direct and manage traffic flow both within your VPC and subnets and outside to the internet. Let's take a deeper look at how they work.

Route tables, NAT gateways, and internet gateways

Let's start with the two different types of gateways before moving onto route tables. As the name suggests, the gateways act as a throughway to external sources such as the internet. Both the **network address translation (NAT)** gateway and internet gateways control access from your subnets to the internet but they are used for different use cases:

- **Internet gateway**: This is a logical device that allows your servers and databases in a *public* subnet to access the internet, and for users and services hosted *outside your VPC* to access your servers inside your VPC. If you do not have an internet gateway, then you are unable to access your devices in the VPC from the internet and you can only use a route directly from within the AWS infrastructure. A VPC can only have one internet gateway across all subnets.
- **NAT gateway**: This is a logical device that allows your servers and databases in a *private* subnet to access the internet, but unlike an internet gateway, there is no inbound route so users or devices outside your VPC cannot reach your services within the VPC. The NAT gateway is routinely used to allow servers and databases in a secure, private subnet to request updates and patches from the internet without having to open access to the wider world, which would open up security issues. A NAT gateway is restricted to a single *AZ* but multiple subnets can connect to it. You can have multiple NAT gateways in a single VPC.

To use either gateway, you need a **route table**. A route table is a set of rules that control and define where your network traffic gets directed. Every VPC has a default route table that is used by all subnets unless overridden. This is called the main route table. Each subnet can only have one route table associated, but multiple subnets can use the same route table. To allow your subnets to use either the NAT or internet gateway, you need to configure the route table so that any requests to an IP address not within your VPC are routed to the gateway. The gateway will then handle the request and route it onto the internet or other AWS services outside of your VPC.

Route tables and VPC networking can become very complicated, but for the AWS Certified Database – Specialty exam, you'll need to understand the following:

- Internet gateways allow access to and from the internet for your public subnets.
- NAT gateways allow access to the internet but not from it for your private subnets.
- Before you can use a gateway, you need to create a rule in your route table to send any traffic with a destination IP address that is not in your VPC to the gateway.

In the AWS Certified Database – Specialty exam, you may be asked questions about problems accessing a database from the internet. You should consider gateways and route tables when thinking about the answer.

Next, we are going to learn about security groups, which are another element of VPC security.

Security groups

Security groups are similar to firewalls within your VPC that work at a resource/instance level. For example, you can create a security group for each server in your VPC. The number of security groups is limited to 2,500 per region. You can use them to control access rules to servers and databases within your VPC. Security groups use two different filters to control access:

- *Ports*: Which ports or protocols do you want to allow? If you are running an Oracle database with a listener on port `1521`, then this will need to be on the allow list, or else no one will be able to connect.
- *Source*: From where do you want to allow traffic? If you have a database running as part of an application, you might want to only allow traffic from the application servers.

Security groups are able to define other security groups in the allow-list rules. This makes management of access much easier as you can define your application servers in one security group, the databases in another, and then configure the rules to allow traffic to flow between them without being concerned about IPs changing or failovers. They will *always* allow outbound traffic from a server or database within a VPC, even to the internet, unless specifically blocked by a security group rule or other rules such as a route table.

Security groups are stateful. This means that they will remember whether an outbound request was made and allowed and if so, they will allow the response to that request to flow inbound even if you have rules restricting that type of inbound traffic. Security groups by default deny all and you need to create allow rules to grant access. You cannot create a deny rule. Security groups restrict access to other AWS services such as **Relational Database Service** (**RDS**) or S3 storage by default. To allow your servers within the VPC to connect to these services, you need to grant permissions to the security group.

Network Access Control Lists (NACLs)

NACLs are firewalls for your entire VPC that work at the subnet level. They have a similar configuration as security groups using ports and sources to control access but they have some major differences.

Firstly, NACLS are *stateless*. This means that they do not remember any outbound requests so you need to specifically allow both outbound and inbound access as required.

NACLs can have both allow and deny rules. This allows you to explicitly deny access from certain IP addresses that cannot be overridden by other NACL or security group rules. This can be useful if you have a rogue server that is sending unauthorized requests to your subnets as you can specifically block it. NACLs also have rule order. Rules are applied from first to last so later rules will override earlier ones. This means you need to create your rules in a specific order to ensure your intended settings are implemented. For example, if you end with a rule that allows all then all other deny rules are overridden, potentially opening a security hole. You can only have one NACL per subnet.

Similar to the previous section, security groups, NACLs, and their configuration are a much larger topic than you will need to know for the AWS Certified Database – Specialty exam, but there is likely to be a question about troubleshooting access problems where a misconfigured security group or NACL could be the correct answer.

Endpoints

A VPC is an isolated area of the cloud for your use, but not every AWS service resides within a VPC. Many AWS services such as **Simple Storage Service** (**S3**), where you can store files and documents, do not reside in any VPC. To access these from within your VPC, you need to either send the request out to the internet via the internet gateway or you can use an **endpoint**. Using an endpoint allows you to connect to non-VPC located services without needing to connect to the internet. This can improve your security as instances or databases located in a private subnet can access these other services without needing a NAT gateway. In addition, the traffic is sent over AWS internal networks ensuring they cannot be intercepted by a third party and typically have greater bandwidth and network speed than the public internet.

We've learned how to set up and configure a basic VPC using subnets, gateways, security groups, NACLs, and endpoints to create a secure and efficient environment for us to deploy a database, but before we start building our VPC, we will now learn how to control user and service access within AWS using AWS Identity and Access Management.

Introducing AWS identity and access management

Identity and access management (**IAM**) is a service that controls users, roles, and access mechanisms for all your AWS services. Security groups secure services at the VPC resource or instance level; IAM secures services at the account level.

IAM has three main areas, called **identities**:

- **Users**: A user is a person who needs to access your AWS services. You can grant a user permission to control what they can and cannot access.
- **Groups**: A group is a collection of users who will have the same permissions. This is often used to make administration easier.
- **Roles**: A role is used to define a set of permissions and who can use it. However, it is not assigned directly to a person or a service, but rather a service or person can utilize it when needed. Roles are temporary and, therefore, offer greater protection than granting permanent permissions via groups or users.

To define the access controls, which you will then give to a user, group, or role, IAM uses **policies**. A policy will contain multiple statements granting **permissions**. A policy is written in either JSON or YAML. Here is an example of an IAM policy document written in JSON that grants full RDS access within the `us-east-1` region. This would mean any user, group, or role granted this policy would only be able to operate RDS instances in the named region and others would be blocked:

```
{
    "Version": "2012-10-17",
    "Statement": [
        {
            "Effect": "Allow",
            "Action": "rds:*",
            "Resource": ["arn:aws:rds:us-east-1:*:*"]
        },
        {
            "Effect": "Allow",
            "Action": ["rds:Describe*"],
            "Resource": ["*"]
        }
    ]
}
```

In the AWS Certified Database – Specialty exam, you may be asked a question about a user being unable to deploy or shut down an RDS instance, and the answer might be linked to IAM permissions.

Now, we've learned the theory behind VPCs and IAM, let's put this into practice with two hands-on labs.

Building a VPC

In the *Virtual Private Cloud overview* section, we learned what a typical VPC looks like with private and public subnets and two AZs. We are now going to build this VPC using both the AWS Console and the AWS Command-Line Interface (`awscli`). If you have not yet created an AWS Account or configured `awscli`, please follow the steps in the *Technical requirements* section of this chapter before continuing.

Using the AWS Console

We are going to deploy a VPC using the AWS Console first. The tasks you will complete are as follows:

- Creating the VPC
- Creating the subnets
- Creating the gateways
- Editing the route tables

Now navigate to the AWS Console: `console.aws.com`.

Creating the VPC

Follow the given steps to create the VPC:

1. Log in to the AWS Console using the account you created earlier (or using an existing one) and check your region at the top right of the console home page. We will be using `eu-west-2` during this lab, but you are free to use any available region.

2. Find the search bar at the top, type `VPC`, and select the purple **VPC** icon from the list:

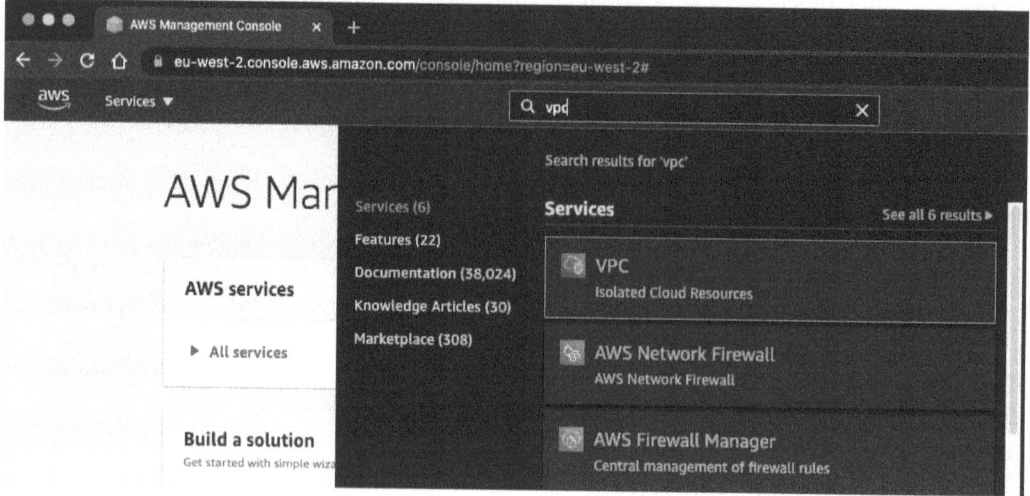

Figure 3.3 – AWS Console showing the VPC service

3. There are two ways to create a new VPC, you can use the VPC wizard or you can create one manually. To enhance our learning, we are going to create one manually. On the VPC home page, click **VPC**. You will see that a VPC already exists, this is a default one created by AWS and it's recommended this is left as the default and all users create their own VPC to customize:

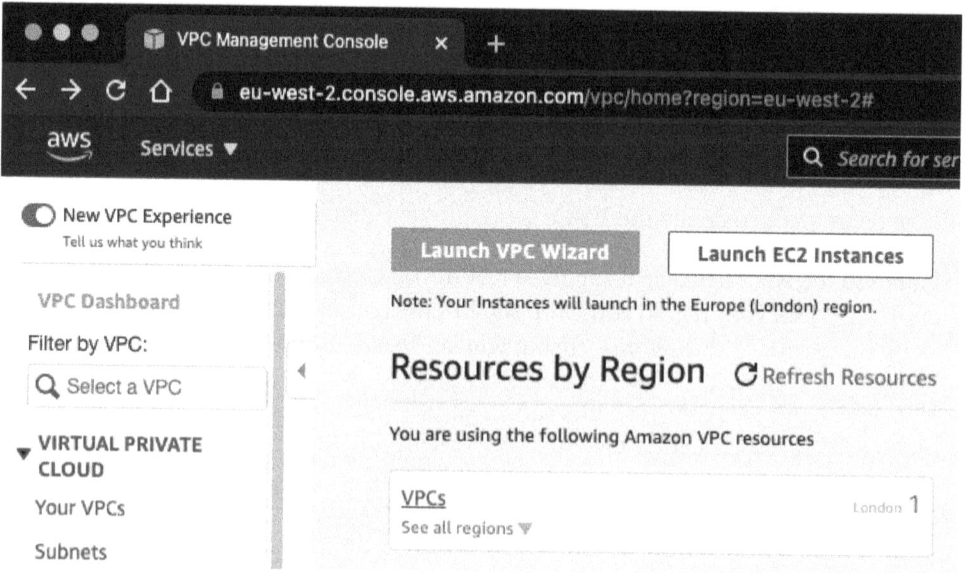

Figure 3.4 – VPC home page

4. At the top right of the new page, click the orange **Create VPC** button.
5. Enter the following to create your VPC:

   A. Name: `dbcert_vpc`

   B. IPv4 CIDR range (IP address range): `10.0.0.0/16`

   Leave everything else as the defaults and click **Create VPC** at the bottom and you will be presented with a page similar to the following, showing the details of your new, empty VPC:

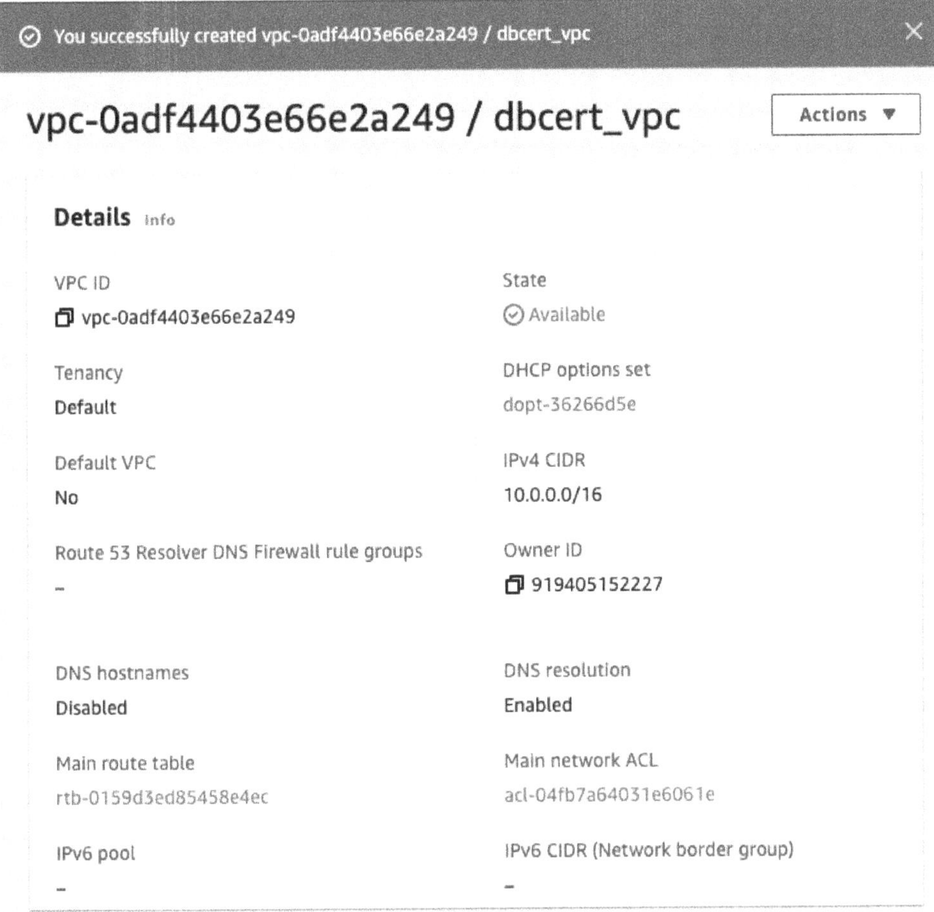

Figure 3.5 – VPC creation confirmation screen

Now we have created an empty VPC with an IP range assigned. Next, we will create the subnets to split our VPC into smaller areas where we can deploy our databases and applications.

Creating the subnets

Now, we need to create the four subnets (two public and two private) needed to hold our servers and databases:

1. Click on **Subnets** in the menu on the left-hand side. You will see that some already exist. These subnets are associated with the default VPC, and they should be left as the default.
2. Select **Create subnet** at the top right of the screen:

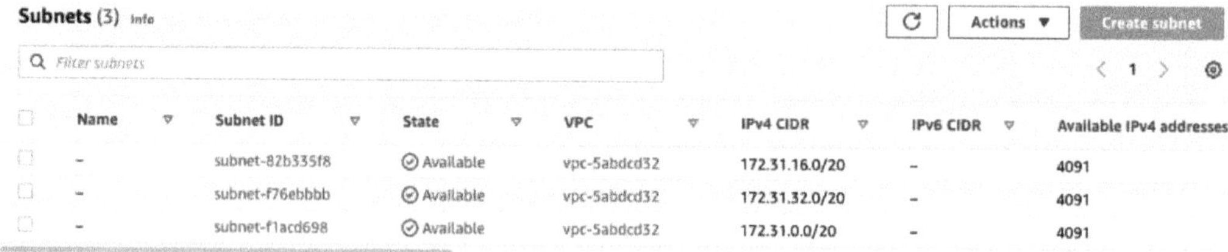

Subnets (3) Info
Actions
Create subnet
Filter subnets
Name
Subnet ID
State
VPC
IPv4 CIDR
IPv6 CIDR
Available IPv4 addresses
subnet-82b335f8
Available
vpc-5abdcd32
172.31.16.0/20
4091
subnet-f76ebbbb
Available
vpc-5abdcd32
172.31.32.0/20
4091
subnet-f1acd698
Available
vpc-5abdcd32
172.31.0.0/20
4091

Figure 3.6 – Subnet home page screen

3. Select the VPC you created from the drop-down list and enter the following details:
   - **Subnet name**: `dbcert-pub1`
   - **Availability Zone**: Choose availability zone **a**. Its name will be the region you are in followed by **a**.
   - **IPv4 CIDR block**: `10.0.1.0/24` (this must be a subset of the larger VPC IP address range you defined earlier).

   Leave everything else as the default and click **Create subnet**. This is how it should appear:

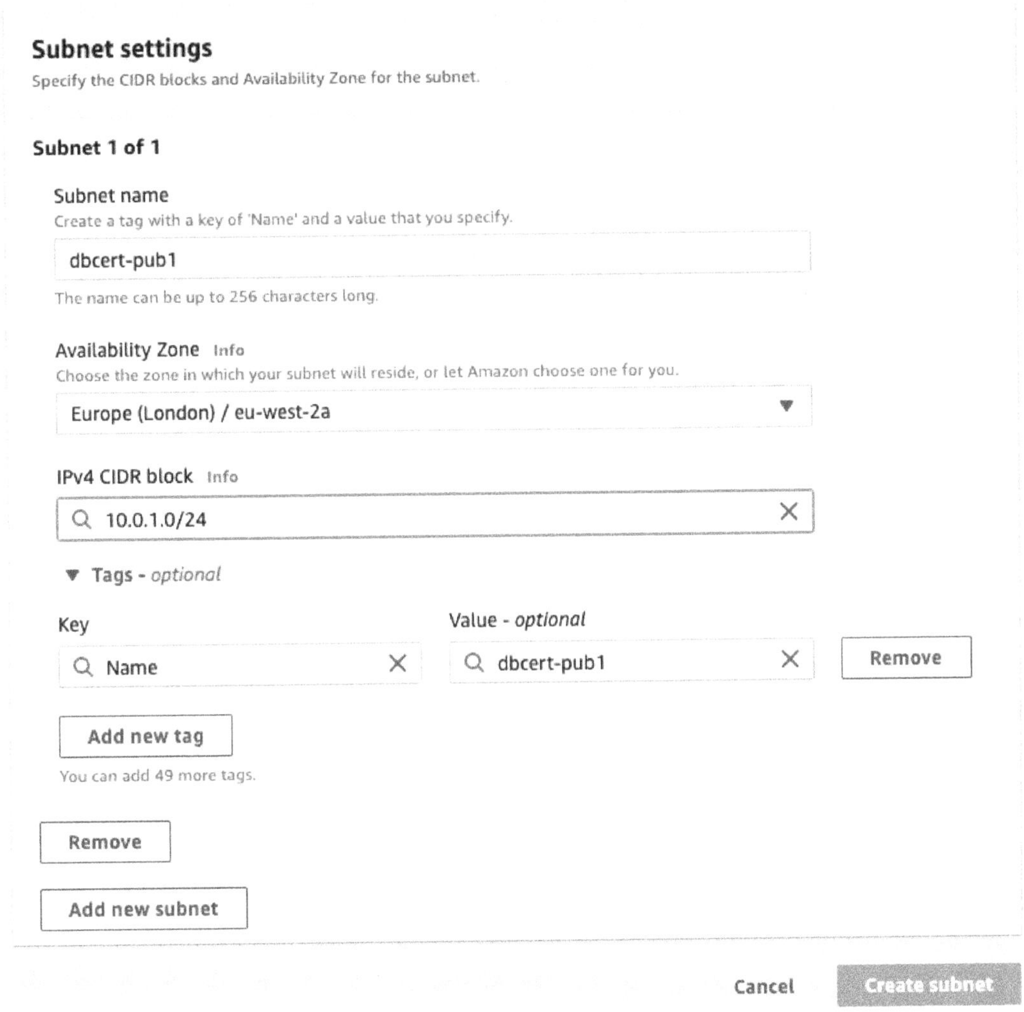

Subnet settings
Specify the CIDR blocks and Availability Zone for the subnet.

Subnet 1 of 1

Subnet name
Create a tag with a key of 'Name' and a value that you specify.
dbcert-pub1
The name can be up to 256 characters long.

Availability Zone Info
Choose the zone in which your subnet will reside, or let Amazon choose one for you.
Europe (London) / eu-west-2a

IPv4 CIDR block Info
10.0.1.0/24

▼ Tags - *optional*

Key: Name
Value - *optional*: dbcert-pub1
Remove

Add new tag
You can add 49 more tags.

Remove

Add new subnet

Cancel Create subnet

Figure 3.7 – Subnet creation

4. Repeat *step 3* to create three more subnets with the following details:

   A. **Subnet name**: `dbcert-pub2`, **Availability Zone**: **b**, **IPv4 CIDR block**: `10.0.2.0/24`

   B. **Subnet name**: `dbcert-priv1`, **Availability Zone**: **a**, **IPv4 CIDR block**: `10.0.3.0/24`

   C. **Subnet name**: `dbcert-priv2`, **Availability Zone**: **b**, **IPv4 CIDR block**: `10.0.4.0/24`

5. When you have finished, your subnet page should look like this:

Subnets (7) Info

Filter subnets

	Name	Subnet ID	State	VPC	IPv4 CIDR
☐	dbcert-pub2	subnet-019ba0f21f96ac44d	Available	vpc-0adf4403e66e2a249 | dbc...	10.0.2.0/24
☐	dbcert-pub1	subnet-074dc3b4aa0ca2210	Available	vpc-0adf4403e66e2a249 | dbc...	10.0.1.0/24
☐	dbcert-priv2	subnet-05f3e713b68480613	Available	vpc-0adf4403e66e2a249 | dbc...	10.0.4.0/24
☐	dbcert-priv1	subnet-0c421af3dfa333492	Available	vpc-0adf4403e66e2a249 | dbc...	10.0.3.0/24

Figure 3.8 – Subnets after all four have been created

We enable auto-assignment of public IPs so that any instance that we create in this subnet will have a public IP by default and therefore will be accessible from the internet.

6. Select one of the public (**dbcert-pub**) subnets and select **Modify auto-assign IP settings** from the **Actions** menu as shown:

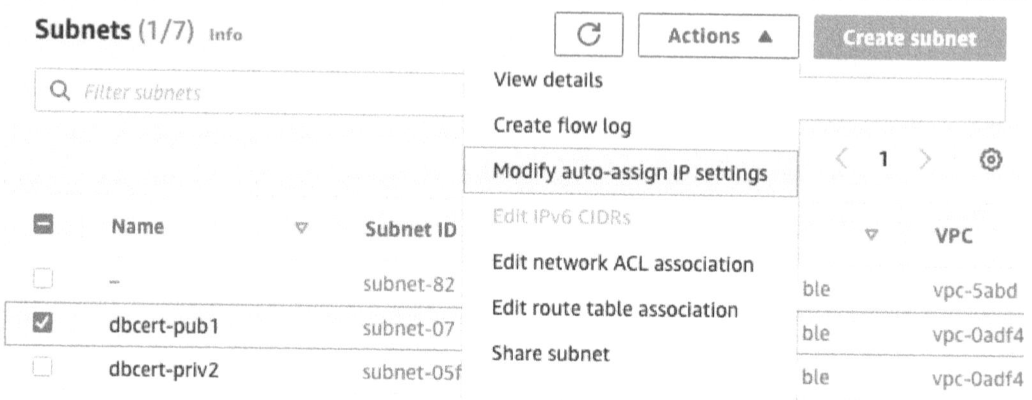

Figure 3.9 – Modify auto-assign IP settings

7. On the screen that opens, click the checkbox for **Enable auto-assign public IPv4 address** and click **Save**. Do *not* enable this for your private subnets.
8. Repeat *steps 6* and *7* for the other public subnet.

Now we have created our subnets into which we will deploy a database, but before we do that, we need to make sure we can reach our public subnets from the internet. Let's learn how to create the two different types of gateways, starting with internet gateways.

Creating the gateways

Next, we will create our gateways and set up our route tables so our services can talk to the internet:

1. Click **Internet Gateways** on the menu on the left and then select **Create Internet gateway** at the top right:

Figure 3.10 – Internet gateways home page

2. Enter `dbcert-igw` as the name and click **Create Internet gateway**.
3. At the top of the confirmation page, select the **Actions** dropdown and click **Attach to VPC**. Without this, our VPC will not be able to use the internet gateway:

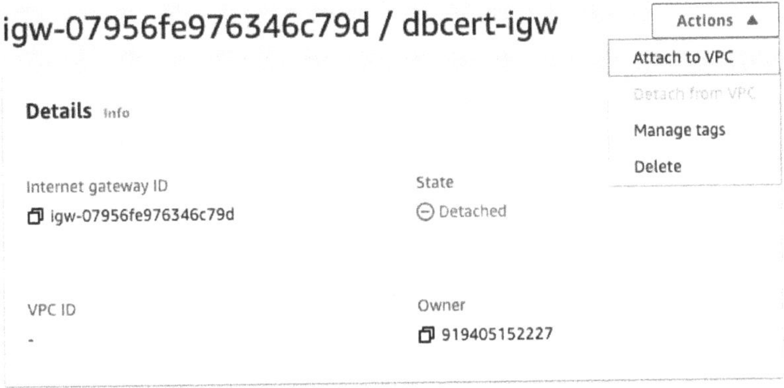

Figure 3.11 – Attach the internet gateway to a VPC

4. Select your VPC from the drop-down list and click **Attach internet gateway**.
5. Select **NAT gateways** from the menu on the left and click **Create NAT gateway** at the top right.

6. Enter `dbcert-nat1` as the name and select **dbcert-pub1 subnet** from the **Subnet** drop-down list. We must create the NAT gateway in a public subnet to allow our private subnets to reach the internet in a secure manner.
7. Set the connectivity type to **Public**. **Private** is used to allow connections between AWS services outside of a VPC, but without allowing full internet access.
8. A NAT gateway must have a public IP address assigned to it so it can communicate with the internet. Click the **Allocate Elastic IP** button to populate this field. The settings should look similar to this:

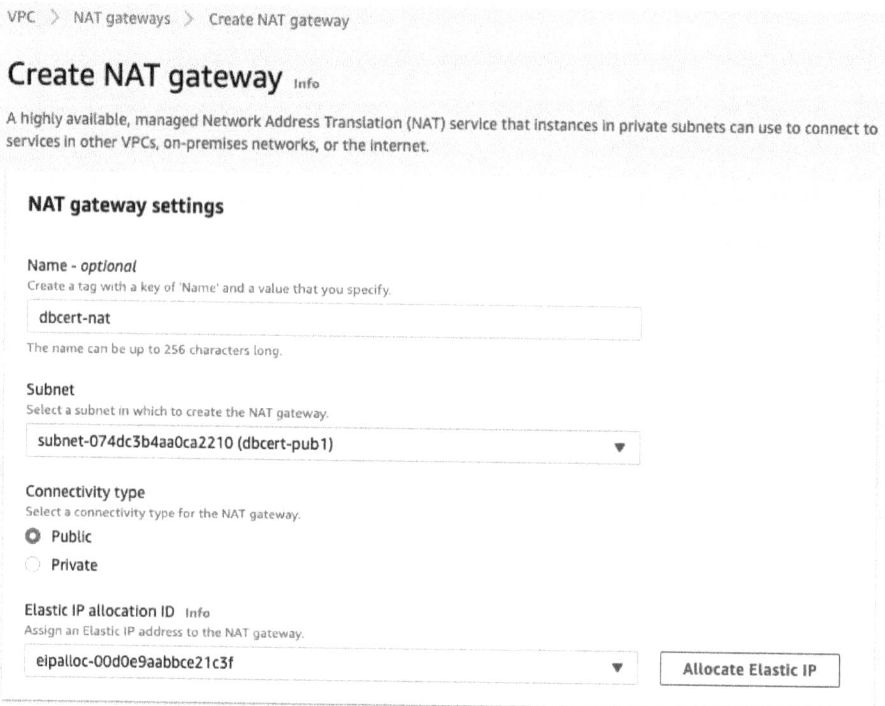

Figure 3.12 – NAT gateway creation screen

9. Click **Create NAT gateway** at the bottom.
10. Repeat *steps 5–9* to create another NAT gateway called `dbcert-nat2` in our other public subnet. This ensures we have resilience, should an availability zone fail. You will need to allocate another elastic IP as you cannot have more than one gateway with the same IP address.

Now we have configured our gateways so our subnets will have controlled access to the internet. To allow our subnets to use the gateways, we next need to amend the route tables so traffic flows to them.

Editing the route tables

The final step in creating our VPC is to update the route tables so that traffic can be correctly routed. We will create a route table for both our public subnet and each of our subnets. We need a different route table for each private subnet because the NAT gateway they are going to send traffic to can only receive requests from the same availability zone as the subnet:

1. Select **Route Tables** from the menu on the left and click **Create route table** at the top right.
2. Use the name `dbcert-rt1` and the VPC is the one we are creating. Click **Create route table**.
3. On the confirmation screen, scroll down to the bottom and select **Edit routes**:

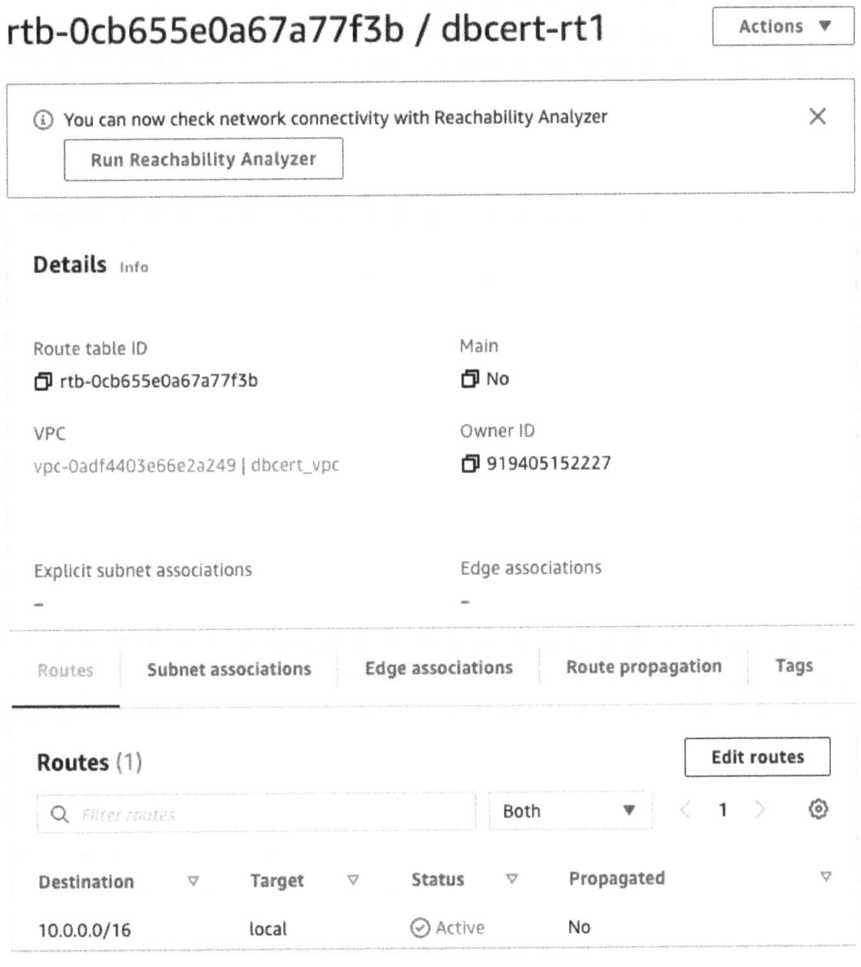

Figure 3.13 – Editing a route table

4. On the **Edit routes** page, leave the first entry in place and click **Add route**. Enter the following:

   A. **Destination**: `0.0.0.0/0` (this means anything not already routed; in other words, anything outside my VPC and on the internet).

   B. **Target**: `Internet gateway`, then select the one that appears. It will be **igw-**<*numbers*>.

   It will look similar to this:

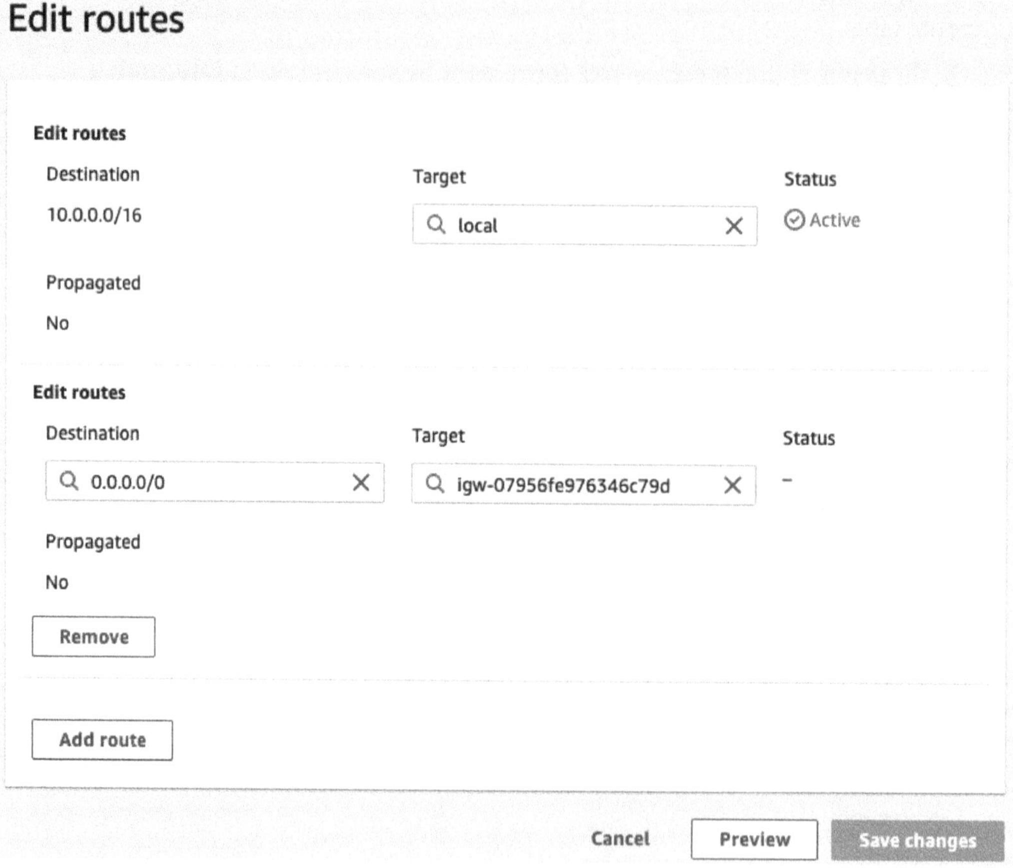

Figure 3.14 – Route table configuration for internet gateway

5. Click **Save changes**.

   We've created a route for our public subnets to use the internet gateway, but we haven't yet told them to use it. We now need to associate our public subnets with that route table.

6. In the routes table at the bottom, click **Subnet associations**:

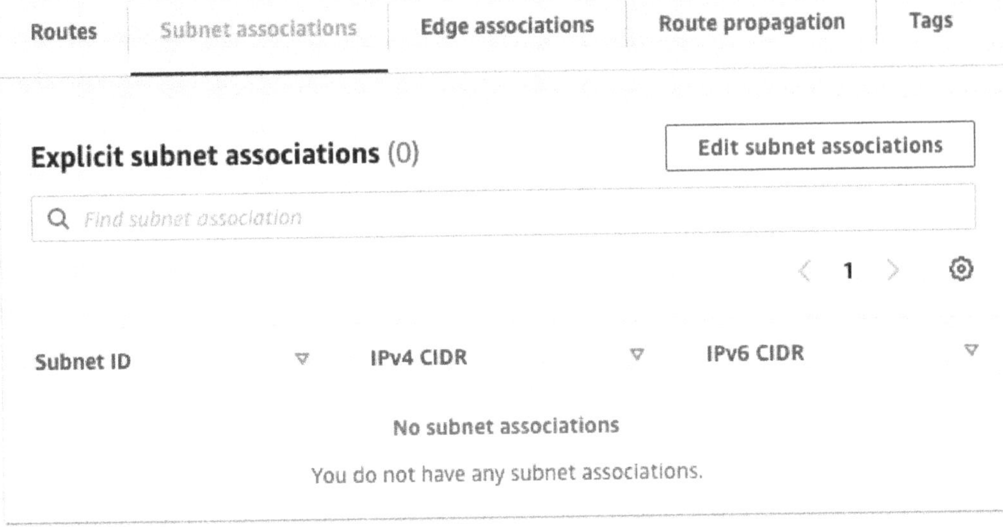

Figure 3.15 – Subnet associations table

7. Select **Edit subnet associations** and check the boxes next to `dbcert-pub1` and `dbcert-pub2`.
8. Click **Save associations**.

   We now need to create a route table for each of our private subnets to be able to communicate with the NAT gateways.

9. Select **Route Tables** from the menu on the left and click **Create route table** at the top right.
10. Use the name `dbcert-rt2` and the VPC is the one we are creating. Click **Create route table**.
11. On the confirmation screen, scroll down to the bottom and select **Edit routes**.
12. On the **Edit routes** page, leave the first entry in place and click **Add route**. Enter the following:

    A. **Destination**: `0.0.0.0/0` (this means anything not already routed; in other words, anything outside my VPC and on the internet).

    B. **Target**: `NAT gateway`, and then select **dbcert-nat1**.

It will look similar to this:

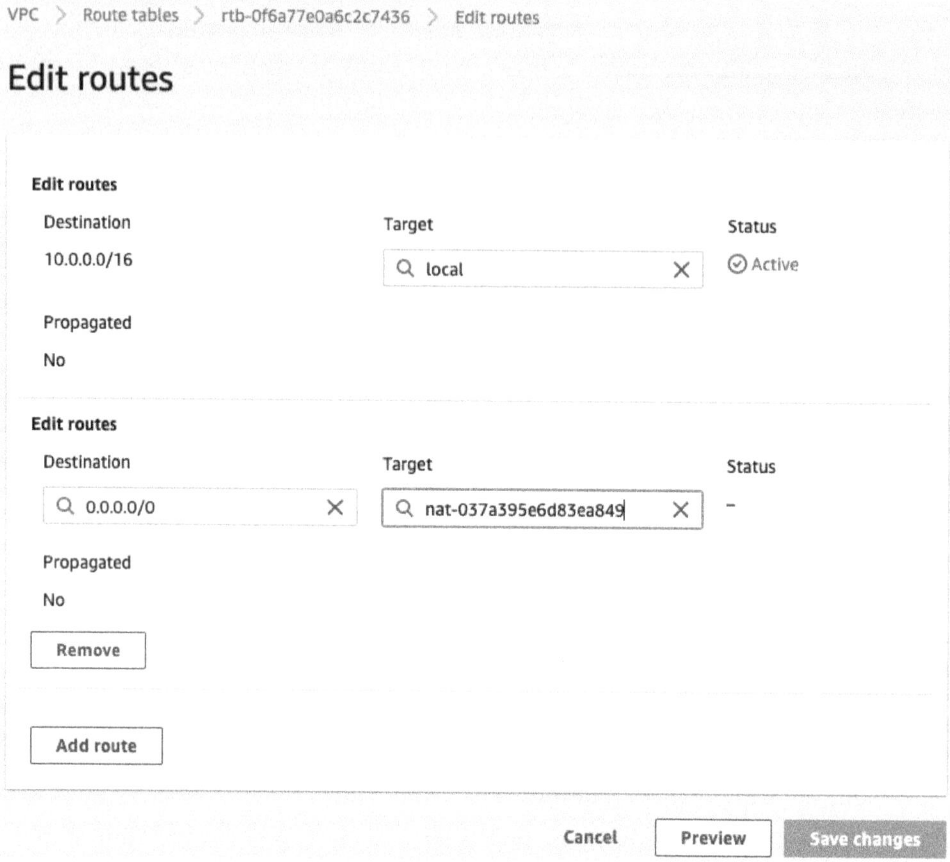

VPC > Route tables > rtb-0f6a77e0a6c2c7436 > Edit routes

Edit routes

Edit routes

Destination	Target	Status
10.0.0.0/16	local	Active

Propagated

No

Edit routes

Destination	Target	Status
0.0.0.0/0	nat-037a395e6d83ea849	-

Propagated

No

Remove

Add route

Cancel Preview Save changes

Figure 3.16 – Route table configuration for NAT gateway

13. Select **Edit subnet associations** and check the boxes next to `dbcert-priv1`.
14. Click **Save associations**.
15. Repeat *steps 9–14* for NAT gateway `dbcert-nat2` and associate it with the `dbcert-priv2` subnet. Use `dbcert-rt3` as the route table name.

This completes the setup of the VPC and its networking. In later chapters, we will set up security groups when we deploy databases. Let's summarize what we have created:

- A VPC called `dbcert`
- Four subnets, two public-facing and two private-facing across two different AZs for resilience
- One internet gateway for our VPC and two NAT gateways for the private subnets

- Route tables for all subnets, with the public subnets having a route to the internet gateway, and the private subnets with a route to the NAT gateway in the same AZ as their own subnet

In the next section, we are going to create the same VPC but using the AWS Command-Line Interface. While this can be faster and allow more automation than using the console, it can be confusing for new AWS users, so it's beneficial to learn how to deploy a VPC using the console first.

Using the AWS Command-Line Interface

We are now going to create another VPC using the **AWS Command-Line Interface** (**awscli**). For this VPC, we are going to create four subnets, two public-facing with an internet gateway and two private. The tasks we will be completing are as follows:

- Creating the VPC
- Creating the subnets
- Creating the gateways
- Editing the route tables

Now open your terminal application for your operating system (for example, Command Prompt or Terminal).

Creating the VPC

Follow the given steps to create the VPC:

1. To create the VPC, we need to define our IPv4 CIDR range. We will use `10.1.0.0/16` so it is different from the VPC we built earlier via the console. Run the following code:

   ```
   aws ec2 create-vpc --cidr-block 10.1.0.0/16
   ```

   In the output, take a note of the `VpcId`:

   ```
   {
       "Vpc": {
           "VpcId": "vpc-4bc7f3bd",
           ...
       }
   }
   ```

Creating the subnets

Follow the given steps to create the subnets:

1. Use the VPC ID from the previous output to edit and run this code. This will create a subnet with a CIDR block of `10.1.1.0/24`:

```
aws ec2 create-subnet --vpc-id vpc-4bc7f3bd --cidr-block
10.1.1.0/24 --availability-zone us-east-2a
```

Make a note of the `subnetId`:

```
{
    "Subnet": {
        ...
        "SubnetId": "subnet-0fca347d",
        ...
    }
}
```

2. Create the other three subnets in the same way, changing the CIDR block range as follows:

```
aws ec2 create-subnet --vpc-id vpc-4bc7f3bd --cidr-block
10.1.2.0/24 --availability-zone us-east-2b
aws ec2 create-subnet --vpc-id vpc-4bc7f3bd --cidr-block
10.1.3.0/24 --availability-zone us-east-2a
aws ec2 create-subnet --vpc-id vpc-4bc7f3bd --cidr-block
10.1.4.0/24 --availability-zone us-east-2b
```

Make a note of these subnet IDs. The first two subnets will be made public and the other two will be private.

Creating the gateways

We now need to create both the internet and NAT gateways to allow our subnets access to the internet:

1. Create an internet gateway:

```
aws ec2 create-internet-gateway
```

In the output, take a note of the `InternetGatewayId`:

```
{
    "InternetGateway": {
        ...
        "InternetGatewayId": "igw-3bb6ac15",
        ...
    }
}
```

2. Using the internet gateway and VPC IDs, attach the internet gateway to your VPC:

```
aws ec2 attach-internet-gateway --vpc-id vpc-4bc7g3bd
--internet-gateway-id igw-3bb6ac15
```

   Before we can create a NAT gateway, we need to create an elastic IP. We did this via the console by clicking the **Allocate Elastic IP** button in the *Creating the gateways* section, but via the CLI we need to do this manually.

3. Create an elastic IP:

```
aws ec2 allocate-address --domain vpc
```

   Make a note of the `AllocationId`:

```
{
    ...
    AllocationId": "eipalloc-03f3e8a",
    ...
}
```

4. Create the NAT gateway using the allocation ID just created and the subnet ID of one of the public subnets:

```
aws ec2 create-nat-gateway --subnet-id subnet-2fc74cea
--allocation-id eipalloc-03f3e8a
```

5. Repeat *steps 3–4* for the other public subnet.
6. Make a note of the `NATGatewayID` that is returned:

```
{
    "NatGateway ": {
        ...
```

```
            "NatGatewayId": "nat-08d48af2",
            ...
        }
}
```

Editing the route tables

Now, we need to create and modify the route tables for the public and private subnets:

1. Create a custom route table for the public subnets:

   ```
   aws ec2 create-route-table --vpc-id vpc-4bc7g3bd
   ```

2. Make a note of the `RouteTableId` that is returned:

   ```
   {
       "RouteTable": {
           ...
           "RouteTableId": "rtb-a7abfa66",
           ...
       }
   }
   ```

3. Add a route for all non-VPC traffic to the internet gateway that you created in the previous section:

   ```
   aws ec2 create-route --route-table-id rtb-a7abfa66
   --destination-cidr-block 0.0.0.0/0 --gateway-id
   igw-3bb6ac15
   ```

4. Repeat *Steps 1–2* for the private subnets. You'll need to create two new route tables, one for each subnet.

5. Add a route for all non-VPC traffic to the NAT gateway that you created in the previous section:

   ```
   aws ec2 create-route --route-table-id rtb-c44e7fc1
   --destination-cidr-block 0.0.0.0/0 --nat-gateway-id
   nat-08d48af2
   ```

6. Repeat *Step 5* for the other private subnet using the other NAT gateway you created.

7. Associate the subnets with the appropriate route tables. First associate the route to the internet gateway with the two public subnets:

```
aws ec2 associate-route-table --subnet-id subnet-0fca347d
--route-table-id rtb-a7abfa66
```

8. Repeat *Step 7* for the other public subnet.
9. Associate the private subnets with the route table with the NAT gateway. Use the route table that points to the NAT gateway in the same AZ as your subnet:

```
aws ec2 associate-route-table --subnet-id subnet-2fc74cea
--route-table-id rtb-c44e7fc1
```

10. Repeat for the other private subnet.
11. Modify the public IP allocation to allow any servers or services you create in the public subnets to receive traffic from the internet:

```
aws ec2 modify-subnet-attribute --subnet-id subnet-
0fca347d --map-public-ip-on-launch
```

12. Repeat for the other public subnet.

We've now created the same VPC configuration that we handled via the console. Feel free to log into the console now and compare the two VPCs.

For the rest of the book, we will use one of these VPCs for our deployments, so feel free to delete one of them to tidy up if you wish, but leave one VPC up and running for the rest of the chapters.

Deleting the VPC

The fastest way to delete one of the VPCs is via the command line. This won't be covered in the AWS Certified Database – Specialty exam so these commands are written to assist you. You'll need to change the IDs to match your own environment:

1. Delete the NAT gateways:

```
aws ec2 delete-nat-gateway --nat-gateway-id nat-id
```

2. Delete the subnets. Repeat this line for all four of them:

```
aws ec2 delete-subnet --subnet-id subnet-id
```

3. Delete the route tables:

```
aws ec2 delete-route-table --route-table-id rtb-id
```

4. Detach the internet gateway from the VPC and delete it:

```
aws ec2 detach-internet-gateway --internet-gateway-id
igw-id --vpc-id vpc-id
```

```
aws ec2 delete-internet-gateway --internet-gateway-id
igw-id
```

5. Delete the NAT gateways:

```
aws ec2 delete-nat-gateway --nat-gateway-id nat-id
```

6. Delete the VPC:

```
aws ec2 delete-vpc --vpc-id vpc-id
```

You can check the VPC has been cleared up by using the console or using the following command:

```
aws ec2 describe-vpcs
```

The completes the clear-up and will leave you with one fully working VPC, complete with two private and two public subnets across two different AZs for resilience, and gateways controlling internet access.

Summary

In this chapter, we learned about how the AWS infrastructure is organized into regions and availability zones and how a VPC gives you an area of AWS infrastructure that is yours to control and configure. We also learned about the different components of a VPC, such as subnets, gateways, and route tables, and we finished by creating VPCs using the AWS Console and awscli.

VPCs are the starting point for any deployments you make within AWS and knowing how they work is critical to be able to successfully deploy, configure, and maintain databases on AWS. Also, during the AWS Certified Database – Specialty exam, your knowledge of VPCs will be tested with questions about troubleshooting access or security problems caused by placing a database into a public subnet.

In the next chapter, we will learn about AWS RDS, and the knowledge we've gained during this chapter about VPCs will be reused in the rest of this book.

Cheat sheet

- AWS infrastructure consists of regions and availability zones.
- A VPC is an area of AWS infrastructure that you can control and configure. You deploy this VPC in a region and across AZs.
- Within the VPC are subnets, internet gateways, route tables, and security groups that control security, access, and routes to the internet.
- Subnets can be private where there is no direct access to them or their contents from outside the VPC, or public where they can be accessed directly from the internet and have public IP addresses.
- Security groups are logical groups to help define access routes between different components within a VPC. They can be used to limit access to databases from application servers only and to limit access only via using specific ports.

Review questions

To check your knowledge from this chapter, here are five questions that you should now be able to answer. Remember the exam techniques from *Chapter 1, AWS Certified Database – Specialty Exam Overview*, and remove the clearly incorrect answers first to help you:

1. A user has deployed a database in a private subnet in their VPC. They have created an internet gateway and a NAT gateway. The database is unable to connect to the internet to check for updates. What is the most likely reason?

    A. An internet gateway with a private IP was used.

    B. The user needs to allow outbound traffic in the security group for port `80` to allow internet updates.

    C. A private subnet can never connect to the internet.

    D. The route tables are updated to point all external traffic to the gateways.

2. A user has created a VPC with a single public subnet. The user has created a security group for that VPC. Which of the following statements is true when a security group is created?

    A. It can connect to AWS services such as S3 and RDS by default.

    B. It will have all inbound traffic allowed.

    C. It will have all outbound traffic allowed.

    D. It will allow traffic to flow on the internet.

3. Which of the following are characteristics of Amazon VPC subnets? Choose two answers.

    A. Each subnet maps to a single availability zone.

    B. A CIDR block mask of `/25` is the smallest range supported.

    C. Instances in a private subnet can communicate with the internet only if they have an elastic IP.

    D. By default, all subnets can route between each other, whether they are private or public.

    E. Each subnet spans at least two availability zones to provide a high-availability environment.

4. When considering a VPC, which of the following statements are correct?

    A. You can associate multiple subnets with the same route table.

    B. You can associate multiple subnets with the same route table, but you can't associate a subnet with only one route table.

    C. You can't associate multiple subnets with the same route table.

    D. None of these.

5. You have launched an Amazon **Elastic Compute Cloud** (**EC2**) instance in a public subnet with a primary private IP address assigned, an internet gateway is attached to the VPC, and the public route table is configured to send all internet-based traffic to the internet gateway. The instance security group is set to allow all outbound traffic but cannot access the internet. Why is the internet unreachable from this instance?

    A. The internet gateway security group must allow all outbound traffic.

    B. The instance does not have a public IP address.

    C. The instance security group must allow all inbound traffic.

    D. The instance *Source/Destination check* property must be enabled.

Answers with explanations can be found in *Chapter 17, Answers*.

Further reading

During this chapter, we have covered a wide range of VPC and networking topics. In the AWS Certified Database – Specialty exam, you will only be expected to know the VPC networking and configuration topics covered in this chapter. However, for a deeper understanding of VPCs, security groups, and subnets, the following books and courses are recommended:

- *AWS MasterClass: Networking And Virtual Private Cloud*: `https://www.packtpub.com/product/aws-masterclass-networking-and-virtual-private-cloud-vpc-video/9781789344981`
- *Practical AWS Networking*: `https://www.packtpub.com/product/practical-aws-networking/9781788398299`
- *AWS Networking Cookbook*: `https://www.packtpub.com/product/aws-networking-cookbook/9781787123243`

Part 2: Workload-Specific Database Design

We are going to spend some time looking at the different database services offered by AWS. This will include understanding the key use cases for each type as well as hands-on labs and examples to build your learning.

This section includes the following chapters:

- *Chapter 4, Relational Database Service*
- *Chapter 5, Amazon Aurora*
- *Chapter 6, Amazon DynamoDB*
- *Chapter 7, Redshift and DocumentDB*
- *Chapter 8, Neptune, Quantum Ledger Database, and Timestream*
- *Chapter 9, Amazon ElastiCache*

4 Relational Database Service

In this chapter, we are going to dive deep into AWS **Relational Database Service** (**RDS**). RDS is a major topic within the AWS Certified Database – Specialty exam and understanding it will not only greatly improve your preparation for the exam, but also help you understand later chapters, which will cover different database types.

This chapter includes a hands-on lab where we will deploy, configure, and explore an RDS instance, including how we can monitor it. During this section, you will need a VPC with a minimum of two subnets. If you have not completed *Chapter 3, Understanding AWS Infrastructure*, please ensure you have a VPC that meets the minimum requirements, as detailed here: `https://docs.aws.amazon.com/AmazonRDS/latest/UserGuide/USER_VPC.WorkingWithRDSInstanceinaVPC.html`.

In this chapter, we're going to cover the following main topics:

- Overview of RDS
- Understanding replicas and multi-AZ
- Configuring backups and running restores
- Maintaining an RDS instance
- Understanding RDS pricing
- Deploying an RDS instance

Let's start by taking a looking at what an RDS instance is, what different versions are available, and how it differs from an on-premises instance. We'll also look at some specific limits within RDS that may come up in the exam.

Technical requirements

You will need an AWS account with root access. Everything we will do in this chapter will be available under the **Free Tier**, which means you can run all the example code without spending any money if your account has only been opened within the last 12 months. You will also need AWS **Command-Line Interface** (**CLI**) access. The AWS guide at `https://docs.aws.amazon.com/cli/latest/userguide/cli-chap-configure.html` will explain the steps required, but I will them summarize here:

1. Create an AWS account if you have not already done so.
2. Download the latest version of the AWS CLI from `https://docs.aws.amazon.com/cli/latest/userguide/welcome-versions.html#welcome-versions-v2`.
3. Create an access key for your administration user at `https://docs.aws.amazon.com/IAM/latest/UserGuide/getting-started_create-admin-group.html#getting-started_create-admin-group-cli`.
4. Run the `aws configure` command to set up a profile for your user.

You will also need a VPC that meets the minimum requirements for an RDS instance (`https://docs.aws.amazon.com/AmazonRDS/latest/UserGuide/USER_VPC.WorkingWithRDSInstanceinaVPC.html`). If you have completed the steps in *Chapter 3*, *Understanding AWS Infrastructure*, then you will already have a VPC that meets these requirements.

Overview of RDS

AWS RDS is a managed database service. What this means is that AWS offers a wrapper around a relational database that manages many of the functions that are normally carried out by a DBA. For example, RDS can take backups by default without the DBA needing to schedule them. RDS aims to reduce the amount of time a DBA spends doing day-to-day administration work, allowing them to focus on areas such as performance tuning.

To use RDS, you need to consider four things:

- Which database type do I want?
- How much **compute** (CPU and memory) do I need?
- How much storage do I need?
- Do I need to consider **high availability** or **disaster recovery** options?

With that information and the VPC that we built in *Chapter 3, Understanding AWS Infrastructure*, you can deploy an RDS that's ready to store the data for your application.

To be able to decide on these four questions, first, let's look at what databases RDS supports.

Supported databases

As the name suggests, RDS only supports relational databases. At the time of writing, these are as follows:

- Oracle Database 12c
- Oracle Database 19c
- Microsoft SQL Server 2012 SP4 onward
- MySQL 5.6 onward
- MariaDB 10.2 onward
- PostgreSQL 9.5 onward

As you can see, as well as limiting the database engines that are supported, there is a restriction on versions. Being a managed service, AWS controls the versions that can be run on their systems to ensure compatibility and security. In general, AWS supports the same database version as the vendor. So, for example, if Oracle no longer offers standard support on a database version, then AWS will not support it either.

Both Oracle and SQL Server require a license to authorize their usage, and this applies to RDS instances as well as on-premises databases. RDS offers two different license models to allow customers to choose the one that's most suited to their needs:

- **License-included**: You pay a monthly fee to AWS to cover the database license costs. AWS is responsible for ensuring compliance for the database software and operating system, but the customer is still required to remain compliant with the data they store within the database.
- **Bring-your-own-license**: You obtain the required licenses for your databases directly from the vendor (Oracle or Microsoft). The customer is responsible for ensuring compliance for the database software and operating system and the customer is still required to remain compliant with the data they store within the database.

Now, let's look at how compute requirements are used in RDS.

Compute

In simple terms, compute is a combination of CPU and memory that's given to a server or needed for a task. For example, your current on-premises database might be using a server that has four CPU cores and 16 GB of memory. When you deploy an RDS instance, you will need to choose how much compute to allocate to it. The more compute you choose, the higher the monthly costs will be.

RDS only allows for certain configurations of compute. For example, you cannot have 15 CPU cores or 19 GB of memory. There is often a direct correlation between the number of CPUs and the amount of memory. For example, if you double the number of CPU cores, you will also need to double the amount of memory. You'll need to consider this when you're choosing the best **instance type** for your database. An instance type is what AWS calls the different compute options. Another consideration for RDS Oracle and RDS SQL Server is licensing. Both Oracle and SQL Server are typically licensed on a **per-core model**, where you pay based on the number of cores you are using. In these situations, it can be more cost-efficient to choose an instance type with a much greater memory to CPU ratio so that you can minimize the licensing costs while maintaining the required performance. This may seem complicated at the moment, but at the end of this chapter is a section called *Understanding RDS pricing* and a hands-on lab, which will help demonstrate the available instance types. Questions around instance types and the most cost-efficient option may come up in your exam, so you must understand how these work.

Now, let's look at the limitations that apply to an RDS instance that may be different from an on-premises database.

Database administration limitations

RDS is a managed service, which means that AWS takes responsibility for many day-to-day administrative tasks. This also means that your access to the database and its functions is also more limited than on an on-premises database. AWS provides a **master user** that can be used as an admin-level account, but it cannot carry out all the same functions as a full admin account that you may have in an on-premises database. Here are some of the main restrictions you will find on RDS compared to on-premises:

- No access to the operating system running the database. All connections must be made at the database layer, such as using SQL*Plus to connect to RDS Oracle or `pgsql` to connect to RDS PostgreSQL.
- Limited access to read or write from the operating system. RDS provides functions at the database level to allow files to be transferred in or out of the underlying operating system, but this requires additional configuration steps.
- No full admin privileges. For RDS Oracle, this will mean no access to the `'sysdba'` account and for RDS SQL Server, there is no SA access.
- Certain functions that you would normally run as an admin user are now used via RDS-provided code, which calls the function on your behalf. This can mean a lot of scripts may need to be changed.
- Database or operating system parameters can no longer be changed using SQL code. To change these settings, you now need to alter **parameter groups**, which we will learn about later in this chapter.

For full details on the commands you can and cannot run within an RDS database, please refer to the AWS documentation at `https://docs.aws.amazon.com/AmazonRDS/latest/UserGuide/UsingWithRDS.MasterAccounts.html`.

It is important to note that AWS takes responsibility for patching and maintaining the underlying servers where your RDS instances run. This removes another task that would commonly fall to the DBA or operations team. Patching or maintenance is carried out during the maintenance window you set when you create the instance (more information can be found in the *Maintaining an RDS instance* section of this chapter), which can cause downtime.

Service limits

RDS also has certain **service limits**. Service limits indicate the maximums that you can use within RDS and includes the maximum amount of storage you can assign to the database, the maximum number of database connections, and even the number of RDS instances you can run in your account. Here are some of the most common limits you may come across. These are often asked about in the exam, so it is worth trying to remember these numbers:

- **Maximum storage allocated to a database**: 16 TiB for SQLServer, 64 TiB for all other RDS types.
- **Maximum number of RDS instances allowed**: 40 (this can be increased via a support request to AWS Support). You are restricted to 10 instances if you choose a license-included model.
- **Maximum number of Data API requests**: 500 (Data API requests will be explained in more detail later in this chapter, but this refers to using `awscli` and similar tools for monitoring by sending requests for information from the database).
- **Maximum file size**: 16 TiB for Oracle, MySQL, and MariaDB. The other databases do not have any limits, so long as there is storage space available.

There are many other less common service limits on RDS, but these will not come up in the exam. Please refer to the AWS documentation for the full list: `https://docs.aws.amazon.com/AmazonRDS/latest/UserGuide/CHAP_Limits.html`.

Now that we understand what RDS is and some of its benefits and limitations, we can start learning about some of its specific features. Let's start with replicas and multi-AZ databases.

Understanding replicas and multi-AZ

Many database deployments require high availability or a failover strategy to meet the **recovery point objectives** (**RPOs**) and **recovery time objectives** (**RTOs**) of the application. RDS offers two different solutions to meet those requirements:

- Multi-AZ deployments
- Read replicas

Both of these technologies offer enhanced protection from a primary database failing and will speed up any database recovery strategy, but they use different methods and have different use cases.

Multi-AZ

In *Chapter 3, Understanding AWS Infrastructure*, we learned about AWS infrastructure, VPCs, and **Availability Zones** (**AZs**). A Multi-AZ deployment is one in which you provision a primary database in one AZ and standby databases in one or more different AZs. The primary and standby databases are kept synchronized either using their native replication technology (Always On for SQL Server, for example) or by using an AWS-specific technology. The syncing process is monitored and managed by AWS on your behalf, and you will not need to configure it further, except if you're considering setting up alerting in case the replication breaks. A multi-AZ deployment can only be located in a single region; there are currently no options for a cross-region multi-AZ deployment. The following diagram shows a typical multi-AZ deployment:

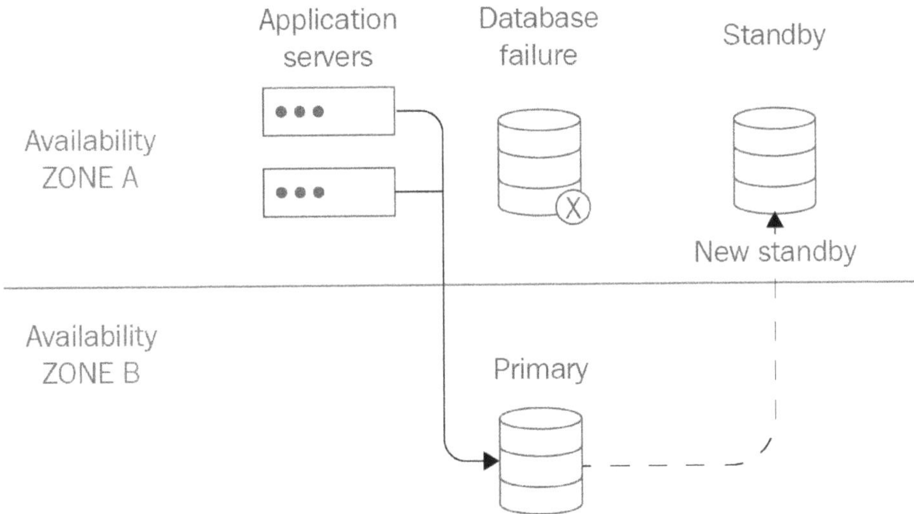

Figure 4.1 – Multi-AZ deployment topology

Using a multi-AZ deployment protects your database in case of a hardware failure in your primary database. The database will be automatically switched over to the standby one with minimal downtime. To decrease any manual steps that must be taken to reconnect the application to the new primary database after a switchover, RDS uses endpoints rather than IPs to connect to the database. An endpoint is similar to a hostname, but the endpoint can be moved between databases using a service called **DNS**. DNS is outside the scope of this book, but further reading can be found at the end of this chapter. When a database is switched over from primary to standby, AWS moves the primary endpoint to the standby database, meaning that no changes need to be made to the connection details on the application, which, in turn, reduces any downtime.

AWS will automatically switch your database over to the standby database if it detects any of these conditions:

- The operating system underlying the RDS database instance is being patched in an offline operation. Here, AWS handles patching during maintenance windows and if the patching requires the database to be rebooted, AWS will perform a switchover to minimize any downtime.
- The primary host of the RDS multi-AZ instance is unhealthy. This means that there has been a hardware failure on the host that's hosting the RDS instance.
- The primary host of the RDS multi-AZ instance is unreachable due to loss of network connectivity. This can be caused by the network being overwhelmed by the instance or a network failure.
- The RDS instance was modified by the customer. Some modifications to an RDS instance require a reboot. Here, AWS will switch over the database to minimize downtime.
- The RDS multi-AZ primary instance is busy and unresponsive. If AWS is unable to receive a response from the primary database within a certain timescale, it will initiate a switchover to minimize downtime.
- The storage volume underlying the primary host of the RDS multi-AZ instance experienced a failure. This means that a storage volume or disk has failed or is corrupt.
- The user requested that a failover occur for the database instance. A user can manually request a reboot with the `failover` command to force a manual switchover.

AWS offers an SLA of 99.95% reliability while using a multi-AZ deployment, with service credits being applied if that SLA is not met. They do not offer a formal SLA for non-multi-AZ deployments. A multi-AZ failover typically takes less than 120 seconds to complete, but this is dependent on transaction levels.

Single-AZ versus multi-AZ failures

While RDS has a 99.95% SLA, it can break. Typically, there are three different outage types on RDS:

- **A storage failure**: The disks storing your database either go offline or become corrupted.
- **A hardware failure**: The server that your RDS instance is running on suffers an outage.
- **An AZ failure**: Typically, this would occur if the data center hosting your instance suffers a failure.

The actions RDS takes to restore your service will depend on whether you have a multi-AZ instance or not. The following table gives a high-level explanation of what RDS does to recover as fast as possible:

Failure Type	Single-AZ	Multi-AZ
Hardware failure	RDS will launch a new instance in the same AZ and attach the disks to the new instance. The endpoint will remain the same. Outage circa 30 minutes.	RDS will fail over to the standby. RDS will launch a new instance in the same AZ and attach the disks to the new instance. Outage time circa 30 seconds.
Storage failure	RDS will not attempt automatic recovery as this may result in data loss. Manual action needs to be taken to recover the database. The outage could be hours.	RDS will fail over to the standby. A new standby can be created from the existing instance manually to replace the broken old primary instance. Outage time circa 30 seconds.
AZ failure	RDS will not attempt automatic recovery as this may result in data loss. Manual action needs to be taken to recover the database. The outage could be hours.	RDS will fail over to the standby. A new standby can be created from the existing instance manually to replace the broken old primary instance. Outage time circa 30 seconds.

Figure 4.2 – Failure recovery methods for single- and multi-AZ deployments

As you can see, a multi-AZ deployment will significantly reduce any downtime that's caused by a hardware failure or maintenance being carried out by AWS.

Read replicas

A read replica is an **asynchronous** copy of your primary database that can only be used for reads. Asynchronous means that the database is not guaranteed to be kept fully in sync with your primary database. Being read-only also means that you cannot use a read replica for any database operations that involve data being inserted, updated, or deleted. The following diagram shows a typical read replica deployment:

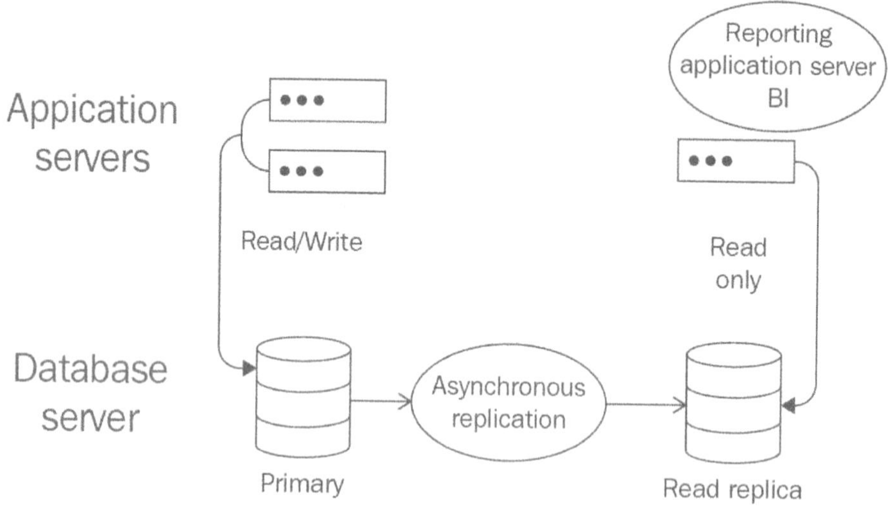

Figure 4.3 – Read replica topology

Read replicas can offer some limited protection from a primary database failure but because they are asynchronous, they are only suitable for databases where the application can tolerate a small loss of data. If you need a guaranteed zero data loss, then they won't meet your needs. In the exam, it is important to remember this as you will often be asked questions about a high availability system where the application needs guaranteed data.

The main use case for read replicas is to help increase the performance of the database through horizontal scaling. As a reminder, horizontal scaling is where the database grows by adding additional servers to it, rather than increasing the amount of compute given to it. To use a read replica successfully, the application will need to be designed to send read-only queries to the read replica while sending any write queries to the primary database. You can also consider configuring reporting applications to use the read replica while keeping the main online transaction processing application using the primary database.

Another major benefit of read replicas is that, unlike a multi-AZ deployment, they can be created in a different region to the primary database instance. This can be used to help reduce latency if applications are connecting from different geographical locations. It can also enhance high availability by offering rapid cross-region restore options.

AWS will not automatically switch over to a read replica, but you can promote a read replica to become a standalone primary database manually. Remember that a read replica is asynchronous, so RDS cannot guarantee zero data loss if you do decide to promote. There are no specific SLAs around read replica availability.

When creating a read replica, it is important to remember these points for the exam:

- Automated backups must be enabled on the source database when the read replica is first created. They can be turned off afterward if you wish. More information on automated backups will be provided in the next section.
- If you are using a Single-AZ deployment, there may be a short outage while creating the read replica due to high I/O requirements. If you are using a multi-AZ deployment, then the read replica is created from the standby and there will be no downtime.

Now that we've learned about the two different options for creating a highly available and scalable RDS database, we need to learn how to protect and restore our data in case of failure. This is done using automated and manual backups.

Configuring backups and running restores

RDS offers a fully managed backup service that will support the rapid restoration and recovery of your databases. These backups can also be used to support making copies of your database to be used in a different account or region. This is also called **cross-region** or **cross-account cloning**. Let's start by looking at RDS automated backups in more depth.

RDS automated backups

AWS manages standard backups for you unless you specifically configure it not to. The backups are taken when the database is running, and they do not cause any downtime. Backups can cause performance overhead as they add additional work to the RDS instance. Due to this, backups are run during backup windows. They are given a default time slot that can be customized if required, typically to avoid peak operating hours. Each RDS instance is allocated the same amount of backup storage as the instance storage, so if you create an RDS instance with 20 GB of storage, you will also get 20 GB of backup storage included in the price. You can control how long the backups are stored by setting a **retention period**. The default retention period is 7 days if your database is created via the AWS console and 1 day if it's created using the AWS CLI, but this can be changed to another whole number between zero and 35. Setting the retention period to zero turns off backups. Changing the backup retention period either to or from zero will cause an outage while this is being configured. The exam commonly features questions around backup retention limits and defaults, as well as outages that are caused by changing a retention period to zero.

RDS automated backups use native backup tools for the database (for example, RMAN for Oracle), and they run at the database layer. This means that for RDS instances with more than one database (for example, it's common for a Microsoft SQL Server instance to host multiple databases), each database will be backed up separately, allowing for a faster recovery where only the impacted database is restored.

In addition to taking regular database backups, AWS also backs up a copy of all the changes that have been made to the database every 5 minutes and stores them for the duration of the retention period. Depending on the database engines, the files holding these changes are called audit logs, transaction logs, or changelogs. This allows you to restore and recover the database to any point in time during the backup retention period. Here, RDS restores the full database backup to before the time you wish to recover to and applies the changes from the changelog from that point forward until the recovery time is reached. This is called **point-in-time recovery** (**PITR**). You can use this method to minimize any data loss by recovering your database to a time just before the incident happened rather than needing to restore only from the last full backup. Using PITRs helps ensure the business's RPOs are met. Because RDS backs up the database changes every 5 minutes, the guaranteed RPO on RDS is also 5 minutes for instances where backups are enabled and operational. We will look at restore procedures in more depth later in this chapter.

RDS backups can utilize a multi-AZ or read replica configuration. If you run a database in multi-AZ mode, then the backups will be taken from the standby database to minimize any performance impact on the primary database.

When you delete an RDS instance, the backups will also be deleted by default. You can override this behavior by setting **Retain automated backups** upon deleting the instance. You can only retain 40 backups if the origin instances have been deleted. The retained backups do not contain any information about the parameter or option groups, so these may need to be recreated if they have been removed and you want to restore them from a retained backup.

Now that we've looked at the first type of backup RDS offers – the automated backup – let's look at a manual backup option that's offered by RDS called a **snapshot**. We'll learn how it differs from an automated backup and when it should be used.

Snapshots

AWS RDS offers a manual backup service called a snapshot. A snapshot differs from an automated backup because it takes a backup of the entire storage volumes as opposed to a database-level backup. In the previous section, we learned that RDS automated backups are taken at the database layer using native backup tools. Snapshots are taken at the storage layer, so they do not separate each database. Snapshots do not have a retention policy and they do not count toward your retained backups count. Snapshots need to be manually deleted to be removed and they are included in the free backup storage amount for the database.

Snapshots are very useful if you plan to make modifications to a database as they can act as a restore point for a quick and easy recovery if you need to roll back the database changes. They can also offer some database deletion protection. If you delete an instance, you have the option to take a snapshot of it. You can use this snapshot to restore the database quickly if you realize you need to get it back.

Snapshots can also be encrypted. This allows you to safely store the backed-up data, even if the original database was not encrypted. Snapshots can be encrypted with KMS keys. This can be used as a quick way to encrypt a database that was created without encryption. The exam will often ask a question about the fastest way to encrypt a database.

Snapshot sharing

Another use of a snapshot is to migrate a database to a different region or account. Unlike automated backups, which are restricted to a single region and only to your account, a snapshot can be shared across regions and accounts.

You can share an encrypted snapshot to another account or VPC in the same region using the same KMS key, but as the KMS keys are region-specific, if you want to share a snapshot across regions, then you need to encrypt the snapshot with a KMS key from the target region. The exam will often ask questions about sharing an encrypted snapshot between accounts and regions, but you will not need to know about KMS in depth.

To share a snapshot with another account, you must obtain the account identifier for the target account and, using the AWS console or AWS CLI, share the snapshot. If the snapshot is encrypted, then the target account will also need access to the KMS key. You can grant access to the KMS key via IAM policies and roles. You can only share a snapshot that has been encrypted using a customer KMS key. You cannot use the default KMS key to share a snapshot with a different account. For the exam, you'll need to remember the high-level steps of sharing an encrypted snapshot, but you won't need to know the specific roles or policies that are required.

Now that we've learned how to take both automated and manual backups for RDS, let's learn how to use those to handle different restore situations.

Restores

One of the major benefits of RDS over a self-managed database is the ease of restoring and recovery. This is a task that can be challenging even for an experienced DBA. Using RDS, this can be done quickly and safely either via the console or the command line.

There are two main types of restore/recovery:

- **Point-in-time recovery (PITR)**: We restore the last full backup and apply transactions logs to roll forward to the chosen recovery time.
- **Snapshot restore**: We use a snapshot to make a complete copy of our database.

First, let's learn about how to carry out a PITR.

Point-in-time recovery (PITR)

A PITR is where you specify the time that you want to restore the database to. This can be any time during the backup retention period, so if it was set for 10 days, you can restore and recover to any point in the previous 10 days. You would commonly use this technique to recover data that has been lost or altered incorrectly.

When you initiate the restore and recovery procedure, RDS creates a new instance for you rather than replacing the existing one. This speeds up the recovery process as it removes the need to overwrite or delete the existing data and it also allows for a comparison to be made against the original database. A typical scenario would be where a developer accidentally drops a database table. They know it was done at around 11 A.M. but can't be sure exactly. By recovering and restoring to a different instance, you can carry out a series of recoveries to find the exact time the table was dropped and restore it. Then, you can copy that table across to your existing database. Here, the dropped table is recovered without it affecting the rest of the database.

You can also decide to keep the new instance and switch across to it rather than trying to merge the changes. If you do this, then the endpoint will change and you will either need to change the application configuration to connect to the new endpoint, or you can drop the old database and rename the new one so that it matches the old one. If you do this, the application doesn't need to change its configuration.

Now, let's look at snapshot restores, which are commonly used to duplicate or clone a database rather than recover from data loss.

Snapshot restores

A snapshot restore is commonly used to duplicate, clone, or migrate an existing RDS instance to a new account or region. It can also be used to encrypt a database that was launched unencrypted.

To restore a snapshot, you can either use the AWS console or the AWS CLI. This option will create a new instance in the same region and account where you are running the tool or console. To clone across regions, you need to move the snapshot, taking into account any encryption that needs to be put in place. Once the snapshot has been copied to the target region, you can run the restore. A similar process is used to restore a snapshot in a new account, where you need to have shared the snapshot with the target account.

A snapshot copy of the database requires the same option and parameter groups to be created. We'll learn more about these in the next section. If a parameter group is missing, then the database will return to the default group, but if an option group is missing, then the restore will fail. Before you begin the restore process, it is recommended that the option and parameter groups are recreated in the new region, account, or VPC. The restored database will also inherit the default security group unless a different one is specified. Typically, you must create a new security group for the DB, so this should be specified during the restore.

With that, we've learned about the different recovery options and scenarios that are available, including how to migrate your database between accounts and regions. In the next section, we will look at common maintenance scenarios you may need to carry out on an RDS instance.

Maintaining an RDS instance

One of the main benefits of using RDS is that a lot of the normal maintenance tasks a DBA would carry out on-premises are handled for you by RDS. However, there are still some tasks that need to be handled.

Let's look at the most common tasks, starting with how to check database logs.

Checking database logs

It's common for databases to suffer from failures or generate errors that need to be investigated. On-premises, a DBA would look at the database logs stored on the server to start troubleshooting. However, on RDS, since there is no access to the operating system, we need to use a different method to access the logs.

There are three different methods we can use to check the database logs:

- Use the RDS instance page on the AWS console.
- Use a SQL query within the RDS instance.
- Use CloudWatch logs.

CloudWatch is only available if you have enabled it. You can enable CloudWatch log publishing while provisioning the RDS instance or while it is running by modifying the instance via the AWS console or AWS CLI.

Each database engine has different logs, so the commands you need to run to access the logs differ between each. We will practice reading the logs from a MySQL database in the hands-on lab at the end of this chapter.

If you publish the logs to CloudWatch, you can also set up incident handling rules that can notify you if specific errors are seen in the logs. We'll cover this in more detail in *Chapter 13, CloudWatch and Logging*.

Now that we know how to check database errors that have been written to the logs, let's look at some actions we may need to take to respond to those errors, starting with what to do if we run out of space or other resources in our database.

Maintaining storage and compute

Monitoring storage and resource usage is one of the most common tasks a DBA needs to carry out. A database that's running out of space or memory at a critical time can cause a significant negative impact on the business. Using RDS can simplify and even automate how additional storage and resources are provisioned to the databases to help them grow to handle a growing or unexpectedly high workload.

The current storage and compute usage can be monitored by using the RDS instance page on the AWS console, by using the AWS CLI, or by using CloudWatch to get detailed statistics. You can create CloudWatch alarms to send notifications if you breach thresholds on resource usage on your instances to allow a DBA to act before it causes an outage. We'll cover this in more detail in *Chapter 13, CloudWatch and Logging*.

First, let's learn how to increase the storage that's allocated to an instance and change the storage type to improve performance.

Working with storage

One of the most common actions a DBA needs to take with their on-premises databases is to extend the storage that's been allocated to the database. This can be a time-consuming task as often, storage needs to be physically added to a server first before the database can be enlarged. On RDS, storage can be added immediately without the need to wait for more physical disks to be set up. As a result, you can extend the storage that's allocated within minutes either by using the AWS console or via the AWS CLI. Adding storage can be done while the database is online without any downtime occurring, but you cannot decrease the storage without migrating the database to a new instance.

Additionally, if you wish to reduce the workload even further for the DBAs, you can configure your databases to **autoscale** their storage. Autoscaling is when RDS is granted permission to extend the database storage when it detects you are running out of free space on the RDS instance. Autoscaling will increase the allocated storage when it detects the following:

- You have less than 10% free space left available.
- You have had less than 10% free space left for more than 5 consecutive minutes – in other words, this isn't just a blip.
- Your database has not had its storage extended in the previous 6 hours – this is to protect you from high bills if something is unintentionally using your storage.

RDS will increase the storage allocated using the greatest value of these three:

- 5 GiB.
- 10% of your total storage – for example, if you have a 500 GiB database, RDS will grow the storage by 50 GiB.
- The predicted storage amount to cover 7 hours' worth of growth at the rate that's been monitored over the last hour.

Autoscaling is extremely useful if your application has an unpredictable or inconsistent growth pattern as it can reduce the time the DBAs spend increasing storage. However, any growth of storage, whether you're autoscaling or manually, will have additional costs, so it is critical to monitor the growth of your databases to ensure it is using space efficiently and you are not increasing the space when it is not required. It is always better to try to reduce the storage requirements through housekeeping than to increase the storage. It is also important to remember that if you are using a multi-AZ database, then any storage increases will be carried out on the standby databases. It must also be an exact physical copy of the primary. Read replicas can amend their storage separately as they are logical copies.

As well as offering options to rapidly increase the allocated storage, RDS also offers different types of storage to handle different needs. RDS offers three different storage types:

- General-purpose SSD (`gp2`)
- Provisioned IOPS (`io1`)
- Magnetic

Magnetic storage is now deprecated but is maintained for older deployments, so it is not recommended that you use it for a new instance. The difference between `gp2` and `io1` is the number of **input and operations you can perform per second** (**IOPS**) and the maximum storage size. For the exam, you will need to know the specific IOPS and how it's calculated for the two main storage types.

gp2 has a limit of 64 TiB of storage for all database engines, excluding SQL Server, which has a maximum of 16 TiB. If you need a larger amount of storage, then you should consider using io1 storage instead. Your database is allocated 3 IOPS per GB of storage, up to a maximum of 16,000 IOPS. If you have a database with less than 1 TiB of storage, you can **burst** up to 3,000 IOPS for short periods. The time you can burst is determined by the number of IOPS credits you have. You are initially given 5.4 million credits when your instance is first created. Credits are given using the following formula:

$$\text{Burst duration in seconds} = \frac{\text{(Credits remaining)}}{\text{(Burst IOPS)} - 3^{*}\text{(Storage size in GiB)}}$$

You may be asked to calculate the burst time for a given scenario in the exam, so practice using this formula.

If you need more IOPS than what's offered by `gp2` for your allocated storage, then you should consider using `io1` storage instead. io1 storage allows you to specify the number of IOPS you need up to a maximum amount. The maximums differ per database engine:

- **Oracle**: 256,000 IOPS and storage between 100 GiB and 64 TiB
- **SQL Server**: 64,000 IOPS and storage between 20 GiB and 16 TiB
- **MariaDB, PostgreSQL, MySQL**: 80,000 IOPS and storage between 100 GiB and 64 TiB

io1 storage is more expensive than gp2. In the exam, you may be given a scenario where a customer has a certain sized database with a specific number of IOPS. You'll need to consider if they should use io1 or gp2 storage. If the question asks for the most cost-effective storage class, then you should choose gp2, so long as none of the values exceed the maximums for that database type. So, you will need to learn them.

The storage type can be configured either when you provision the instance or any time it is running. Unlike adding additional storage, there will be downtime if you change between gp2 and io1 storage. This downtime is minimized if you are using a multi-AZ deployment as the instance will fail over to the standby while the primary instance is being modified.

Now, let's learn how to increase the compute that's available for the database if required.

Working with compute options

Being able to add more memory or CPU quickly and efficiently to an instance is a huge benefit of RDS over an on-premises database. To change the amount of compute that's allocated to a database instance, you can change the instance class. An instance class can be changed to a larger size, reduced to a smaller size, or you can change the type of instance to a different type of architecture.

The main things you must consider before changing your instance class are as follows:

- Do you have the correct licenses for the new instance? If you are using your own licenses for your databases, these are often linked to the number of cores being used. If you move your database to a larger instance, you will likely be using more cores.
- Changing an instance class will result in downtime. This will be reduced if you are using a multi-AZ deployment as the instance will fail over to minimize any outage.
- When do you want the change to take place? You can choose to apply the change immediately or opt to wait until the scheduled maintenance window.

Thus change can be made either via the AWS console or using the AWS CLI. It is important to note that not all instance classes are available in every region or for every database engine. For more information on the latest supported instance classes for your database engine, please go to the following AWS page: `https://docs.aws.amazon.com/AmazonRDS/latest/UserGuide/Concepts.DBInstanceClass.html#Concepts.DBInstanceClass.Support`.

RDS does not support autoscaling for the instance classes, so any changes will need to be made manually.

So far, we've learned how to modify storage amounts and type and compute, and have looked at how to set up autoscaling for the storage to ensure we never run out of space. Now, we are going to learn how to modify database parameters and how to install additional database features.

Parameter and option groups

You have no access to the operating system on an RDS instance or access to the admin account options to change them at the database layer. Due to this, you need to use different methods to make changes to them.

First, we'll look at option groups.

Working with option groups

An option group is used to control which features are enabled on your databases. Every RDS database is associated with an option group when it is provisioned. The default groups are created for each database engine and version. You can create custom options groups and each one can only be associated with databases that have been deployed with the same engine and version. For example, you will need two different option groups to support both an Oracle 19 version database and an Oracle 12 version database.

To add options to the option group, you simply select them from the list shown and apply the changes. Some examples of the options available are as follows:

- **Oracle**: APEX, OEM, OEM Agent, S3 integration, and AWR reports
- **SQL Server**: SQL Server Audit, SSIS, and SSAS
- **MySQL**: Memcached
- **MariaDB**: MariaDB auditing

Some of these options will require downtime to be applied, so you can choose to deploy the changes immediately or wait until the maintenance window. Any changes you apply to an option group will affect all the databases associated with that option group, so it can be a quick way to add options to a large number of databases. However, be aware that any downtime will affect every database in that group.

Now, let's learn about parameter groups.

Working with parameter groups

Parameter groups are used to modify the system and database settings that are applied to your database. They are used to make the same changes you'd make on-premises using an `ALTER SYSTEM` command on Oracle or a `SET` command on MySQL.

Every RDS database is associated with a parameter group when it is provisioned. The default groups are created for each database engine and version. You can create custom parameter groups and each one can only be associated with databases that have been deployed with the same engine and version. For example, you will need two different parameter groups to support both a MySQL 5.6 version database and a MySQL 8.0 version database.

Some of the parameter changes will require downtime to be applied, so you can choose to deploy the changes immediately or wait until the maintenance window. To identify which changes required downtime, there is a flag stating if the change is dynamic (immediate and does not need a restart) or not. Any changes you apply to a parameter group will affect all the databases associated with that parameter group, so it can be a quick way to add options to a large number of databases. However, be aware that any downtime will affect every database in that group.

Now that we've learned how to work with both option groups and parameter groups to make configuration changes to our RDS databases, let's learn how to upgrade the databases to a newer version.

Upgrading an RDS instance

RDS has two main types of database version upgrades – minor and major. Each database engine has a numbering system, but for MySQL, a minor upgrade would be going from version 5.6.22 to version 5.6.23, whereas a major upgrade would be going from version 5.6 to version 5.7. Different methods are involved for minor and major upgrades.

Applying a minor version upgrade

There are two options for handling minor upgrades within RDS – you can ask RDS to automatically upgrade it for you during a maintenance window or you can do it manually. An automatic upgrade will be triggered if RDS sets a newer minor version to be the preferred version. RDS only changes the preferred version once it has been fully tested and confirmed to be reliable. The upgrade will be done during a maintenance window, and it will incur downtime while it is applied. You can minimize the downtime by using a multi-AZ deployment as the database will switch over to the standby instance while the primary is being upgraded. If you have a backup retention time set to a value greater than zero, RDS will take a snapshot just before the upgrade to provide a restore point; another snapshot will be taken just after the upgrade completes.

If you decide to manually upgrade the database, you can select the version you wish to upgrade to either via the AWS console or the AWS CLI. The upgrade process is the same as the automated method; you just have more control over when the upgrade is carried out.

Applying a major version upgrade

The main real difference when you're applying a major version upgrade is that RDS doesn't let you handle these automatically. This is because a major version upgrade often changes the way the databases work beyond bug fixes, which can cause your application to fail or for performance to degrade. You need to fully test any major upgrades before applying them to a production database.

When you begin the upgrade, you will be asked to provide a new option and parameter group for the instance. Remember that option and parameter groups are dependent on the version of the database. Before you begin the upgrade, you should create new option and parameter groups with the same values as for the existing version. This will reduce any additional configuration after the upgrade completes and will remove one of the main reasons for an upgrade failure.

You will incur downtime when the upgrade is running and RDS will be unable to switch over to the primary, even if you have multi-AZ enabled. This is because both database instances need to be upgraded simultaneously.

When the upgrade completes, the database's status will return to `AVAILABLE` and you will be able to connect and run any tests that are required.

Encryption

RDS offers two different types of encryption:

- **Encryption at rest**: This means that the data that's saved on disk is encrypted. If someone was to gain access to the physical disks holding your database, they would not be able to access the data on them without the encryption key.
- **Encryption in transit**: This means that the data that's being sent to and from the database from the application or other users is encrypted and that if it was intercepted, it would be unreadable without the encryption key.

Encryption at rest is the default choice when creating an RDS instance. AWS will create and store a **key management service** (**KMS**) key for you, which is used to decrypt the data stored on the disk when the instance is started.

> **Changing RDS encryption**
>
> You cannot modify the encryption status of an RDS instance after it is created. To add encryption you need to create a snapshot, create an encrypted copy of this snapshot and then restore the snapshot to a new instance.

Encryption in transit uses SSL/TLS encryption. Each database engine has a different method to configure this connection type, but for all databases, you will need to download the root certificate from AWS for your Region and provide this to the client you're encrypting the connection for. The following page holds all the certificates that are required and details of how to configure encryption for each database: `https://docs.aws.amazon.com/AmazonRDS/latest/UserGuide/UsingWithRDS.SSL.html#UsingWithRDS.SSL.RegionCertificates`.

With that, we've learned how RDS handles databases upgrades and how we can do them manually. In the next section, we will learn how RDS is priced, what you pay for, and how you can reduce those costs.

Understanding RDS pricing

RDS pricing is dependent on many things that make up its total cost:

- What instance class are you using and what is its size?
- Which database engine are you using?
- Are the license costs included or are you using your own license?
- How large is the storage that's been allocated?
- Are you using `gp2` or `io1` storage?
- Are you using a multi-AZ deployment or read replicas?

The instance class and its size are often the largest cost of your database. As the instance class increases and you are using more compute, the costs will also increase. The instance class costs increase linearly, so if you double the compute, you'll also double the cost. If you have a performance problem with your database, increasing the instance size can alleviate it but at a great cost. So, before you increase the instance sizing, you should look at other potential ways to improve performance. The instance sizing can also affect the costs of the database if you decide to use a licensing-included model. In this case, the number of CPUs will also dictate the costs of the licensing you will have to pay. RDS offers memory-optimized instance types that have much more memory per CPU than standard classes to help reduce the license costs that are incurred while offering good performance.

Another large cost of RDS is the storage that's allocated. You are charged a fixed price per GB for the allocated storage, regardless of whether you're using it or not. Given the speed and simplicity of adding additional storage, you should generally avoid over-allocating storage. There is a situation where it would be more cost-efficient to over-allocate storage where your IOPS needs are higher than the baseline provided by RDS (3 IOPS per GB), but you can increase the storage that's allocated to obtain the IOPS that's needed as it will increase in line with the storage that's been allocated. Provisioned IOPS storage is more expensive than general-purpose storage and you need to pay for the IOPS that's been provisioned, as well as the storage amount. For example, if you need 100 GB of storage but need more than the 300 IOPS provided with that storage, you could consider increasing the storage allocation to a higher amount rather than switching to `io2` storage.

If you are using a multi-AZ deployment, then all of your costs will double as the multi-AZ standby is an exact physical copy of your primary instance. A read replica will add to your costs but as you can give it a different instance class, size, and storage compared to the primary instance, the costs will be different.

Now that we've learned what RDS is, what it does, and how to maintain it, it's time to put this into practice by creating an instance.

Deploying an RDS instance

Now that we've learned about RDS and its features, let's deploy an instance to practice and learn how the topics we've covered in this chapter work together. We will be deploying an RDS instance using the MySQL engine. After that, we will take a snapshot and restore it before creating and making changes to a parameter group. We'll be using both the AWS console and the AWS CLI for this.

Provisioning an RDS instance

We'll start by provisioning an RDS MySQL instance. We'll be using the Ohio (us-east-1) region. Let's get started:

1. Open the AWS console in an internet browser and log in using an account that has the privileges to create and modify an RDS instance.
2. Navigate to the **RDS** section.

3. Click the orange **Create database** button in the middle of the page:

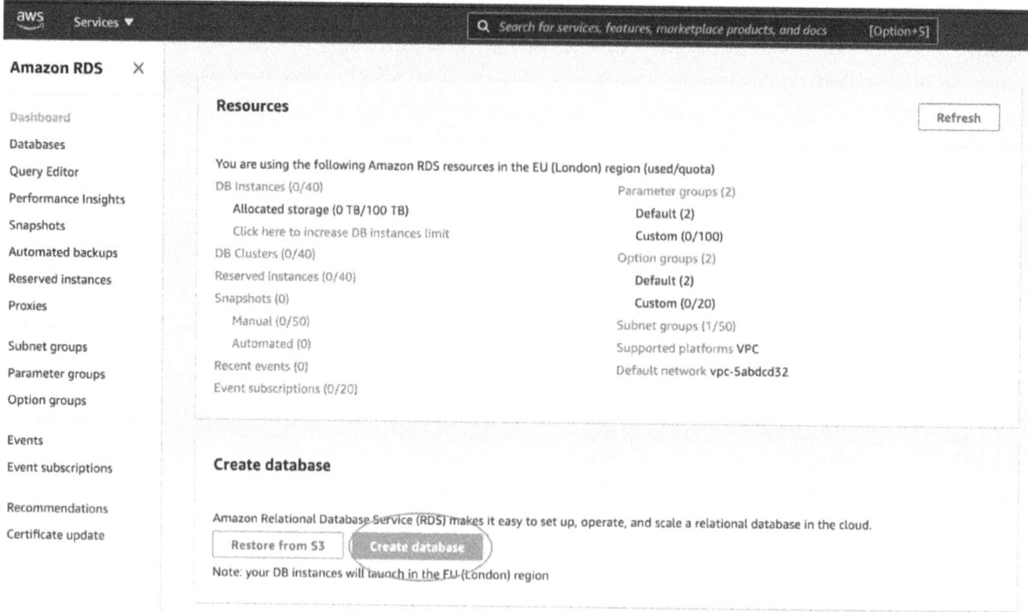

Figure 4.4 – AWS console

4. This will open a page where you can enter details about the database you want to create. Choose the following options. Leave any that are not mentioned here as-is:

   - Choose database creation method: **Standard create**.
   - Engine type: **MySQL**.
   - Edition: **MySQL Community**.
   - Version: Choose the default.
   - Templates: **Free tier**.
   - Database instance identifier: `dbcertdb1`.
   - Master password: Choose your own.
   - Database instance class: Burstable classes – `db.t3.micro`.
   - Virtual private cloud: Choose the one you created earlier.

- Public access: No.
- VPC security group: Create new.
- New VPC security group name: `dbcertdbsg`.
- Additional configuration: Leave all as-is but open this section to review the options.
- Click **Create database**.

5. The database will take around 10 minutes to create and its status will go through various status changes, including `MODIFYING`, `BACKING-UP`, and `AVAILABLE`.
6. Using the AWS CLI, we can check the database's status while it is being created:

```
aws rds describe-db-instances
```

You will see an output similar to the following:

```
{
    "DBInstances": [
        {
            "DBInstanceIdentifier": "dbcertdb1",
            "DBInstanceClass": "db.t3.micro",
            "Engine": "mysql",
            "DBInstanceStatus": "available",
            ...
        }
    ]
}
```

With that, we have created an RDS instance. We will now practice taking a snapshot of it and restoring it.

Taking a snapshot and restoring

Once the database has become `AVAILABLE`, we can take a snapshot of it and create a new instance from it. Let's get started:

1. From the Amazon RDS dashboard page, click **DB Instances**, and then click on the database we just created. You'll see a screen that's similar to the following:

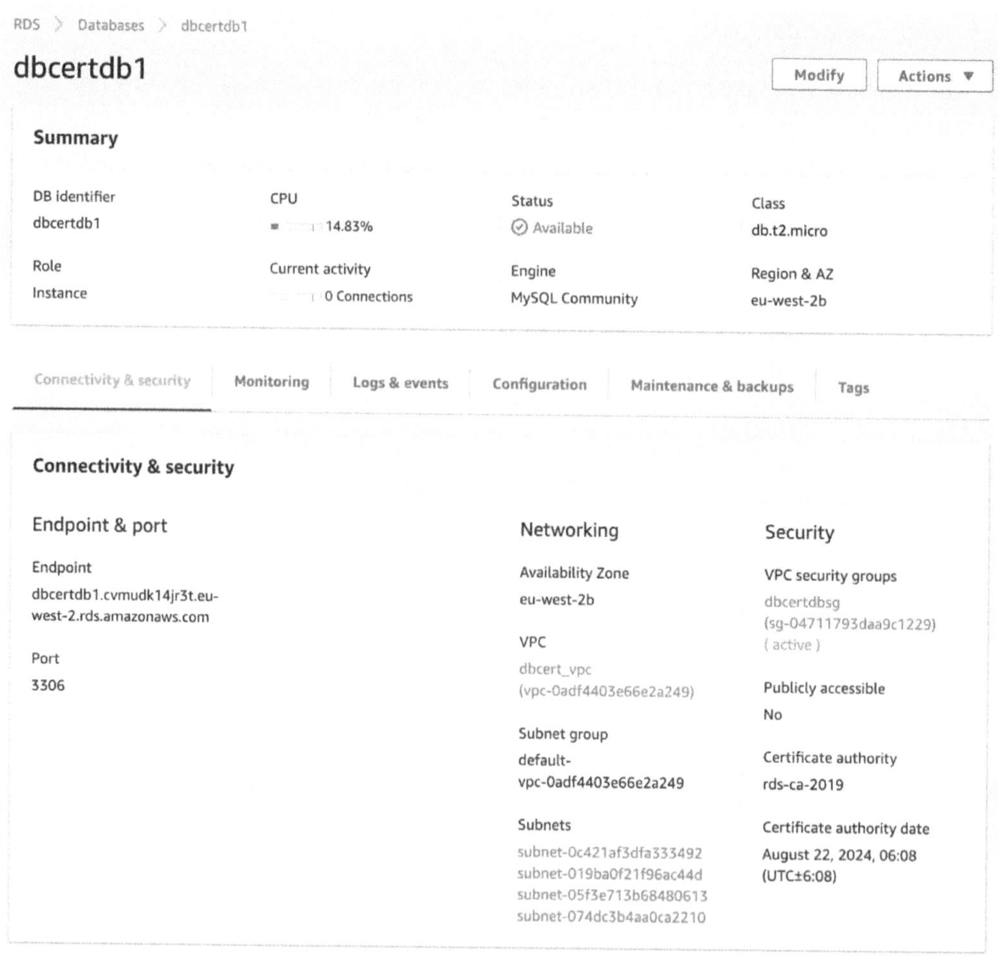

Figure 4.5 – AWS console

2. Click on **Actions** at the top left of the screen and choose **Take snapshot** from the drop-down list.
3. Enter `dbcert-snap1` as the name and click **Take snapshot**:

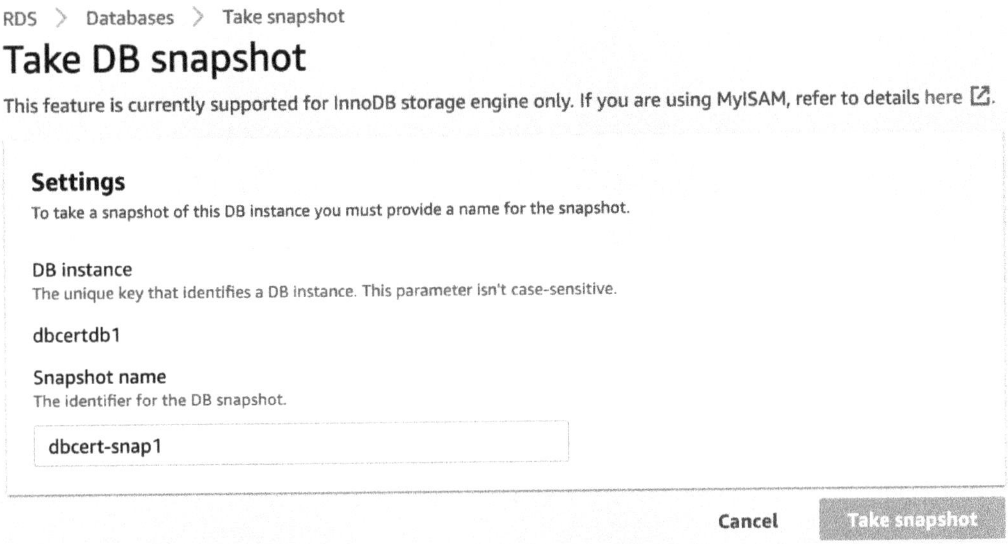

RDS > Databases > Take snapshot

Take DB snapshot

This feature is currently supported for InnoDB storage engine only. If you are using MyISAM, refer to details here.

Settings

To take a snapshot of this DB instance you must provide a name for the snapshot.

DB instance

The unique key that identifies a DB instance. This parameter isn't case-sensitive.

dbcertdb1

Snapshot name

The identifier for the DB snapshot.

dbcert-snap1

Cancel Take snapshot

Figure 4.6 – AWS console

4. The snapshot will take a while to create, depending on the size of the database. You can check the current status of the snapshots that have been created by using the AWS CLI:

```
aws rds describe-db-snapshots
```

You will see an output similar to the following:

```
{
    "DBSnapshots": [
        {
            "DBSnapshotIdentifier": "dbcert-snap1",
            "DBInstanceIdentifier": "dbcertdb1",
            "SnapshotCreateTime":
"2021-09-11T22:28:08.598Z",
            "Engine": "mysql",
            ...
            "Status": "available"
```

```
    ...
            }
        ]
    }
```

5. You can also take a snapshot using the AWS CLI:

```
aws rds create-db-snapshot --db-instance-identifier
dbcertdb1 --db-snapshot-identifier dbcert-snap2
```

6. Once the snapshot has been created, click on the snapshot's name link.
7. Click **Actions** at the top right and select **Restore snapshot** from the drop-down list.
8. Fill in the page with the following details. Leave any that are not mentioned as-is:
   - Database instance identifier: `dbcert-db2`
   - VPC security group: Choose existing
   - Existing VPC security groups: `dbcertdbsg`
   - Database instance class: Burstable classes – `db.t3.micro`
9. Click **Restore DB instance.**
10. The new instance will take a similar time to create as the original instance.

Now that we've created an instance, taken a snapshot of it, and restored it, let's modify a parameter group and apply it to our database.

Modifying a parameter group

Now, let's make a new parameter group that we can make changes to before applying it to our databases. Let's get started:

1. Return to the RDS dashboard and select **Parameter groups** from the menu on the left:

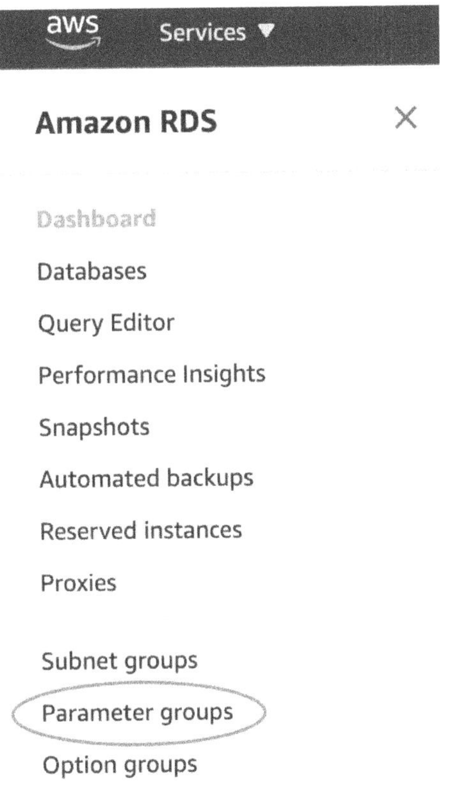

Figure 4.7 – AWS console parameter groups

2. Click **Create parameter group** at the top right.
3. Fill out the page that appears with the following information. Leave any options not mentioned as-is:

   - Parameter group family: `mysql8.0`
   - Group name: `mysql8pg`
   - Description: Parameter group for MySQL 8.0

4. Click **Create**. Then, click the **Parameter groups** name link when the dashboard appears:

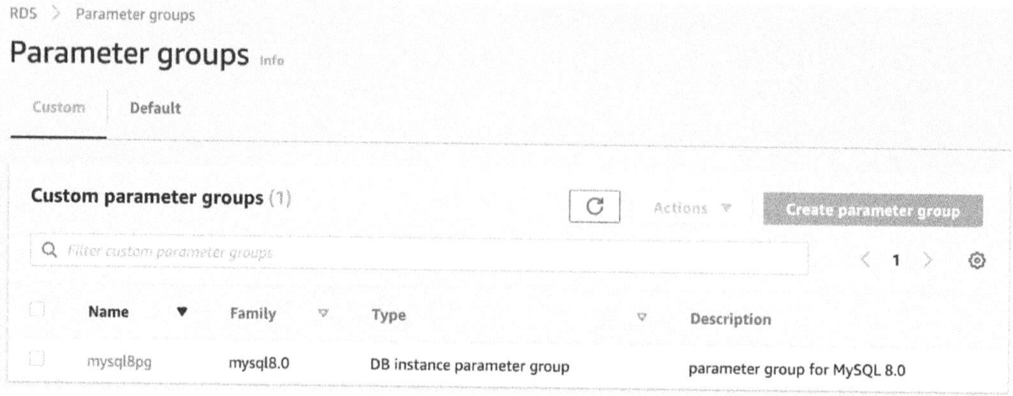

Figure 4.8 – AWS console parameter groups

5. Under the **Parameters** section, click **Modify**.
6. Find the `wait_timeout` parameter and change its value to `1`.
7. Scroll to the bottom of the page and click **Continue**.
8. Click **Apply changes**.

   Now, we need to assign the parameter group to our databases.

9. Click **Databases** from the left-hand menu and select one of the databases we've created.

   Click on the **Configuration** tab and scroll down to check the current parameter group:

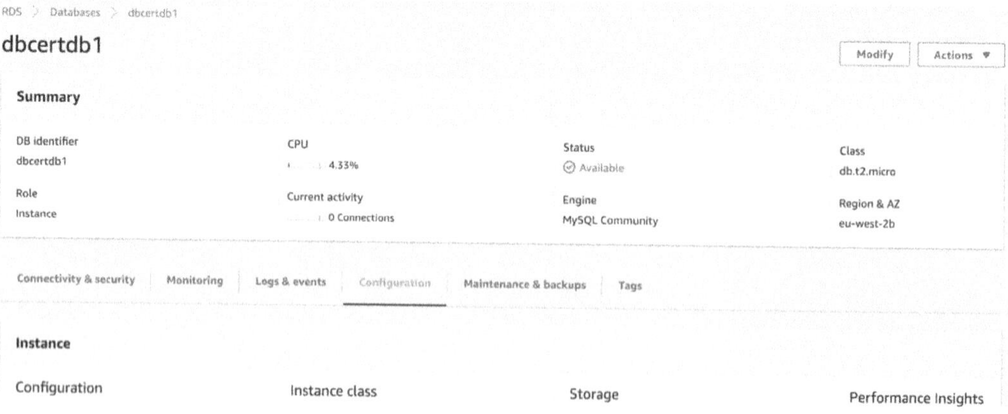

Figure 4.9 – AWS console DB configuration tab

10. Click **Modify**.

11. Scroll down to the **Additional configuration** section and change the parameter group to the one we just created:

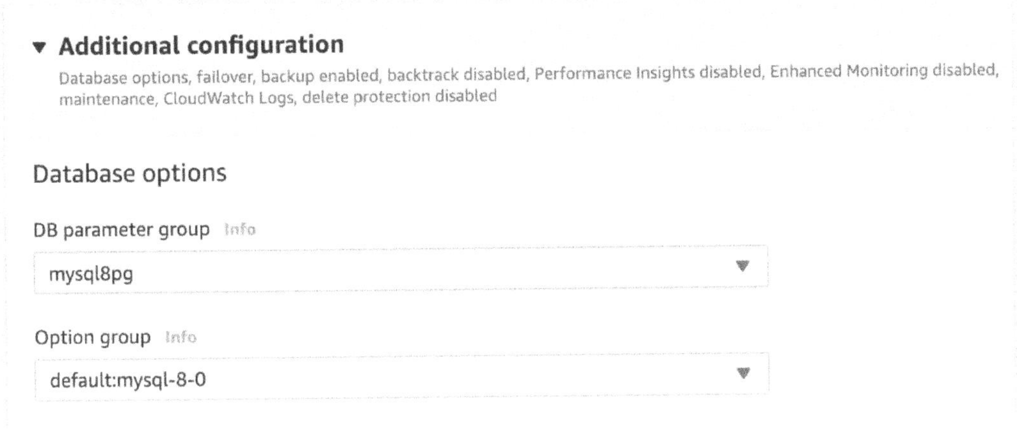

▾ **Additional configuration**

Database options, failover, backup enabled, backtrack disabled, Performance Insights disabled, Enhanced Monitoring disabled, maintenance, CloudWatch Logs, delete protection disabled

Database options

DB parameter group Info

mysql8pg

Option group Info

default:mysql-8-0

Figure 4.10 – AWS console additional configuration

12. Click **Continue** at the bottom of the page.
13. Select **Apply immediately** and click **Modify DB Instance**.

Once you've done this, check whether the new parameter group has been applied. This can be seen on the **Configuration** page of the database instance.

With that, we've gone through some of the basic admin tasks you may need to perform on an RDS instance, including creating a database and modifying it, as well as taking and restoring a snapshot. Since we created the database in the **Free Tier**, it will not accrue any costs at this point, so you can leave it running to learn more about RDS.

Deleting RDS instances

When you are ready to remove the RDS instances, you can use the AWS CLI to do so. Let's get started:

1. Obtain the current status of your database instances:

```
aws rds describe-db-instances
```

You'll see an output similar to the following:

```
{
    "DBInstances": [
        {
            "DBInstanceIdentifier": "dbcertdb1",
```

```
                "DBInstanceClass": "db.t3.micro",
                "Engine": "mysql",
                "DBInstanceStatus": "available",
                ...
            }
        ]
    }
```

2. Obtain the *DB identifier* from the output and run the `delete` command:

```
aws rds delete-db-instance --db-instance-identifier
dbcertdb1
```

3. You can keep running the `describe-db-instances` command to check the status of the database while it deletes.
4. Repeat this for any other databases you want to delete.

   We also need to remove the snapshot we took because, unlike the automated database backups, it will not be deleted with the instance.
5. Obtain the current list of snapshots:

```
aws rds describe-db-snapshots
```

You'll see an output similar to the following:

```
{
    "DBSnapshots": [
        {
            "DBSnapshotIdentifier": "dbcert-snap1",
            "DBInstanceIdentifier": "dbcertdb1",
            ...
            "Status": "available"
          ...
        }
    ]
}
```

Obtain `DBSnapshotIdentifier` from the output and run the `delete` command:

```
aws rds delete-db-snapshot --db-snapshot-identifier
dbcert-snap1
```

6. You can keep running the `describe-db-snapshots` command to check the status of the snapshot while it deletes.

Now, let's summarize what we've learned in this chapter and answer some practice exam questions to ensure we have a good understanding of the topics that have been covered.

Summary

In this chapter, we learned about AWS RDS. We learned what database types are supported, how to deploy and connect to an RDS instance, and how to carry out some common maintenance and configuration tasks. We learned how to use both the AWS console and AWS CLI to interact with our databases.

During the AWS Certified Database – Specialty exam, your knowledge of RDS will be tested heavily with questions around troubleshooting, service limits, upgrade procedures, and sharing snapshots.

In the next chapter, we will learn about Aurora, which is a special version of RDS that was created by AWS. We will continue to use the knowledge we've learned in this chapter to interact with Aurora as it has many similarities to RDS.

Cheat sheet

This cheat sheet summarizes the key points from this chapter:

- AWS RDS is a managed database service for the MySQL, PostgreSQL, Oracle, SQL Server, and MariaDB relational database engines.
- RDS uses endpoints for connections so that you do not need to configure your application connection strings after a failover.
- RDS automates many of the daily administrative functions that are typically carried out by a DBA. These include backups, log rotation, patching the operating system and database, and autoscaling storage.
- You can take manual backups called snapshots, which can be used to create copies of your database in different regions or a different account if they are shared.
- RDS supports encryption at rest and can enforce encrypted traffic between the client and the database using SSL/TLS.
- Using a multi-AZ deployment will greatly reduce any downtime during a database failure, upgrade, or maintenance period that requires the instance to be restarted. This is because RDS will automatically switch over to the standby mode to maintain the database service.

- Read replicas can be used to horizontally scale the database to offload some read-only queries away from the primary instance.

Review

To check your knowledge of this chapter, here are five questions that you should be able to answer. Remember the exam techniques from *Chapter 1, AWS Certified Database – Specialty Exam Overview*, and remove the incorrect answers first to help yourself:

1. A customer is developing a new application. Information will be uploaded from a large number of different devices. The customer is concerned about unexpectedly high volumes of data being loaded and exceeding the storage that's been allocated to the database. What steps can they take to simply and cost-effectively solve this issue?

   A. Migrate from RDS to EC2 and turn on autoscaling for the instance's compute.

   B. Use S3 to store the incoming data and build a lambda function to merge the updates to RDS.

   C. Enable storage autoscaling for the RDS instance.

   D. Create a read replica and send the read-only traffic to it.

2. You are using a new RDS PostgreSQL database. You are unable to connect to the database using `pgsql`. What is the most likely cause?

   A. You are not using the admin user account.

   B. The inbound rules on your instance security group do not allow your connection.

   C. The outbound rules on your instance security group do not allow your connection.

   D. You have not deployed a NAT gateway to allow connections from the internet.

3. You have deployed a multi-AZ RDS SQL Server database. Your manager wants to know the impact that upcoming RDS OS upgrade work will have on the availability of the database. What should you tell them?

   A. The primary instance will be worked on first; the standby will be promoted to be the new primary until the upgrade is complete. When the primary upgrade is complete, the standby will be upgraded. There will be no downtime.

   B. Both the primary and standby database servers will be upgraded at the same time. There will be downtime during the upgrade.

C. The standby instance will be upgraded first; the instance will then failover and the primary instance will be upgraded. There will be downtime during the failover process.

D. The standby instance will be worked on first and then promoted to be the primary while the upgrade completes. The primary will then be upgraded. There will be no downtime.

4. A company is growing into a new region, and they want to create a copy of their database to be shared with a different account. They have high-security requirements, so all their databases and snapshots are encrypted. What should they do to share the snapshot with a new account to allow for a restore?

   A. Add the target account to a customer KMS key. Copy the snapshot using the customer KMS key and then share the snapshot with the target account.

   B. Add the target account to a customer KMS key. Copy the snapshot using the default KMS key and then share the snapshot with the target account.

   C. Download the snapshot and use FTP to send it to the new location. Restore the snapshot to the new account.

   D. Add the target account to a default KMS key. Copy the snapshot using the default KMS key and then share the snapshot with the target account.

5. You are migrating an on-premises MySQL to RDS. You need to create a procedure for handling the backups to ensure you are meeting your compliance targets. Which of the following is true?

   A. The default retention period for backups is 7 days if you create your database using either the AWS CLI or console.

   B. The default retention period for backups is 30 days if you create your database using the console and 7 days if you use the AWS CLI.

   C. No default retention periods are defined.

   D. The default retention period for backups is 7 days if you create your database using the console and 1 day if you use the AWS CLI.

The answers to these questions, along with explanations, can be found in *Chapter 17, Answers*.

Further reading

In this chapter, we covered the most common RDS topics. In the AWS Certified Database – Specialty exam, you will be expected to know about and understand how other areas of AWS interact with RDS, which we will cover in more depth later in this book. However, if you wish to have a deeper understanding of KMS and encryption, *AWS: Security Best Practices on AWS*, is recommended: `https://subscription.packtpub.com/book/virtualization_and_cloud/9781789134513/2/ch02lvl1sec19/aws-kms`.

5
Amazon Aurora

Amazon Aurora is a fully managed relational database offered by **Amazon Web Services (AWS)**. It has many similarities to Amazon **Relational Database Service** (**RDS**), which we learned about in the previous chapter, but it also has many exclusive features. Aurora is a major topic within the AWS Certified Database – Specialty exam and as it features many of the same technologies as RDS it is highly recommended that you study *Chapter 4*, *Relational Database Service*, before this one.

In this chapter, we will learn about Amazon Aurora's architecture and how it differs from RDS, how we can achieve high availability and design Aurora to allow rapid disaster recovery, and we'll learn about some advanced options and features that only exist within Aurora.

This chapter includes a hands-on lab where we will deploy, configure, and explore an Aurora cluster, including how we can monitor it.

In this chapter, we're going to cover the following main topics:

- Overview of the Amazon Aurora service
- Understanding Aurora clusters and replicas
- Backing up and restoring Aurora
- Using Aurora's Global Database and Serverless options
- Understanding Aurora pricing
- Deploying an Aurora cluster

Let's start by making sure we understand what Aurora is, which database types it supports, and how it differs from RDS.

Technical requirements

You will require an AWS account with root access; everything we will do in this chapter will be available as **Free Tier**, which means you can run all the example code without spending any money as long as your account has only been opened within the last 12 months. You will also require AWS **Command-Line Interface** (**CLI**) access. The *AWS CLI Configuration Guide* (`https://docs.aws.amazon.com/cli/latest/userguide/cli-chap-configure.html`) will explain the steps required, but I will summarize them here:

1. Open an AWS account if you have not already done so.
2. Download the AWS CLI latest version (*AWS CLI version 2*) from the following link: `https://docs.aws.amazon.com/cli/latest/userguide/cli-chap-welcome.html`.
3. Create an access key for your administration user: `https://docs.aws.amazon.com/IAM/latest/UserGuide/getting-started_create-admin-group.html#getting-started_create-admin-group-cli`.
4. Run the `aws configure` command to set up a profile for your user.

You will also require a VPC that meets the minimum requirements for an RDS instance, which you can read about here: `https://docs.aws.amazon.com/AmazonRDS/latest/UserGuide/USER_VPC.WorkingWithRDSInstanceinaVPC.html`. If you completed the steps in *Chapter 3, Understanding AWS infrastructure*, you will already have a VPC that meets the requirements.

Overview of the Amazon Aurora service

Amazon Aurora is a managed database service. This means that AWS offers a wrapper around a relational database that handles many of the functions normally carried out by a **Database Administrator** (**DBA**). Where Aurora differs from RDS is that Aurora always speeds up the database functionality, and it can run up to five times faster than a non-Aurora version of the same database. Aurora manages such fast speeds by using a distributed storage system to avoid bandwidth and disk-read bottlenecks. Aurora has many benefits compared to RDS:

- **Faster scaling**: Aurora can almost instantly add additional read replicas whereas with RDS these can take some time to provision.
- **Read replicas**: Aurora supports up to 15 **replicas** compared to five on RDS.

- **High durability**: Aurora stores your data in six different locations across three **Availability Zones** (**AZs**) by default, so it has very high resilience as standard.
- **Rapid disaster recovery**: Aurora can recover faster from a failure. It can recreate what they call a compute node almost instantly to get your database back up and running if there was a failure.
- **Storage costs**: Aurora does not pre-provision storage. All storage is auto-scaled, which keeps costs efficient.
- **Serverless**: Aurora can be run in **Serverless** mode, which means you no longer need to define your computer requirements.

However, Aurora is more limited in the databases it supports compared to RDS and it can be harder to accurately calculate how much it will cost in advance.

Let's take a look at what database types Aurora supports and how this is decided.

Supported databases

Aurora is a type of RDS, so, therefore, it also only supports relational databases. However, because of the way in which Aurora works, it is described as being compatible with a database engine rather than using it. Currently, only two different database engines are compatible with Aurora:

- MySQL 5.6, 5.7, and 8.0 – InnoDB storage engine only
- PostgreSQL 9.6 onward

As you can see, compared to RDS, the choices are much more limited with Aurora. You will also find that newer versions of PostgreSQL and MySQL typically take longer to be supported in Aurora than RDS because the Aurora code wrapper has to be rewritten to support any changes.

As Aurora only supports open source databases, there are no licensing considerations to worry about. With Aurora, you only pay for what you use and you do not need a third-party license.

Compute and limitations

Aurora is very similar to RDS for both compute and access restrictions so we'll give a brief reminder here. If you are not using a Serverless Aurora cluster (which we will talk about in more depth in the *Using Aurora's Global Database and Serverless options* section of this chapter.), then the compute considerations are the same as for RDS. You will need to decide the size of the instance you need to handle your workload. The instance class can be changed after the database has been created.

Aurora also has similar restrictions on access as RDS; there is no access to the operating system or to root or sys accounts, and some functionality you would have on-premises has been changed to use Aurora-specific functions instead.

Service limits

Aurora also has certain **service limits**. Service limits indicate the maximums that you can use within RDS and includes the maximum amount of storage you can assign to the database, the maximum number of database connections, and even the number of Aurora instances you can run in your account. Here are some of the most common limits you may come across. These are often asked in the exam so it is worth trying to remember these numbers:

- **Maximum storage allocated to a database**: 128 tebibytes
- **Largest table size**: MySQL: 64 tebibytes, PostgreSQL 32 tebibytes
- **Maximum number of Aurora instances allowed**: 40 (this can be increased via a support request to AWS Support)
- **Maximum number of Data API requests**: 500 (Data API requests will be explained in more detail later in this chapter; however, this refers to the use of the `awscli` and similar tools that can be used for monitoring by sending requests for information from the database)
- **Maximum number of read replicas**: Five (this can be increased to a maximum of 15 via a Support Request to AWS Support)
- **Maximum storage size for all DB instances**: 100,000 (this can be increased to a maximum of 15 via a Support Request to AWS Support)

There are many other less-common service limits on Aurora but these will not come up in the exam. Please refer to the *AWS documentation* for the full list, which you can find at the following link: `https://docs.aws.amazon.com/AmazonRDS/latest/AuroraUserGuide/CHAP_Limits.html`.

Now that we understand what Aurora is and some of its benefits and limitations, we can start to learn some of the specific features, starting with clusters and replicas.

Understanding Aurora clusters and replicas

Amazon Aurora has been designed to benefit from cloud technology and as a result, it can use cloud ideologies such as auto-scaling (both horizontal and vertical) and decoupling of different parts of the application to improve resilience in a deeper manner than RDS. Let's take a closer look at an Aurora cluster to see how it decouples the compute layer and the storage layer to offer high redundancy and fast scaling.

Aurora clusters

An Aurora cluster is made up of two different types of nodes:

- **Database instance**: This is the power of the database and is where the database application sits and the processing of the data happens.
- **Cluster volume**: This is the storage layer spanning three AZs to offer the six data storage locations.

The following diagram shows how an Aurora cluster is arranged:

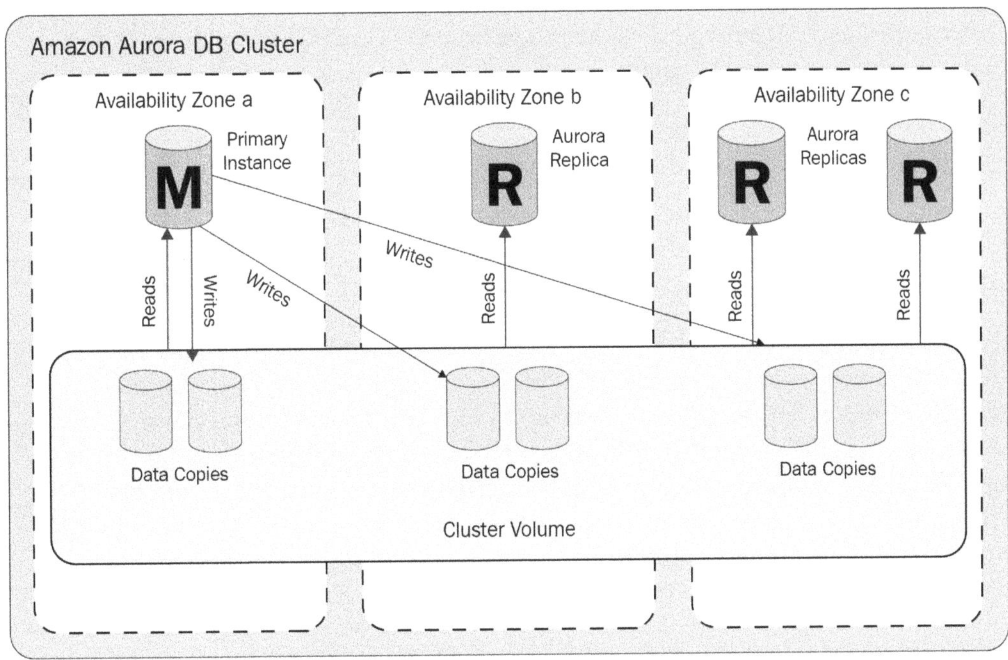

Figure 5.1 – Amazon Aurora cluster topology

All of the data is stored within the cluster volumes, and the database instances themselves only hold transient data in memory, which is lost if the instance reboots. The database instances can be read/write (primary) nodes or read replicas, and they communicate with the cluster volumes in the same AZ to improve latency and minimize cross-AZ traffic. The cluster volumes handle all replication, removing this from the database layer to further aid performance and to access the benefits of using the AWS storage backbone network. The database instances do not share data with each other. It is worth noting that even if you have a single database instance, it is still called a cluster as it will contain the single database instance and six cluster volumes. However, an Aurora cluster can contain up to 15 read replicas, which we will learn about now.

Read replicas

Amazon Aurora allows the creation of up to 15 read replicas, sometimes called **reader instances**, in the same region as the **primary/writer instance**. The reader instances can be used for two purposes:

- **Performance**: The application can be reconfigured to send read-only requests to the reader instances, reducing traffic against the writer instance.
- **Resilience**: A reader instance can be rapidly promoted to become a writer instance automatically if the original writer instance fails. This offers fast recovery of your databases. Amazon Aurora uses an endpoint that is automatically moved to the new writer instance, meaning no manual steps need to be carried out at the application layer to reconnect to the databases.

A reader instance can be a different instance class to the writer instance, allowing you to optimize the compute capabilities between reads and writes.

Let's look in more depth at what happens when a writer instance fails.

Failover

In the case of a failure of the writer instance, Aurora will automatically **promote** one of the reader instances to become the writer. Promote means to change the instance type from a reader to a writer. As you can create up to 15 reader instances, you can control the order in which the reader instances will be promoted first by assigning a **tier** to each reader instance. The lowest tier number denotes the highest priority for promotion, starting at tier zero. If more than one reader instance has the same tier, then Aurora will promote the instance that is the same instance class size as the original writer if one exists, and if not, it will pick one at random. This process takes less than 30 seconds to complete.

If you do not have a reader instance running when the writer instance fails, Aurora will recreate the writer instance for you. This will have considerably longer downtime than promoting a reader instance.

You can also manually promote a reader instance at any time without a failover. This creates a new standalone Aurora cluster to which you can now add reader instances.

We've looked at how read replicas or read instances work with Aurora but we haven't learned how we connect to them and how an application will send its read-only traffic to the right database instance. We do this via endpoints.

Endpoints

We learned in the previous section that Aurora uses a cluster endpoint that points to the writer instance. This endpoint is automatically moved if the writer instance fails and a reader instance is promoted. You can also create additional reader endpoints that will act as a load balancer to all the reader instances in your cluster.

You are also able to create custom endpoints for specific scenarios. For example, if you had a web application with read and write traffic and a reporting server with only reads, you might want to ensure the read traffic from both goes to different reader instances to balance the load. This method is also useful if you create reader instances of different sizes to suit different applications, so the reporting server might need to connect to the reader instance larger than the web application. You can use custom endpoints to create groups of reader and writer instances as well allowing for a highly specific configuration. Aurora will automatically stop traffic going to a promoted, deleted, or shut-down instance. You can also tell Aurora to add new instances to a custom endpoint automatically based on the exclusion and static list.

An example of how the endpoints can be configured is shown in the following diagram:

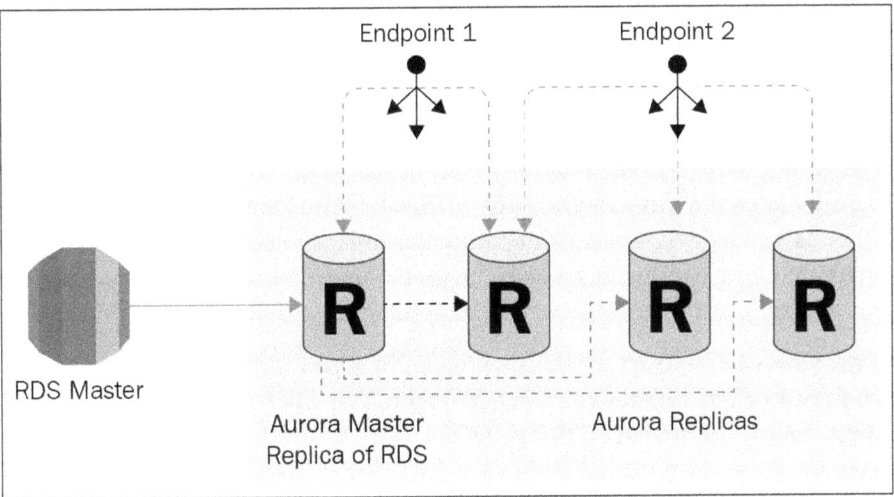

Figure 5.2 – Amazon Aurora endpoints

In this section, we've learned how an Aurora cluster works, how endpoints are used to control and configure access to the Aurora instances, and how they work with reader instances to split application traffic. In the next section, we are going to look at how Aurora is backed up and restored, and how you can migrate from RDS.

Backing up and restoring Aurora

Ensuring your data is secure and can be restored rapidly is a critical part of any reliable and resilient database system. Aurora has multiple options for backup and recovery strategies.

Backing up an Aurora cluster

Amazon Aurora is backed up continually and automatically as well as a system backup taken daily. The continual backups are taken throughout the day and do not have an impact on the performance of the database; this is a major advantage of the cluster volumes Aurora uses. The daily backup is taken during the backup window defined and this can have a low impact on performance, so the backup window should be chosen during a non-peak time. The backups are held in S3 until the retention time is reached, when they are deleted. The retention time can be set between one and 35 days and the default is one day regardless of whether the database is provisioned by the console or `awscli`.

You can also make ad-hoc backups at any time. These are called *snapshots* and they are not deleted unless done so manually, so these are often used to hold a backup beyond the retention period. The snapshots can also be used to create a new Aurora cluster and they can be shared with other accounts.

Restoring an Aurora cluster

An Aurora cluster can be restored from any Aurora snapshot. To restore the system, you use the snapshot to create a new cluster, which allows you to change the name. The new cluster will be associated with the default parameter unless you override it. If you need the same parameters or parameter group to be used, it is recommended that you do not remove the old group as the new cluster can be associated with it again.

A snapshot can only be restored in the same region or account it is currently stored in. If you wish to restore to a different account or region, you will need to copy or share the snapshot first. Let's learn how to do that now.

Copying and sharing a snapshot

First, let's look at copying a snapshot to a different Region in the same account.

To share a snapshot to a different region, you simply copy it and put the new region as the destination. If the Aurora cluster is encrypted, then all the backups will be too. As **Key Management Service** (**KMS**) keys are region-specific, the snapshot will need to be encrypted with a KMS key from the target region before you can copy it. Once the snapshot has been copied, you can use it to create a new Aurora cluster in the new region.

The snapshots do not automatically expire, so you will need to manually delete them to clear space if required; however, you must ensure the transfer has been completed fully before deleting the source snapshot, as its removal while the cross-region transfer is taking place can cause it to fail.

You can also share a snapshot with other AWS accounts within the same region. You can share an unencrypted snapshot publicly, which means any other AWS accounts can access it. If you wish to share an encrypted snapshot, you must also share the KMS key it was encrypted with to the other account. For security reasons, you cannot share an encrypted snapshot that was encrypted with the account default KMS key as this may grant access to decrypt other databases or systems that used the same key. By default, you can share a snapshot with up to 20 other AWS accounts.

If you wish to share with a different account in a different region, you must take a two-step approach, by doing either of the following:

- Share the snapshot to the new account in the same region; the recipient then copies the snapshot to the target region.
- Copy the snapshot to the target region, then share the snapshot to the new account from the target region.

Now we've learned how to work with Aurora backups, let's learn how to migrate an RDS database to Aurora.

Migrating from RDS to Aurora

Amazon Aurora is fully compatible with RDS MySQL and PostgreSQL. This means you can quickly and easily migrate from RDS to Aurora with minimal downtime. An RDS instance allows you to create an Aurora read replica instance that is solely designed for you to migrate.

When you first create an Aurora read replica, AWS takes a snapshot of your RDS instance and copies this to Aurora. This can take some time, several hours per tebibyte. When the read replica is created, RDS will start sending the transaction logs to Aurora so that the data is updated. This is an *asynchronous* replication, which means that the databases will not always be in sync, and at busy times you can get lag drift. You should monitor the lag and when it is at zero, you can promote the Aurora read replica to become a standalone Aurora cluster. At this point, you can switch the application to use the new Aurora cluster and you can delete the RDS database.

> **Backtrack**
>
> Aurora MySQL offers a feature called **Backtrack**, which lets you rewind a database to a prior point in time without having to restore the entire database. If you are used to working with Oracle databases, you can consider it as a similar feature to Oracle Flashback. You can enable Backtrack at any time by setting the Backtrack window for your database. Backtrack has a maximum window of 72 hours.
>
> If you need to rewind the database, you can choose the exact moment at any time in your Backtrack window and the database will be put back as it was.

After migrating from RDS to Aurora, you can take advantage of two Aurora-specific features that do not exist in RDS: Global Database and Serverless. Let's learn about them now.

Using Aurora's Global Database and Serverless options

Aurora offers two advanced features that can make a huge difference for certain use cases. In particular, customers who have a worldwide customer base can use Global Database options to reduce the latency between the database and applications around the world, improving performance. Customers with unpredictable or intermittent workloads can benefit from Aurora Serverless, where they can use a database without having to define the compute. Let's start by looking at Aurora Global Database in more depth.

Aurora Global Database

Aurora Global Database allows you to create a cross-region Aurora cluster where you can send read requests all over the world. This allows you to have read replicas in the same regions as your applications and users to greatly reduce latency times and improve the performance of your applications.

Aurora Global Database can also offer rapid recovery from a region outage, as any of the secondary/read regions can be promoted to a primary writer region in under a minute.

There is no performance impact in enabling Global Database as the replication is handled at the cluster volume layer. The cross-region replication is asynchronous but typically suffers lag times of under a second, making it a good solution for read-heavy global workloads.

You are limited to a maximum of five secondary regions, allowing you to operate in six regions at any one time (including the primary region). The nodes in the secondary regions can differ in size and type from the primary, allowing for high customization to fit your use case and usage patterns. For example, if you wanted to run in three regions but the third region had far fewer customers, you could provision a `t3.medium` instance there instead of an `m5.xlarge` instance in the other two regions.

Let's now look at another feature of Aurora: Aurora Serverless.

Aurora Serverless

Aurora Serverless is an on-demand, auto-scaling version of Aurora. This means that you do not need to specify the compute or instance class for it as Aurora Serverless is not run on a virtual machine, but runs on AWS hardware instead. Aurora Serverless automatically scales in a fraction of a second and goes from being able to handle a few hundred transactions to hundreds of thousands. Aurora Serverless will also pause when not in use, making it cost-efficient. When Aurora Serverless pauses, it can take several seconds for it to *wake up* and allow transactions to start again. This is important as the restart period is not instant and therefore you need to carefully decide whether your workload will operate effectively with Aurora Serverless. The best use cases for Aurora are when your workload is unpredictable with sharp spikes and drops in usage. Aurora can almost instantly scale up and down to maintain the same performance level for the end users, regardless of the workload.

Aurora Serverless offers the same features as Aurora, including global tables and read replicas. You can also mix a cluster to feature both Serverless and standard provisioned nodes. This can be used to rapidly add fully automated scaling to any Aurora cluster, even one that's already running.

We've now learned about the key features of Aurora and how they can be used to meet different use cases. Questions around global tables and Aurora Serverless do appear in the exam. Let's now look at how Aurora is priced for both provisioned mode and Serverless.

Understanding Aurora pricing

Aurora pricing is different between provisioned mode and Serverless. In provisioned mode, Aurora is priced in a similar way to RDS, where you decide how much resources (CPU and memory) you need, as well as how much storage. In Serverless, you are billed based on the **Aurora Capacity Units** (**ACUs**), which are priced as a combination of CPU and memory. In addition, you pay for any specific features you use such as global tables and Backtrack. In addition, you pay for read/write I/O usage in Aurora, which is included as standard in RDS.

To calculate your total Aurora costs, you will need to choose an instance size, database engine (MySQL or PostgreSQL), storage size, and I/O requirements. You can use the AWS Calculator to help you build your estimate. The following screenshot shows the figures you need to add to the Calculator for storage and I/O rates:

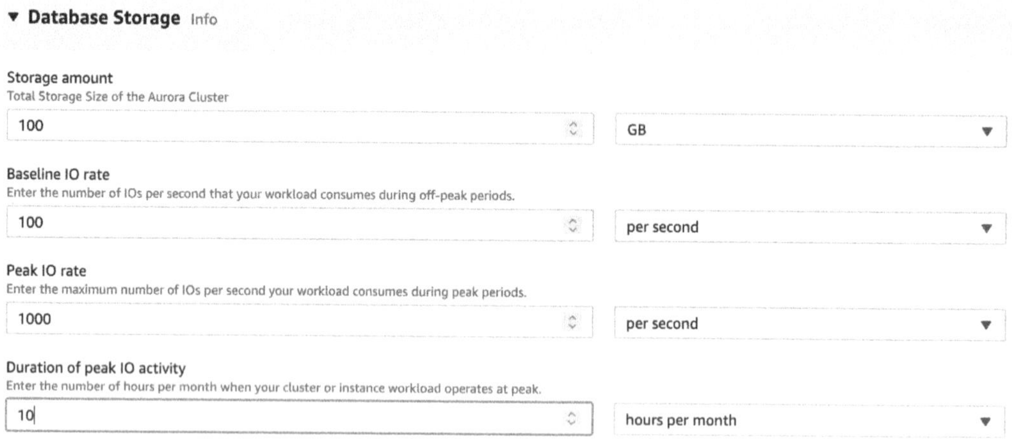

▼ **Database Storage** Info

Storage amount
Total Storage Size of the Aurora Cluster
100 | GB

Baseline IO rate
Enter the number of IOs per second that your workload consumes during off-peak periods.
100 | per second

Peak IO rate
Enter the maximum number of IOs per second your workload consumes during peak periods.
1000 | per second

Duration of peak IO activity
Enter the number of hours per month when your cluster or instance workload operates at peak.
10 | hours per month

Figure 5.3 – AWS Calculator

The Calculator URL is `https://calculator.aws/`.

Aurora provisioned pricing is very similar to RDS, which we covered in *Chapter 4, Relational Database Service*, so let's look more closely at Aurora Serverless pricing to understand how it differs.

Aurora Serverless pricing

You do not choose an instance class for Aurora Serverless; instead, you can set two optional parameters to control the minimum and maximum amount of CPU and memory resources available to your database. The resources are called ACUs. If you do not set these ACU values, then your Aurora instance can grow from zero ACUs (that is, the database will be shut down) up to 256 ACUs, which equates to an `r5.16xlarge` instance class. On top of this, Aurora can also automatically scale your reader nodes to the same size. If you recall, you can have 15 reader nodes, giving you the equivalent in processing power of 16 `r5.16xlarge` instances, which is enough to consistently manage 96,000 simultaneous connections.

Aurora bills each ACU's usage by the second, so you will only pay for what you use. If the database is shut down because it is not being used, you will only pay for the storage being used and no charges will apply for any ACUs.

Global tables pricing

If you decide to use global tables, you will need to pay for any resource usage for the secondary regions in the same way as your primary region. This could be Aurora Serverless ACUs or provisioned compute. In addition, you will need to pay **transfer fees**. Transfer fees are paid when data is moved between regions or is moved outside of an AWS data center, for example, if your application sends data back to an on-premises server. To calculate the charges for global tables, you need to work out the write I/O on your primary region and then multiply those by the number of secondary regions. Once you have this figure, you can use the AWS Pricing Calculator to find out the specific cost for your regions.

High-level pricing questions come up in the exam, often focused on how a customer is billed for using Serverless and what they would need to consider when using global tables, so it's important to understand these costs, but you will not be asked to calculate the actual costs.

We've now looked at all the key Aurora features, how it differs from RDS, and how it's priced. Aurora questions are featured heavily in the exam and you will often be asked workload-specific questions where you need to be able to differentiate between a workload only suitable for RDS versus when you might want to use Aurora Serverless. Let's now practice creating and working with an Aurora cluster in a hands-on lab.

Deploying an Aurora cluster

Now we have learned about Aurora and its features, let's deploy our own cluster to practice and to see how the topics we've covered in this chapter work together. We will be deploying an Aurora cluster using the MySQL engine in Serverless mode and we'll then add Global Database. We'll use both the console and `awscli` for these steps.

Provisioning an Aurora cluster

We'll start by provisioning an Aurora MySQL cluster. We'll be using the Ohio (`us-east-1`) region. It is important to switch off encryption for this cluster, otherwise we will get an error when creating a global database. In a production environment, we would create a custom KMS key to be used for our multi-region databases, but for now, we will turn off encryption:

1. Open the AWS console in an internet browser and log in using an account that has privileges to create and modify an RDS instance.
2. Navigate to **Amazon RDS** (remember Aurora is a specific type of RDS).
3. Click **Create database** in the middle of the page.

4. This will open a page allowing you to enter the details of the database you want to create. Choose the following options. Any that are not mentioned here, leave as default:

   A. **Choose database creation method**: `Standard create`.
   B. **Engine type**: `Amazon Aurora`.
   C. **Edition**: `Amazon Aurora MySQL-Compatible Edition`.
   D. **Capacity Type**: `Provisioned`.
   E. **Version**: Choose the default.
   F. **DB instance identifier**: `dbcertaur1`.
   G. **Master password**: Choose your own.
   H. **Availability and durability**: `Don't create an Aurora Replica`.
   I. **DB instance class**: `Burstable classes - db.r5.large`.
   J. **Virtual private cloud**: Choose the one you created earlier.
   K. **Public access**: `No`.
   L. **VPC security group**: `Use existing - dbcertdbsg`.
   M. **Enable encryption**: Untick.
   N. **Additional configuration**: Leave all as default, but open this section to review the options.
   O. Click **Create database**.

5. The database will take around 10 minutes to create and its status will change through various statuses, including `MODIFYING`, `BACKING-UP`, and finally `AVAILABLE`.
6. Using `awscli`, we can check the database status while it is being created, as shown in the following:

```
aws rds describe-db-instances
```

You will see output similar to the following:

```
{
    "DBInstances": [
        {
            "DBInstanceIdentifier": "dbcertaur1",
            "DBInstanceClass": "db.r5.large",
            "Engine": "mysql",
```

```
                "DBInstanceStatus": "available",
                ...
            }
        ]
    }
```

Once the database has been provisioned and shows an `AVAILABLE` status, we can modify it.

Adding a read replica auto-scaling policy

We are now going to add a new reader instance to our cluster, but we are going to deploy it using an auto-scaling policy:

1. Open the AWS console in an internet browser and log in using an account that has privileges to create and modify an RDS instance.
2. Navigate to the RDS section (remember that Aurora is a specific type of RDS).
3. Find the provisioned Aurora cluster you created earlier and select the **Actions** dropdown, then click **Add replica auto-scaling**:

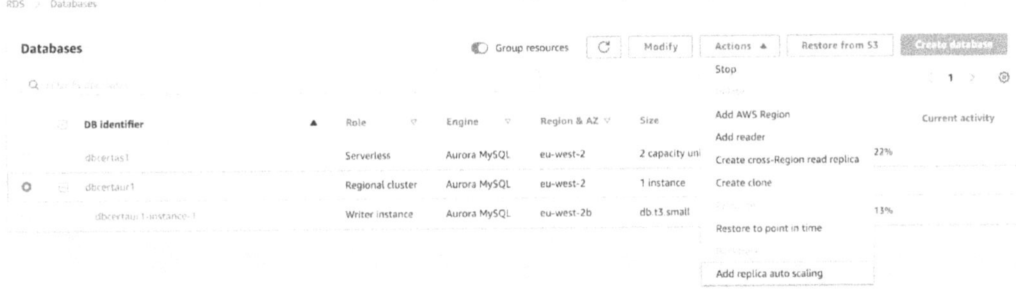

Figure 5.4 – Add replica auto-scaling

4. Enter `dbcertscale` for the policy name and the target value as `75% CPU`. Leave everything else as default.

> **Note**
>
> Take a look at the settings and options to ensure you understand what they mean and what they do before continuing.

5. When you return to the console screen, you should see that a new reader instance is being created. This is because the minimum number of reader instances was set to one, therefore the Aurora cluster will need to immediately create a reader, as shown in the following screenshot:

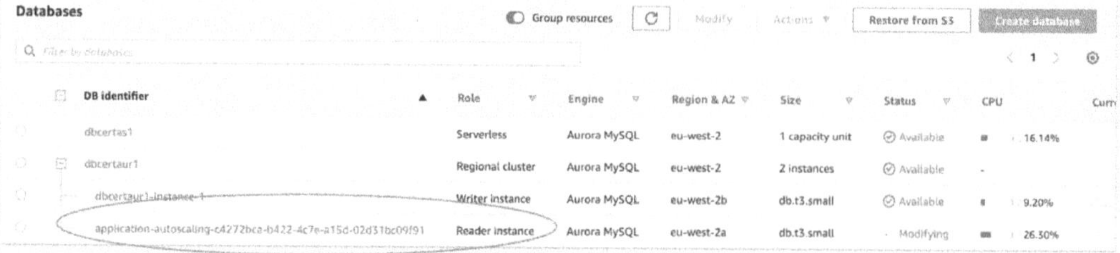

Figure 5.5 – AWS console showing the reader instance

If this is not visible immediately, go to the DB instance, and then the **Logs and Events** tab. You should see two entries like this, showing that the auto-scaling policy and the event to create a new read replica have been triggered:

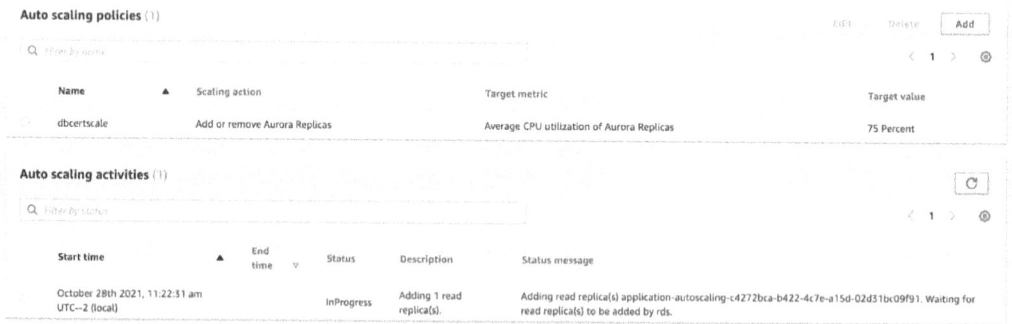

Figure 5.6 – Auto-scaling policies

Now we've got our cluster up and running with read replicas, let's make it global.

Adding global databases

Now we have our Aurora cluster running and we have the read replicas auto-scaling policy in place, let's create some global databases. The first thing we need to do is to change to a self-managed key; AWS default keys cannot be shared cross-region so we would hit an error if we tried to use one:

1. Open the AWS console in an internet browser and log in using an account that has privileges to create and modify an RDS instance.
2. Navigate to the RDS section (remember Aurora is a specific type of RDS).

3. Highlight the `dbcertaur1` database, click the **Actions** dropdown, and select **Add AWS Region**, as shown in the following screenshot:

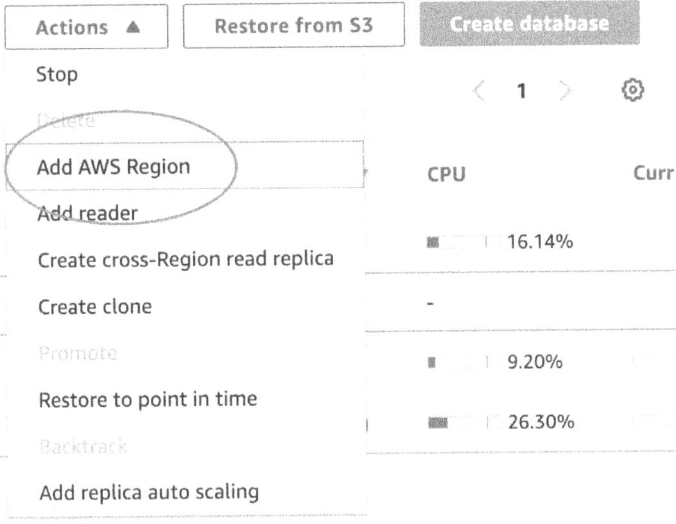

Figure 5.7 – Add AWS Region

You may get an error saying that the database version chosen doesn't meet the requirements for global databases. If this is the case, then click the **Modify** button and change to a supported type. You can see the supported types for Global Database by selecting the option. You may also need to change the instance size to a higher class if you did not select the `r5.large` option:

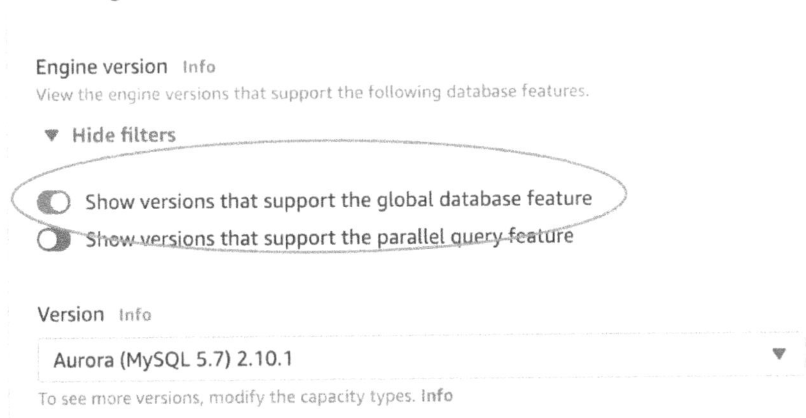

Figure 5.8 – Show only versions that support Global Database

The compatible options change regularly so you'll need to refer to the AWS guides (`https://docs.aws.amazon.com/AmazonRDS/latest/AuroraUserGuide/Concepts.DBInstanceClass.html`) to find the right combination.

4. Give the global database a name: `dbcertglob`.
5. Select any region in which you would like to deploy (make a note of which region you choose so you can check the database later. The AWS console is region-dependent).
6. Select an instance class from the drop-down menu. The larger the class, the more it will cost, so for this hands-on lab, you should choose the smallest available. This will depend on which region you deploy, as shown here:

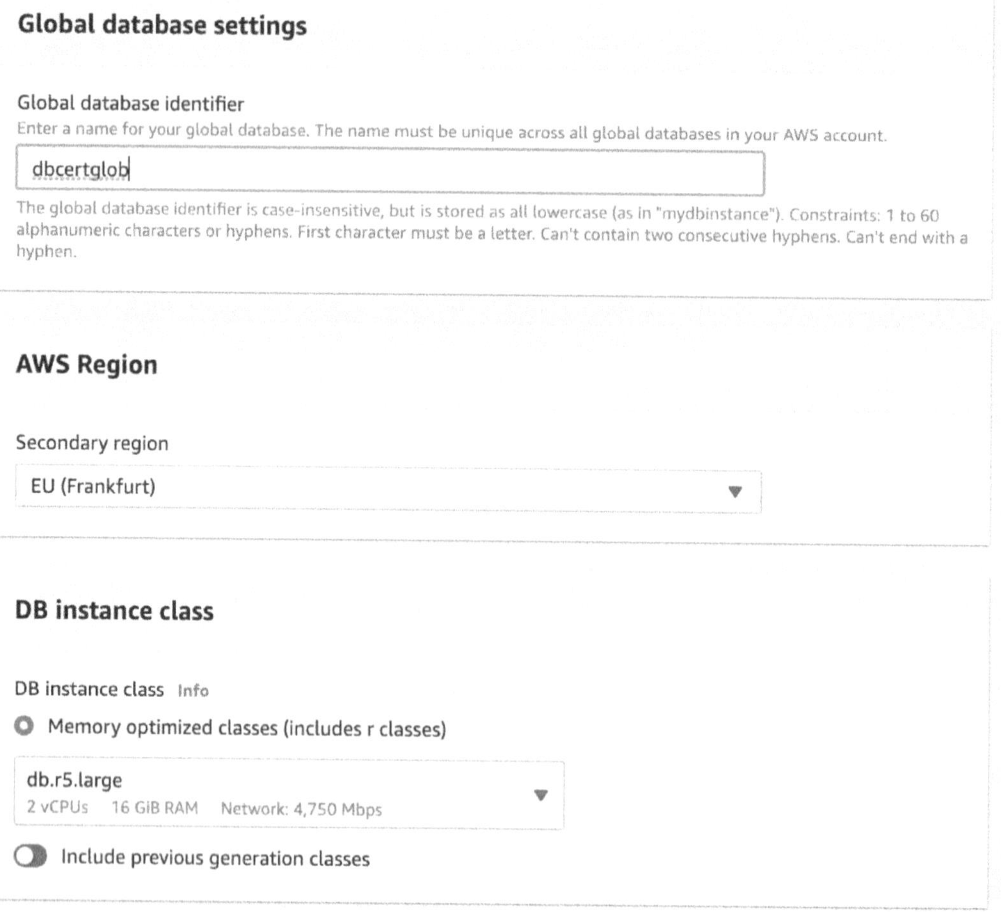
Global database settings
Global database identifier
Enter a name for your global database. The name must be unique across all global databases in your AWS account.
dbcertglob
The global database identifier is case-insensitive, but is stored as all lowercase (as in "mydbinstance"). Constraints: 1 to 60 alphanumeric characters or hyphens. First character must be a letter. Can't contain two consecutive hyphens. Can't end with a hyphen.
AWS Region
Secondary region
EU (Frankfurt)
DB instance class
DB instance class Info
Memory optimized classes (includes r classes)
db.r5.large
2 vCPUs 16 GiB RAM Network: 4,750 Mbps
Include previous generation classes

Figure 5.9 – Creating a global database

7. Leave the connectivity options as default but make sure you understand them. As we have not created our own VPC in another region, we will use the default Amazon provides. This would not be good practice in a production system and you should set up a VPC manually first for more security and control.
8. If it appears under the **Encryption** heading, turn encryption off to match the source database. If you enabled encryption on the source database, you will get an error. If this happens, go back to the *Provisioning an Aurora cluster* section and recreate the cluster without encryption to continue.
9. Expand the **Additional Configuration** options and uncheck **Enable Performance Insights** and **Enable Enhanced monitoring** as we won't be using these and they have charges associated:

Backup
Backup retention period Info
Choose the number of days that RDS should retain automatic backups for this instance.
1 day
Copy tags to snapshots
Performance Insights Info
Enable Performance Insights
Monitoring
Enable Enhanced monitoring
Enabling Enhanced monitoring metrics are useful when you want to see how different processes or threads use the CPU.
Maintenance
Auto minor version upgrade Info
Enable auto minor version upgrade
Enabling auto minor version upgrade will automatically upgrade to new minor versions as they are released. The automatic upgrades occur during the maintenance window for the database.
Maintenance window Info
Select the period you want pending modifications or maintenance applied to the database by Amazon RDS.
Select window
No preference
Cancel
Add region

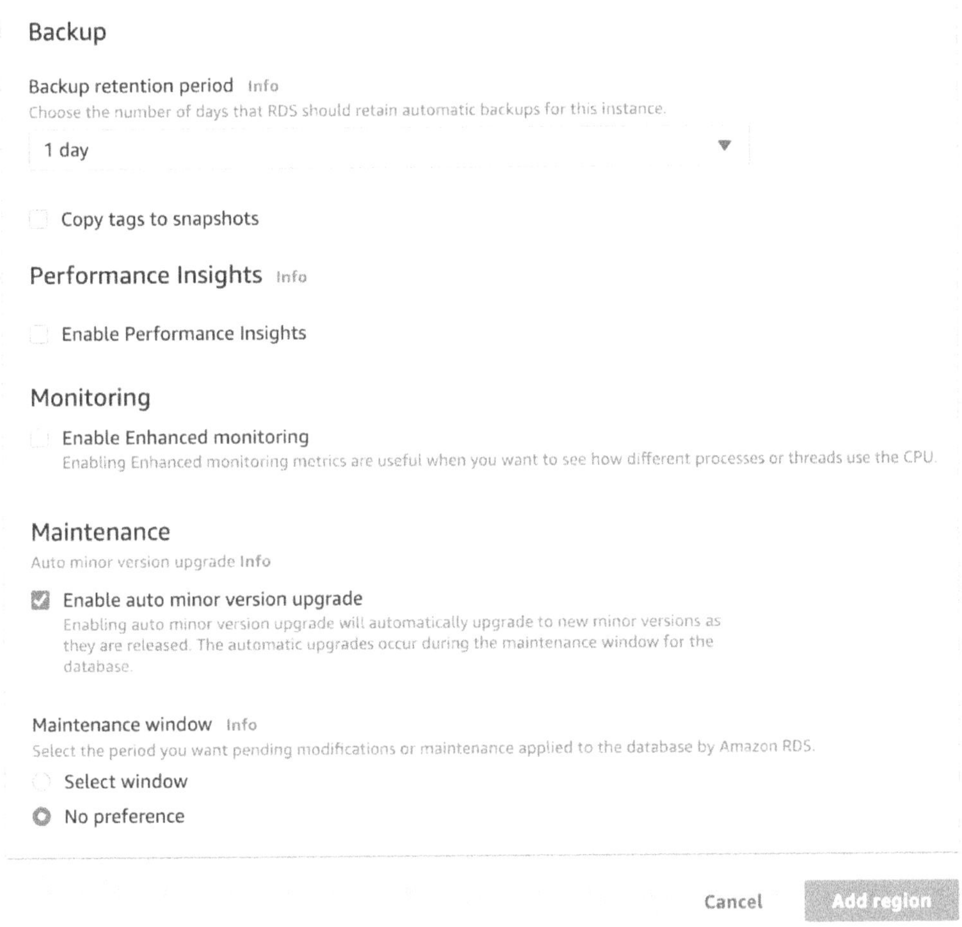

Figure 5.10 – Additional configuration options

10. Click **Add region**.
11. AWS will create a new Aurora cluster in the new region. This will take around 10 minutes to complete.

You've now created an Aurora global database across two regions. If you wish, you can now delete the Aurora cluster to save costs, as Aurora is not available on the Free Tier.

Summary

In this chapter, we have learned about Amazon Aurora. We have learned how Aurora differs from RDS, what database types are supported, how to deploy both a provisioned and Serverless Aurora cluster, and how to carry out some common maintenance and configuration tasks. We learned how to use both the AWS console and `awscli` to interact with our databases. These skills will enable us to work with Amazon Aurora databases confidently, as well as describe the use cases and benefits of Aurora compared to RDS.

During the AWS Certified Database – Specialty exam, your knowledge of Aurora will be tested heavily with questions around troubleshooting, service limits, Serverless and Global Database features, and migrating from RDS.

In the next chapter, we will be learning about AWS DynamoDB, which is a NoSQL database designed and fully managed by AWS. DynamoDB is very different from both RDS and Aurora as it supports unstructured data and does not rely on complex queries with joins.

Cheat sheet

This cheat sheet reminds you of the high-level topics and points covered in this chapter and should act as a revision guide and refresher:

- Amazon Aurora is a managed database service created by AWS that offers a database compatible with MySQL or PostgreSQL.
- An Aurora cluster features reader and writer instances with their own endpoints, allowing you to split your application workload between reads and writes.
- You do not define the storage capacity for Aurora as it can scale instantaneously and automatically. You also do not need to define any **Input/Output Operations Per Second (IOPS)** or throughput as you always get the maximum available with any Aurora instance or storage size.
- You can have up to 15 reader instances in any one cluster, but only one writer instance.

- Aurora automates many of the daily administrative functions typically carried out by a DBA. These include backups, log rotation, and patching of the operating system and database, and can include auto-scaling of the storage, the sizing of the writer instance, and the number and size of any reader nodes.
- Aurora is automatically a Multi-AZ deployment with six copies of your data being stored across three AZs.
- Aurora Serverless allows you to provision an Aurora cluster without specifying the instance size you need. Instead, you allocate maximum and minimum Aurora capacity units and the Serverless instance will scale automatically to handle any load.
- Global Database lets you quickly and easily offer a multi-region deployment to reduce latency between a global application and the database.
- Aurora Backtrack allows you to put the database back to how it was at any time in the Backtrack window without recovering from a backup.

Let's now check your knowledge of what you have learned during this chapter.

Review

To check your knowledge from this chapter, here are five questions that you should now be able to answer. Remember the exam techniques from *Chapter 1, AWS Certified Database – Specialty Exam Overview*, and remove the clearly incorrect answers first to help you:

1. You have an application that has an Amazon Aurora MySQL backend database. The customer wants to grant access to a reporting tool. How can you modify the existing database to give access to the reporting tool, which must be highly available without impacting the performance of the online application in the most cost-efficient way?

    A. Create a cross-region Multi-AZ deployment and create a read replica in the second region.

    B. Move the instance to Amazon EC2 and create and manage snapshots manually.

    C. Create a Multi-AZ Aurora read replica of the Aurora DB instance.

    D. Create a Single-AZ Aurora read replica of the Aurora DB instance. Create a second Single-AZ Aurora read replica from the replica.

2. You are managing a web application used by users in the United Kingdom and America. The application includes a database tier using a MySQL database hosted in `eu-west-2` (London). The web tier runs from `eu-west-2` and `us-east-1` (Ohio), which has routing to direct users to the closest web tier. It has been noted that American customers are complaining of slow response times to queries. Which changes should be made to the database tier to improve performance?

    A. Migrate the database to Amazon RDS for MySQL. Configure **Multi-AZ** in the Ohio region.

    B. Migrate the database to Amazon Aurora. Use Aurora global tables to enable replication to additional regions.

    C. Deploy MySQL instances in each region. Deploy an Application Load Balancer in front of MySQL to reduce the load on the primary instance.

    D. Migrate the database to an Amazon Aurora global database in MySQL compatibility mode. Configure read replicas in Ohio.

3. An application requires a Postgres database, which will only be used a few times a week for periods of less than an hour. The database needs to provide automatic start-up and scaling. Which database service is most suitable?

    A. Amazon Aurora

    B. Amazon Aurora Serverless

    C. Amazon RDS MySQL

    D. Amazon EC2 instance with MySQL database installed

4. You are the DBA for a financial company that currently has data hosted in an Amazon Aurora MySQL DB. Since this database stores critical financial data, there is a need to ensure that it can be made available in another region in the case of a disaster. How can this be achieved in the most cost-efficient and simplest way?

    A. Create a read replica of Amazon Aurora in another region.

    B. Make a copy of the underlying EBS volumes in the Amazon cluster in another region.

    C. Enable Global Database for the Aurora database and provision in another region.

    D. Create an EBS snapshot of the underlying EBS volumes in the Amazon cluster and then copy them to another region.

5. A large television company is running a critical application that uses Amazon RDS for PostgreSQL in Multi-AZ. The database size is currently 45 tebibytes. The head of IT wants to migrate the database to Amazon Aurora with minimal disruption to the business. What is the simplest and most resilient migration plan to meet these requirements?

    A. Use the **AWS Schema Conversion Tool** (**AWS SCT**) to copy the database schema from RDS for PostgreSQL to an Aurora PostgreSQL DB cluster. Create an AWS DMS task to copy the data.

    B. Create a manual script to continuously back up the RDS instance using `pg_dump`, and restore the backup to an Aurora PostgreSQL DB cluster using `pg_restore`.

    C. Create a read replica from the existing RDS instance. Check that the replication lag is zero and then promote the read replica as a standalone Aurora DB cluster.

    D. Create an Aurora replica from the existing RDS instance. Stop the writes on the master, check that the replication lag is zero, and then promote the Aurora replica as a standalone Aurora DB cluster.

Answers with explanations can be found in *Chapter 17*, *Answers*.

Further reading

In this chapter, we have covered the most common Aurora topics. In the AWS Certified Database – Specialty exam, you will be expected to know and understand how other areas of AWS interact with Aurora, which we will cover in more depth in later chapters. However, for a deeper understanding of how the underlying storage and network configuration of Aurora works, refer to the book *AWS: Security Best Practices on AWS* (`https://subscription.packtpub.com/book/virtualization_and_cloud/9781789134513/2/ch02lvl1sec19/aws-kms`).

6 Amazon DynamoDB

In this chapter, we are going to look at the first of the **NoSQL** databases that **AWS** offers, **DynamoDB**. DynamoDB is a major topic in the AWS Certified Database – Specialty exam, and for a large number of **Database Administrators** (**DBAs**) who have come from a relational database background, it can be one of the most difficult to understand given how differently it works to a SQL database.

This chapter will include hands-on labs where we will deploy, configure, and explore a DynamoDB table, and we will spend some time learning how to interact with a DynamoDB table using code. DynamoDB does not require a **Virtual Private Cloud** (**VPC**) to be deployed in.

In this chapter, we are going to cover the following main topics:

- Overview of DynamoDB
- Querying and scanning a
- DynamoDB table
- Working with DynamoDB records
- Understanding consistency modes
- Understanding high availability and backups
- Understanding DynamoDBadvanced features
- Maintaining and monitoring a DynamoDB table
- Understanding DynamoDB pricing and limits
- Deploying and querying a DynamoDB table

Let's begin by checking the technical requirements for this chapter before looking at an overview of DynamoDB.

Technical requirements

You will require an AWS account with root access. Everything we will do in this chapter will be available with the **Free Tier**, which means you can run all the code examples without spending any money as long as your account has only been opened within the last 12 months. You will also require a **command-line interface** (**CLI**) with AWS access. The AWS CLI Configuration Guide, found at `https://docs.aws.amazon.com/cli/latest/userguide/cli-chap-configure.html`, explains the steps required, but I will summarize them here:

1. Open an AWS account if you have not already done so.
2. Download the AWS CLI latest version from here: `https://docs.aws.amazon.com/cli/latest/userguide/welcome-versions.html#welcome-versions-v2`.
3. Create an access key for your administration user here: `https://docs.aws.amazon.com/IAM/latest/UserGuide/getting-started_create-admin-group.html#getting-started_create-admin-group-cli`.
4. Run the `aws configure` command to set up a profile for your user.

The code for this chapter can be downloaded from this book's GitHub repository here:

`https://github.com/PacktPublishing/AWS-Certified-Database---Specialty-DBS-C01-Certification`

Overview of DynamoDB

Amazon DynamoDB is a fully managed NoSQL and serverless database service that supports key-value and document data structures. It is a proprietary database engine only offered by AWS. You may recall from *Chapter 2, Understanding Database Fundamentals*, that a NoSQL database is a database designed to store semi-structured or non-structured data without a concrete schema. DynamoDB is a **key-value database**, meaning that all data is stored with a key that acts as an identifier for the data, and the values, which are the attributes. A serverless database is one for which you do not need to define the compute requirements. When you provision an RDS instance, you need to calculate the number of CPUs and amount of memory you will need. When you provision DynamoDB, you do not need to do so and you can opt to run in **on-demand mode**, where AWS will manage your table capacity for you. DynamoDB uses the amount of data that your application reads and writes to work out your charges rather than the compute requirements.

A DynamoDB table can store data in the following formats:

- **String**: A value that can contain letters and numbers:

```
"Name": { "S": "Kate" }
```

- **Number**: A value that can only contain numbers including a decimal point:

```
"Score": { "N": "1045" }
```

- **Binary**: A value that can store complex data types in `base64` format. You can store images or documents using this:

```
"Image": { "B": "bXkgc3VwZXIgc64jcmV0IHRlehrsh" }
```

- **Boolean**: A value that can only be `true` or `false`:

```
"Parent": { "BOOL": "false" }
```

- **Null**: A value that can be `true` or `false`:

```
"Empty": { "NULL": "true" }
```

- **List**: An array of values of the same or differing types such as strings or numbers:

```
"Objects": { "L": [ "Book", "98" ] }
```

- **Map**: A collection of key-value pairs allowing for nested data:

```
"ChildrenDetails": {
    "M": {
        "Dave": {
            "Relationship": "Son",
            "Age": 12
        },
        "Amy": {
            "Relationship": "Daughter",
            "Age": 9,
            "HairColour": "Brown"
        }
    }
}
```

- **String set**: A list of strings:

```
"Children": { "SS": [ "Dave", "Amy" ] }
```

- **Number set**: A list of numerals:

```
"Codes": { "NS": [ "16436", "98464" ] }
```

- **Binary set**: A list of binary values:

```
"Images": { "BS": [ "aGVbG93b3JsZA==", "c2VjcmV0cw==" ] }
```

While DynamoDB can have an undefined schema, meaning you can create new attributes at runtime that differ for each record in the table, you need to ensure that the attribute types are consistent. For example, you cannot insert a string into a number attribute.

To use DynamoDB, you need to consider the following things:

- What key do I want to use for my table?
- How much data will I read and write to my table?
- How much storage will I need?
- Do I need to consider **high availability** or **disaster recovery** options?

DynamoDB is a serverless database so you do not deploy it within a VPC. To be able to make a decision on these four questions, let's first look at how a DynamoDB table is designed.

DynamoDB tables

A DynamoDB table has four components:

- A **partition key**
- A **sort key**
- **Attributes**
- **Indexes**

Only the partition key is required and for a very simple use case, this can be all you need. A partition key is used to define where the data is stored on a disk, a physical partition. All data with the same partition key is stored together, making retrieval from a single partition extremely fast. A sort key is used to order the data within the partition. You can use the sort key to store the data in the order you are likely to retrieve it in, so perhaps you might store it in date order with the newest first.

A typical DynamoDB table would look similar to the following example of a video game high score list:

PlayerID	GameName	HighScore	PlayerName
1	BugHunt	342	John Smith
1	SpaceMission	4553	John Smith
2	BugHunt	643	Sally Jones
2	SpaceMission	7332	Sally Jones
2	WarGame	8	Sally Jones
3	WarGame	12	Tom Brown

Figure 6.1 – A typical DynamoDB table

In the table, `PlayerID` is a partition key, and `GameName` is the sort key. There are other attributes that can be different for each item in the table. You can see that having unstructured data allows for different columns to be created for each item, which allows for multiple different types of data to be stored in one table. The table key for this example is a composite one, made up of both the partition key and the sort key. The key must be unique within the table, so for scenarios where you would want to store multiple entries linked to one user or one product, you will need a sort key as well as the partition key to guarantee uniqueness.

A DynamoDB table can also contain two different types of indexes:

- A **global secondary index** (**GSI**)
- A **local secondary index** (**LSI**)

A GSI allows you to specify a different key to be searched, which can improve the performance of your queries where you need to search for attributes that are not included in the original key. They can also reduce costs when used in the correct situations. We will cover DynamoDB pricing later on in this chapter. A GSI can be created either during the table provisioning or afterward, allowing for great flexibility. A GSI also has its own provisioned capacity, allowing you to split the costs between the different access patterns and decide whether they will use the base table or the GSI.

An LSI allows you to create a new composite key to be searched, which must have the same partition key as your original table but will have a different sort key. Like the GSI, this can speed up queries on attributes not included in the original key for the table but that still use the table partition key. An LSI must be defined at table creation time and cannot be created afterward. The capacity for an LSI comes from the base table and it does not have its own provisioned capacity. A table with an LSI is also limited to a maximum size of 10 GB.

The exam will not go into depth about how you design a DynamoDB table, but you need to understand the basic method. Firstly, you need to work out which questions need to be answered by your database; for example, the following questions might be asked about our high score table in *Figure 6.1*:

- What was the highest score for John Smith on Space Mission?
- What was the highest score of all time for Bug Hunt?
- Who has the highest score on Space Mission?

To understand why these questions are important to ensuring the table is designed correctly, we need to understand how DynamoDB querying works.

Querying and scanning a DynamoDB table

DynamoDB has two different methods of retrieving data:

- **Query**
- **Scan**

DynamoDB is designed to be queried only by the key attributes. This means that if you wanted to query an attribute that wasn't a part of the key, then you would need to scan the entire table. This is fine for small tables, but as they grow in size the performance of the queries will rapidly decline. If you are from a SQL database background you can think of this in similar terms to a query being run against a table without an index. In addition to performance concerns, in DynamoDB, the more data you access in a table the more it costs, so queries that involve scanning the entire table can become costly. A query method can only be used if you are querying against the partition key, and a scan method is used if you are not using the partition key.

Let's take a look at an example using our high score table. If we want to get the high score for a player for a certain game we can do so via a query, as `PlayerID` is our partition key and `GameName` is our sort key, but to find out what the highest score ever was for a certain game, it would require a full scan as we are not using the partition key of `PlayerID`. The same would be true for any other attributes where we are not using `PlayerID`.

In the previous section, we learned about two different indexes we can use to help with our table design, GSI and LSI. To allow us to obtain the highest score ever for a certain game, we would need `GameName` to be a partition key, and a GSI lets us do that. We can also set the `Score` column to be the sort key, which orders the query results for us allowing us to only return the top one in descending order to get the highest score for the `GameName` we chose. The GSI would also contain the partition key of the base table as an attribute, so we would also be able to return the ID of the player who had that high score by using a query rather than a scan.

The exam may ask a question about how you would advise a customer to build a table for a certain use case, and you would need to identify whether the use case can be answered with the current table structure or by adding additional indexes, but you will not be asked to design a DynamoDB table. It's important that you understand the differences between the two different index types and how they are used.

Partitions

We learned about partition keys and how they can be used in querying to improve performance, but the partition keys have an even greater role in controlling how the data is physically arranged and stored on disk.

DynamoDB runs across a huge fleet of computers and your data is spread across them in a technique called **sharding**. The partition key defines the data that should be located together within the same partition, and therefore, the same physical location. This allows queries that return a large number of records with the same partition key to be returned from one location, which greatly improves the speed of the query as less data is queried. This also optimizes your costs, as we will learn how DynamoDB uses read and write requests based on the size of the items being accessed for charging, with the fewer the items accessed, the lower the cost.

For some tables with only a partition key as the primary key, you cannot use this technique, as all primary keys must be unique. This means that your data will be spread across all the partitions. However, using partition keys to control the location of data can result in some partitions being more heavily utilized than others. For example, imagine that you have a partition key with 80% of the values being the same. This would create one large partition with the majority of the data in one place. This can cause a bottleneck called a **hot partition** and can be responsible for performance issues. It is important to ensure that you choose a partition key that has well-balanced and well-spread values to avoid this issue.

The records in the partitions are sorted by the sort key `defined`. This can also speed up queries where you are likely to retrieve the first records most frequently. An example here is to use a date as the sort key so that the most recent dates are first to be retrieved.

Now that we understand the basic structure of a DynamoDB table and how queries and scans work, let's look at how you insert, delete, retrieve and modify records in a DynamoDB table.

Working with DynamoDB records

DynamoDB uses an **application programming interface** (**API**) to control how you access it. We've used the AWS API before in previous chapters to create and work with other databases, but unlike an RDS instance, you can also use the API to run queries and to create and modify data within a DynamoDB table.

DynamoDB has seven main API methods for data manipulation and retrieval:

- `PutItem`
- `GetItem`
- `UpdateItem`
- `DeleteItem`
- `ExecuteStatement`
- `Query`
- `Scan`

PutItem

The `PutItem` API allows you to load records into the database. You can use the following syntax:

```
aws dynamodb put-item \
    --table-name GameScores \
    --item '{
      "PlayerID": {"S": "KateG"}
    }' \
```

The first line tells DynamoDB what action you will be taking: `put-item`. The next line identifies the table you will be writing to, and then the final lines contain the information of the record itself. In our example, we are only writing the `PlayerID` attribute, but you can add multiple attributes here if you wish. The syntax follows JSON standards, which are common across the AWS APIs.

GetItem

The `GetItem` API allows you to return a single record based on its key. You would use the following syntax:

```
aws dynamodb get-item \
    --table-name GameScores \
```

```
    --projection-expression "Score, PlayerID" \
    --key '{
      "PlayerID": {"S": "KateG"}
    }' \
```

The first line tells DynamoDB what action you will be taking: `get-item`. The next line identifies the table you will be reading from. The final lines contain the key details of the record itself you want to return. There is an extra line compared to the `PutItem` code, `--projection-expression "Score, PlayerID"`. This line allows you to filter the attributes that are returned, and in our example, only `PlayerID` and `Score` would be returned.

UpdateItem

The `UpdateItem` API allows you to modify a single record based on its key. It has four options you can use:

- `SET` – Sets the value of an attribute of a record. The attribute does not need to exist in the table before it is added as DynamoDB is designed for unstructured data. Attributes are only created when new records with new attributes are added. You do not manually add them.
- `REMOVE` – Removes the value of an attribute of a record.
- `ADD` – Adds a value to a set (we are referring to the DynamoDB types string set, number set, or binary set), which is a special attribute similar to an array.
- `DELETE` – Removes a value from a set.

Let's look at these options in more depth as each one requires a different syntax.

SET

The `SET` syntax lets you update an attribute of a record. You would use the following syntax:

```
aws dynamodb update-item \
    --table-name GameScores \
    --key '{
      "PlayerID": {"S": "KateG"}
    }' \
    --update-expression 'SET Score = :s' \
    --expression-attribute-values '{
```

```
        ":s": {"N": "4523"}
    }' \
```

The first line tells DynamoDB what action you will be taking: `update-item`. The next line identifies the table you will be writing to, and then the third line contains the key details of the record itself you want to update. The next lines tell DynamoDB which attribute to update. The line `--update-expression 'SET Score = :s'` tells DynamoDB what to do with that record, in this case `'SET Score = :s'`. Now, `:s` is a variable that we pass in the next line, `--expression-attribute-values '{":s": {"N": "4523"}`.

REMOVE

The `REMOVE` syntax lets you remove an attribute of a record. You would use the following syntax:

```
aws dynamodb update-item \
    --table-name GameScores \
    --key '{
        "PlayerID": {"S": "KateG"}
    }' \
    --update-expression "REMOVE Score"\
    }' \
```

The first line tells DynamoDB what action you will be taking: `update-item`. The next line identifies the table you will be writing to, and then the third line contains the key details of the record itself you want to update. The next lines tell DynamoDB which attribute to remove. The line `--update-expression "REMOVE Score"` is telling DynamoDB to delete the value stored in the attribute.

DELETE and ADD

These two options are for working with sets and allow you to delete and add values to an existing set. A set is an array of values of the same type.

DeleteItem

The `DeleteItem` API allows you to delete a single record based on its key. You would use the following syntax. This differs from the delete function used in the `UpdateItem` API as that deletes a value from a set, but the `DeleteItem` API removes an entire record:

```
aws dynamodb delete-item \
    --table-name GameScores \
```

```
    --key '{
      "PlayerID": {"S": "KateG"}
    }' \
    --condition-expression "Score < :a" \
    --expression-attribute-values '{
      ":a": {"N": "5000"}
    }' \
```

The first line tells DynamoDB what action you will be taking: `delete-item`. The next line identifies the table you will be writing to, and then the final lines contain the key details of the record itself you want to return. There is an extra line `--condition-expression "Score < :a"`. This line allows you to only delete the record if certain conditions exist, in this instance, only delete `KateG` if their score is less than `5000`.

ExecuteStatement

The `ExecuteStatement` API allows you to run queries against the DynamoDB table using the `PartiQL query` syntax. The `PartiQL query` syntax follows standard SQL syntax, allowing you to use `SELECT`, `INSERT`, `UPDATE`, and `DELETE` type statements.

Query

We talked about querying a DynamoDB table earlier in the chapter, but now we will look at the code you would use to do so and what you can and cannot query against. A query is extremely fast, even on a table with millions of rows, as it can go directly to the row required. Do not forget that a GSI adds additional key values, and so if you have an attribute you need to query that is not included in the base table keys, adding a GSI can help improve performance.

A query against a DynamoDB table can only be performed against the partition key, so in our `GameScores` table, we can only use the `PlayerID` and `GameName` columns for a query to filter on. An example query to get the scores for a certain player who played a certain game is as follows:

```
aws dynamodb query \
    --table-name GameScores \
    --key-condition-expression "PlayerID = :playerid AND 
GameName = :gamename"\
    --expression-attribute-values '{
        ":playerid": { "S": "KateG" },
```

```
        ":gamename": { "S": "Space Mission" }
    }'
    --projection-expression "PlayerID, GameName"
```

Note the syntax for the query, especially `--projection-expression "PlayerID, GameName"`. This line controls what attributes are returned to the user or application and can be useful to speed up queries if you have a large number of attributes. This line can be used on all other retrieval type commands used within DynamoDB, such as `get-item` and `scan`.

Scan

We briefly learned how a scan differs from a query earlier in this chapter, but let's take a deeper look at the syntax and when you would use it.

A scan is used when you need to filter against an attribute that is not included in any table or index keys. It can be useful if you do not regularly need to filter against this attribute and therefore, a GSI or LSI may not be a sensible design decision.

To run a scan, you can use syntax similar to the following to return all records where the high score is greater than 5,000:

```
aws dynamodb scan \
     --table-name GameScores \
     --filter-expression "Score < :score" \
     --expression-attribute-values '{":score":{"S":"5000"}}'
```

A scan will read every single record in your table, and this can quickly get very expensive, as you will see when we look at how DynamoDB is priced. In general, scans should be avoided unless it is a genuine one-off use case that cannot be answered using a query.

Now we have learned how to work with DynamoDB data stored in a table, let's look at how DynamoDB handles consistency and transactions.

Understanding consistency modes

DynamoDB offers two different data consistency modes to handle different use cases:

- **Eventually consistent reads** – This is the default.
- **Strongly consistent reads**

Let's start by learning about eventually consistent reads.

DynamoDB is typically used for cases where data consistency is not critical to the application. For example, website session data can be lost without major impact; the user may have to log in again or they may have to add items back into their shopping cart but unlike a banking transaction, which must fully succeed and be consistent without exception, session data is classified as transient. As a result, DynamoDB defaults to what is called an eventually consistent read. An eventually consistent read means that each read request might not get data that has recently been updated. This is due to how DynamoDB stores its data; it does not wait for the write request to be written to each storage location before it confirms it as successful. This means if your write request has not been written to all the storage locations before you try to read the data again from the table, you will retrieve the old data.

If your application cannot handle an eventually consistent model, then DynamoDB offers a strongly consistent read instead. This means that DynamoDB will guarantee the latest data is returned, but there are some downsides to this model:

- If there is any network issue or outage then the read may fail with an **HTTP 500** error. (Please see the *Maintaining and monitoring a DynamoDB table* section for more information on DynamoDB errors.)
- Strongly consistent reads have higher latency and will therefore return data slower.
- They are not supported on GSIs.
- They use more throughput capacity than eventually consistent reads, which may affect your costs.

In addition, DynamoDB also uses a standard write model by default. This means that a request to write data is handled in a different transaction from the one reading it. This can cause issues if you have numerous updates being handled simultaneously, as the data may have been changed by another session. DynamoDB offers transaction-level querying to ensure the consistency of data during the transaction in a similar manner to a **Relational Database Management System** (**RDBMS**). Using the transactional model can cause conflicts that need to be handled. For example, if an `UpdateItem` request is made while a transaction is running against the same item, you will receive a `TransactionConflictException` error.

We've learned how to handle different consistency models within DynamoDB, so now let's look at how backups and resilience work in DynamoDB and what options you have for high availability.

Understanding high availability and backups

Like other databases, DynamoDB will often become a critical part of your application, and your data needs to be resilient and recoverable to meet your application service level agreements. DynamoDB offers two methods to improve resilience and reliability:

- Global tables
- Backups

Let's start by looking at global tables.

Global tables

As DynamoDB is serverless and doesn't run in a VPC, the options you have for making it highly available are different from other AWS services. You cannot have a multi-AZ deployment here. DynamoDB offers a service called **global tables** to overcome this. Global tables allow you to configure a multi-region and active-active database deployment. DynamoDB will create an exact replica of your database across all the regions you specify, allowing you to create a highly available database system. If a table fails or becomes unavailable in one region, the traffic will automatically be routed to one of the remaining tables. DynamoDB uses **eventually consistent writes** to keep the global tables in sync. If you rely on strongly consistent reads, you will need to configure your application to use a single table, as the data may not propagate instantly and may cause data reconciliation issues.

> Note
>
> DynamoDB used to offer a service called cross-region replication, but this has been replaced by global tables and will not feature in the exam.

Backup and restore

Once you load data in DynamoDB it will become important to ensure the data is protected and can be recovered in case of a failure with the DynamoDB instance or its storage. AWS offers a backup-and-restore functionality as part of DynamoDB. DynamoDB has two different backup types offered:

- **On-demand**
- **Point-in-time recovery (PITR)**

On-demand backups are one-off ad hoc backups, typically taken as a restore point for changes that are made to allow for a rapid recovery. PITR backups are taken continuously in the background, allowing you to recover your database to any point in the last 35 days.

To take a backup, you can either use the console or API to trigger the backup. To check whether PITR backups are turned on and the latest restore time available, you can use the following code:

```
aws dynamodb describe-continuous-backups --table-name
GameScores
```

The output will look like the following, where you can see the recovery windows times in Unix epoch standard:

```
    "ContinuousBackupsDescription": {
        "PointInTimeRecoveryDescription": {
            "PointInTimeRecoveryStatus": "ENABLED",
            "EarliestRestorableDateTime": 1719256518.0,
            "LatestRestorableDateTime": 1620018613.01
        },
        "ContinuousBackupsStatus": "ENABLED"
    }
```

> **Note**
>
> If you wish to restore your DynamoDB table from a backup, you must create a new table and you cannot overwrite the existing one. This is to protect you from accidental data loss.

To run a restore, you can use the following command where you specify the Unix epoch time you wish to restore:

```
aws dynamodb restore-table-to-point-in-time \
    --source-table-name GameScores \
    --target-table-name GamesScoresRecovered \
    --no-use-latest-restorable-time \
    --restore-date-time 1619257264.0
```

When you restore your DynamoDB table, you are also able to change some of the table settings, such as switching the billing mode (**PAY-PER-REQUEST** or **PROVISIONED**), removing GSIs (you cannot remove LSIs due to the technical limitations of DynamoDB), changing the encryption key, or even restoring a table to a different AWS region, which can be a useful method of copying data between regions quickly and efficiently.

In this section, we've learned how to protect our DynamoDB data via multi-region replication global tables and how to take and restore backups. Now we will look at some more advanced options for DynamoDB, such as streams and time to live.

Understanding DynamoDB advanced features

DynamoDB has several additional features that can be used to help support auditing and compliance requirements. Often, companies have a requirement to audit all changes made to database tables, especially the ones containing **personally identifiable information** (**PII**) such as customer names and addresses. These are the three tools that can be used:

- **DynamoDB Streams**
- **CloudTrail**
- **Time to live** (**TTL**)

Additionally, for some very large (multi-TB) datasets or applications needing extremely fast microsecond response times, they can consider using **DynamoDB Accelerator** (**DAX**).

Let's start by looking at DynamoDB Streams and how it can be used for auditing purposes and to trigger other actions.

DynamoDB Streams

DynamoDB Streams is a time-ordered sequence of events affecting the items in your DynamoDB table. This includes inserts, deletes, and updates. The changes are written to a log, which can then be read and used by other parts of the application to trigger other actions. For example, if your application needs to send an email. If a user's email address is updated you can create code to look out for an email update in the DynamoDB stream and then send the email when the event occurs. It is common for these application triggers to be written in a coding language called **AWS Lambda**. AWS Lambda is outside the scope of this book. However, at the end of this chapter in the *Further reading* section, there are some book suggestions for beginners to learn AWS Lambda, as it's a powerful tool. In the AWS Certified Database – Specialty exam, you will not need to know about Lambda, beyond knowing that DynamoDB Streams can trigger AWS Lambda events and security, which will be covered in depth in *Chapter 12, AWS Database Security*.

CloudTrail

CloudTrail is a unified auditing tool that works for many AWS services, including DynamoDB. When configured for DynamoDB, it will automatically log any access attempts to DynamoDB, including any changes made at the data level. This audit trail is stored in an **S3 bucket**, which in turn can be queried using tools such as **Amazon Athena** (which we will learn about in *Chapter 11, Database Task Automation*) or used by a third-party tool such as **Splunk**. CloudTrail can also be configured to write the events into **CloudWatch**, which also monitors the performance of your DynamoDB, to give a complete view of your table activities in one location.

TTL

TTL is a method of automatically removing entries older than a certain time. It can be useful for login use cases where you want a user's session to only last for 15 minutes before they need to log in again, or if you have a data retention time and want to remove older records automatically. To use this, you need to add an attribute that stores a timestamp in Unix epoch format. This timestamp indicates when you want the record to be removed, so if you only want a record to last for 15 minutes you would add a timestamp of 15 minutes into the future. Using TTL, DynamoDB will remove any records where the timestamp value is older than the current time. These events are logged into the DynamoDB stream as well, so you can trigger further application or Lambda actions, such as prompting the user to log in again as their session has expired.

Now we've learned how to use some of the extra DynamoDB features to assist with compliance and data removal, let's look at a performance enhancement feature that can help with very large datasets, DAX.

DAX

DynamoDB is designed to give millisecond response times, but there are certain use cases that need microsecond response times for large datasets. DAX is a *caching service* available for DynamoDB to speed up data retrieval by holding data in memory, avoiding reading from a disk, which is slower.

DAX offers the following benefits:

- It reduces response times of eventually consistent reads from milliseconds to microseconds.
- It uses the same API as DynamoDB so there is no need to rewrite your application code.

- It can lower costs by reducing the number of reads from a disk as the data will be stored in the cache.
- It uses the same encryption standards as the source table, ensuring compliance is maintained.

DAX sits in front of a DynamoDB cluster and is by default deployed within the same VPC as your application (remember that DynamoDB itself does not sit in a VPC):

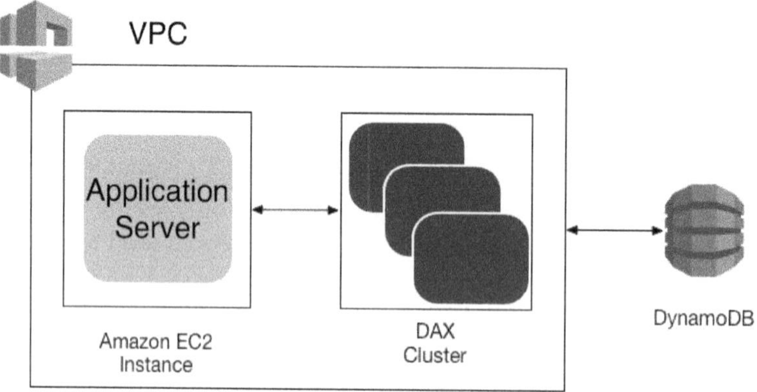

Figure 6.2 – A DAX cluster

DAX consists of nodes that form a cluster. You can have a single node or up to a maximum of 10 per cluster, but for production systems, the recommendation is a minimum of three for resilience. Your application will send the DynamoDB API request to the DAX cluster using a DAX client that is installed alongside the application. The DAX cluster will see whether it can answer the API call with data it holds in memory and if it can't, it pushes the request to the DynamoDB instance automatically. DAX then adds the response from the DynamoDB instance to its memory so that repeated calls can be answered from the cache. Any *strongly consistent read* will always be sent to the DynamoDB instance to ensure the latest version of the data is sent back. Any write requests are sent straight through to the DynamoDB instance as DAX is only designed for faster read requests. DAX also cannot process any table-level requests such as `CreateTable`; these need to be sent directly to DynamoDB rather than via the DAX client, as the DAX client is limited to read and write requests.

DAX itself has provisioned capacity, and if this limit is reached, you will start to suffer performance degradation and `ThrottlingException` errors. If this happens, you should consider adding more nodes to your DAX cluster or increasing the instance class size in use.

We've now learned about the advanced features available with a DynamoDB table, so let's look at how we monitor the performance of our DynamoDB table.

Maintaining and monitoring a DynamoDB table

The main tools you will use for monitoring a DynamoDB table are CloudWatch and CloudTrail. CloudWatch monitors the performance metrics of the table, such as the number of reads and writes and throughput metrics, while CloudTrail watches and records the actual data access patterns, stores, and audit trail of changes made.

One of the main areas you will need to closely monitor with DynamoDB is the amount of data being read and written to the table. We will look at the pricing in the next section, but DynamoDB is billed based on reads and will start getting errors stating `'ProvisionedThroughputExceededException'`. For the full list of common DynamoDB errors, please see `https://docs.aws.amazon.com/amazondynamodb/latest/APIReference/CommonErrors.html#CommonErrors-ThrottlingException`.

The following figure shows an example of the metrics you can monitor in CloudWatch. This diagram shows that we are using more write capacity than we have provisioned so we are being throttled:

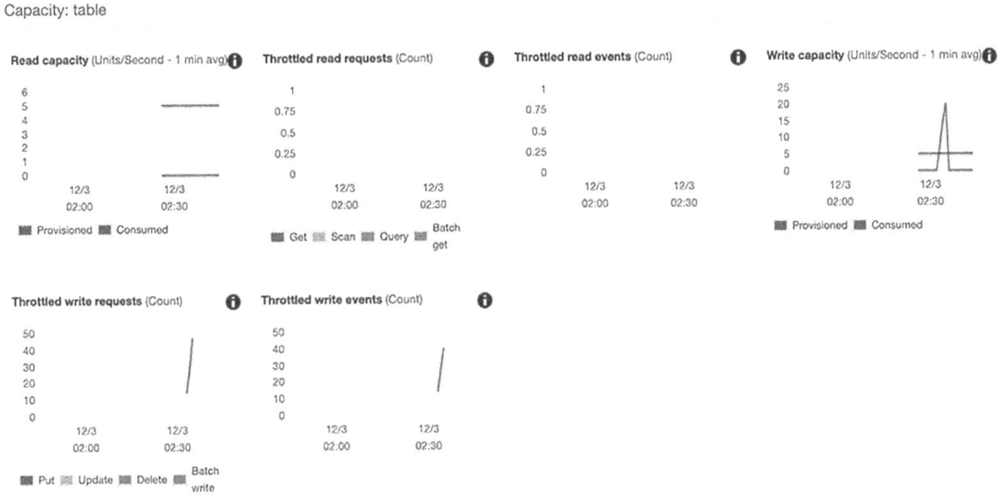

Figure 6.3 – DynamoDB monitoring in CloudWatch

Earlier in this chapter, we learned that GSIs have their own provisioned capacity separate from the base table. You can monitor the metrics against the GSI within CloudWatch as well. GSIs can suffer from capacity issues in the same way as the base table and so they should be monitored closely to ensure the performance is met.

We've learned how to monitor table and index usage but why is it important? Let's learn how DynamoDB is priced and why controlling the reads and writes matters.

Understanding DynamoDB pricing and limits

DynamoDB is a serverless managed service, which means you do not pick an instance size to control the performance. Instead, DynamoDB is charged based on how much data you read and write to your table. DynamoDB has four main components to its pricing:

- Read **request units**
- Write request units
- Storage
- Additional features such as DAX, global tables, and streams

Let's start by looking at read and write capacity units.

Request units

Request units are the main usage mechanism within DynamoDB. The number of requests you need for each task will depend on the amount of data being returned as well as the read/write type:

- *One read request* will give you *one* strongly consistent read request or *two* eventually consistent requests for every 4 KB of data.
- *Two read requests* will give you *one* transactional read for every 4 KB of data.
- *One write request* will give you *one* standard write for every 1 KB of data.
- *Two write requests* will give you *one* transactional write for every 1 KB of data.

In the AWS Certified Database – Specialty exam, you may be asked to calculate how many read request units will be needed for a certain use case. For example, how many read requests will be needed to read 100 items of 5 KB each from a DynamoDB table in strongly consistent mode? In this case, you need one read request for each 4 KB of data in strongly consistent mode, so given each item is 5 KB, you will need two per item, so you'd need 200 read requests.

DynamoDB offers two different modes for calculating your usage costs, on-demand and provisioned.

In provisioned mode, your usage is calculated on read and write requests per second, called capacity units. Calculating your usage accurately is highly important in provisioned capacity mode as, if you exceed the amount you have paid for the DynamoDB, table performance will decline and you will start to receive errors stating `ProvisionedThroughputExceededException`.

On-demand mode does not require you to pre-define the capacity units you expect to use. However, if you run in on-demand mode, you will pay more than in provisioned mode for each read and write request, but the table will not be throttled. If you are unable to accurately calculate your data usage needs or if the application has spiky usage (where it is high for short periods and then quiet), it is advisable to use on-demand mode to avoid either overpaying for high capacity to handle the peaks and then not using it during the troughs of demand or to avoid hitting throttling limits if you are under-provisioned.

If you use provisioned mode, DynamoDB supports autoscaling of capacity units for tables and GSIs. You can define a lower and upper limit for the autoscaling and allow DynamoDB to manage the capacity requirements. This can be a useful method of utilizing provisioned capacity mode but avoiding hitting throttling limits for an unexpected spike in load.

Storage

The other main element of billing on a DynamoDB table is storage. DynamoDB offers 25 GB of storage for free. This storage includes the table data and any indexes. Unlike RDS, backups are not included in your storage allocation and are charged separately using the same pricing model as database storage.

Additional features

The additional features of DynamoDB are all billed in a different manner related to how the data is used:

- Global tables are billed based on the number of replicated records per month.
- Streams offer 2,500,000 read events for free each month and you are then charged for the read requests after that.
- DAX is charged in a similar manner to RDS or EC2, where you choose an instance class with a specific compute resource and you pay for each hour that node is running. The data transfer between your application VPC and DynamoDB is free.

We've learned about the theory around DynamoDB, how a table is made, how you query it, and how the pricing works. Now let's put that into practice with a hands-on lab.

Deploying and querying a DynamoDB table

Now that we have learned about DynamoDB and its features, let's deploy our own DynamoDB table to practice using the console and API. We will be using the `GameScores` table we've seen in some of the examples in this chapter to build a simple leaderboard database. We'll be using both the console and the AWS CLI for these steps.

Provisioning a DynamoDB table

We'll start by provisioning a DynamoDB table. We'll be using the **Ohio** (**us-east-1**) region:

1. Open the AWS console in an internet browser and log in using an account that has privileges to create and modify a DynamoDB table.
2. Navigate to the DynamoDB section.
3. Click the orange **Create table** button on the right side of the screen:

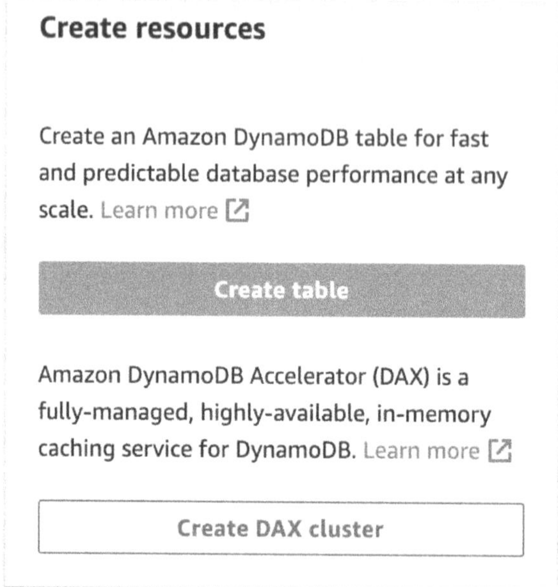

Figure 6.4 – Screenshot of Create resources

4. This will open the **Create table** page, allowing us to enter the details of our table. Choose the following options. Any options that are not mentioned here, leave as default:

   A. **Table name**: `GameScores`.

   B. **Partition key**: `PlayerID`.

C. **Sort key**: `GameName`.

D. **Settings**: Customize settings.

E. **Read/write capacity settings**: `on-demand`.

F. **Secondary indexes**: Leave blank.

G. **Encryption at rest**: Owned by Amazon DynamoDB.

H. Click **Create table**.

Notice that we didn't add any attributes except the partition and sort keys, as these are only added when new records are created in the table due to DynamoDB's ability to handle unstructured data.

5. The table is created immediately.
6. We can use the AWS CLI to check the table status:

```
aws dynamodb describe-table -table-name GameScores
```

We will get output similar to the following:

```
{
    "Table": {
        "AttributeDefinitions": [
            {
                "AttributeName": "PlayerID",
                "AttributeType": "S"
            },
            {
                "AttributeName": "GameName",
                "AttributeType": "S"
            }
        ],
        "TableSizeBytes": 0,
        "TableName": "GameScores",
        "TableStatus": "ACTIVE",
        "KeySchema": [
            {
                "KeyType": "HASH",
                "AttributeName": " PlayerID "
            },
```

```
                {
                    "KeyType": "RANGE",
                    "AttributeName": " GameName "
                }
            ],
            "ItemCount": 0,
            "CreationDateTime": 1621886952.043
        }
    }
```

We have now created our table called `GameScores` and we are ready to add some items, which we will do in the next section.

Adding items

Now we have our empty table, we can add some items. We can use the API to do this or we can use the console. Let's start with the console:

1. From the DynamoDB dashboard, click **Tables** on the left-hand side and click on the `GameScores` table.
2. Click **View items** in the top left of the screen:

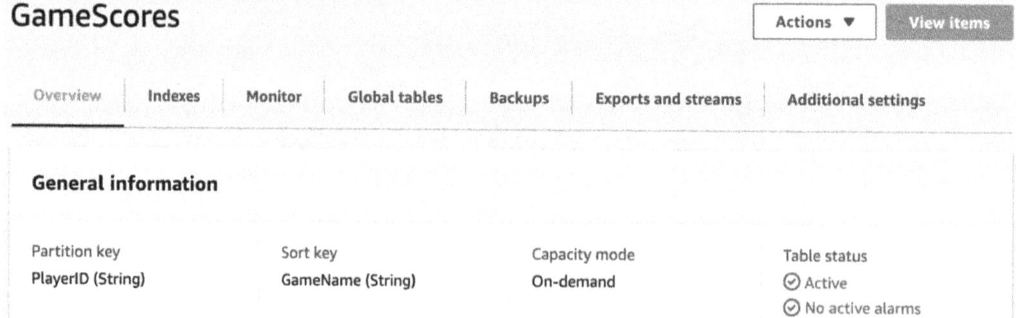

Figure 6.5 – Viewing items

3. This opens a page allowing us to run queries against the DynamoDB table, but first, we need to add some items. Click **Create item** as shown in the following screenshot:

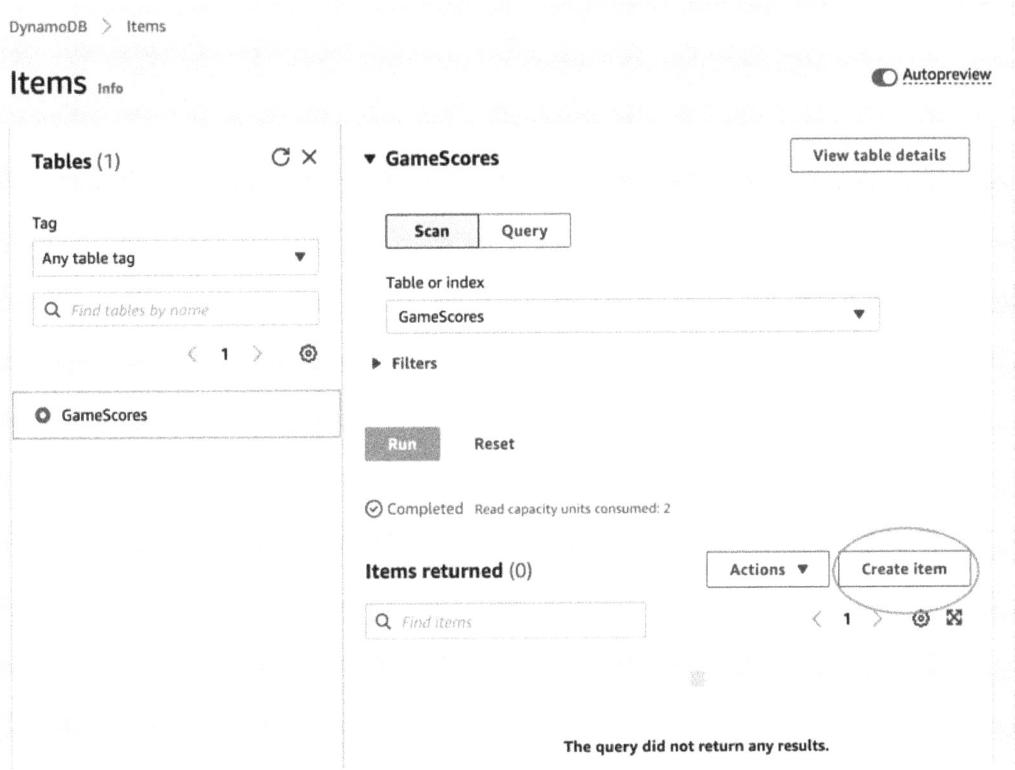

Figure 6.6 – Run queries against the DynamoDB table

4. Add some items to the table; we will need to add both `PlayerID` and `GameName`. We will also add an attribute at this point. Click on the **Add new attribute** drop-down menu and select **Number**. We will call this `HighScore`. Fill in all three fields and then click **Add item**. If we wish, we can repeat this step to add more records.
5. Once done, we can see the items created in the table. Note the message in the middle of the page that says the following:

   Read capacity units consumed: 2

6. Let's add a record using the API as well:

```
aws dynamodb put-item --table-name GameScores\
--item'{
"PlayerID": {"S": "JohnS"},
"GameName": {"S": "Bug Hunt"},
"HighScore": {"N": "753"}
}'\
```

Return to the console to see the new record we created.

Querying and scanning the table

Now we have a couple of records in our table, we can start to run a query and scans to see how they behave.

Query

We are going to use the API to run the query. Here, we are going to query the *JohnS* score in the *Bug Hunt* game:

```
aws dynamodb query \
    --table-name GameScores \
    --key-condition-expression "PlayerID = :playerid AND 
GameName = :gamename"\
    --expression-attribute-values '{
        ":playerid": { "S": "JohnS" },
        ":gamename": { "S": "Bug Hunt" }
    }'
    --projection-expression "PlayerID, GameName, HighScore"
```

Note that we can only query items that are a part of the key, but we can filter on other attributes if they are returned in the original dataset. So, for example, we can add an additional filter to only get the scores larger than 1,000:

```
aws dynamodb query \
    --table-name GameScores \
    --key-condition-expression "PlayerID = :playerid AND 
GameName = :gamename"\
    --expression-attribute-values '{
        ":playerid": { "S": "JohnS" },
```

```
        ":gamename": { "S": "Bug Hunt" }
    }'
    --filter-expression "HighScore > :score"\
    --projection-expression "PlayerID, GameName, HighScore"
```

We've now learned how to use queries to quickly retrieve records using the partition key, so now let's learn how to use scan commands to retrieve records using other columns than the partition key.

Scan

We want to find out all the players who scored over 100, but as the `HighScore` attribute is not part of the key, we cannot get this via a query, so we need to use a scan. Remember that scans involve checking every item in the table, so it can be slow and expensive and should be avoided if possible:

```
aws dynamodb scan \
    --table-name GameScores \
    --filter-expression "HighScore > :score" \
    --projection-expression "PlayerID, GameName" \
    --expression-attribute-values '{":score":{"N":"1000"}}'
```

A better way of doing this type of query would be to add a GSI and use that instead of relying on a scan. Let's do that now.

Creating a new index

In the previous section, we had to use a scan to get the data we wanted as `HighScore` was not part of our key. If we add a new GSI to the table, we can make `HighScore` become a key. First, think about how we want the data to be returned. As we are storing data for multiple games, it's unlikely we'll want our query to return all scores, but rather the scores for a specific game, so we should create a GSI with `GameName` as the partition key and `HighScore` as the sort key. The benefit of doing this is that the scores are stored in sorted order, so if we want to get a `HighScore` instance, we can simply get the first key:

1. Use the API (or the console if you prefer) to create a new GSI:

```
aws dynamodb update-table \
    --table-name GameScore \
    --attribute-definitions '[
```

```
{AttributeName=GameName,AttributeType=S},
{AttributeName=HighScore,AttributeType=N}
]'\
    --global-secondary-index-updates '[
{"Create": {"IndexName": "GameTitleScores","KeySchema":[
{"AttributeName":"GameName","KeyType":"HASH"},":
{"AttributeName":"HighScore","KeyType":"RANGE"}],
"Projection":{"ProjectionType":"ALL"}}
]'
```

2. Now we have the new index, we can run a query to get the highest score for our game; unlike the case with a SQL database, we need to specifically tell DynamoDB which index to use. Remember that the `HighScore` attribute is sorted, so we can just get the first value returned by using the `no-scan-index-forward` setting to reverse the order:

```
aws dynamodb query \
    --table-name GameScores \
    --index-name GameTitleScores
    --key-condition-expression "GameName = :game\
    --expression-attribute-values '{
        ":gamename": { "S": "Bug Hunt" }
    --projection-expression "PlayerID, HighScore" \
    --no-scan-index-forward
    --max-items 1
    }'
```

We have now learned how to create a DynamoDB table, insert items, query them, and use a scan. Let's now review what we've learned in this chapter.

Summary

In this chapter, we have learned about Amazon DynamoDB. We have learned how to create a DynamoDB table and how to use different index types to query the data. We also learned how to scan the table for cases where we cannot use an index. We learned how DynamoDB is priced and some techniques to minimize costs.

In the AWS Certified Database – Specialty exam, your knowledge of DynamoDB will be tested heavily with questions around common error codes, service limits, index types and their key features, and backup and restore methods.

In the next chapter, we will be learning about Redshift and DocumentDB, which are both AWS databases with specific use cases. We will continue to use the knowledge learned in this chapter to interact with Redshift and DocumentDB, as they have many similarities with DynamoDB.

Cheat sheet

This cheat sheet reminds you of the high-level topics and points covered in this chapter and should act as a revision guide and refresher:

- Amazon DynamoDB is a low-latency, managed, and serverless NoSQL database created by AWS offering millisecond response times.
- DynamoDB is serverless, which means you do not need to specify the compute needed for your workload; instead, you define capacity units that control how much data can be read and written.
- You can run the table in on-demand mode, but the costs are generally higher than provisioned mode.
- If you exceed the amount of capacity reserved, you can receive errors around throttling and the performance of your queries will drop.
- DynamoDB stores data in items that must have a key to define them.
- DynamoDB relies on two different index types, GSI and LSI, to control access to the items.
- You can take manual backups or use PITR backups.
- You can use global tables to provision your DynamoDB table across multiple regions.
- You can use DynamoDB Accelerator to act as a cache in front of DynamoDB to speed up read queries.

Review

To check your knowledge from this chapter, here are five questions that you should now be able to answer. Remember the exam techniques from *Chapter 1, AWS Certified Database – Specialty Exam Overview*, and remove the clearly incorrect answers first to help you:

1. You are working as a developer for a small company with a DynamoDB table. The company is complaining of poor performance after increasing the number of records in the table and they say they are seeing "throttling errors." What is the most cost-efficient option for them to consider?

   A. Enable TTL against a timestamp attribute.

   B. Implement DAX.

   C. Turn on Dynamo Streams.

   D. Turn on autoscaling.

2. You are designing a new DynamoDB table and need to calculate how many **Capacity Units (CUs)** to provision. Each item is 3 KB in size and you expect to read a maximum of 100 items and write 10 per second. You will only be using eventually consistent reads and standard writes.

   A. 50 RCUs and 30 WCUs

   B. 100 RCUs and 10 WCUs

   C. 50 RCUs and 30 WCUs

   D. 300 RCUs and 30 WCUs

3. How much free storage is offered per account for DynamoDB?

   A. 10 GB.

   B. 1 GB.

   C. None, it is all charged.

   D. 25 GB.

4. Which of the following correctly describes the two different index types available on a DynamoDB table?

   A. GSIs can only be created when the table is provisioned. LSIs must contain the partition key of the base table.

   B. LSIs can only be created when the table is provisioned. GSIs can contain entirely different keys to the base table.

C. LSIs can only be created when the table is provisioned. LSIs can contain entirely different keys to the base table.

D. GSIs can only be created when the table is provisioned. GSIs must contain the partition key of the base table.

5. You receive the following error, `ThrottlingException`, while using your DynamoDB table. What action should you take to resolve it?

   A. Set up autoscaling.

   B. Switch from provisioned mode to on-demand.

   C. Increase the number of nodes in your DAX cluster.

   D. Set up global tables.

Answers with explanations can be found in *Chapter 17, Answers*.

Further reading

This chapter covers all you will need to know for the AWS Certified Database – Specialty exam but you may enjoy learning some additional information about DynamoDB. The following books can teach you more about AWS Lambda and about working with DynamoDB from a developer's point of view:

- *Mastering AWS Lambda*:

  `https://www.packtpub.com/product/mastering-aws-lambda/9781786467690`

- *DynamoDB Cookbook*:

  `https://www.packtpub.com/product/dynamodb-cookbook/978178393755`

7 Redshift and DocumentDB

In this chapter, we are going to learn about two different AWS database technologies: **Redshift** and **DocumentDB**.

This chapter includes a hands-on lab where we will deploy, configure, and explore Redshift and DocumentDB instances, including how to monitor them. To do this, you will need a VPC with a minimum of two subnets. If you have not completed *Chapter 3*, *Understanding AWS Infrastructure*, please ensure you have a VPC that meets the minimum requirements, as detailed here: `https://docs.aws.amazon.com/AmazonRDS/latest/UserGuide/USER_VPC.WorkingWithRDSInstanceinaVPC.html`.

In this chapter, we're going to cover the following main topics:

- Overview of Amazon Redshift
- Performance tuning and maintaining a Redshift cluster
- Connecting Redshift to other AWS services
- Deploying a Redshift cluster
- Overview of DocumentDB
- Performance tuning and maintaining DocumentDB
- Deploying a DocumentDB cluster

Let's start by making sure we understand what Amazon Redshift is, when you should use it, and how it works differently from RDS, Aurora, or DynamoDB.

Technical requirements

You will need an AWS account with root access. Everything we will do in this chapter will be unavailable in the **Free Tier**, which means it will cost you a small amount to follow the hands-on sections. You will also require AWS **Command-Line Interface** (**CLI**) access. The AWS guide at `https://docs.aws.amazon.com/cli/latest/userguide/cli-chap-configure.html` explains the steps that are required, but I will summarize them here:

1. Create an AWS account if you have not already done so.
2. Download the latest version of the AWS CLI from `https://docs.aws.amazon.com/cli/latest/userguide/welcome-versions.html#welcome-versions-v2`.
3. Create an access key for your administration user by going to `https://docs.aws.amazon.com/IAM/latest/UserGuide/getting-started_create-admin-group.html#getting-started_create-admin-group-cli`.
4. Run the `aws configure` command to set up a profile for your user.

You will also need a VPC that meets the minimum requirements for an RDS instance (`https://docs.aws.amazon.com/AmazonRDS/latest/UserGuide/USER_VPC.WorkingWithRDSInstanceinaVPC.html`). If you completed the steps in *Chapter 3, Understanding AWS Infrastructure*, you will already have a VPC that meets these requirements.

Overview of Amazon Redshift

Amazon Redshift is a data warehouse managed service that's offered by AWS as an enterprise-class relational database query and management system. A data warehouse is a special type of database that's designed to handle large data loads and provide rapid response times to complex queries. Amazon Redshift uses a combination of massively parallel queries, columnar data storage, and data compression to maximize the query's speeds while minimizing storage costs. For more general information on columnar databases, please refer to *Chapter 2, Understanding Database Fundamentals*.

Let's take a closer look at the architecture of a Redshift cluster.

Redshift architecture

Similar to RDS Aurora, Redshift operates a cluster topology, which allows it to use multiple nodes to scale and split (or **shard**) the workload. The following diagram shows a high-level view of how Redshift is deployed:

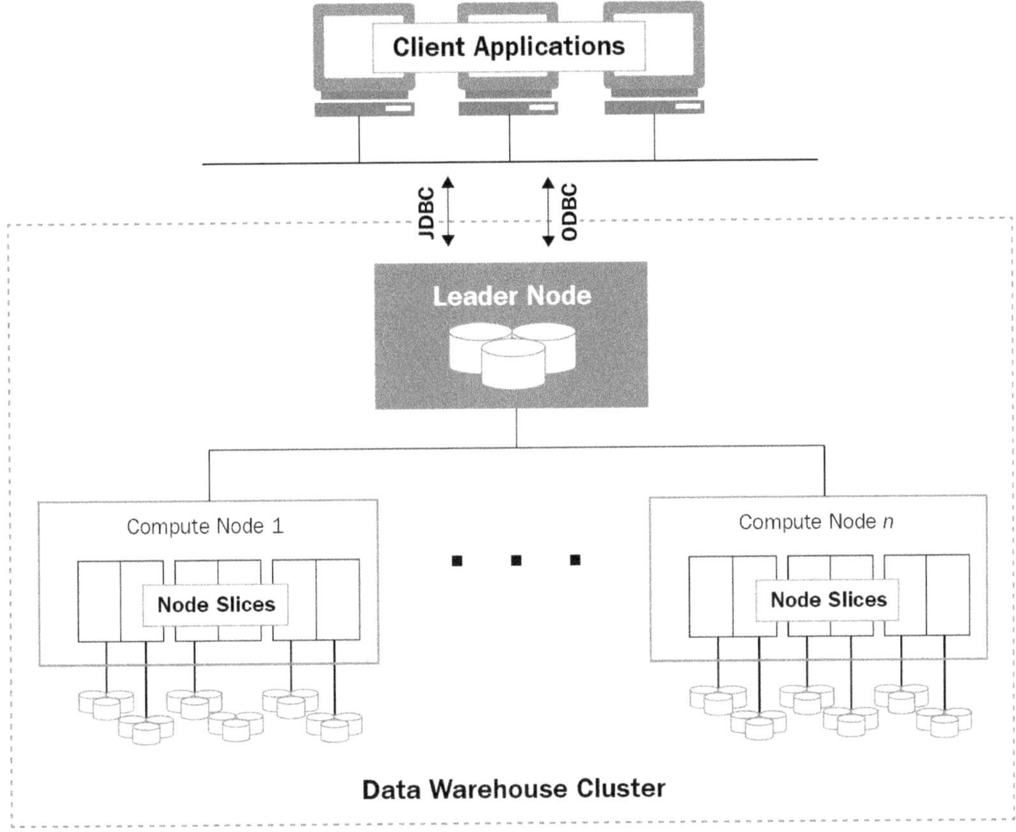

Figure 7.1 – Redshift cluster topology

In the preceding diagram, you can see *leader nodes* and *compute nodes*.

A leader node manages all the communication to and from the client and acts as an orchestrator to ensure the query is handled as efficiently as possible. It will send requests to different compute nodes and combine any sharded datasets before forwarding them to the client. This is called **aggregation**.

A compute node executes the queries it is asked to by the leader node. A compute node contains *node slices*. A node slice is a portion of the memory and disk space of each compute node. The node slices work in parallel and are controlled by the leader node. The number of node slices is determined by the size of the compute node, where the larger the compute node, the more slices are available. The workload is split between each node slice based on the **distribution key**. Each table that's loaded into a Redshift cluster has a distribution key and should be carefully selected to ensure it has a wide range of values. For example, a distribution key for gender would have a small number of values, so it would only use a small number of the available node slices, whereas a distribution key for age would have a much wider range of values and would be able to efficiently split the workload across all of the node slices. The user data is stored on the disks that are attached to the compute nodes.

Each leader and compute node has CPU and memory assigned. You can change the size of each node by changing the instance type and size; you can add additional nodes to match your workload requirements.

Redshift uses a PostgreSQL engine as its relational database management system. As such, Redshift can support SQL querying and can operate as an **online transaction processing** (**OLTP**) system (see *Chapter 2, Understanding Database Fundamentals*, for more information). Redshift has been optimized for high-performance analysis and reporting large datasets, so an OLTP workload would be inefficient.

Now that we've learned how an Amazon Redshift cluster and its components work, let's learn how to optimize performance while minimizing costs.

Performance tuning and maintaining a Redshift cluster

Tuning an Amazon Redshift database can make a huge difference to the costs and performance of your application. Amazon Redshift has six main areas you should consider when tuning it:

- Massively parallel processing
- Columnar data storage
- Data compression

- Query optimizer
- Result caching
- Compiled code

We will start by looking at massively parallel processing, which we mentioned briefly in the *Overview of Amazon Redshift* section.

Massively parallel processing

Parallel processing is when your workload is split across multiple strands to allow for faster querying. In theory, it will be quicker for your work to be done by four different strands simultaneously than by one, even with the overhead of merging the individual strands at the end. With most RDBMSs, the parallelism is contained in a single node, so the maximum speed of the query is limited by the overall resource to that one node, and limits such as storage speed are often the bottlenecks. Redshift overcomes this limitation by having multiple compute nodes, all of which have storage. This is what gives it **massively parallel processing** (**MPP**) capabilities; not only can it run in parallel on each compute node, but it can also run in parallel across nodes.

The critical factor when it comes to maximizing performance is to have good data distribution. Redshift offers three different ways to store data on the node slices on the compute nodes:

- **All**: All the data is stored on each node. This can result in the data being returned quickly but at high storage costs.
- **Even**: The data is stored in a round-robin fashion across the node slices. This is useful if your data doesn't have a key with a balanced distribution and a wide number of values.
- **Key**: The data is stored according to the distribution key values. This can be useful if you have a good key with a balanced and wide number of values and if your queries and reports will use that key.

The following diagram shows what these distribution options would look like when stored on disk:

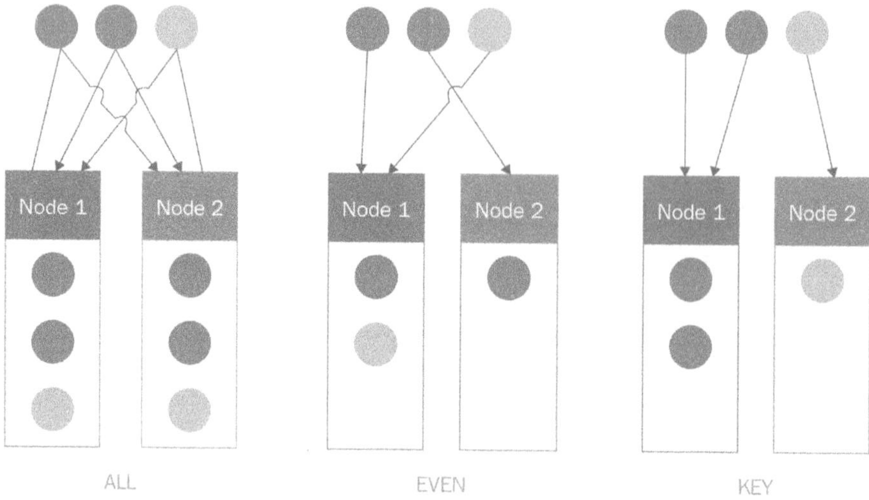

Figure 7.2 – Data distribution on Redshift

Which method you use will depend on your data and how you intend to query it. For the exam, you will not need to know about advanced performance tuning, but you will often be asked about the key performance techniques that are used in a Redshift database and how you could make improvements.

Now, let's look at columnar data storage and how this helps improve performance.

Columnar data storage

In an OLTP database, the data is stored in rows. This is because, in general, you return a subset of rows for your query but often use all or most of the columns. Let's consider an online shopping application. When you search for a product, you only return a small number of the products that they have available, and a lot of data such as the item's name, supplier, price, and picture is returned. When you run an analytics database such as Redshift, you are typically looking for an aggregated view across all the rows in your table but against specific columns. Looking at the online shop again, a typical analytics query would be looking at the average sales price of certain products. To do that, you'd need to look at every item that's been sold and its price – all the rows but only a few columns. This matters because of how databases retrieve records from disk. If you store the data in row order and you want to return a small number of columns from all the rows, then you need to scan the entire table, which incurs large **input/output** (**I/O**) and can cause performance to slow down. If you store it in column order, you only scan the columns you need, which drastically reduces the I/O.

To get the best performance, the table columns need to be sorted so that the ones that will be used in the most queries are stored first. This is known as a sort key.

Data compression

Data compression reduces the amount of space that's required to store the data on the disk. This can reduce I/O requirements as less data is being sent back and forth to the storage layer. However, the data needs to be decompressed before it can be used, which can cause a bottleneck during processing. Redshift uses a technique called adaptive compression, which allows for different levels of compression to be used based on a column's usage. This can be managed automatically.

Query optimizer

Like other RDBMSs, Redshift uses an optimizer to identify the fastest way to return the data to the requestor. It is aware of any resource bottlenecks and can adapt each query to the current state and usage of the Redshift cluster in real time.

Result caching

Redshift utilizes an in-memory cache to store commonly accessed data without having to retrieve it from the disk. Reading from memory is much faster than from disk, so any data that can be obtained from the cache will speed up a query. Data held in the cache is marked as invalid if any of the underlying tables have DML run against them. Caching is particularly useful if you are likely to run the same query repeatedly and if the data is uploaded in bulk or batch operations so that the table won't be updated between queries. This would invalidate the cached data.

As well as result caching, Redshift offers the use of **materialized views** (**MVs**). An MV allows the result of a query to be stored in a virtual table, either for future querying or to avoid the overhead of processing a large query again. Redshift allows MV auto-refresh by default, meaning that if the underlying tables that are used in the MV are updated, that data is automatically updated in the MV as well.

Compiled code

When you send a query to the Redshift database, the leader node processes it and turns it into compiled code. Compiled code is code that the database can read without having to process it further and without having to run it through a query optimizer again. This means that once the leader node has processed it, the compute nodes can all immediately run the code with no further overhead. The more nodes you have, the greater the overhead saving. The compiled code is also cached, so the same query would not be reprocessed and further time would be saved.

On top of these main areas, Redshift also offers two automatic tuning tools:

- Redshift Advisor
- Auto **workload management** (**WLM**)

Redshift Advisor can manage almost all of the performance tuning features of your database. It can automatically create distribution keys on the most optimal columns, it can handle adaptive data compression, and it can even organize your column sorting. It can also monitor your cluster's performance, provide advice on problems, and specify what action should be taken to improve them.

Redshift uses WLM to control the order and priority of queries that are allowed to run. You can configure WLM manually or you can create up to eight different queues with different priorities and let Redshift control it automatically. For example, if you had a large number of small queries that could run at the same time without running out of memory, it may make more sense to run those first to hold a larger query until they have finished. If enabled, Redshift will carefully manage the workload to ensure it remains within the resource limits while maximizing the query's throughput. You can set a queue to either `NORMAL` or `HIGHEST` priority to control which queue Redshift will focus on first. This can be useful if you have critical queries that are getting stuck behind less critical ones. You can create a separate critical queue with the priority set to `HIGHEST` to ensure these are run first.

Explaining how to tune a Redshift database could take a book on its own, but for the exam, you will only need to know the high-level concepts and automation Redshift offers. If you wish to know more, please review the books specified in the *Further reading* section at the end of this chapter.

Connecting Redshift to other AWS services

One of the main benefits a data warehouse offers is that it provides a single location for all the data required for reporting and analytics. Your users don't need to go to multiple different places for the information as it's all in one place. AWS offers several methods that allow you to load data from other sources quickly and efficiently. First, let's look at Redshift Spectrum, which offers connectivity from an S3 bucket.

Redshift Spectrum

Redshift Spectrum is a feature that allows you to query data from an S3 bucket directly from Redshift using a SQL query. Before Spectrum was released, you would have had to load the data from S3 into Redshift before it could be queried, but now, you can query it in situ. To use Redshift Spectrum, you must configure your S3 bucket as an external table that you can then call in a query. You can even use joins to create a complex query involving multiple S3 buckets and files, as well as data held within tables in the Redshift database itself.

Amazon Kinesis Data Firehose

Amazon Kinesis Data Firehose (**Firehose**) is a tool that's used to load streamed data into various AWS services, including Redshift. Firehose can be an extremely simple and useful method to load real-time data into a Redshift cluster. Firehose can capture information from other systems and send that data securely and efficiently to Redshift. This allows you to easily connect a wide range of other systems directly to Redshift without having to write code or batch processes. Firehose is a fully managed system that automatically scales when needed.

Now, let's learn how to use another AWS tool to use the data within Redshift instead of pushing data to it.

Amazon QuickSight

Amazon QuickSight is a graphical analytics tool that's used for business intelligence. QuickSight connects natively with Redshift to allow you to quickly create graphical dashboards from your data. The following screenshot shows an example of the information QuickSight can offer:

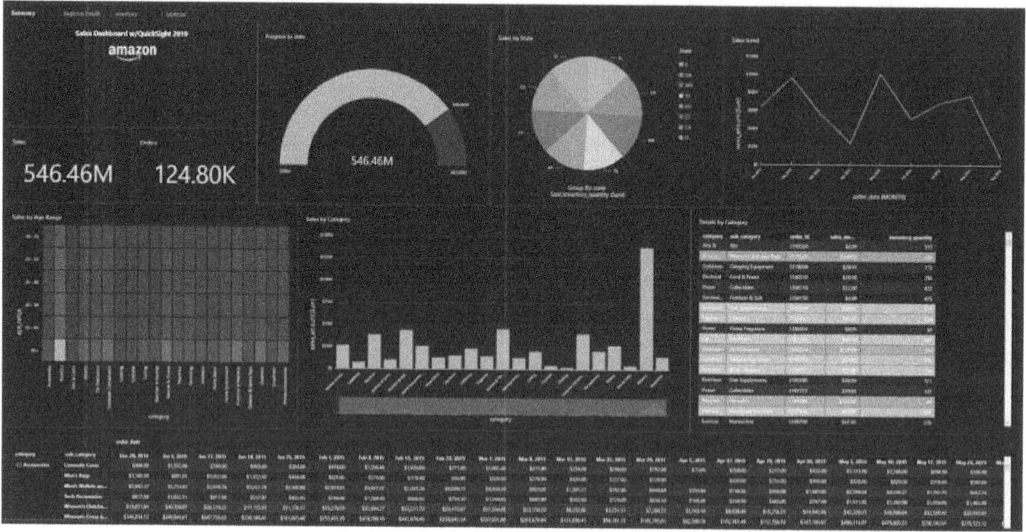

Figure 7.3 – Amazon Quicksight dashboard

As you can see, there are multiple ways to connect Redshift to other AWS and on-premises tools to allow for faster data ingestion, data queries outside of Redshift by using Spectrum, and to utilize the data to get value from it through analytics tools.

Now, let's create a Redshift cluster and place some data in an S3 bucket to demonstrate how to use Redshift Spectrum.

Deploying a Redshift cluster

Let's start by deploying our Redshift cluster, before configuring Redshift Spectrum to access data in S3:

1. Log into the AWS console and navigate to Amazon Redshift.
2. Select **Create cluster**.
3. Enter a name for your cluster and, if available, select the **Free trial** option:

Cluster configuration

Cluster identifier

This is the unique key that identifies a cluster.

dbcertred

The identifier must be from 1-63 characters. Valid characters are a-z (lowercase only) and - (hyphen).

What are you planning to use this cluster for?

Production
Configure for fast and consistent performance at the best price.

Free trial
Configure for learning about Amazon Redshift. This configuration is free for a limited time if your organization has never created an Amazon Redshift cluster.

When the free trial ends, delete your cluster to avoid incurring charges at on-demand rate for compute and storage. If you want to take a final snapshot of your cluster and store the snapshot on an S3, our on-demand rate applies.

Figure 7.4 – Redshift cluster creation

4. Enter a password and click **Create cluster**.
5. The console will now show a connection screen, explaining how to connect to your cluster, as well as the cluster's status at the bottom:

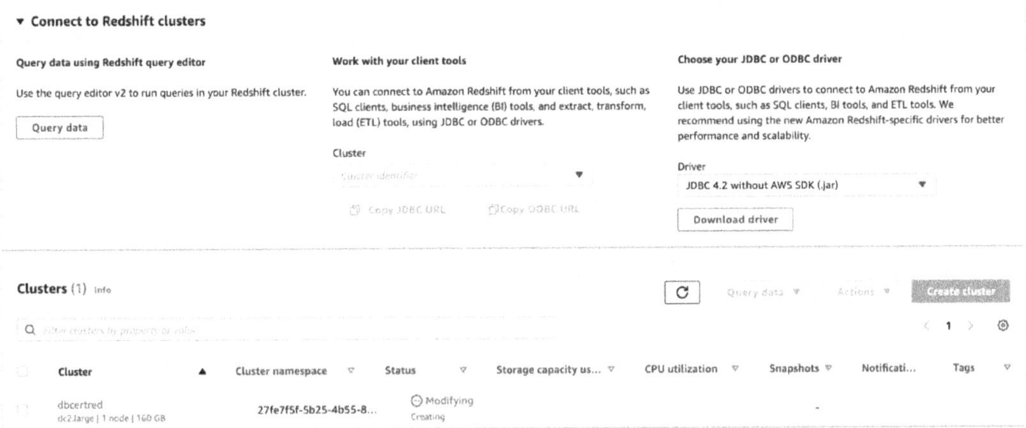

Figure 7.5 – Redshift dashboard

When the cluster appears as **Available**, we can configure Redshift Spectrum.

Configuring Redshift Spectrum

Amazon hosts test data in a public S3 database. We will use that in this lab. We can access it using Redshift Spectrum. To configure Redshift Spectrum, we need to complete three tasks:

- Configure an IAM role – we will cover IAM in *Chapter 12, AWS Database Security*.
- Create or identify an S3 bucket we can use – we will use a publicly available bucket with sample data.
- Create an external table.

Let's start by setting up IAM:

1. Open the AWS console and navigate to the **IAM** section.
2. Click **Roles** from the left-hand menu.
3. Click **Create role**:

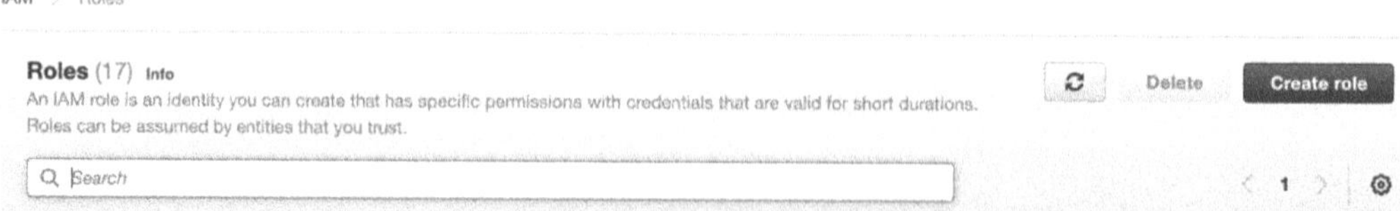

Figure 7.6 – The Create role button

4. Select **Redshift** from the list at the bottom of the page:

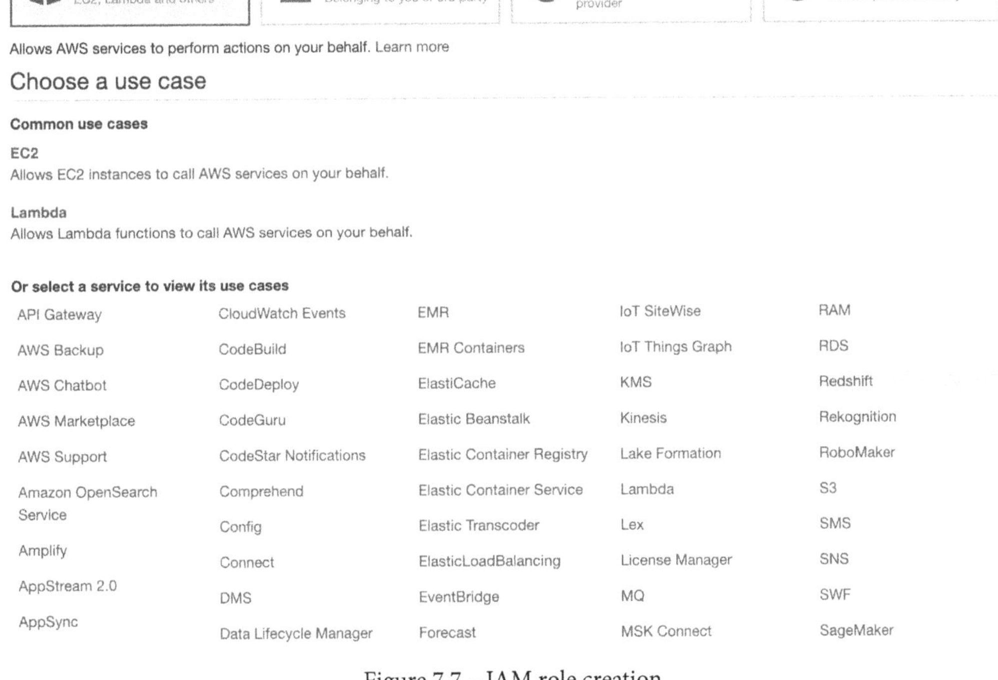

Figure 7.7 – IAM role creation

5. Click **Redshift – customizable** and then **Next: Permissions**:

Select your use case

Redshift
Allows Redshift clusters to call AWS services on your behalf.

Redshift - Customizable
Allows Redshift clusters to call AWS services on your behalf.

Redshift - Scheduler
Allow Redshift Scheduler to call Redshift on your behalf.

* Required Cancel Next: Permissions

Figure 7.8 – IAM Redshift role

6. Choose **AmazonS3ReadOnlyAccess** and **AWSGlueConsoleFullAccess** and click **Next: Tags**, then **Next: Review**.

7. Give it a name and then click **Create role**:
8. Return to the Redshift dashboard.
9. Check the box next to the cluster and click the **Actions** dropdown menu. Select **Manage IAM roles** (you may need to scroll through the menu):

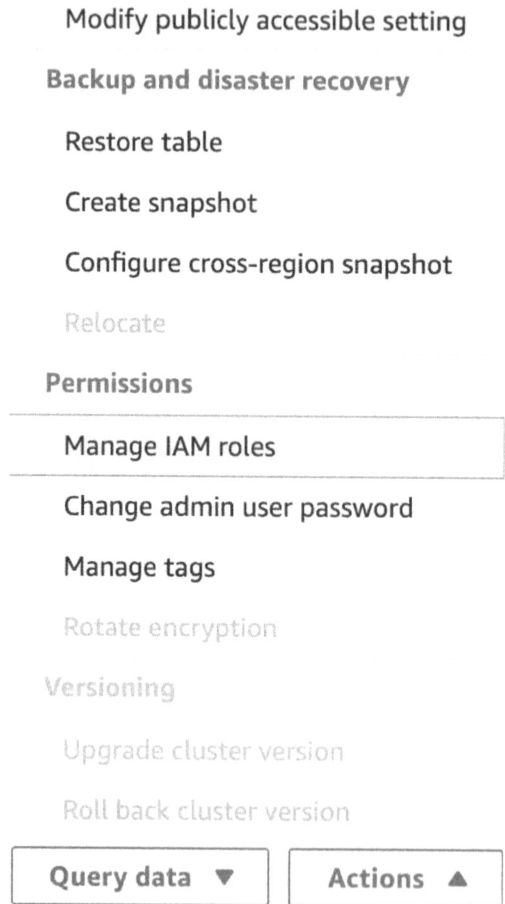

Figure 7.9 – Redshift – Manage IAM roles

10. Select the IAM role you just created from the drop-down box and click **Associate IAM role**. Then, choose **Save changes**:

Cluster permissions

Your cluster needs permissions to access other AWS services on your behalf. For the required permissions, add IAM roles with the principal "redshift.amazonaws.com". You can associate up to 50 IAM roles with this cluster. Learn more

Available IAM roles Info

Choose an IAM role | Associate IAM role

Associated IAM roles	Status	
redshifts3 arn:aws:iam::919405152227:role/redshifts3	Not applied	Remove

Cancel | Save changes

Figure 7.10 – Redshift IAM association

11. When the dashboard reloads, click **Editor** via the menu on the left and click **Connect to database**.
12. Enter the necessary DB details. **Database name** should be `dev` and **Database user** should be `awsuser`. Then, click **Connect**:

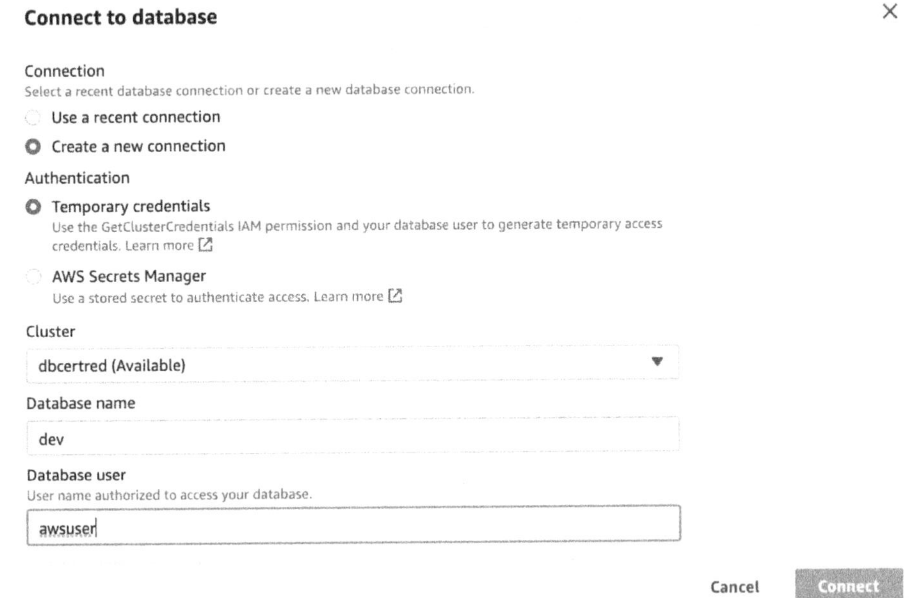

Figure 7.11 – Redshift Spectrum connection

13. Run the following code to create an external schema and table we can query. Change the highlighted line so that it matches the ARN of the IAM role you created. You can find this in the **Roles** area of IAM:

```
create external schema spectrum_dbcert
from data catalog
database 'dev'
iam_role 'arn:aws:iam::919405152227:role/redshifts3'
create external database if not exists;
```

You should see an output similar to the following. If you get an error about strings, double-check your quotes:

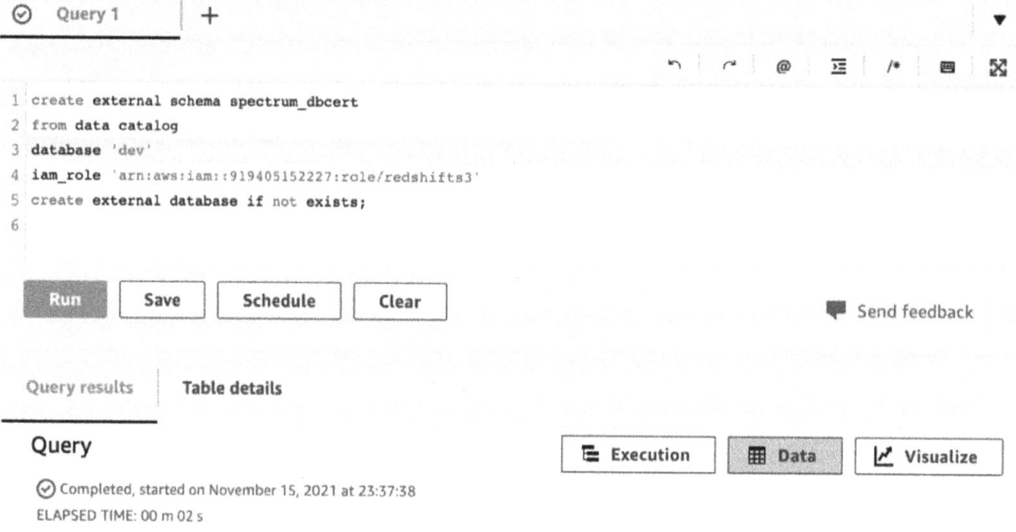

Figure 7.12 – Creating an external schema

14. Run the following code to create a table based on the S3 data that we can query. Change the highlighted part so that it matches the name of the schema you just created:

```
create external table spectrum_dbcert.sales(
salesid integer,
listid integer,
sellerid integer,
buyerid integer,
eventid integer,
```

```
dateid smallint,
qtysold smallint,
pricepaid decimal(8,2),
commission decimal(8,2),
saletime timestamp)
row format delimited
fields terminated by '\t'
stored as textfile
location 's3://awssampledbuswest2/tickit/spectrum/sales/'
table properties ('numRows'='172000');
```

You should see an output similar to the following:

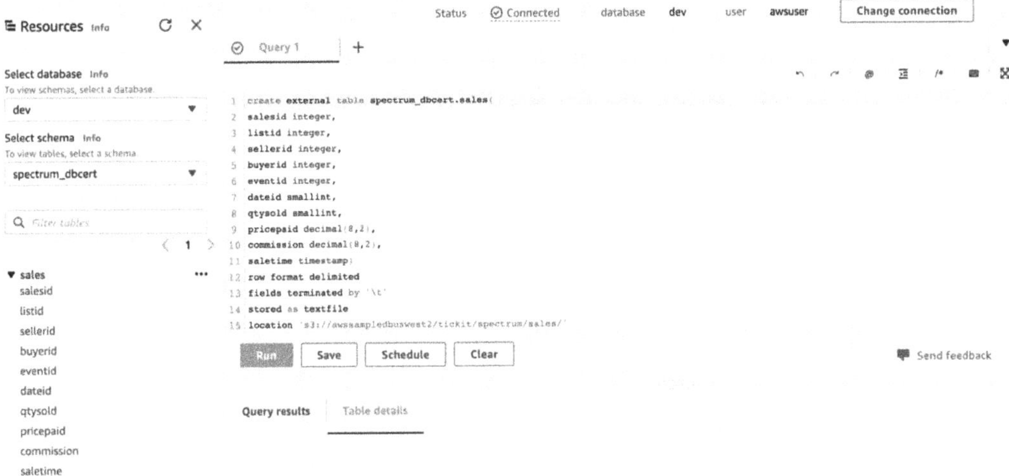

Figure 7.13 – Redshift external table

15. From the **Select schema** dropdown, you will now be able to see a schema with the same name you used. Selecting this will show a table called `sales`. This table is being read from a `.csv` file hosted in S3. You can run standard SQL queries against this data if you wish.

This completes the hands-on section for Redshift. You can delete this database if you wish or continue to use it to explore more options.

Now that we've learned all the Redshift information we will need for the AWS Database Certified Specialty exam, let's take a look at DocumentDB.

Overview of DocumentDB

Amazon DocumentDB is a fully managed and scalable NoSQL database designed to store and query semi-structured data such as JSON documents. JSON documents are pieces of information saved in a format structure called **JavaScript Object Notation** (**JSON**). The fixed structure of a JSON document allows all the data and fields within it to be queried similarly to an RDBMS table.

DocumentDB is compatible with another popular document database called MongoDB. This makes it a good choice for customers who are looking to move to an open source document database while currently using MongoDB.

DocumentDB is similar to DynamoDB in that they are both NoSQL databases, but while DynamoDB is tuned for key-value data retrieval operations, DocumentDB is more tuned to favor fast query handling. Also, DocumentDB is provisioned in a similar way to RDS, where you define an instance size to handle your workload as opposed to DynamoDB, which uses read/write capacity units. However, both can store and query JSON documents, so the correct one to use will depend on the type of querying that's required and the cost structure. For example, in the exam, you may be asked to choose which database is correct for storing and querying JSON documents. Since you've been asked to query JSON, DocumentDB would be a better fit. If the exam asked you to choose which database is correct for storing JSON documents to be retrieved using key-value lookups, then DynamoDB would be a better fit.

DocumentDB architecture

DocumentDB has a similar architecture to RDS: it is deployed within a VPC, it has a separate storage layer, and it can be configured with read replicas. A typical topology for DocumentDB is as follows:

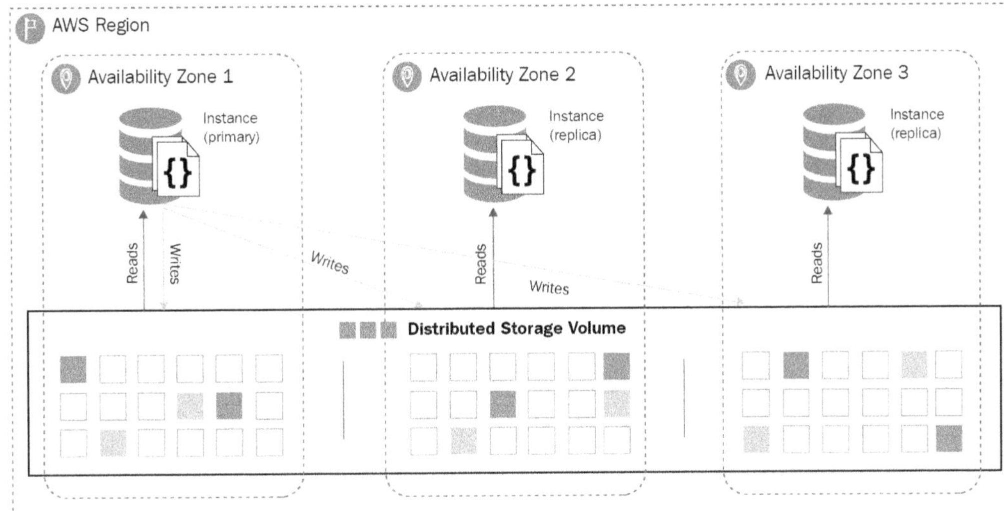

Figure 7.14 – DocumentDB topology

As you can see, when a write is issued to the database, it gets sent to all of the replicas, as well as the primary instance. This means that all of the read replicas are synchronously updated and are strongly consistent. Again, this differs from DynamoDB, which favors eventual consistency.

The separate storage layer means that a single instance is highly resilient. If the compute node fails, AWS will automatically provision a new one and reconnect the storage so that no data is lost.

Now, let's at performance tuning and how to maintain a DocumentDB cluster in more depth.

Performance tuning and maintaining DocumentDB

DocumentDB is a very specialized database, so tuning methods that are used on other systems are not that effective. It is important to choose the right size instance for your DocumentDB as this controls the resources it is given. Without sufficient memory and CPU, your performance will be poor and queries will be slow. If you are migrating from MongoDB, it is recommended to match the resource that was allocated to your MongoDB cluster initially as a start and tune from there. For a new workload, it can be different to accurately estimate the resources needed. For those cases, you need to test different instance sizes as extensively as possible before launching your production or critical workloads.

Once your primary instance has been sized correctly, you can consider some other performance tuning options such as read replicas.

Read replicas

DocumentDB allows for up to 15 read replicas per cluster. A read replica is a copy of your primary database in the same region that only allows data to be read. Read replicas can massively improve the performance of your database by allowing reads and writes to be split, so read queries are not queued or slowed while a write is committed. They also allow your database to scale horizontally, which splits the I/O across multiple nodes. I/O can often be the main bottleneck in any database system as reading from disks is considerably slower than reading from memory, and there can be limited bandwidth between each server and the disks. Splitting the reads across multiple servers increases the bandwidth and reduces the likelihood of slowdowns caused by I/O.

In addition to same-region read replicas, DocumentDB also offers read replicas that can support cross-region. These are called global clusters.

Global clusters

Standard read replicas can only be created in the same region as the primary one. Global clusters remove that restriction, allowing you to create up to five read-only clusters in different regions. Unlike read replicas, which have millisecond latency, global clusters can take up to 1 second to keep in sync, so they are useful when eventually consistent reads are acceptable.

Global clusters can have different parameter groups associated with each cluster. This allows you to configure each region differently for a specific use case.

The final main performance tuning tool you can use with DocumentDB can help you create indexes. If you are migrating from MongoDB, you need to use a special tool to create these indexes before you load the data.

DocumentDB Index Tool

When you want to migrate your data from MongoDB to DocumentDB, the indexes are not automatically created using either the AWS Data Migration Service or using `mongorestore`. To create these, AWS provides a DocumentDB Index Tool, which obtains the index information from your existing MongoDB cluster and creates index creation scripts you can run on your target DB.

Parameter groups

DocumentDB uses parameter groups to control the settings for the database. This allows you to customize each cluster so that they match your needs. You can customize parameters such as how the profiler (a tool that helps speed up queries) works, whether the database automatically logs to an external audit, and whether connections must use TLS security.

Time to live (TTL)

DocumentDB allows records to be automatically deleted when they reach a certain age. TTL can be useful in keeping your storage costs low, speeding up queries, and ensuring you are compliant with data regulations that may require you to remove data that's older than a certain number of years or days.

Now that we've learned the theory behind DocumentDB, let's provision a DocumentDB cluster and enable global clusters.

Deploying a DocumentDB cluster

Let's start by creating our DocumentDB cluster:

1. Open the AWS console and navigate to the **Amazon DocumentDB** section.
2. Click **Launch Amazon DocumentDB**.

3. Complete the form by giving it a name. Select `db.r5.large` as the instance type (this is the lowest cost usable for ours) and change the number of instances to **1**. At the bottom of the screen, toggle the **Advanced options** switch. Review the settings but don't change any of them. Then, click **Create cluster**:

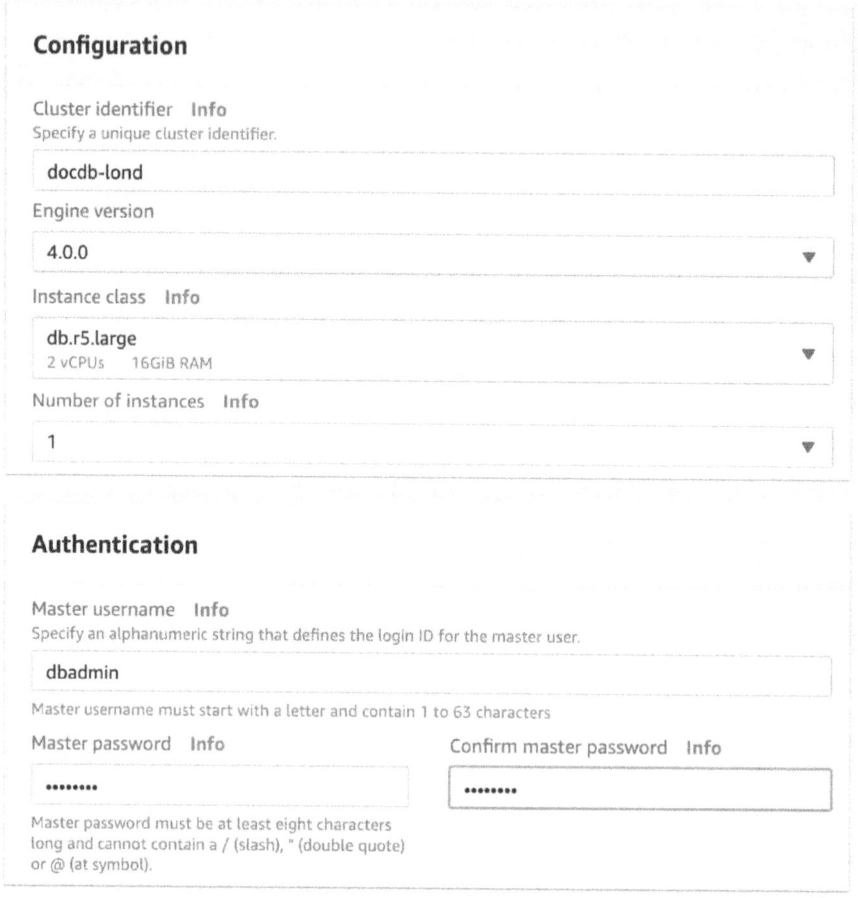

Figure 7.15 – AWS console – DocumentDB creating a cluster

4. The console will show the cluster being created and becoming **available**:

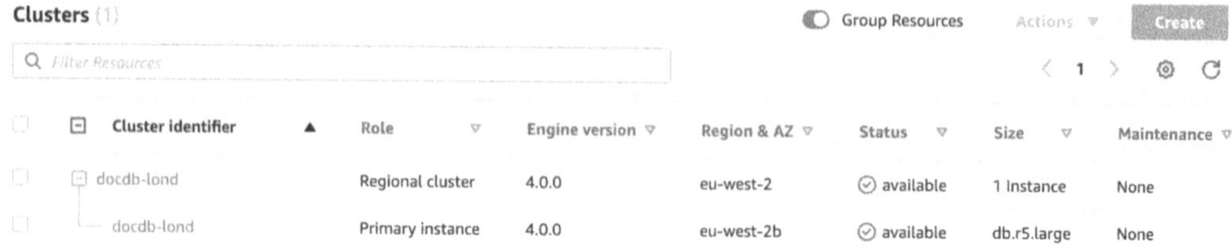

Figure 7.16 – DocumentDB dashboard

5. Once the cluster shows as **available**, we can create a second cluster in a different region to make it a global cluster. Check the box for the **Regional cluster** node and click the **Actions** dropdown. Then, select **Add region**.
6. Complete the form that opens. You can select any region you like. The cluster names must be unique. Select the smallest instance class available and select a single instance to keep costs low. Then, click **Create cluster**:

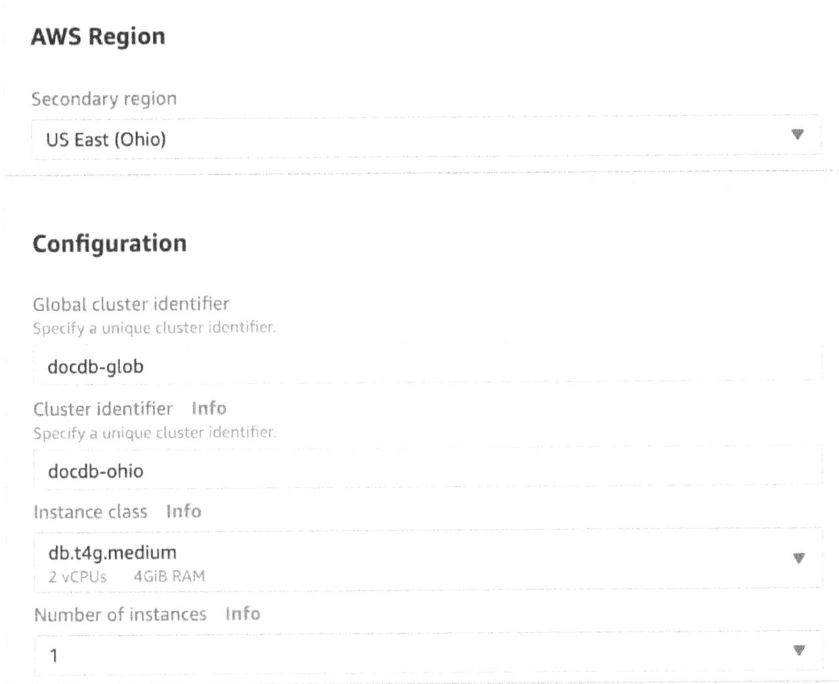

Figure 7.17 – Global cluster creation

7. The dashboard will now show the two clusters you made in the different regions:

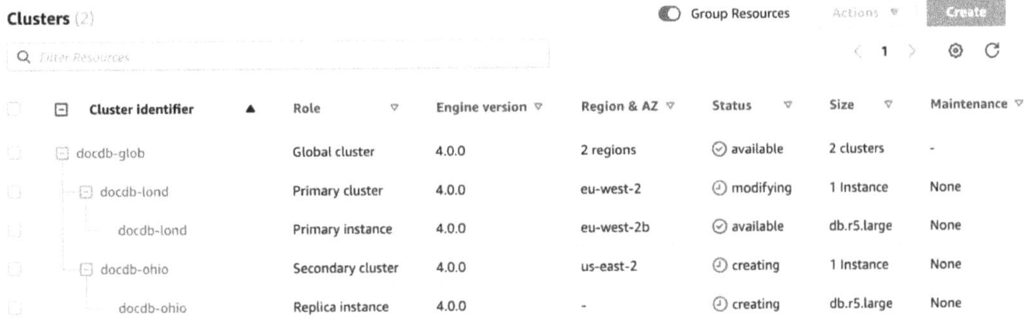

Figure 7.18 – DocumentDB dashboard

This completes the hands-on section for DocumentDB. If you wish to save on costs, feel free to delete the two clusters you created and ensure you don't choose to save a final snapshot.

Now, let's summarize what we have learned in this chapter.

Summary

In this chapter, we learned about two new databases offered by AWS – Redshift and DocumentDB. We learned that Redshift is a columnar database store based on PostgreSQL that is fully managed by AWS. We also learned how to use Redshift Spectrum to query data directly from S3 without having to import it.

Regarding DocumentDB, we learned about some of the differences between it and DynamoDB, how it is provisioned, and some key areas regarding its performance. We also learned how to deploy a global cluster, which allows us to run read replicas in multiple regions.

In the next chapter, we are going to learn about three more AWS databases: **Neptune**, **Timestream**, and **Quantum Ledger DB**. By doing this, we will build upon the themes and knowledge we've gained in this chapter.

Cheat sheet

This cheat sheet summarizes the key points from this chapter:

- Redshift is a fully managed, columnar, analytics, and reporting database based on PostgreSQL.
- Redshift uses multiple nodes and data sharding to underpin its massively parallel feature, which ensures its rapid response times to complex queries.
- It is important to correctly design your Redshift storage and column sort order to maximize performance.
- Redshift can query data directly from S3 using Redshift Spectrum.
- You can quickly import data in real time into Redshift using AWS Kinesis Firehose.
- DocumentDB is a NoSQL database designed for JSON document-based workloads.
- DocumentDB is deployed into a VPC.
- You can deploy up to 15 read replicas for DocumentDB and it supports cross-region replicas using the global cluster feature.

- You can use parameter groups to control DocumentDB's features and options.
- DocumentDB has a TTL feature so that you can automatically delete documents that are older than the configured age.

Review

Now, let's practice with a few exam-style questions:

1. A company uses Amazon Redshift for its data warehousing needs. ETL jobs run every night to load data, apply business rules, and create aggregate tables for reporting purposes. The company's data analysis, data science, and business intelligence teams use the data warehouse during regular business hours. Workload management is set to auto, and separate queues exist for each team with the priority set to `NORMAL`. Recently, a sudden spike of read queries from the data analysis team has occurred at least twice a day, and queries wait in line for cluster resources. The company needs a solution that enables the data analysis team to avoid query queuing without impacting latency and the query times of other teams.

   Which solution meets these requirements?

   A. Increase the query priority to `HIGHEST` for the data analysis queue.

   B. Configure the data analysis queue to enable concurrency scaling.

   C. Create a query monitoring rule to add more cluster capacity for the data analysis queue when queries are waiting for resources.

   D. Use workload management query queue hopping to route the query to the next matching queue.

2. A marketing company has data in Salesforce, MySQL, and Amazon S3. The company wants to use data from these three locations and create mobile dashboards for its users. The company is unsure how it should create the dashboards and needs a solution with the least possible customization and coding. Which solution meets these requirements?

   A. Use Amazon Athena federated queries to join the data sources. Use Amazon QuickSight to generate the mobile dashboards.

   B. Use AWS Lake Formation to migrate the data sources into Amazon S3. Use Amazon QuickSight to generate the mobile dashboards.

C. Use Amazon Redshift federated queries to join the data sources. Use Amazon QuickSight to generate the mobile dashboards.

D. Use Amazon QuickSight to connect to the data sources and generate the mobile dashboards.

3. A company has a Redshift cluster for a very large, multi-petabyte, data warehouse. The data within the cluster can easily be recreated from data stored in Amazon S3. The company wants to reduce the overall total cost of running this Redshift cluster. Which scenario would best reduce the total overall ownership of the cluster?

   A. Instead of implementing automatic daily backups, write a CLI script that creates manual snapshots every few days. Copy the manual snapshot to a secondary AWS region for disaster recovery situations.

   B. Enable automated snapshots but set the retention period to a lower number to reduce storage costs.

   C. Implement daily backups, but do not enable multi-region copies to save data transfer costs.

   D. Disable automated and manual snapshots on the cluster.

4. A large multinational company wants to run a new application in several AWS regions to support a global user base. The application will need a database that can support a high volume of low-latency reads and writes that are expected to vary over time. The main data that will be stored is JSON documents that have fields that will be queried. The data must be shared across all of the regions to support dynamic company-wide reports. Which database meets these requirements?

   A. Use Amazon Aurora Serverless and configure endpoints in each region.

   B. Use Amazon RDS for MySQL and deploy read replicas in an auto-scaling group in each region.

   C. Use Amazon DocumentDB and configure global cluster read replicas in an auto-scaling group in each region.

   D. Use Amazon DynamoDB global tables and configure DynamoDB auto-scaling for the tables.

5. A customer is trying to upload a document that's 20 MB in size to a newly created DocumentDB but they are receiving an error. What is the most likely problem?

   A. They are trying to upload to a read replica endpoint rather than the primary.

   B. The document is corrupt and should be recreated.

C. DocumentDB has used all its available storage.

D. The document is too large.

Further reading

Here are a couple of resources you can refer to for further reading:

- *Amazon Redshift Cookbook*: `https://www.packtpub.com/product/amazon-redshift-cookbook/9781800569683`
- *Hands-On Amazon Redshift for Data Warehousing* [Video]: `https://www.packtpub.com/product/hands-on-amazon-redshift-for-data-warehousing-video/9781838558888`

8

Neptune, Quantum Ledger Database, and Timestream

In this chapter, we are going to explore and learn about three different **Amazon Web Services** (**AWS**) database technologies: **Neptune**, **Quantum Ledger Database** (**QLDB**), and **Timestream**. Each of these databases supports a specific workload type. All three are fully managed, and QLDB and Timestream are serverless databases.

Neptune is a graph database that allows you to run queries to quickly find out the connections and relationships between data items. QLDB is a database that works like an audit trail and does not allow any data to be deleted or changed. Timestream is a time-series database that allows you to work with data closely connected to timestamps, allowing you to keep an ordered record of events.

This chapter includes a hands-on lab where we will deploy, configure, and explore Neptune, QLDB, and Timestream instances, including how we can monitor and access them.

In this chapter, we're going to cover the following main topics:

- Overview of Amazon Neptune
- Working with Neptune
- Deploying a Neptune cluster
- Overview of Amazon QLDB
- Accessing a QLDB database
- Deploying a QLDB database
- Overview of Amazon Timestream
- Accessing a Timestream database
- Loading data into Timestream
- Deploying a Timestream database

Let's start by making sure we understand what Amazon Neptune is, when you would use it, and how it works differently from a **Relational Database Service** (**RDS**), Aurora, or DynamoDB.

Technical requirements

You will require an AWS account with root access; everything we will do in this chapter will be unavailable in free tier, which means it will cost a small amount to follow the hands-on sections. You will also require **command-line interface** (**CLI**) AWS access. The AWS guide (`https://docs.aws.amazon.com/cli/latest/userguide/cli-chap-configure.html`) will explain the steps required, but I will summarize here, as follows:

1. Open an AWS account if you have not already done so.
2. Download the AWS CLI latest version from here:

   `https://docs.aws.amazon.com/cli/latest/userguide/welcome-versions.html#welcome-versions-v2`

3. Create an admin user by going to the following link:

   `https://docs.aws.amazon.com/IAM/latest/UserGuide/getting-started_create-admin-group.html#getting-started_create-admin-group-cli`

4. Create an access key for your administration user by visiting this link:

   `https://docs.aws.amazon.com/IAM/latest/UserGuide/id_credentials_access-keys.html`

5. Run the `aws configure` command to set up a profile for your user. Refer to the following link for more information:

   `https://docs.aws.amazon.com/cli/latest/userguide/cli-configure-quickstart.html#cli-configure-quickstart-creds`

You will also require a **virtual private cloud** (**VPC**) that meets the minimum requirements for an RDS instance (`https://docs.aws.amazon.com/AmazonRDS/latest/UserGuide/USER_VPC.WorkingWithRDSInstanceinaVPC.html`). If you completed the steps in *Chapter 3*, *Understanding AWS Infrastructure*, you will already have a VPC that meets the requirements.

Overview of Amazon Neptune

Amazon Neptune is a graph database. As we learned in *Chapter 2*, *Understanding Database Fundamentals*, a graph database stores information as nodes and relationships rather than in tables and indexes or documents. You use a graph database when you need to know how things connect together, or if you need to store data that has a large number of links between records and you want to improve performance when running queries to find out those links. You can have queries in a **relational database management system** (**RDBMS**) that traverse multiple tables, but the more tables and links you add to the query, the worse the performance becomes, and this is where a graph database can make a big difference.

Let's start by looking at Neptune architecture and how it is deployed within AWS in the Cloud.

Neptune architecture and features

Amazon Neptune is deployed within a VPC. When it is deployed, you control access to it using **subnetworks (subnets)** and security groups. Neptune can be deployed as a cluster with **Multi-AZ** options, and its configuration is controlled using parameter groups in a similar manner to RDS instances. It is common to use Neptune in conjunction with other AWS services such as AWS Lambda (a serverless programming tool that allows you to run code without creating a server). A typical Neptune cluster across two **Availability Zones (AZs)** connecting these services can be seen in the following diagram:

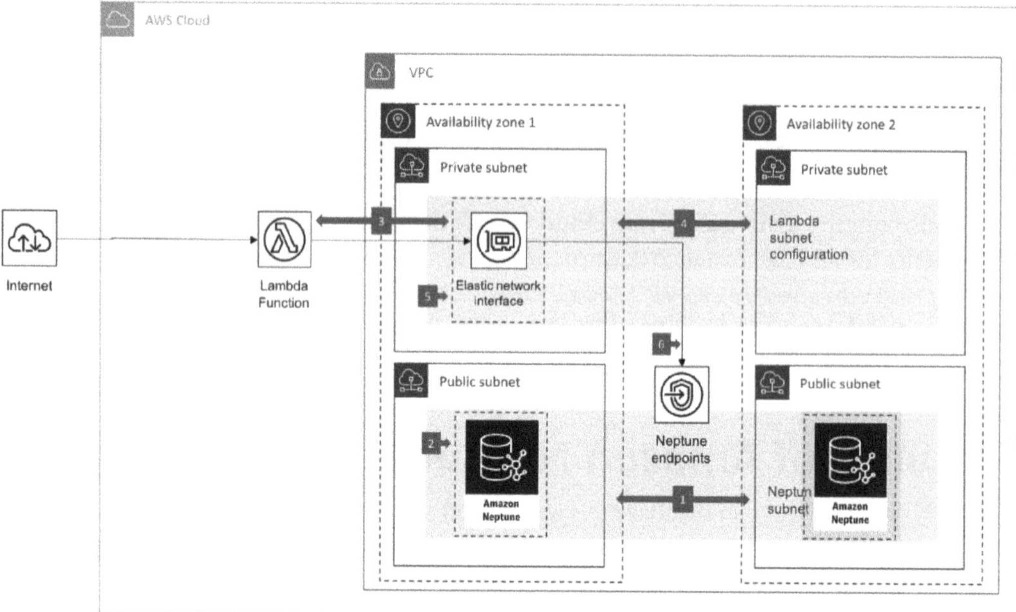

Figure 8.1 – Amazon Neptune Multi-AZ deployment with AWS Lambda

Amazon Neptune also supports cross-region replication using a service called Neptune Streams, which you can enable after you have created your Neptune cluster and copied a backup of your Neptune cluster across to the target region.

Now we've learned about Neptune topology and some key features, let's learn how to use Neptune data, including how to load and query data and how to work with graph data.

Working with Neptune

One of the first things to understand about graph databases is how they store data and, specifically, how Neptune stores data. Unlike RDBMS and some NoSQL systems (such as DynamoDB), graph databases do not use **Structured Query Language** (**SQL**) for querying. Instead, Neptune supports two different graph query languages: Gremlin and **SPARQL Protocol and RDF Query Language** (**SPARQL**). You can only use one language at a time in your database, and each language has its own requirements for how the data will be stored within Neptune and how you can utilize it. If you use Gremlin, the data stored will be using the **Property Graph** data framework, and if you choose SPARQL, you will be using the **Resource Description Framework** (**RDF**). SPARQL looks similar to SQL with `SELECT` and `INSERT` statements, but has some major differences with how it handles `WHERE` clauses and the syntax. Gremlin will appear unfamiliar to **database administrators** (**DBAs**) as it uses a structure more similar to programming languages such as Java or Python. Knowing the two different types of frameworks and languages you can use is important for the exam, but you will not need to know the specific differences between them.

Each item stored in Neptune consists of four elements, as outlined here:

- `subject (S)`—This can either refer to the name of the item or to the source item of a relationship (remember: graph databases focus closely on relationships, so they are defined specifically and stored, unlike in RDBMSs).
- `predicate (P)`—This describes the type of property that is being stored or the type of relationship. Consider this as a verb or a property description. Examples for relationships could be "*likes*," "*bought*," "*owns*" or, for a property of an item, "*color*," "*name*," or "*person*."
- `object (O)`—For a relationship, this will refer to the target item, and for a property, it will be the value you want to store.
- `graph (G)`—This is an optional parameter that can be used to create a *named graph* **identifier** (**ID**), or it can store an ID value for a relationship that's been created.

By using the preceding syntax, you can build up a diagram of items with properties such as descriptions of a person, as well as relationships to other items, such as books they own. The following diagram shows a simple representation of how that could look:

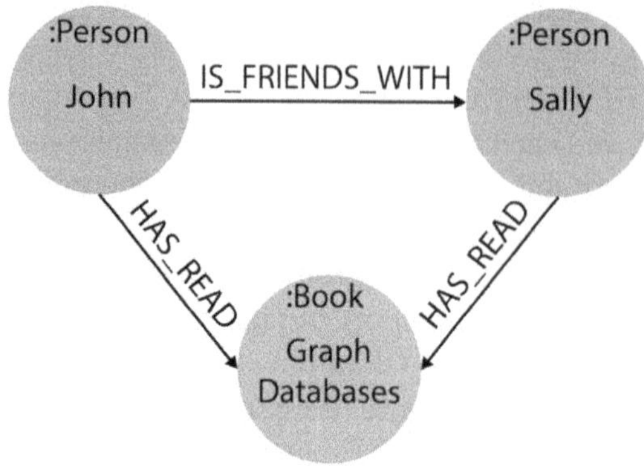

Figure 8.2 – Graph database showing people who have read a book

So, we now understand how Neptune stores data, but how do we load it? Let's look at how we can load data into a Neptune tool.

Loading data into Neptune

You can add data via SPARQL `INSERT` statements or their Gremlin equivalents, `addE` and `addV`. This approach would take a large amount of time for large datasets, and therefore Amazon offers the **Neptune Bulk Loader**. The Neptune Bulk Loader can read files hosted in a **Simple Storage Service** (**S3**) bucket and process them rapidly over the internal AWS network. The Neptune Bulk Loader tool takes advantage of endpoints (see *Chapter 2, Understanding Database Fundamentals*) to allow you to read and load data directly from an S3 bucket without having to open up your database subnets or security groups to the internet. It also allows you to use the AWS internal network, which operates at 10 **gigabits per second** (**Gbps**) and is often much faster than an AWS Direct Connect connection and faster than moving data via the public internet. You can also load data into Neptune using a tool called AWS **Database Migration Service** (**DMS**). DMS allows you to convert from an RDBMS database engine into Neptune. We will look at DMS in depth in *Chapter 10, The AWS Schema Conversion Tool and AWS Database Migration Service.*

Using Neptune Jupyter notebooks

One of the main use cases for using a graph database is the ability to quickly produce a graphical representation of your data. A graph database lends itself to producing a graphical model very quickly and easily because of how the data is stored; you don't need a complex data model to be able to see all the data connections as the connections themselves are stored as data items in the database. AWS offers a tool called Notebook that connects with Neptune and allows you to create graphs of your data rapidly. The notebooks use a framework called Jupyter, which is a graphical development environment designed for the web. You won't need to know any more about Jupyter for the exam.

Here is an example of how Neptune notebooks can visualize data based on your queries:

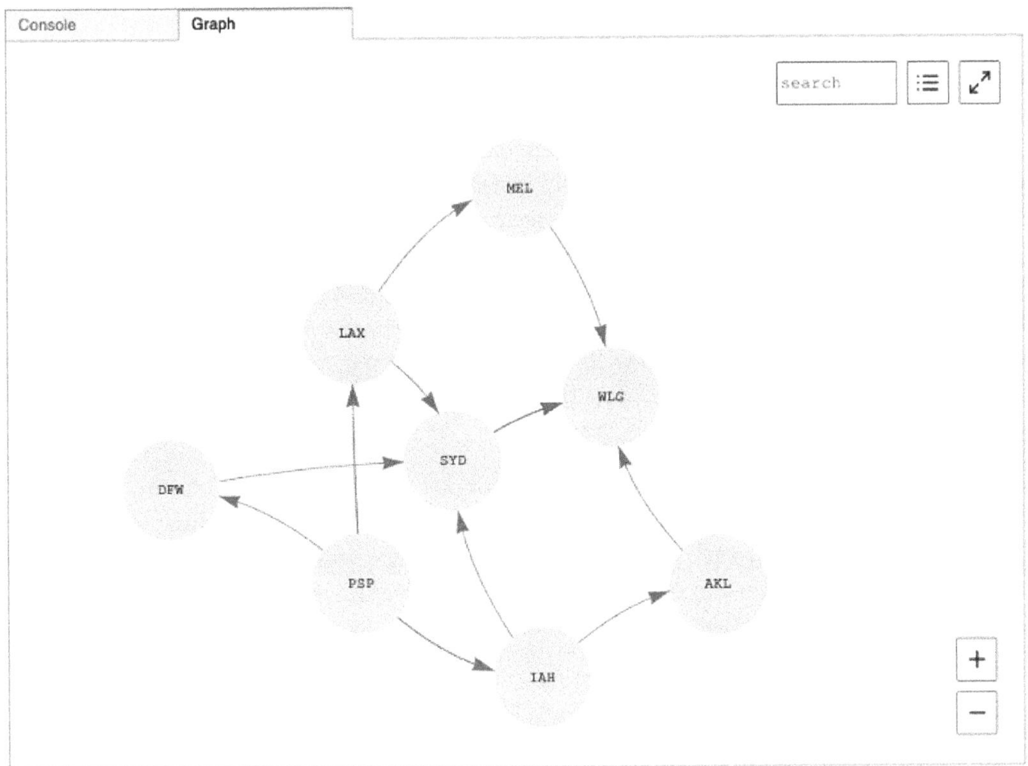

Figure 8.3 – Neptune notebook data visualization

The notebooks that are created run through another AWS service called **Sagemaker**. Sagemaker is a **machine learning** (**ML**) platform that is outside of the scope of the exam, but there may be a question on Neptune that mentions Sagemaker notebooks.

We've learned some of the key features of Neptune, how to load data, and how to query the data in a visual way, but how do you manage it? Let's look at that now.

Managing a Neptune cluster

Neptune is a fully managed database system, meaning that patching and backups are handled by AWS within the maintenance window and backup retention policies you set. However, areas such as instance sizing and read replicas remain under your control.

A Neptune instance can have up to 15 read replicas within the same region to allow you to scale your cluster horizontally. You can also change the instance class of both your primary database and read replicas at any time to make sure they are appropriately sized for your workload. Neptune supports auto-scaling of read replicas via an auto-scaling group, but it does not support auto-scaling of the instance class—this must be changed manually. Neptune sends logs by default to CloudWatch, allowing you to monitor its performance closely. CloudWatch also allows you to set up alarms against specific metrics to warn you if a cluster needs to be modified to handle a larger-than-expected workload.

Neptune will automatically scale your storage as your database grows, up to a maximum of 64 **tebibytes** (**TiB**). When it is first provisioned, you are given 10 **gigabytes** (**GB**) of storage, which will automatically grow as needed. Storage will not automatically shrink if data is deleted, but the Neptune database will instead try to optimize the storage. As the storage grows, Neptune updates the **high-water mark** (**HWM**). The HWM is the value used to calculate your storage costs. Neptune makes size copies of your data, but you are only charged for one, so if your database reaches 100 GB in size, you are only billed for 100 GB and not 600 GB as you may expect, given there are six copies of your data (two copies in three different AZs). If you wish to reduce the storage size and reduce your storage costs, you need to export the data from the database and import it into a new Neptune database; you cannot do this in situ.

Neptune uses parameter groups to control the configuration of a Neptune cluster. There are two types of parameter groups: database and cluster. Database groups allow you to set different parameters for each database, but cluster groups will affect all databases, including read replicas. You can override a cluster group parameter by modifying the database group last, as the latest changes take precedence.

We've now learned the main features of an Amazon Neptune database and cluster, including how to load data. Now, let's deploy a Neptune cluster and load some data into it.

Deploying a Neptune cluster

The first step we are going to do is to create a single, standalone Neptune cluster. Once the cluster is provisioned, we will load some data and install and configure a Gremlin client to allow us to query the data in the database.

> **Note**
>
> Neptune is not included in the AWS free tier, so following this lab will be chargeable by AWS. This lab is designed to keep costs at a minimum while learning the critical elements required for the exam.

Let's start by creating our Amazon Neptune cluster, as follows:

1. Log in to the AWS console and navigate to **Neptune**.
2. Click **Launch Amazon Neptune**, as illustrated in the following screenshot:

Graph database

Create an Amazon Neptune database cluster

Launch Amazon Neptune

Figure 8.4 – Launch Amazon Neptune

3. Complete the **Create database** form, as follows. If a value is not mentioned, please leave it as its default:
   - **Settings | DB cluster identifier**: `dbcert-neptune`
   - **Templates**: `Development and Testing`
   - **DB instance size | DB instance class**: `db.t3.medium`
   - **Connectivity | Virtual Private Cloud (VPC)**: Select the VPC you created in *Chapter 2, Understanding AWS Fundamentals*
   - **Connectivity | Additional connectivity configuration|VPC security group**: Create a new one and enter `dbcert-neptune-sg`
   - **Notebook configuration**: Uncheck **Create notebook**
   - Additional configuration—**Log exports**: Uncheck **Audit log**

4. Click **Create database**. The database will take around 10 minutes to show an **Available** status, which you can see in the following screenshot:

Figure 8.5 – Neptune dashboard screen

5. You will be able to see the cluster and a single `Writer` node.

Now we have our Neptune database up and running, we will load some data and run some queries. We'll start by loading data into an S3 bucket and granting Neptune read permissions. Proceed as follows:

1. Navigate to the `https://github.com/PacktPublishing/AWS-Certified-Database---Specialty-DBS-C01-Certification/tree/main/ch8` GitHub **Uniform Resource Locator** (**URL**) and download two files, `airports.csv` and `flight_routes.csv`.
2. Return to the AWS console and navigate to **S3**.
3. Click **Create bucket** on the right-hand side, as illustrated in the following screenshot:

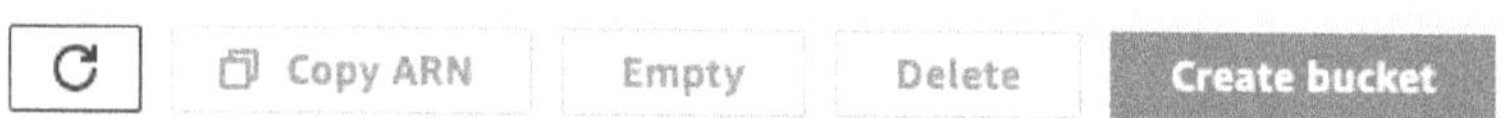

Figure 8.6 – Creating an S3 bucket

4. Complete the **Create bucket** form, as follows. Leave any values not mentioned as default:
   - **General configuration|Bucket name**: `dbcert-s3-<your name>`. S3 buckets must have unique names globally.
   - **General configuration|AWS Region**: `EU (Ireland) eu-west-1`.
5. Click **Create bucket**.
6. Click the bucket name you just created from the dashboard and select **Upload**, as illustrated in the following screenshot:

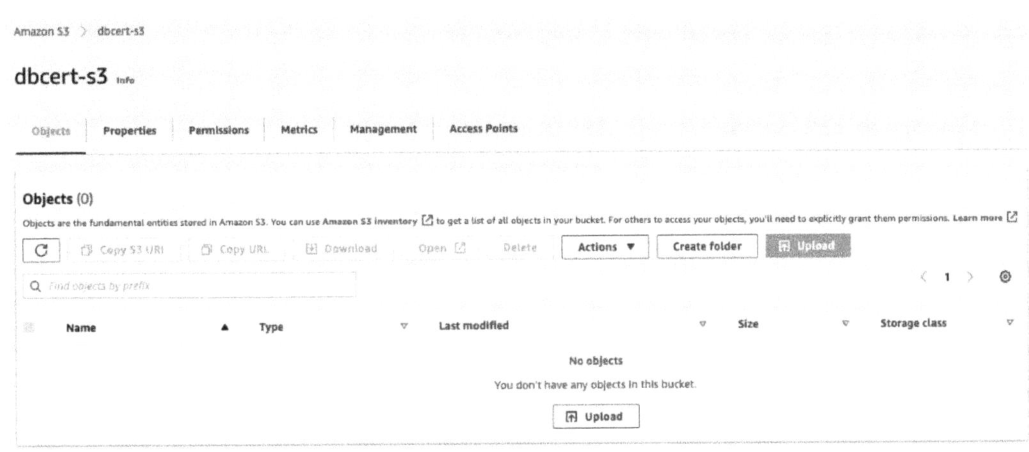

Figure 8.7 – S3 bucket upload

7. Locate the two `.csv` files you downloaded and upload those into the bucket, as illustrated in the following screenshot:

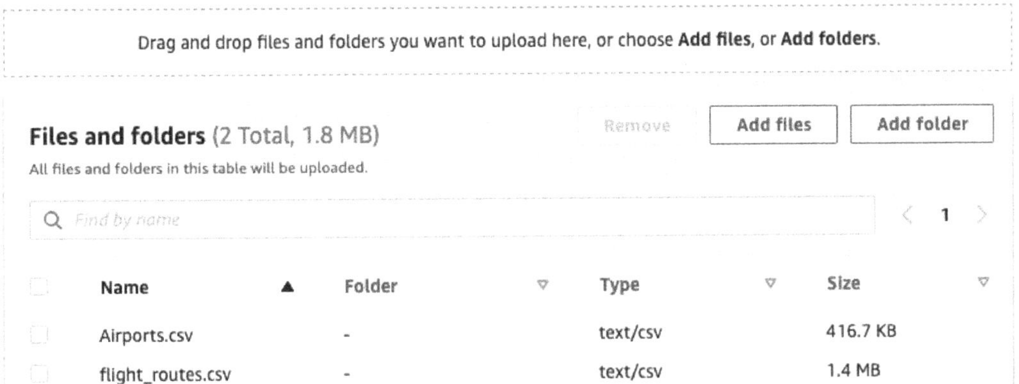

Figure 8.8 – S3 upload files

8. Click **Upload** at the bottom and wait for the transfer to complete. It will take around a minute on a standard internet connection. Wait until both files show as **Succeeded**.

We now need to create an S3 endpoint so that Neptune can access the data in the bucket. Proceed as follows:

1. Navigate to **VPC service** in the AWS console.
2. In the left navigation pane, choose **Endpoints**.
3. Click **Create Endpoint**.
4. Enter `s3` in the search bar and select `com.amazonaws.eu-west-1.s3` for the **Service name** value. Choose a value for **Gateway type**.
5. Choose the VPC that contains your Neptune database instance.
6. Select the checkbox next to the route tables that are associated with the subnets related to your Neptune database cluster. If you only have one route table, you must select that box.
7. If you wish, review the policy statement that defines this endpoint.
8. Click **Create Endpoint**.
9. An endpoint will be created immediately and you will see it in the dashboard view, as illustrated in the following screenshot:

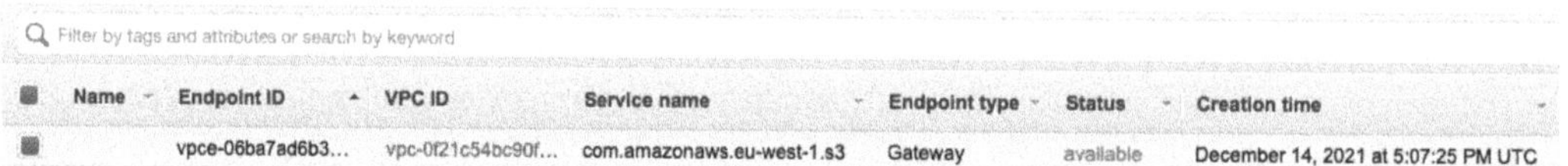

Figure 8.9 – Endpoint dashboard

The next step is to set up **identity and access management** (**IAM**) roles to allow the Neptune instance to communicate with the S3 bucket. Proceed as follows:

1. Log in to the AWS console and navigate to **IAM**.
2. Click **Roles** from the menu and then select **Create role**.
3. Click the **AWS service** button and then select **S3** from the list, as illustrated in the following screenshot. Select **S3** again in the **Select your use case** option at the bottom, and then click **Next: Permissions**:

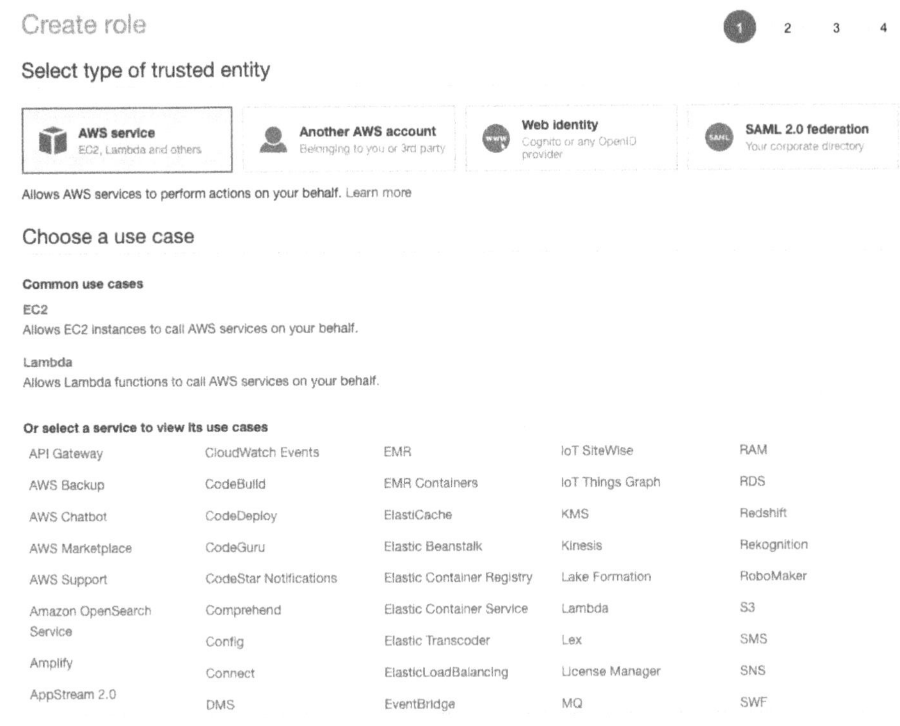

Figure 8.10 – Selecting the S3 service

4. Enter `AmazonS3ReadOnlyAccess` in the search box and then check the checkbox in the table below, as illustrated in the following screenshot. Then, click **Next: Tags**:

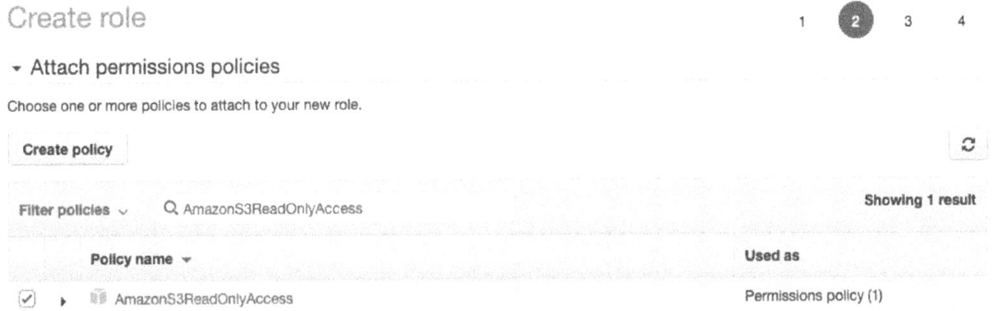

Figure 8.11 – Adding role permissions

5. Click **Review**.
6. Enter a name for the role, such as `dbcert-neptune-s3`, and click **Create role**.
7. Once the role has been created, click **Roles** from the left-hand menu and enter the name of the role you just created in the search box. Click the role name you created.

8. Click the **Trust relationships** tab, as illustrated in the following screenshot:

Figure 8.12 – Adding a trust relationship

9. Click **Edit trust relationship** and replace the code with the following code:

```
{
  "Version": "2012-10-17",
  "Statement": [
    {
      "Sid": "",
      "Effect": "Allow",
      "Principal": {
        "Service": [
          "rds.amazonaws.com"
        ]
      },
      "Action": "sts:AssumeRole"
    }
  ]
}
```

This code allows an RDS instance (of which Neptune is classified) to use this role.

10. Click **Update trust policy**.

11. Make a note of the **Role ARN** value, as shown in the following screenshot, as we will need it later on:

Roles > dbcert-neptune-s3

Summary

Role ARN arn:aws:iam::653375240923:role/dbcert-neptune-s3

Figure 8.13 - Making a note of the Role ARN value

12. Navigate to **Neptune** from the AWS console.
13. Select the database with the cluster role you created earlier, and then select **Manage IAM roles** from the **Actions** dropdown, as illustrated in the following screenshot:

Figure 8.14 – Assigning the IAM role to Neptune

14. Select the role you just created and click **Done**.

We will now create an **Elastic Compute Cloud** (**EC2**) instance from which we can run commands against the Neptune database. Proceed as follows:

1. Log in to the AWS console and navigate to **EC2**.
2. Click **Launch instance** from the **EC2** dashboard.
3. Select **Amazon Linux 2 AMI**, as illustrated in the following screenshot. Any kernel version is fine. Your **Amazon Machine Image** (**AMI**) details will vary depending on the region you choose:

Amazon Machine Image (AMI)

Amazon Linux 2 AMI (HVM) - Kernel 5.10, SSD Volume Type — Free tier eligible
ami-0e8cb4bdc5bb2e6c0 (64-bit (x86)) / ami-00cf3a525c4693c5f (64-bit (Arm))
Virtualization: hvm ENA enabled: true Root device type: ebs

Description

Amazon Linux 2 Kernel 5.10 AMI 2.0.20220406.1 x86_64 HVM gp2

Architecture: 64-bit (x86)

AMI ID: ami-0e8cb4bdc5bb2e6c0

Figure 8.15 - The Elastic Compute Cloud dashboard

4. Choose `t2.micro`, which is part of the free tier, as illustrated in the following screenshot:

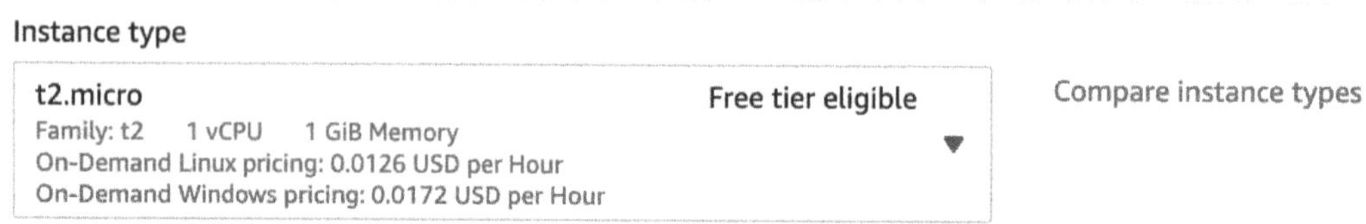

Figure 8.16 – Choosing the right EC2 instance size

5. Click **Next: Configure Instance Details.**

   Under **Network**, select the same VPC that the Neptune database was launched in. The VPC we built in *Chapter 2*, *Understanding Database Fundamentals*, will meet the requirements. Select any public subnet from the **Subnet** dropdown, as illustrated in the following screenshot—you can tell if it's a public subnet if the **Auto-assign Public IP** default value is **(Enable)**. This is important so that we can connect to this EC2 instance. Leave all other values as default and click **Review and Launch**:

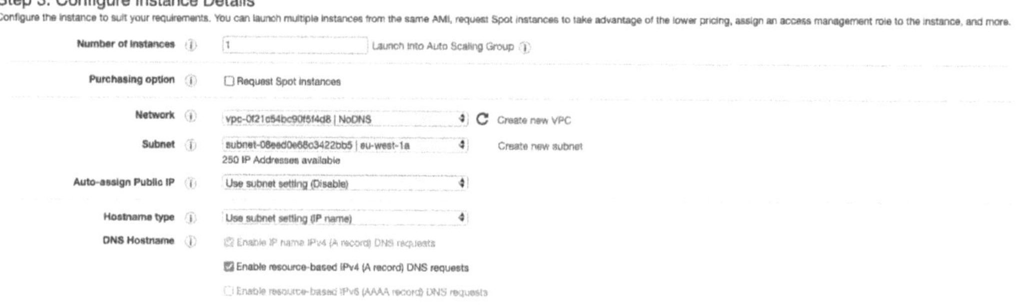

Figure 8.17 – EC2 launch configuration

6. On the **Review Instance Launch** page, click **Edit security groups.**
7. Create a new security group called `dbcert_neptune_ec2_sg`. Edit the rule to allow **Secure Shell** (**SSH**) on port `22` from your **Internet Protocol** (**IP**) address. This is so that we will be able to access the instance. The process is illustrated in the following screenshot:

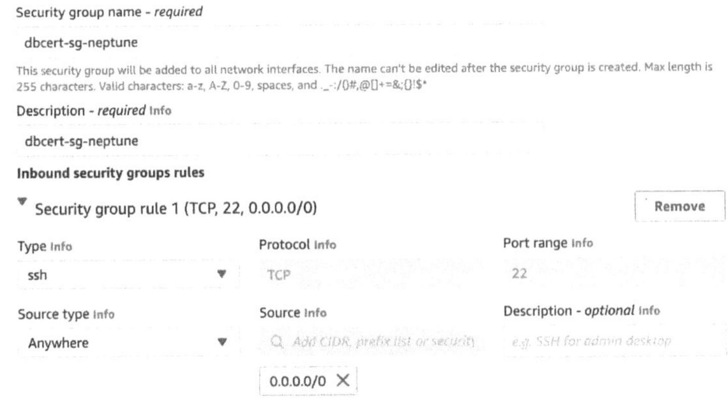

Figure 8.18 – Security group configuration

8. Click **Review and Launch** and then click **Launch**.
9. Select **Create a new key pair** from the dropdown and enter a name, such as `dbcert-neptune-kp`. Click **Download Key Pair** and then **Launch Instances**.
10. Return to the **EC2 Dashboard** and wait for the **Instance State** value to show as **Running**. This will take a few minutes.
11. We now need to add a rule to our Neptune database cluster security to allow the EC2 instance to connect to it. Navigate to the **VPC** service from the console main menu.
12. Select **Security groups** from the left-hand menu and locate your Neptune security group, which we called `dbcert_neptune_sg`.
13. Add a rule to allow `dbcert_neptune_ec2_sg` to connect to it on port `8182`.

Once the instance is running, we will try to connect to it using the EC2 instance connect tool. You can also try to use an `ssh` command from your local computer, but this is beyond the scope of this lab. Proceed as follows:

1. Select the instance you just created, and then click **Connect**.
2. Select **EC2 Instance Connect** and leave the username as `ec2-user`, as illustrated in the following screenshot:

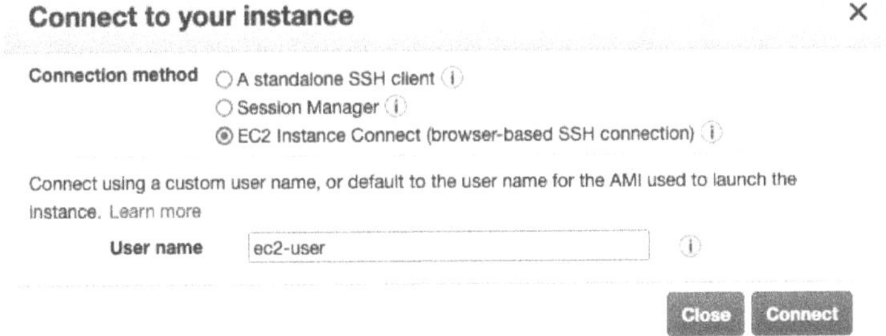

Figure 8.19 – Connecting to an EC2 instance

3. Click **Connect**.

   A screen similar to this should appear:

```
Amazon Linux 2 AMI

https://aws.amazon.com/amazon-linux-2/
6 package(s) needed for security, out of 14 available
Run "sudo yum update" to apply all updates.
[ec2-user@ip-172-30-1-251 ~]$
```

Figure 8.20 – EC2 terminal

   We are now going to use a tool called `curl` that allows to you run commands using **HyperText Transfer Protocol** (**HTTP**). You won't need to know about `curl` beyond this lab for the exam, but there is a recommendation in the *Further reading* section if you wish to know more.

4. In a different browser window or tab, navigate to the **Neptune** dashboard.
5. Click on the `Writer` node and make a note of the **Endpoint** and **Port** values under the **Connectivity & security** tab.
6. Return to your EC2 session and run the following `curl` command. You will need to modify the sections highlighted to match your own values:

```
curl -X POST \
    -H 'Content-Type: application/json' \
    https://dbcert-neptune-instance-1.cdhcmbt6wawh.
eu-west-1.neptune.amazonaws.com:8182/loader -d '
    {
      "source" : "s3://dbcert-s3-kgawron",
      "format" : "csv",
```

```
        "iamRoleArn" : "arn:aws:iam::653375240923:role/
dbcert-neptune-s3",
        "region" : "eu-west-1",
        "failOnError" : "FALSE",
        "parallelism" : "MEDIUM",
        "updateSingleCardinalityProperties" : "FALSE",
        "queueRequest" : "FALSE"
    }'
```

You will get the following output, showing the import is running:

```
{
    "status" : "200 OK",
    "payload" : {
        "loadId" : "03edf947-9702-48f5-8fa3-e2f1f31ba749"
    }
```

Now we have some data in the database, we need to install Gremlin to be able to run it.

7. From your EC2 instance, install Java, like so:

   ```
   sudo yum install java-1.8.0-devel
   ```

8. Now, download and install the Gremlin console, as follows:

   ```
   wget https://archive.apache.org/dist/tinkerpop/3.4.8/
   apache-tinkerpop-gremlin-console-3.4.8-bin.zip

   unzip apache-tinkerpop-gremlin-console-3.4.8-bin.zip
   ```

9. Change directory to `apache-tinkerpop-gremlin-console-3.4.8`.
10. Download and install Amazon certificates. Neptune uses a **Secure Sockets Layer** (**SSL**) connect, so to connect to it, we need an SSL certificate. Change the Java location to match the one you have downloaded. The code is illustrated in the following snippet:

   ```
   wget https://www.amazontrust.com/repository/SFSRootCAG2.
   cer
   mkdir /tmp/certs/
   ```

```
cp /usr/lib/jvm/java-1.8.0-openjdk-1.8.0.312.b07-1.
amzn2.0.1.x86_64/jre/lib/security/cacerts /tmp/certs/
cacerts
sudo keytool -importcert \
             -alias neptune-tests-ca \
             -keystore /tmp/certs/cacerts \
             -file  /home/ec2-user/apache-tinkerpop-
gremlin-console-3.4.8/SFSRootCAG2.cer \
             -noprompt \
                 -storepass changeit
```

11. Change into the `conf` directory and create a file called `neptune-con.yaml` with the following contents. You will need to change the values highlighted to match your own Neptune database. `[]` brackets are needed:

```
hosts: [dbcert-neptune.cluster-cdhcmbt6wawh.eu-west-1.
neptune.amazonaws.com]
port: 8182
connectionPool: { enableSsl: true,  trustStore: /tmp/
certs/cacerts }
serializer: { className: org.apache.tinkerpop.gremlin.
driver.ser.GryoMessageSerializerV3d0, config: {
serializeResultToString: true }}
```

12. Go back to the `apache-tinkerpop-gremlin-console-3.4.8` directory and run `bin/gremlin.sh`. This will load the Gremlin console.
13. At the `gremlin>` prompt, enter the following code to load your Neptune configuration and then tell Gremlin to use it:

```
:remote connect tinkerpop.server conf/neptune-con.yaml
:remote console
```

14. We can now run Gremlin queries, such as finding out how many components there are, as follows:

```
g.V().label().groupCount()
```

Or, we can find out where we can fly direct to from London Heathrow, as in this example:

```
g.V().has('code','LHR').out().path().by('code')
```

Feel free to review the *Further reading* section, which has a guide on more detailed Gremlin queries if you wish. When you are finished, type `:exit` to quit the Gremlin console.

15. You can now clear up the environment, including the EC2 instance you created.

Now we've learned about Neptune and have completed a hands-on lab covering all the topics that may come up in the exam, let's learn about another purpose-built database offered by AWS—QLDB.

Overview of Amazon QLDB

Amazon QLDB is a fully managed, transparent, immutable, and cryptographically verifiable transaction log database. What does this really mean? If you consider running an `UPDATE` or `DELETE` statement against a typical RDBMS, what happens? If you have logging enabled, then that transaction should be stored in the logs, but there will be no record of the change within the database. It would be fairly simple for someone to make changes and for those logs to be deleted or lost (how long are transaction logs kept for before being deleted?), and then all record of that change is also lost. QLDB not only stores the latest version of a record after it's been updated or deleted but also stores all the previous versions within the database itself. Additionally, the database ensures that every new version of a record contains an algorithmic reference to the previous version, meaning that any attempt to modify a record without making a record of the change will cause the algorithm to fail, and hence alert that someone has tampered with the system. As a result, QLDB is the perfect database to use when you need to have absolute guarantees over the accuracy of data; use cases such as financial transactions or medical cases are commonly cited when considering QLDB.

A QLDB table will look similar to this:

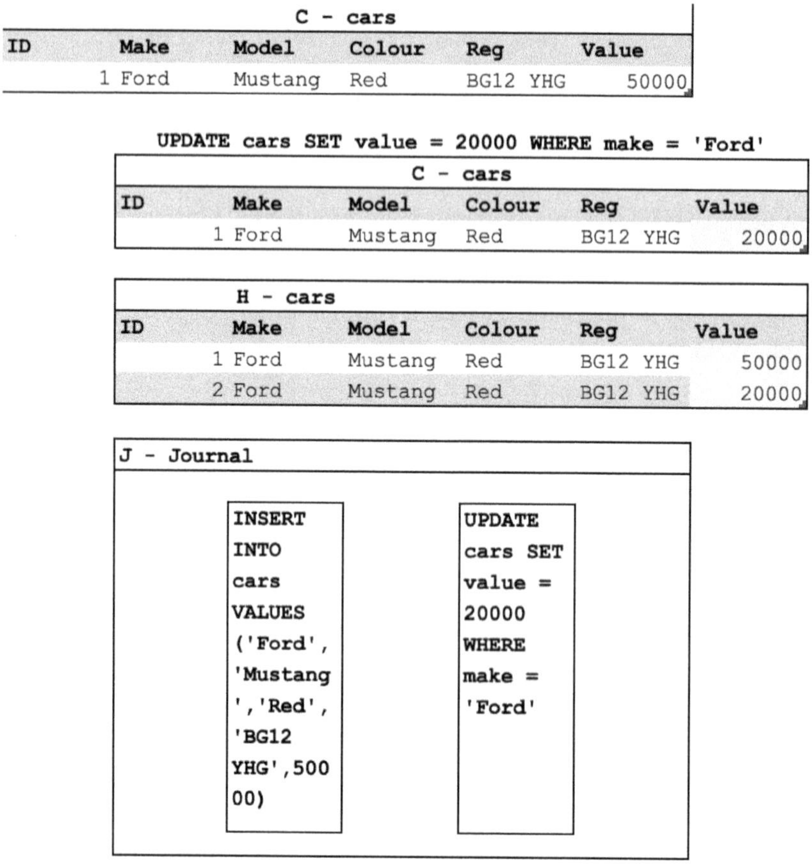

C - cars

ID	Make	Model	Colour	Reg	Value
1	Ford	Mustang	Red	BG12 YHG	50000

UPDATE cars SET value = 20000 WHERE make = 'Ford'

C - cars

ID	Make	Model	Colour	Reg	Value
1	Ford	Mustang	Red	BG12 YHG	20000

H - cars

ID	Make	Model	Colour	Reg	Value
1	Ford	Mustang	Red	BG12 YHG	50000
2	Ford	Mustang	Red	BG12 YHG	20000

J - Journal

```
INSERT
INTO
cars
VALUES
('Ford',
'Mustang
','Red',
'BG12
YHG',500
00)
```

```
UPDATE
cars SET
value =
20000
WHERE
make =
'Ford'
```

Figure 8.21 – QLDB schema view

The **C** table holds the current state of a record, the **H** table holds all the historical values that the record had, and the **J** table holds a log of all changes that have been made. The **J** table contains what are called digests. These are alphanumeric strings known as a **hashchain**. A hashchain is added to every time a record is amended. Each new entry contains all the previous entries, so the values grow as the database changes. As each entry contains all the previous entries too, any entry to the journal must match; otherwise, the change will be seen by the database and the verification will fail. Changing any data in the database without it being tracked requires every journal entry for that record to also be changed at the same time. This would require computing power that doesn't currently exist, therefore a QLDB instance is classed as immutable and cryptographically verifiable. You can query any of three tables at any time, depending on the data you require.

Let's take a look at the QLDB architecture and how you deploy it within AWS.

QLDB architecture

QLDB is deployed by default across multiple AZs, with multiple copies of the data also being stored in each AZ. This makes it both resilient to a software failure and fast to recover from and durable if storage is lost. A write to QLDB is only committed once the data has been successfully written to multiple storage locations in more than one AZ.

QLDB is a serverless database. This means that you do not need to provision compute capacity or storage amounts for it as it will auto-scale seamlessly with demand.

One of the main benefits of QLDB is its interconnectivity with other AWS services. You can quickly and easily connect QLDB to tools such as Amazon Kinesis Data Streams, which monitors the logs of the database and takes actions based on them. For example, you can configure Amazon Kinesis to forward all data modifications to an RDS instance. Due to how QLDB manages the data, it can be much slower to query than an equivalent non-immutable database in RDS, so connecting the two systems together in this way would allow you to run faster read-only queries against the RDS system, but have an immutable copy of the data stored in QLDB for verification purposes. Here is an example of that architecture, whereby QLDB is used for all writes, and reads are from an Aurora RDS database:

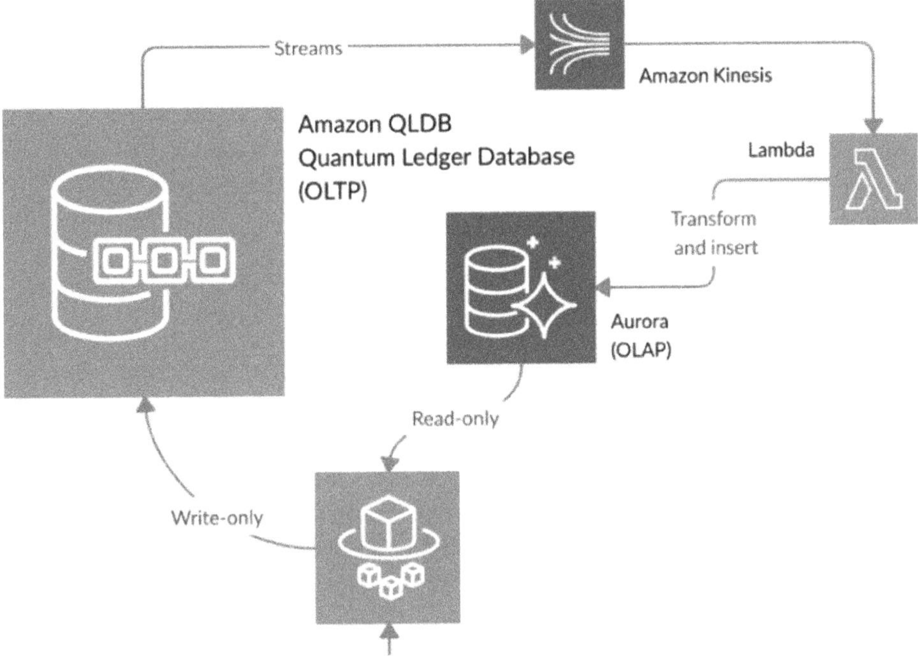

Figure 8.22 – QLDB and Aurora architecture example

Now we've learned how Amazon QLDB works and is provisioned, let's look at how you access and query it.

Accessing a QLDB database

QLDB has three methods to query data, as follows:

- **AWS console**—QLDB has a built-in graphical query tool.
- **Amazon QLDB shell**—You can use a downloadable shell and connect from your local machine to the QLDB instance and run queries.
- **AWS application programming interface (API)**—You can download a QLDB driver and make calls to the QLDB instance using a variety of coding languages such as Java, .NET, and Python.

These methods all use a language called **PartiQL** (pronounced *particle*) to run queries. PartiQL uses a similar structure to SQL queries, allowing you to run `SELECT`, `UPDATE`, and `DELETE` statements complete with `WHERE` clauses. Here's an example of this:

```
SELECT * FROM Cars AS c WHERE c.Reg IN ('BG12 YHG', 'D150
GWE');
```

Here is the output for the previous query. It follows a syntax called Amazon Ion, which closely resembles **JavaScript Object Notation** (**JSON**) syntax:

```
{
    Make: "Ford",
    Model: "Mustang",
    Color: "Red",
    Reg: "BG12 YHG",
    Value: 20000
}
```

You can use PartiQL for joining tables, doing aggregation queries (for example, `MAX` or `AVG`). You can also use PartiQL to obtain the metadata of a record. *Metadata* refers to information about the record itself rather than the data within it. Metadata might include the `RecordID` value, the date it was added or modified, or the size of the record. QLDB allows you to query this metadata by querying system tables. For example, to obtain all the metadata and data for the latest committed version of a specific record, you can use this query (note the addition of `_ql_committed_` to the table name):

```
SELECT * FROM _ql_committed_Cars AS c WHERE c.Reg IN ('BG12
YHG', 'D150 GWE');
```

This query will return the hash value for that record as well as its version number (the number of times it's been updated since first inserted) and the block address (which is the physical location on the storage). It also returns a metadata ID value, which can be used to query historic versions of that record. This is an example output you would see:

```
{
     blockAddress:{
          strandId:" 5PLf9SXwndd631PaSIa0O6",
          sequenceNo:9
     },
     hash:{{LuCf20C1fBB0s7HRV5m28FSx1xn94Z9o3FbePOCF8WO=}},
     data:{
          Make: "Ford",
     Model: "Mustang",
     Color: "Red",
     Reg: "BG12 YHG",
     Value: 20000
     },
     metadata:{
          id:"QgSrP4SPSwUWI0RjxureT3",
          version:0,
          txTime:2021-12-08T11:15:261d-3Z,
          txId:"KaYBkLjAtV0HQ41NYdzX60"
     }
}
```

As QLDB stores the details of all changes made in the history table, you can write a query to see all previous values of a record or limit it to a time range, as in the following example:

```
SELECT * FROM history(Cars, `2021-12-07T00:00:00Z`,
`2021-12-10T23:59:59Z`) AS h WHERE h.metadata.id =
'QgSrP4SPSwUWI0RjxureT3'
```

The output would show you all changes made between those dates, as illustrated here:

```
{
     blockAddress:{
          strandId:" 5PLf9SXwndd631PaSIa0O6",
          sequenceNo:9
```

```
        },
        hash:{{LuCf20C1fBB0s7HRV5m28FSx1xn94Z9o3FbePOCF8WO=}},
        data:{
            ...
          Value: 50000
        },
        metadata:{
            id:"QgSrP4SPSwUWI0RjxureT3",
            version:0,
            txTime:2021-12-08T08:43:321d-3Z,
            txId:"KaYBkLjAtV0HQ41NYdzX60"
        }
    },
    {
        blockAddress:{
            strandId:" 5PLf9SXwndd631PaSIa0O6",
            sequenceNo:12
        },
        hash:{{Qleu1L9OQuqvZP57n9nw5aCqNrIDW7ywAb8QX1ps1Rx =}},
        data:{
            ...
          Value: 20000
        },
        metadata:{
            id:"QgSrP4SPSwUWI0RjxureT3",
            version:1,
            txTime:2021-12-08T11:15:261d-3Z,
            txId:" 7nGrhIQV5xf5Tf5vtsPwPq"
        }
    }
```

Note how the `txId` (transaction ID) value changes, but not the metadata ID value. The version number increases with every change, with version `0` being the first committed version.

Quotas and limits for QLDB

QLDB has some limits you may need to be aware of for the exam. The key ones are noted here:

- **Number of active ledgers in any one region**—5
- **Maximum concurrent session in any one ledger**—1,500
- **Maximum number of active tables**—20
- **Maximum number of tables active or inactive** (dropped tables are called inactive, so count toward this limit)—40
- **Maximum document size**—128 **kilobytes (KB)**

Now we've learned how to access and query QLDB and found out about some of the limits that may come up in the exam, let's put our knowledge to use in a hands-on lab, deploying a QLDB ledger.

Deploying a QLDB database

Let's now use the AWS console to deploy, load data into, and query a QLDB database. First, we will create our ledger.

> **Note**
>
> QLDB is not included in the AWS free tier, so following this lab will be chargeable by AWS. This lab is designed to keep costs at a minimum while learning the critical elements required for the exam.

Proceed as follows:

1. Go to the AWS console and navigate to **Amazon QLDB**.
2. Click **Create ledger**.
3. Enter `dbcert-qldb` as a value for **Ledger name** and leave all other values at their default settings. Click **Create ledger** at the bottom of the page.
4. The database will take a few minutes to create, so wait until the **Status** column shows as **Available**.

   Now, we need to load data into our ledger. We will use sample data provided by AWS for testing.

5. Click on **Getting started** from the menu on the left-hand side and scroll down until you find the **Sample application data** section, as illustrated in the following screenshot:

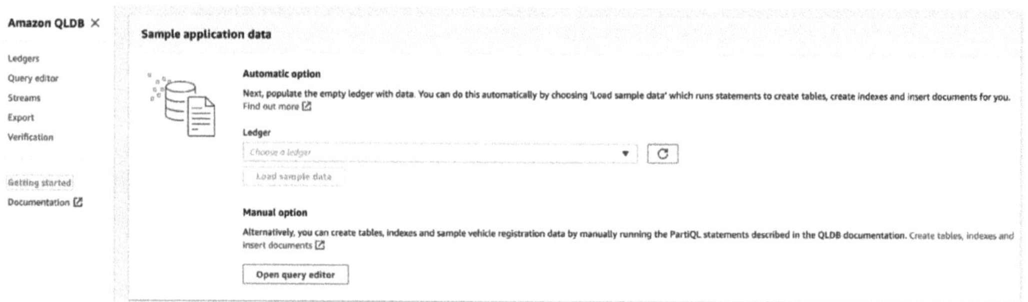

Figure 8.23 – Loading sample data

Select your ledger from the dropdown and click **Load sample data.**

6. Once the data has loaded click **Query editor** on the left-hand menu
7. Select your ledger from the dropdown and wait for a list of tables to be loaded.
8. Click on the table names to view indexes from which you can build your queries. Type the following command into the query window and then click **Run**:

```
select VIN from Vehicle
```

You will receive the following output:

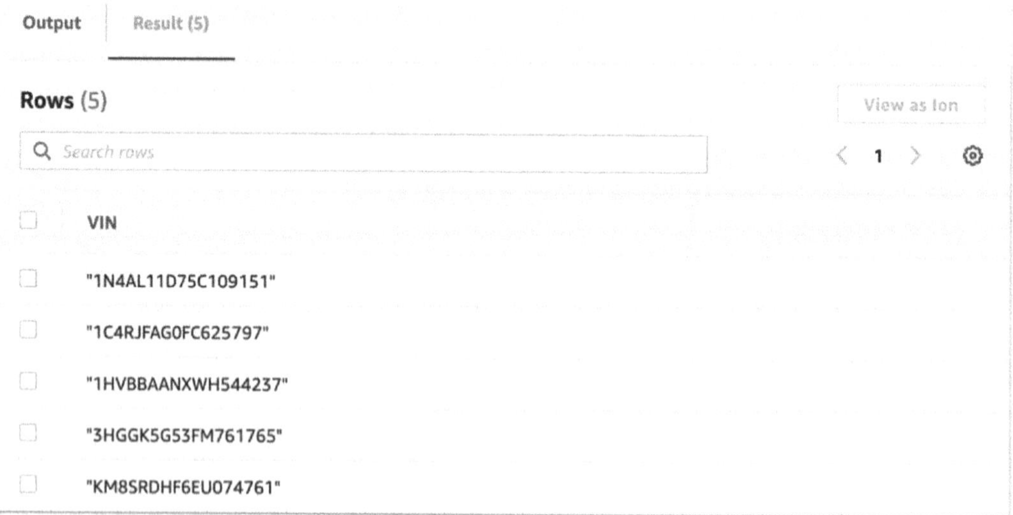

Figure 8.24 – Query output

9. Experiment with different queries against `_ql_committed_` tables, as follows:

```
select * from _ql_committed_Vehicle
```

10. When you are finished, you can delete the QLDB ledger. You will need to modify the ledger to remove **Deletion protection** before you can do so.

We've now learned all the key features you will need to know on QLDB for the exam. Let's now learn about the final purpose-built database AWS offers: Amazon Timestream.

Overview of Amazon Timestream

Amazon Timestream is a time-series database. A time-series database is optimized for storing and querying data saved in key pairs of time and value. It is often used when data is being stored from sensors or operations with a timestamp and associated value that need to be tracked for trending analysis.

Timestream is a fully-managed, serverless, and scalable database service specifically customized and optimized for **Internet of Things** (**IOT**) devices and application sensors, allowing you to store trillions of events per day up to 1,000 times faster than via an RDBMS. Being serverless means you do not need to define your compute values, as Timestream will automatically scale up and down depending on the current workload.

Timestream features a tier-storage solution that moves older and less frequently accessed data to a cheaper storage tier, saving costs. Timestream has its own adaptive query engine that learns your data access patterns to optimize query retrieval speed and can access all the different storage tiers at the same time, making querying simpler and more efficient. Timestream also auto-scales your storage so that you do not need to pre-allocate storage space, as Timestream will grow the storage as required.

Let's look at Timestream architecture and how it differs from other databases.

Timestream architecture

Timestream features two main components: an in-memory data store for fast writes and reads, and a permanent data storage layer for redundancy and resilience. The following diagram shows the architecture used:

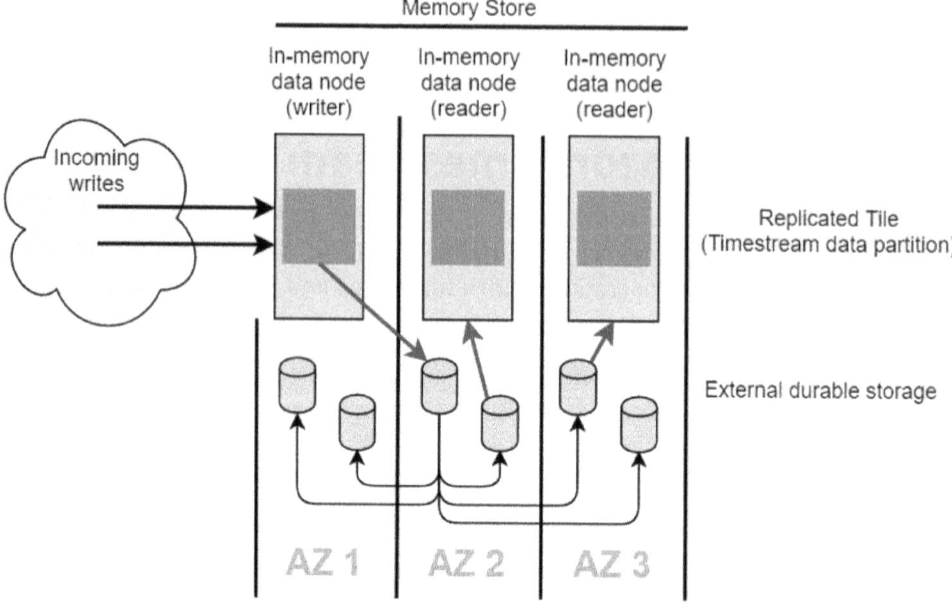

Figure 8.25 – Timestream architecture

Timestream will automatically move data from the memory store to the durable storage based on lifecycle policies you can set. For example, you can tell Timestream to move any data older than 24 hours to durable storage. Data being read from durable storage will be much slower than from memory, but storing in memory is more expensive. Managing lifecycle policies correctly will allow you to handle most queries from data held in the fast memory store while not holding rarely queried data, thereby increasing your costs.

Timestream does not require you to create a schema before using it. Timestream will automatically create tables for you based on the dimensions and attributes you ask it to store. Here is an example of a Timestream table:

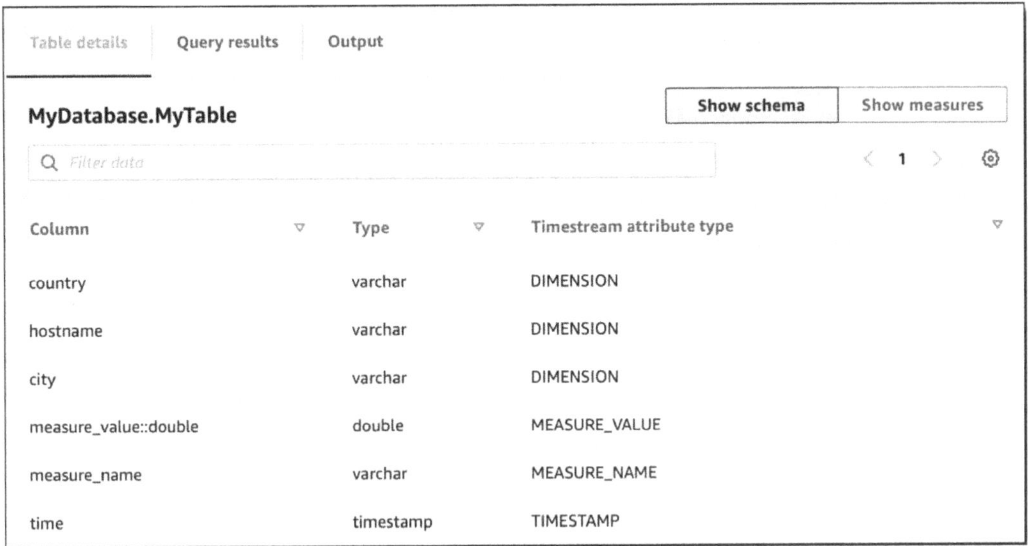

Figure 8.26 – Timestream schema

You can see column names, types, and the Timestream attribute type. The Timestream attribute type will be one of four, as outlined here:

- `DIMENSION`—This is metadata about the entry and contains extra information about the data that is being stored.
- `MEASURE_NAME`—This is the name of the measure that is being taken. This could be something such as weight, size, speed, and so on.
- `MEASURE_VALUE`—This is the value that has been measured.
- `TIMESTAMP`—This is the time the value was taken.

This is an example of how data could look using that schema:

Rows returned (8)

country	hostname	city	measure_value::double	measure_name	time
UK	MyHostname	London	5.7	disk_utilization	2020-09-18 15:06:03.424000000
UK	MyHostname	London	46.8	cpu_utilization	2020-09-18 15:06:03.424000000
UK	MyHostname	London	64.1	memory_utilization	2020-09-18 15:06:03.424000000
UK	MyHostname	London	73.8	swap_utilization	2020-09-18 15:06:03.424000000
UK	MyHostname	London	44.1	cpu_utilization	2020-09-18 15:06:02.420000000
UK	MyHostname	London	5.7	disk_utilization	2020-09-18 15:06:02.420000000
UK	MyHostname	London	64.2	memory_utilization	2020-09-18 15:06:02.420000000
UK	MyHostname	London	73.8	swap_utilization	2020-09-18 15:06:02.420000000

Figure 8.27 – Timestream query

Timestream stores data in time order sorted by dimensions. For example, in the previous query, the data would be first organized by country, hostname, and city, and then it would be sorted in timestamp order. As most queries will contain a `WHERE` clause filtering on one or more dimension values, this will ensure the highest performance as all of those values will be located together in the same memory or durable storage area, allowing them to be returned simultaneously without multiple disk reads.

Timestream natively supports the forwarding of data to other AWS services vis Amazon Kinesis. It is common for Timestream to be connected to graphically querying tools such as Amazon QuickSight or Grafana to use visualization to aid trending and analysis.

We've learned about the high-level architecture and schema design of a Timestream database, but how do we query it and load data? Let's learn how to do that now.

Accessing a Timestream database

Timestream can be queried using three different methods, as follows:

- **AWS console**—Timestream has a built-in graphical query tool.
- **AWS CLI**—You can use the AWS CLI to run both write and read queries from your local computer.

- **AWS API/software development kit (SDK)**—You can download a **Java Database Connectivity** (**JDBC**) driver and make calls to Timestream using a variety of coding languages such as Java, .NET, and Python.

Timestream supports queries written in SQL, allowing you to run `SELECT` and `INSERT` statements combined with `WHERE` clauses to filter. You *cannot* run a `DELETE` statement from Timestream, nor run an `UPDATE` statement against an existing entry, as this will break the time pattern. You can also run a scheduled query. Given the time-sensitive nature of Timestream use cases, it's common to create daily or weekly reports showing trends, patterns, and exceptions. Scheduled queries are used to create views that can then in turn be queried. This can greatly improve the performance of your queries as the aggregated data has already been collated, and therefore you are only querying against a subset held in memory. A typical use case for scheduled queries is to connect an ML tool such as AWS SageMaker to identify exceptions that may point to fraud or sensor failure.

Loading data into Timestream

Timestream doesn't have any method to bulk-load data as it is designed to receive a large amount of data from sensors in real time rather than as a bulk data load. You can import a sample dataset for testing when you deploy Timestream.

Let's do that now—we'll learn how to deploy a Timestream database, import some sample data, and then run some queries.

Deploying a Timestream database

Let's now use the AWS console to deploy, load data into, and query a Timestream database. First, we will create our table.

> **Note**
>
> Timestream is not included in the AWS free tier, so following this lab will be chargeable by AWS. This lab is designed to keep costs at a minimum while learning the critical elements required for the exam.

Proceed as follows:

1. Go to the AWS console and navigate to **Amazon Timestream**.
2. Click **Create database**.

3. Choose **Sample database**. Enter `dbcert-timestream` as the **Database name** value and leave all other values at their default values. Click **Create database** at the bottom of the page.
4. A database will take be created immediately, complete with sample data loaded.
5. Click **Query editor** on the left-hand menu.
6. Select your database from the dropdown and wait for a list of tables to be loaded.
7. Click on the table names to view columns from which you can build your queries. Type the following command into the query window and then click **Run**:

```
select truck_id from "dbcert-timestream.IotMulti"
```

You will receive the following output:

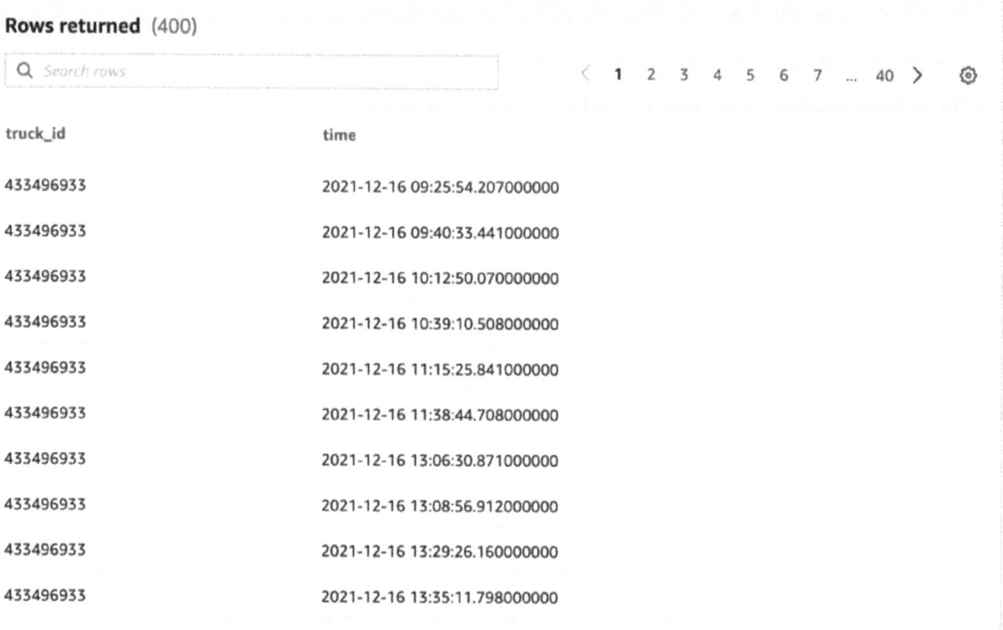

Rows returned (400)

Search rows

< 1 2 3 4 5 6 7 ... 40 >

truck_id	time
433496933	2021-12-16 09:25:54.207000000
433496933	2021-12-16 09:40:33.441000000
433496933	2021-12-16 10:12:50.070000000
433496933	2021-12-16 10:39:10.508000000
433496933	2021-12-16 11:15:25.841000000
433496933	2021-12-16 11:38:44.708000000
433496933	2021-12-16 13:06:30.871000000
433496933	2021-12-16 13:08:56.912000000
433496933	2021-12-16 13:29:26.160000000
433496933	2021-12-16 13:35:11.798000000

Figure 8.28 – Timestream query output

You can see many entries for the same `truck_id` value. This data isn't very useful, so let's add some aggregation to the query, as follows:

```
SELECT truck_id, fleet, fuel_capacity, model, load_
capacity, make, measure_name FROM "dbcert-timestream".
IoTMulti GROUP BY truck_id, fleet, fuel_capacity, model,
load_capacity, make, measure_name
```

8. Experiment with different queries. Sample queries are accessible via the **Sample queries** tab. Make sure you only select `IoTMulti` queries, else you will receive an error.
9. When you are finished, you can delete the Timestream database. You will need to delete the tables before you can delete the database. You can delete tables from the **Tables** option on the left-hand side of the screen.

We've now learned all the key features of Amazon Timestream, as well as how to deploy and query a Timestream database.

This completes our learning around the different databases offered by AWS that you will need to know for the exam. Let's now review our learning from this chapter.

Summary

In this chapter, we have learned about the final three new databases offered by AWS: Neptune, QLDB, and Timestream. We have learned that Neptune is a graph database fully managed by AWS and is used to define connections between records. We also learned how to use Gremlin and the Neptune Bulk Loader to query and load data.

For QLDB, we discovered what immutable means and how QLDB stores data and all historical versions, making it impossible for it to be changed without leaving a record.

Finally, we learned how to store large amounts of time-value data in Timestream that optimizes storage and queries of data from sensors or IoT devices.

We have now learned about all the different databases that AWS offers and that are covered in the exam. We have practiced working with the AWS console and the AWS CLI to create, query, and delete the databases. We have also learned how to work with other AWS services such as S3 and IAM.

In the next chapter, we are going to learn about how to use two database migration tools offered by AWS: **Schema Conversion Tool** (**SCT**) and **Database Migration Service** (**DMS**).

Let's now review the key points of this chapter in the *Cheat sheet* section.

Cheat sheet

This cheat sheet summarizes the main key points from this chapter, as follows:

- Neptune is a graph database optimized for storing and querying connections between items.
- You can use the Neptune Bulk Loader to import data in various formats from an S3 bucket using S3 endpoints.
- Neptune supports querying using the SPARQL language, which is similar to SQL, as well as Gremlin, which is a specific graph querying language.
- Neptune is a highly redundant, fully managed database system with options for both Multi-AZ and cross-region replication using Neptune Streams.
- QLDB is an immutable centralized ledger database optimized for workloads that require verifiable data chains with all historic versions and modifications.
- QLDB uses the PartiQL query language and returns data in Amazon ION format.
- QLDB does not offer any backup or restore functionality, but you can export to S3.
- QLDB scales automatically, so you do not need to provision compute or storage for it.
- Timestream is a fully managed, scalable database service optimized for time-series data, typically from sensors or IoT devices.
- Timestream creates a schema for you dependent on the data you load, so it allows for fully customized tables created at runtime.
- Timestream offers data management policies to store data on cheaper magnetic storage for less frequently accessed data, while frequently accessed data is stored with memory for rapid querying.
- Timestream supports querying using SQL syntax, allowing for complex aggregated queries.

Review

Let's now review your knowledge with this quiz:

1. You are working as a database consultant for a health insurance company. You are constructing a new Amazon Neptune database cluster, and you try to load data from Amazon S3 using the Neptune Bulk Loader from an EC2 instance in the same VPC as the Neptune database, but you receive the following error message: `Unable to establish a connection to the s3 endpoint. The source URL is s3://dbcert-neptune/ and the region code is us-east-1. Kindly confirm your S3 configuration.`

   Which of the following activities should you take to resolve the issue? (Select two)

   A. Check that a Neptune VPC endpoint exists.

   B. Check that an Amazon S3 VPC endpoint exists.

   C. Check that Amazon EC2 has an IAM role granting read access to Amazon S3.

   D. Check that Neptune has an IAM role granting read access to Amazon S3.

   E. Check that Amazon S3 has an IAM role granting read access to Neptune.

2. You are working with an Amazon Timestream database and are trying to delete records that have been loaded incorrectly. When running the `DELETE FROM "dbcert-timestream"."test-table"` statement, you receive the following error: `The query syntax is invalid at line 1:1.`

   What is the most likely reason for the error?

   A. The quotes are wrong in the SQL statement

   B. The table name is incorrect

   C. You cannot run a `DELETE` statement on a Timestream database

   D. You do not have the correct IAM permissions

3. You are a DBA for a large financial company that is exploring QLDB. You have created a QLDB with 20 tables and are trying to create another one via the QLDB shell when you receive an error.

   What is the most likely cause?

   A. Someone has dropped the ledger you were working on.

   B. The QLDB service is currently unavailable.

   C. There are too many active sessions currently connected.

   D. You have hit the maximum number of active tables.

4. Which query languages are supported by the Amazon Neptune engine? (Choose two)

   A. Gremlin

   B. PartiQL

   C. SQL

   D. Amazon Ion

   E. SPARQL

5. You are working as a DBA for a financial company that is being audited. The auditors want to see the full history of changes made to certain records in your QLDB ledger. Which table/function do you need to query to provide this information?

   A. `_ql_committed_<table_name>`

   B. `history (table_name)`

   C. `information_schema`

   D. `digest`

Further reading

To learn the topics of this chapter in detail, you can refer to the following resources:

- Apache TinkerPop documentation—Gremlin language:

  `https://tinkerpop.apache.org/gremlin.html`

- `curl` reference guide:

  `https://curl.se/docs/httpscripting.html`

- *Learn Amazon SageMaker – Second Edition*:

  `https://www.packtpub.com/product/learn-amazon-sagemaker-second-edition/9781801817950`

9

Amazon ElastiCache

So far in this book, we have learned about relational and NoSQL database engines, but there is another category of database that doesn't fit into either – caching databases. Database caching can be a useful technique to speed up query read performance by storing frequently accessed information in an area that offers very fast access.

During the AWS Certified Database – Specialty exam, you will likely need to answer questions about performance issues or a specific configuration that uses a high level of caching; this chapter will explain how to answer those types of questions. You will also be able to complete a hands-on lab to practice the theory you will learn.

In this chapter, we're going to cover the following main topics:

- Understanding database caching
- An overview of Amazon ElastiCache
- Redis versus Memcached
- Adding caching to a database system

Let's start by learning about database caching before we move on to the two different engines you can use for caching within AWS.

Technical requirements

You will require an AWS account with root access; not everything we do in this chapter may be available in Free Tier, which means it may cost you a small amount to follow the hands-on sections. You will also require access to the AWS **Command-Line Interface** (**CLI**). The AWS guide (`https://docs.aws.amazon.com/cli/latest/userguide/cli-chap-configure.html`) explains the steps required, but I will summarize them here:

1. Open an AWS account if you have not already done so.
2. Download the latest version of the AWS CLI from here: `https://docs.aws.amazon.com/cli/latest/userguide/welcome-versions.html#welcome-versions-v2`.
3. Create an admin user: `https://docs.aws.amazon.com/IAM/latest/UserGuide/id_credentials_access-keys.html`.
4. Create an access key for your administration user: `https://docs.aws.amazon.com/IAM/latest/UserGuide/getting-started_create-admin-group.html#getting-started_create-admin-group-cli`.
5. Run the `aws configure` command to set up a profile for your user: `https://docs.aws.amazon.com/cli/latest/userguide/cli-configure-quickstart.html#cli-configure-quickstart-creds`.

You will also require a **Virtual Private Cloud** (**VPC**) that meets the minimum requirements for an **Relational Database Service** (**RDS**) instance: `https://docs.aws.amazon.com/AmazonRDS/latest/UserGuide/USER_VPC.WorkingWithRDSInstanceinaVPC.html`. If you completed the steps in *Chapter 3*, *Understanding AWS Infrastructure*, you will already have a VPC that meets the requirements.

Understanding database caching

Caching is a term used across many computing scenarios when you use a high-speed storage layer to store a subset of your data, which can be accessed much faster than if you needed to go directly to a database or application to retrieve it. Databases already include caching within them – for example, Oracle uses the buffer cache to store data frequently requested from the database within **Random-Access Memory** (**RAM**) on the server. Typically, RAM storage is much quicker than accessing data on disk, but it is also more expensive. RAM is also known as volatile storage, meaning it is lost when the server or database is stopped. This type of caching is known as internal caching, meaning it is controlled and maintained directly by the database.

> **Caching Is Typically Read-Only**
>
> It is important to understand that caching is only used for reads. To write any changes, you typically need to send the write to the underlying database. Some caching solutions will let you do a query write-through where the cache is updated at the same time as the database, but not all, so you may need to redesign your application to split read and write traffic in a similar way to using read replicas.

Caching can also be handled externally. Using an external cache allows you to decouple it from a database and, therefore, allows the cache to be tuned or configured in a different manner. For example, if you have a single-node database, you can set up external caching across multiple nodes, allowing you to scale your system horizontally without incurring additional database license costs or hitting the restrictions on multi-node deployments. External caching also allows you to control an unexpected load on your database. Caching databases can be auto-scaled more easily than your database servers, so an unexpectedly high workload would cause your cache to scale first, protecting your databases from becoming overloaded.

Caching methods can also be used to allow you to operate in multiple regions from a single database. This can be a very useful technique if you have a multinational organization with people logging in from all over the world, as it will equalize the user experience. If your database is located in Europe, then typically, you will find that non-Europe-based users will suffer slower performance due to latency (the time it takes for the information to reach the database and back again). By using a multi-region cache, you can create a local copy of commonly accessed data in the same region as the users, reducing latency and improving performance. The AWS exam will often ask questions about poor performance for geographically separated users, and using a caching solution could be the right answer.

An overview of Amazon ElastiCache

Amazon ElastiCache is a fully managed database caching solution that offers two different caching technologies, Redis and Memcached. We will look in more depth at these different engines in the next section. By being a fully managed service, AWS takes ownership of any patching of databases and virtual machines on which they are running. ElastiCache uses a specialized instance class called `cache`, which is optimized for memory to allow the caching service to work as efficiently as possible.

You can think of ElastiCache in a similar way to RDS in that it is a service wrapper that handles the day-to-day tasks, such as patching, backups, and the monitoring of a database engine, rather than being a database engine itself. RDS offers a choice of several different database engines, such as PostgreSQL and Oracle, in the same way that ElastiCache offers Redis and Memcached. As such, the features available will differ depending on which engine you chose.

ElastiCache can be provisioned both inside and outside a VPC, so it can be used for applications or services that do not use a VPC, such as DynamoDB, without having to configure one. If you use ElastiCache outside of a VPC, then you can secure it using special security groups called cache security groups.

ElastiCache is created as a cluster. A cluster is a group of nodes that operate in a unified way and can be deployed across multiple AZs if required. Each node can either contain all of the same data in a duplicated pattern, or you can place a subset of data on each one in a technique called sharding. Sharding is only available with Redis, so we will cover it in more depth in the next section.

The following diagram shows a simple architecture of how you can deploy an ElastiCache cluster to support an application that uses an RDS database. You can see how ElastiCache sits alongside the RDS instance as opposed to in front of it. In most instances, you will need to reconfigure your application to query the cache first and let the cache request the data from the database if it was not in the cache already:

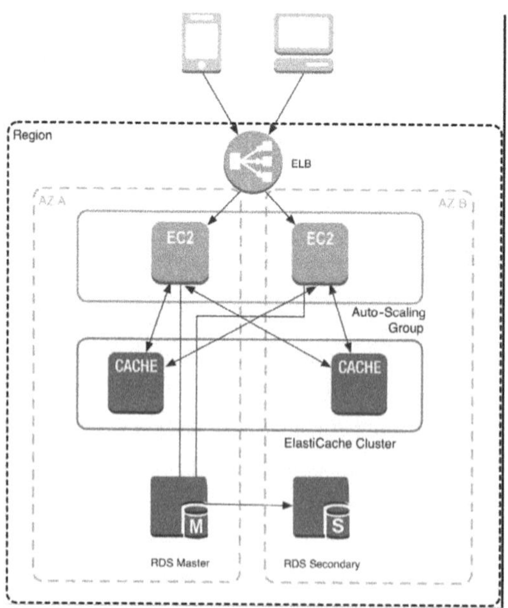

Figure 9.1 – ElastiCache architecture in front of RDS

You can also use ElastiCache as a non-durable database for data that does not need to be persistent, such as a session or gaming data. Both Redis and Memcached support the creation of data objects in them as opposed to being used as a data cache, but Memcached offers limited support. This will be covered more in the next section.

Now that you've learned an overview of ElastiCache, you can see that Memcached and Redis differ greatly. Let's take a deeper look at the different options available and then finish this section with a side-by-side comparison.

Redis versus Memcached

ElastiCache supports both Redis version 2.8 onward and Memcached 1.4 onward. These two database engines both support caching operations, but how they do that and what features they support differs. Let's start by looking at Redis.

Redis

Redis can be used as both a caching database and a non-durable data store due to its ability to store key-value pairs in a similar manner to other NoSQL databases. Redis also offers a wide range of features that NoSQL databases typically support, such as sharding, read replicas, and backups.

Read replicas are nodes that are only able to handle read operations. A primary node can handle both reads and writes. Redis uses a system called a shard, which contains one primary node and up to five read replicas. Redis can create up to 500 shards when running in cluster mode. In non-cluster mode (or with cluster mode disabled), Redis will create a single shard. The main benefit to running with cluster mode disabled is that Redis supports scaling of the instance type, adding additional read replicas and modifications to the cluster without suffering an outage in most cases. With cluster mode enabled, you are unable to make such modifications with a significant outage, so you need to plan the needs of your cluster in advance; however, cluster mode allows you to spread your workload across multiple nodes, helping to reduce any bottlenecks and improve performance.

ElastiCache Redis allows you to make daily backups. You might not require any backups if you are only using the database for caching, as all of the data is stored in the underlying database, but if you are using Redis as a data store, a backup strategy might be required. Backups on Redis can be resource-intensive and cause performance issues. To help control this, you can set a `reserved_memory_percentage` parameter to control how much memory you make available for non-query tasks such as backups; the more you reserve, the faster backups will run, but you are more likely to suffer performance problems during the backup cycle. If you do not set a value, the backups can take all of the memory on the node.

A Redis cache can be controlled and updated through various options. Redis can be configured to automatically update data within its cache on a time-based cycle (time to live), or you can use lazy loading. This only retrieves data from the database when it is first requested, and that data will then be stored in the Redis cache. Data will only be updated when it is requested and is found to be out of date. This can improve the performance of your Redis cluster for frequently accessed and rarely modified data, but if you have ad hoc queries, you will find the performance drops. You can monitor how effectively this strategy works by monitoring cache hits. A higher cache hit means more data is being retrieved from Redis without needing to update the database.

Redis also supports write-through queries. Once you have write-through enabled, any updates or inserts are applied to the Redis cache as well as being sent to the database. This means that the cache is kept up to date in real time with changes made in the source database. The disadvantage of this approach is that a lot of data will never be read and so takes up space unnecessarily in the Redis cache.

If you run Redis with cluster mode disabled, you are able to promote a read replica to become a primary node if a primary node fails. As all of the data in a shard is shared between a primary node and read replicas, this can protect you from any data loss, as the promoted primary node will have all of the data. To do this, you first must disable a Multi-AZ deployment if you are running it before promoting the read replica. This is to stop the cluster from trying to fail over during the promotion steps, as it detects a failure.

Let's now look at Memcached and how it differs from Redis.

Memcached

Memcached is a highly specialized caching database. While you can use it to store other non-durable data, you are restricted to only storing strings and integers, which will limit its usage outside of a caching use case. Memcached does not support clusters, read replicas, and sharding, and you cannot run automated backups. You would only use Memcached if you have a simple data caching use case. Memcached is a much simpler implementation than Redis, and you will need to do a lot less tuning of the cache to make it perform optimally. Memcached also supports the same cache configuration options as Redis, such as **Transistor–Transistor Logic** (**TTL**), write-through, and lazy loading.

Redis versus Memcached

Let's summarize the differences between Redis and Memcached to help you in the exam. While both run under the ElastiCache service, they operate very differently and are used for different scenarios. It is also important to understand the differences between Redis with cluster mode disabled and Redis with cluster mode enabled. You will often be asked which cache to use based on a specific use case:

Feature	Memcached	Redis (cluster mode disabled)	Redis (cluster mode enabled)
Data types	Simple ‡	2.8.x - complex *	3.2.x and later - complex †
Complex †			
Data partitioning	Yes	No	Yes
Cluster is modifiable	Yes	Yes	Limited
Online resharding	No	No	Limited
Encryption	No	Limited	Limited
Node type upgrade	No	Yes	Yes
Engine upgrading	Yes	Yes	Yes
High availability (replication)	No	Yes	Yes
Automatic failover	No	Optional	Required
Pub/Sub capabilities	No	Yes	Yes
Sorted sets	No	Yes	Yes
Backup and restore	No	Yes	Yes

Figure 9.2 – A comparison of Memcached and Redis

Now we have learned the theory of ElastiCache and understand the different engines available, let's complete a hands-on lab so that you can see how to provision and manage an ElastiCache database.

Adding caching to a database system

In this hands-on lab, we are going to provision a Redis database to act as a cache for an existing RDS instance. We will create a Redis cluster and configure it to act as our cache, and then we will create and run some simple code on an EC2 instance that will connect to it to demonstrate the caching.

If you do not have an existing VPC and RDS MySQL database provisioned, then please create those first, following the guides from earlier chapters if required. The MySQL database should contain the `Sakila` sample tables.

Firstly, we are going to create our Redis cluster:

1. Log in to the AWS Management Console as an admin user.
2. Navigate to ElastiCache from the main menu.

3. From the ElastiCache dashboard, select **Get Started Now**. If this page does not appear, you can select **Redis** from the left-hand menu and then click **Create**:

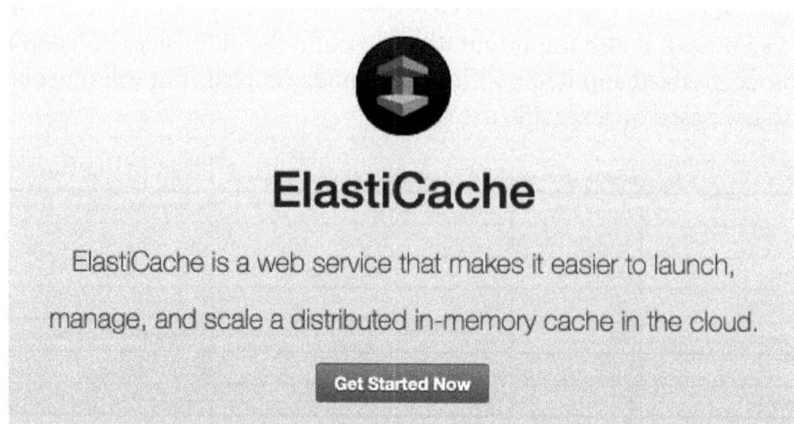

Figure 9.3 – Create ElastiCache

4. Complete the form with the following options. If an option is not mentioned, leave it as default:

    - **Cluster engine**: `Redis`
    - **Cluster Mode enabled**: *unchecked*
    - **Choose a location: Amazon Cloud**
    - **Name**: `dbcert-redis`
    - **Description**: `cache`
    - **Node type**: `t3.micro`
    - **Multi-AZ**: *unchecked*

    Under **Advanced Redis settings**, enter the following:

    - **Subnet group**: **Create new**
    - **Name**: `dbcert-app`
    - **Description**: `app security group`
    - **Subnets**: *select all*
    - **Backups**: *unchecked*

5. Click **Create**. While that creates, we will provision an EC2 instance from where we will install our application code.

6. Navigate to **EC2** from the main menu.
7. Click **Launch instance**.
8. Select the latest **Amazon Linux 2 AMI (HVM)** option from the list.
9. Select **t2.micro** and click **Next** until you get to the **Configure Security Group** screen.
10. Select the same security group that you used for the Redis cluster. You may need to review the security group to ensure that it allows access to the Redis cluster from the EC2 instance on port `6379` and also that it allows SSH access from your IP to allow you to connect to it. You can refer to *Chapter 3, Understanding AWS Infrastructure*, for a reminder on how to work with security groups if required.
11. Select **Next** and then **Launch**.
12. Select **Create a new key pair** and download the key pair:

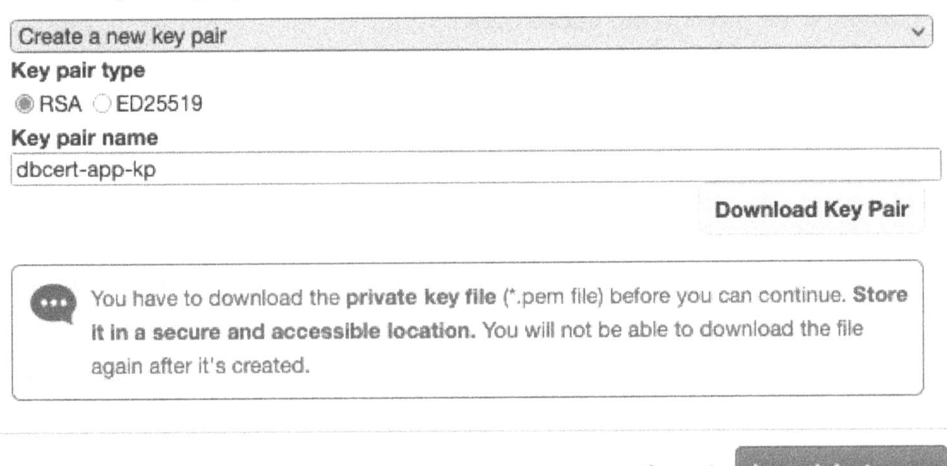

Figure 9.4 – Download the key pair

13. Select **Launch Instances**.
14. When the EC2 instance has a status of **Running**, you can connect to it using an SSH client such as PuTTY on Windows or directly from the terminal if using a Mac.
15. Run the following commands to download and install our application:

```
sudo yum install git -y
sudo yum install mysql -y
sudo yum install python3 -y
pip3 install --user virtualenv
git clone https://github.com/PacktPublishing/
AWS-Certified-Database---Specialty-DBS-C01-Certification
cd AWS-Certified-Database---Specialty-DBS-C01-
Certification/ch9
virtualenv venv
source ./venv/bin/activate
pip3 install -r pip_install.txt
```

16. Next, we need to configure the connection details for our cache and our MySQL database. We will add these as environment variables so that we can reuse them easily. Modify the following code lines to reflect your database and cache connection information:

```
export REDIS_URL=redis://<redis_endpoint>:6379/
export DB_HOST=<db_endpoint>
export DB_USER=admin
export DB_PASS=<password>
export DB_NAME=sakila
```

17. We can now test our caching and our database query. First, make sure your security has been configured correctly and that you can reach the Redis cache. If this does not return `True`, you will need to check your security group before continuing:

```
$python
>>> import redis
>>> client = redis.Redis.from_
url('redis://<endpoint>:6379')
>>> client.ping()
True
>>> quit()
```

18. We can now run our small test. Run `sakila_redis.py` twice to see what happens. You should see the following:

```
(venv) [ec2-user@ip ch10]$ python sakila_redis.py
Retrieved from DB
{'first_name': 'PENELOPE', 'last_name': 'GUINESS'}
Retrieved from DB
{'first_name': 'NICK', 'last_name': 'WAHLBERG'}
Retrieved from DB
{'first_name': 'ED', 'last_name': 'CHASE'}
(venv) [ec2-user@ip ch10]$ python sakila_redis.py
Retrieved from cache
{b'first_name': b'PENELOPE', b'last_name': b'GUINESS'}
Retrieved from cache
{b'first_name': b'NICK', b'last_name': b'WAHLBERG'}
Retrieved from cache
{b'first_name': b'ED', b'last_name': b'CHASE'}
```

Note how the first time the queries are run, they are retrieved from the database, but the second time, they are now pulled from the cache.

19. Within the `sakila_redis.py` code, there is a line that sets TTL on the data within the cache. If you wait more than 10 seconds before running the code again, you will see that the queries go to the database once more. This is because TTL deletes old records from the cache to recover space.

This completes the hands-on lab for this chapter. You can now delete and clear up the environment if you wish.

Let's now review the chapter, starting with the summary.

Summary

In this chapter, we have learned about Amazon ElastiCache and how you can use it to help with performance problems on a database, minimize geographic latency, and help speed up query times for end users. We've learned that ElastiCache is a fully managed service and offers two types of caching databases, Redis and Memcached, which have different features and are used for different scenarios.

It's very important to know the differences between the two different engines and also between cluster mode enabled and cluster mode disabled for Redis, as the exam will ask questions about which version you can use for a given scenario.

In the next chapter, we will learn how to migrate a database to AWS and the tools that are available to help you – that is, AWS **Schema Conversion Tool** (**SCT**) and AWS **Database Migration Service** (**DMS**).

Cheat sheet

This cheat sheet summarizes the main key points from this chapter:

- Amazon ElastiCache is a fully managed caching service.
- ElastiCache supports two different caching technologies, Redis and Memcached.
- Redis has two modes, cluster mode enabled and cluster mode disabled.
- ElastiCache supports read replicas on both engines.
- ElastiCache can be provisioned both inside and outside of a VPC to meet your needs.
- Redis supports sharding and complex data types and can run in Multi-AZ.
- Caching can feature TTL, which ages out older records to save space and to ensure that the latest data is available in the cache.
- Techniques such as write-through and lazy loading can be used to control the speed that the cache updates, balancing new data and saving space.

Review

Let's now practice a few exam-style questions:

1. An application development team complains that they are experiencing performance issues with ElastiCache Redis. You discover that the performance issues occur during the automated backup window. What actions can you take to improve backup performance? (Select two.)

    A. Schedule an automated backup window to occur at midnight.

    B. Set the `reserved-memory-percentage` parameter.

    C. Create backups from a read replica.

    D. Create additional read replicas.

    E. Increase the number of shards.

2. An application team wishes to use ElastiCache Redis to improve its application performance. The application has a requirement that the data must always be the most recent. Which caching strategy should the team utilize?

    A. Write-through
    B. Lazy loading
    C. Cache-aside
    D. Read-through

3. You are advising a company on how to plan a deployment of ElastiCache Redis with cluster mode disabled. What is the maximum number of shards and read replicas that the cluster can have?

    A. 1 shard and 5 read replicas
    B. 5 shards and 0 read replicas
    C. 1 shard and 90 read replicas
    D. 90 shards and 0 read replicas

4. Your company is running ElastiCache for Redis with cluster mode enabled, and it wishes to expand the scope of its caching. Each shard is planned to have five read replicas. What is the maximum number of shards that can be deployed?

    A. 5
    B. 15
    C. 100
    D. 500

5. After an outage, you urgently need to manually promote a read-replica node in an ElastiCache Redis (cluster mode disabled) cluster to a primary node. What step must a specialist perform before they can promote the node to a primary?

    A. Enable Multi-AZ with automatic failover.
    B. Disable Multi-AZ with automatic failover.
    C. Create a manual backup.
    D. Stop the cluster.

The answers can be found in *Chapter 17, Answers*.

Further reading

To understand the concepts of this chapter in further detail, you can refer to the following sources:

- *Redis Essentials*:

  `https://www.packtpub.com/product/redis-essentials/9781784392451`

- *Getting started with Memcached*:

  `https://www.packtpub.com/product/getting-started-with-memcached/9781782163220`

Part 3: Deployment and Migration and Database Security

Once you understand the use cases for your database, the next steps are to migrate them. This chapter will walk through the different options for data migration. We will also take a deep dive into critical database security techniques and how to apply best practices on AWS.

This section includes the following chapters:

- *Chapter 10, The AWS Schema Conversion Tool and AWS Database Migration Service*
- *Chapter 11, Database Task Automation*
- *Chapter 12, AWS Database Security*

10
The AWS Schema Conversion Tool and AWS Database Migration Service

In the previous chapters, we learned about the different databases that are offered by AWS and the key features and use cases for each. Now, we are going to learn how to migrate a database to AWS and the tools that are available to help you – that is, AWS **Schema Conversion Tool** (**SCT**) and AWS **Database Migration Service** (**DMS**).

AWS SCT is a tool that allows you to assess a database's ability to migrate to AWS RDS and whether you can convert the database from a commercial database engine, such as Oracle, into an open source database. Then, it helps you convert the database objects and code for the new database engine.

AWS DMS can also help convert from one database engine into another, but its main role is to move the data within your database from on-premises to AWS or between AWS databases. It offers both bulk load and **Change Data Capture** (**CDC**) modes to support different types of migrations.

This chapter will include a hands-on lab where you can practice using SCT and DMS to convert and migrate a database to AWS.

In this chapter, we will cover the following topics:

- Overview of SCT
- Assessing a database using SCT
- Converting a database using SCT
- Overview of DMS
- Setting up DMS
- Running a DMS task via SCT
- Monitoring and tuning DMS
- Converting and migrating a database to AWS

Let's start by learning what SCT is and does and how to use it to assess and convert databases.

Technical requirements

To complete this chapter, you will need an AWS account with root access. Everything we will do in this chapter will be unavailable in Free Tier, which means it will cost you a small amount to follow the hands-on sections. You will also require command-line interface (CLI) AWS access. The AWS guide at `https://docs.aws.amazon.com/cli/latest/userguide/cli-chap-configure.html` explains the necessary steps, but I will summarize them here:

1. Create an AWS account if you have not already done so.
2. Download the latest version of the AWS CLI from `https://docs.aws.amazon.com/cli/latest/userguide/welcome-versions.html#welcome-versions-v2`.

3. Create an admin user by going to `https://docs.aws.amazon.com/IAM/latest/UserGuide/id_credentials_access-keys.html`.
4. Create an access key for your administration user: `https://docs.aws.amazon.com/IAM/latest/UserGuide/getting-started_create-admin-group.html#getting-started_create-admin-group-cli`.
5. Run the `aws configure` command to set up a profile for your user: `https://docs.aws.amazon.com/cli/latest/userguide/cli-configure-quickstart.html#cli-configure-quickstart-creds`.

You will also require a VPC that meets the minimum requirements for an RDS instance: `https://docs.aws.amazon.com/AmazonRDS/latest/UserGuide/USER_VPC.WorkingWithRDSInstanceinaVPC.html`. If you completed the steps in *Chapter 3*, *Understanding AWS Infrastructure*, then you will already have a VPC that meets the minimum requirements.

You will also need a copy of the Microsoft SQL Server Northwinds sample database: `https://github.com/microsoft/sql-server-samples/blob/master/samples/databases/northwind-pubs/instnwnd.sql`.

Overview of SCT

AWS **Schema Conversion Tool** (**SCT**) is a downloadable program that's designed to help you change from one database engine to another. For example, you can use it to help convert database objects and database code from Oracle into PostgreSQL. It can also be used to carry out a migration assessment to both calculate the effort involved in converting the database engine and also to check for any features that are being used that are incompatible with RDS versions of the database. As we learned in *Chapter 4*, *Relational Database Service*, RDS does not support all the features of every database engine. SCT is available on Windows, Ubuntu Linux, and Fedora Linux.

SCT can carry out assessments and convert from the following database types:

- Oracle
- SQL Server
- Apache Cassandra
- Azure SQL Database

- IBM Db2
- MySQL
- PostgreSQL
- SAP/Sybase ASE

SCT can carry out assessments and convert from the following Data Warehouse types:

- Amazon Redshift
- Azure Synapse Analytics
- Greenplum Database
- Netezza
- Oracle Data Warehouse
- SQL Server Data Warehouse
- Snowflake
- Teradata
- Vertica

The database you are converting/migrating from is known as the source, and the destination is the target. Each source database engine has a limited number of targets you can convert to, depending on its type. For example, any Data Warehouse can only be converted into Amazon Redshift and any database can only be converted into AWS RDS or AWS Aurora. Apache Cassandra is a NoSQL database that can only be converted into Amazon DynamoDB.

SCT allows you to either run an open assessment where you do not know the target type and want SCT to offer suggestions based on the migration complexity, or you can be specific and choose the target database's type, which allows SCT to run the assessment faster. In general, most assessments are done against all the available target databases to get a full picture of your migration options. Once you have assessed your source database and chosen the target database type, you can use SCT to automatically convert source storage items such as tables, indexes, and database code such as stored procedures or functions and apply them to the target. For any items that cannot be converted automatically, SCT offers a graphical user interface that can assist in manually converting any remaining code. Typically, SCT does not move any data (unless it's used in conjunction with DMS tasks, as we'll see later in this chapter) – it only works with schema-level objects.

A migration that uses the same database engine for both the source and the target is called a **homogenous** migration, while a migration where the database engine is changed is called a **heterogenous** migration. These terms may appear in the exam, so you must understand what they mean.

First, let's learn how to assess a database with SCT and what the report will show you.

Assessing a database using SCT

SCT allows you to assess various source databases to check how much effort it takes to convert to either an open source target database that AWS supports in RDS, Amazon DynamoDB, or Amazon Redshift, or to assess a migration from an on-premises Oracle database to RDS Oracle, or from an on-premises Microsoft SQL Server to RDS Microsoft SQL Server.

To run the assessment, you must download the SCT program for your operating system from AWS and install it. Then, you must provide the connection and login details for the source database. SCT will show you a list of all the schemas/users it finds and you can choose the ones to assess, which lets you filter out unused or old schemas.

Once the report is complete, it will show the following information:

- A summary of the source database
- The license evaluation of the source database, including an assessment of whether you can change to a standard edition license from an enterprise edition one
- AWS Cloud compatibility, highlighting any features in the source database that are not available on the target
- The recommended target DB engine
- Specific changes that are needed for the database to run in RDS, such as linked server changes or features that need to be removed
- The amount of effort that it will take to modify or write new code for your target DB engine that can't be converted automatically

The following screenshot shows an example of an SCT report showing the summary of an Oracle database being converted into an RDS PostgreSQL database:

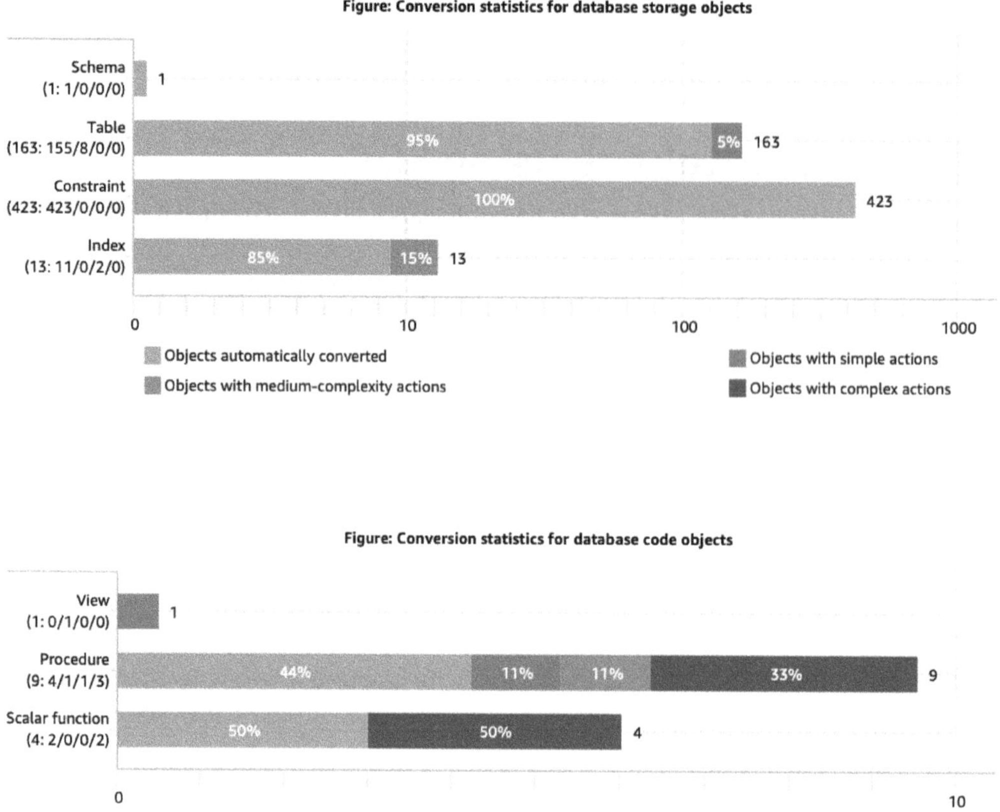

Figure 10.1 – SCT report summary

Here, you can see how the report splits all the different database components into separate sections to help you understand the changes that need to be made for the conversion to occur. The report features an interactive mode, which allows you to click on the bar chart so that you can look at an in-depth report that explains every conversion change that needs to be made, as well as guidance on how to tackle conversions that cannot be done automatically by SCT. You can also review the report in SCT's GUI window. The following screenshot shows the GUI for a Microsoft SQL Server report, where you can see more information about specific database objects:

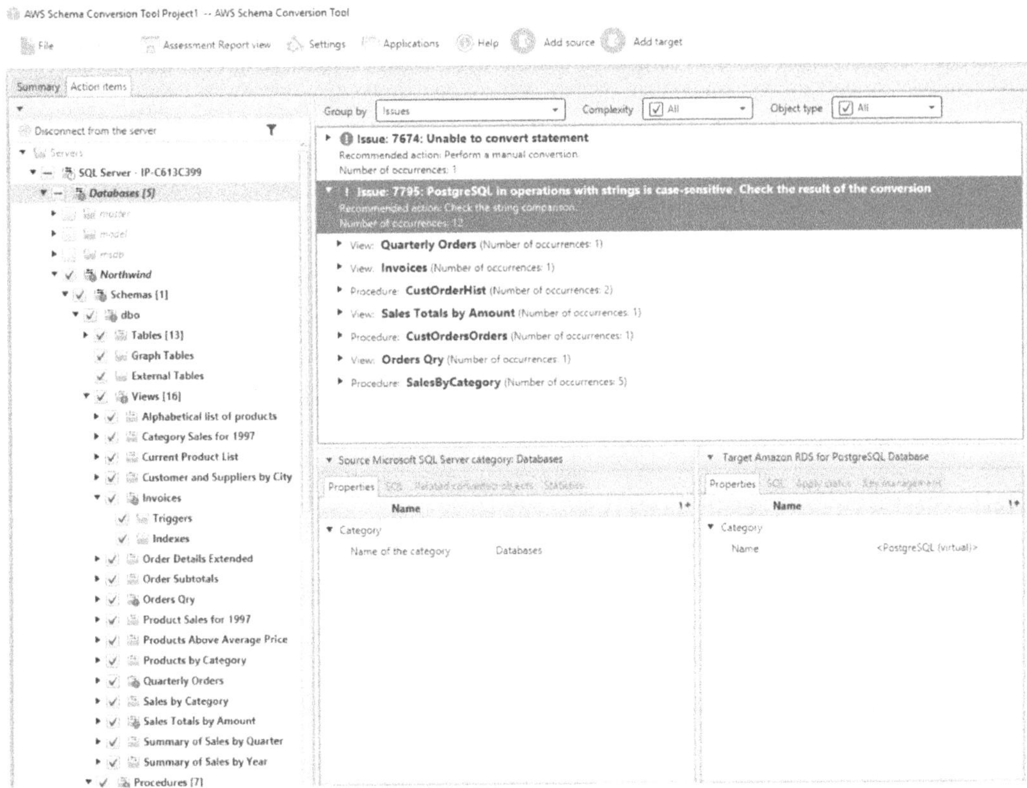

Figure 10.2 – SCT GUI report

Due to the types of information that SCT needs to access, a large amount of information must be sent from the source database, which could potentially include data that must be encrypted. SCT allows you to use an encrypted connection between both the source and target databases. Let's learn how to configure that.

Encryption

SCT lets you use SSL connections to encrypt all the traffic between SCT and the source and target databases. To set this up, you must import the certificates into the key store for your operating system. For Windows, this is the Trusted Root Certification Authorities store, while for Linux, this will be the Java key store. If you are using RDS as a source or target, you will need to obtain the AWS RDS root certificate from `https://s3.amazonaws.com/rds-downloads/rds-ca-2019-root.pem`.

Once the relevant certificates have been added, you can configure SCT to use the key store, which will enable SSL connectivity for the in-scope databases.

> **SCT Permissions**
>
> SCT requires specific read-only permissions on all source databases. If you encounter problems with connecting or errors in the SCT reports mentioning a data access error, you should check that the user account you are using has the correct permissions, as detailed here:
>
> `https://docs.aws.amazon.com/SchemaConversionTool/latest/userguide/CHAP_Source.html`.

Apart from encryption, SCT lets you assess a large number of servers simultaneously. This can be very useful if your application has more than one database or if you need to assess a collection of databases at once. Let's learn how to configure and run a multi-server assessment.

Multi-server assessments

Multi-server assessments let you pass the details of more than one database to SCT for assessment at the same time. SCT produces an aggregated report for all the database servers and schemas that are in scope, allowing you to quickly obtain an overview.

The multi-server assessor requires the database details to be passed to SCT in a CSV file in a specific format. The following is an example of such a file:

```
Name,Description,Server IP,Port,Service Name,SID,Source Engine,Schema Names,Login,Password,Target Engines
ORACLE_DMS_SAMPLE, TEST_APP,10.103.56.32,1521, ORCL1, ,ORACLE,DMS_TEST,SYS,password,ORACLE;AURORA POSTGRESQL
MS_SQL_Server_DB, DEV2,67.17.93.164,1433, , ,MSSQL,northwinds.dbo;northwinds.reporting,reporting_user,password,MSSQL;POSTGRESQL
```

Here, you can see that not every column is needed and that the file allows blanks. The required fields are highlighted. If the port is not given, then SCT will try to use the published default ports for the database engine. You can also see that some fields allow multiple values to be used with a `;` separator. This allows you to define more than one schema per database in a single line, as well as multiple target engine types.

Be aware that the more schemas and target database engines you request for assessment, the longer it will take. It is not uncommon for a single database schema to take 24 hours or more to be assessed if you request all the possible target database engines and you are using a standard personal computer. SCT can be installed on a server with more computing power to speed up the assessments if required.

Now that we have learned how to use SCT to assess a database for a potential database engine conversion, let's learn how SCT is used to convert to a target database.

Converting a database using SCT

Once you have completed the assessments and decided on a target database, you can use SCT to assist in converting the database objects and code. SCT carries out the following tasks:

- SCT installs an extension pack that contains common functions that can be used in converted database code. This extension pack is supplied within the SCT program.
- SCT checks all DDL statements in the source database and attempts to recreate those in the language of the target. This includes tables, views, indexes, and more.
- SCT attempts to convert the database's code into the target database's code.
- For those who cannot automatically convert either using the native code of the target database or via the added extension pack functions, it provides a report that shows where the issues with the conversion are and what action you need to take to resolve them.

Figure 10.2 showed some example output of an assessment report for a SQL Server source database being converted into RDS PostgreSQL format. Looking at the report, we can see that two issues were flagged where the conversion could not be handled manually. SCT allows us to drill down into those objects and see the suggested converted code for ourselves to ensure it is correct and make modifications if needed. The following screenshot shows the code conversion window for an object that SCT was unable to fully convert automatically:

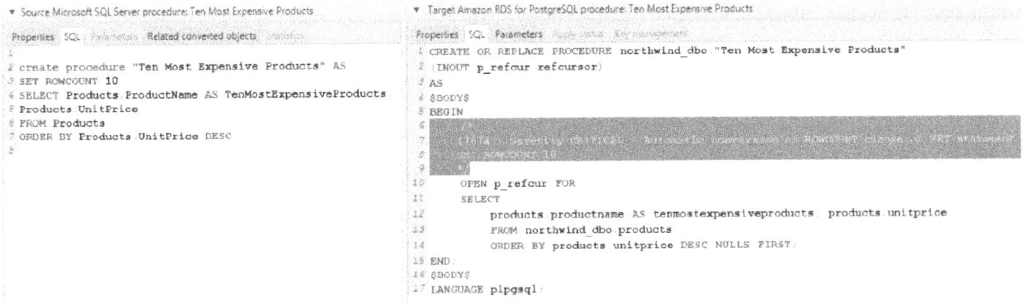

Figure 10.3 – Code conversion

In the highlighted section of the preceding screenshot, you can see that SCT has given a `Severity CRITICAL` warning for the `SET ROWCOUNT 10` line. This means that it has been unable to convert that line into a PostgreSQL-compatible version, so the DBA needs to take action. You can either ignore the error and apply the code with that line commented out (as it is currently) or you can try to resolve it manually. In this example, `SET ROWCOUNT` is used in the same way as the `LIMIT` command is in PostgreSQL, so you could consider rewriting the target DB code so that it includes `LIMIT 10`:

```
CREATE OR REPLACE PROCEDURE northwind_dbo."Ten Most Expensive Products" (INOUT p_refcur refcursor)
AS
$BODY$
BEGIN
    OPEN p_refcur FOR
    SELECT products.productname AS tenmostexpensiveproducts, products.unitprice
        FROM northwind_dbo.products
        ORDER BY products.unitprice DESC
  LIMIT 10;
END;
$BODY$
LANGUAGE plpgsql;
```

Once you are happy with the code, you have a few options – you can save the new SQL statements to a file that you can run manually against your target database or if you have connected SCT to your chosen target database, you can apply the changes directly to the target database, which instructs SCT to run the DDL for all the selected objects and create your target schema, ready to import your data into.

As well as database-level code, SCT also allows you to assess and convert application code that contains SQL statements. Let's learn how to do that now.

Converting application code

Using SCT to assess and convert your application code follows a process that's similar to the one we used for the database code. First, you need to create your database project, as detailed in the previous section, as SCT cannot access application code that's not been matched to a database. Once you've done that, you must load your application code files into SCT. The code can be in any programming language as SCT can perform syntax-based lookups to find SQL code, but it works best with the Java, Python, and C family programming languages. To load the code, you can click the **Application** button within SCT and select **New Application**:

Figure 10.4 – Converting application code

Then, you must select the database and schema(s) that the code must apply to before letting SCT analyze the code. SCT will extract all the SQL code in the files, allowing you to assess it for compatibility with your target database engine. SCT produces a report similar to the database-level reports, showing what can and cannot be automatically converted.

Once you have reviewed the reports, you can request SCT to convert the code where possible. After that, you can review any code that wasn't automatically converted and modified. Once you have made the necessary changes, you can apply them to the code and SCT will amend the code file with the modifications.

Finally, you may need to migrate any **Extract-Transform-Load** (**ETL**) jobs to the target database. AWS offers a tool called AWS Glue (see *Chapter 11*, *Database Task Automation*), which can handle ETL functions.

Converting ETL jobs with AWS Glue

Many Data Warehouse applications use ETL jobs to handle how data is loaded from diverse sources. SCT supports the migration of these jobs to AWS Glue in specific cases:

- Oracle to Redshift and Glue
- SQL Server SSIS to Glue

SCT can import ETL jobs from an Oracle or SQL Server SSIS source and create scripts that you can load into AWS Glue to replicate its rules and functions.

To perform the conversion, Glue creates a holding database on both the source and target databases. Once the conversion has been done, SCT creates a script that you must copy to an S3 bucket that the AWS Glue service can use to create the jobs. If you define access keys within the SCT configuration, SCT can connect to your AWS account to upload the scripts for you and create the Glue jobs without needing to do so manually. If you don't have an access key or don't want to use it with SCT, then you will need to move the script to S3 and run the Glue wizard manually.

With that, we've learned about SCT, including what it does and how to use it to help migrate a database to AWS and convert a database into a new database engine type. We also learned how SCT can be used to assess application code and how to migrate ETL jobs to a service called AWS Glue. SCT only migrates and converts objects, so to migrate the data that's within our database to the target, we need to use DMS.

Overview of DMS

AWS **Database Migration Service** (**DMS**) is a tool for moving your data between databases. DMS can be used to migrate data between databases of the same type or between different database engines. If you use it to migrate between different database engines, it will convert the data for you so that it fits the target. DMS can also create target database tables for you, if they do not already exist, in a similar way to SCT. However, it is much less powerful and only converts the minimal database objects that are required for a successful migration. You would still need to manually create most indexes, views, and database code.

DMS has three main components:

- **Endpoints**: These allow DMS to connect to databases that are hosted in different VPCs and on-premises.
- **Replication Instance**: This is an EC2 instance that's used to run the migration.
- **Tasks**: These are the jobs that control and manage the migration process.

To use DMS, you must provide a source endpoint, target endpoint, and replication instance. Then, you must configure the task to tell DMS how to handle data conversion, how to rename tables, and more. DMS has a large number of transformations it can manage, including the following:

- Changing the case of object and column names
- Adding prefixes or suffixes to object and column names
- Renaming objects and columns entirely

- Changing data types (for example, VARCHAR2 to CHAR)
- Adding or modifying a primary key to/for a table

As well as migrating and converting database objects and data, DMS can run in CDC mode to keep the source and its target database in sync. This can be useful for production database migrations where the window for downtime is very short. You can use DMS to do an initial data migration to check that everything is correct and working; then, you can use CDC to keep the target database in sync with the source. This means that you can switch over to the target database without having to wait for either the database to resync with all the changes on the source or having to migrate all the data again. DMS can run in CDC even when converting between database engines.

> **DMS Studio**
>
> At the time of writing, AWS had released a new tool called DMS Studio in preview. DMS Studio can create data collectors to find, collate, and assess large numbers of databases simultaneously. Given DMS Studio is still in Preview in certain regions only, it will not feature in the exam. However, further information is provided in the *Further reading* section at the end of this chapter.

Now that we've learned the basics of DMS and how it works, let's learn how to set up some of its components, such as its endpoints and replication instances.

Setting up DMS

To start a DMS task, we need to configure the DMS environment. This involves creating a replication instance, as well as the source and target endpoints, and setting up the task itself with the transformation rules we want to apply. The first component we must create is the replication instance.

Replication instances

A replication instance is an EC2 instance that's preconfigured with the DMS application code. Its role is to provide compute resources to any data conversions that need to be handled, as well as store data that's ready to be applied during a CDC mode task. The replication instance can handle multiple tasks simultaneously and can be sized according to your needs. You can monitor the performance and resource usage of a replication instance while tasks are running to help you assess whether the instance is sized correctly. You can also have multiple replication instances per account, but only one can be assigned to a task at once; there is no option to scale horizontally.

Replication instances can be created as multi-AZ instances, which increases the resilience of your replication tasks. This is especially useful for CDC tasks, where a loss of the replication instance may result in data loss on the target DB and the need for a new full load to be taken, which will impact your migration timeline.

When you create a replication instance, you need to specify the DMS version you want to run. Like any software, DMS is upgraded and improved at regular intervals, so you typically want to run the latest version. However, if you are running multiple tasks for one database and have more than one replication instance running the tasks, you will want to ensure the version of DMS is the same across all instances to guarantee the same behavior is applied by DMS. You also need to specify the instance's size. The DMS replication instance is an EC2 instance that uses a special AMI provided by AWS.

A replication instance is created within a VPC, so it will be subject to all the security groups, NACLs, and other restrictions that are configured within that VPC. If you need to connect to databases in other VPCs, you will need to ensure that your replication instance is set to `public`. This means it will be granted a public IP and will ensure that databases outside of the VPC can connect to it. If you do not set it as public, you will only be able to connect to databases within your VPC, which severely limits the usability of DMS.

Once you have created a replication instance, the next thing that needs to be configured for DMS is its endpoints. These endpoints are the connection details of the source and target databases that will allow DMS to migrate the data.

Endpoints

DMS has two types of endpoints – source and target. You must define each endpoint specifically as a source or target, which means that if a database is both a source and a target, then you must define it twice – this is a highly uncommon scenario. This separation is designed to reduce the likelihood of you accidentally configuring DMS to migrate data the wrong way, from target to source, which may overwrite a live database. To create an endpoint, you must fill in a form that asks for the connection details for your database.

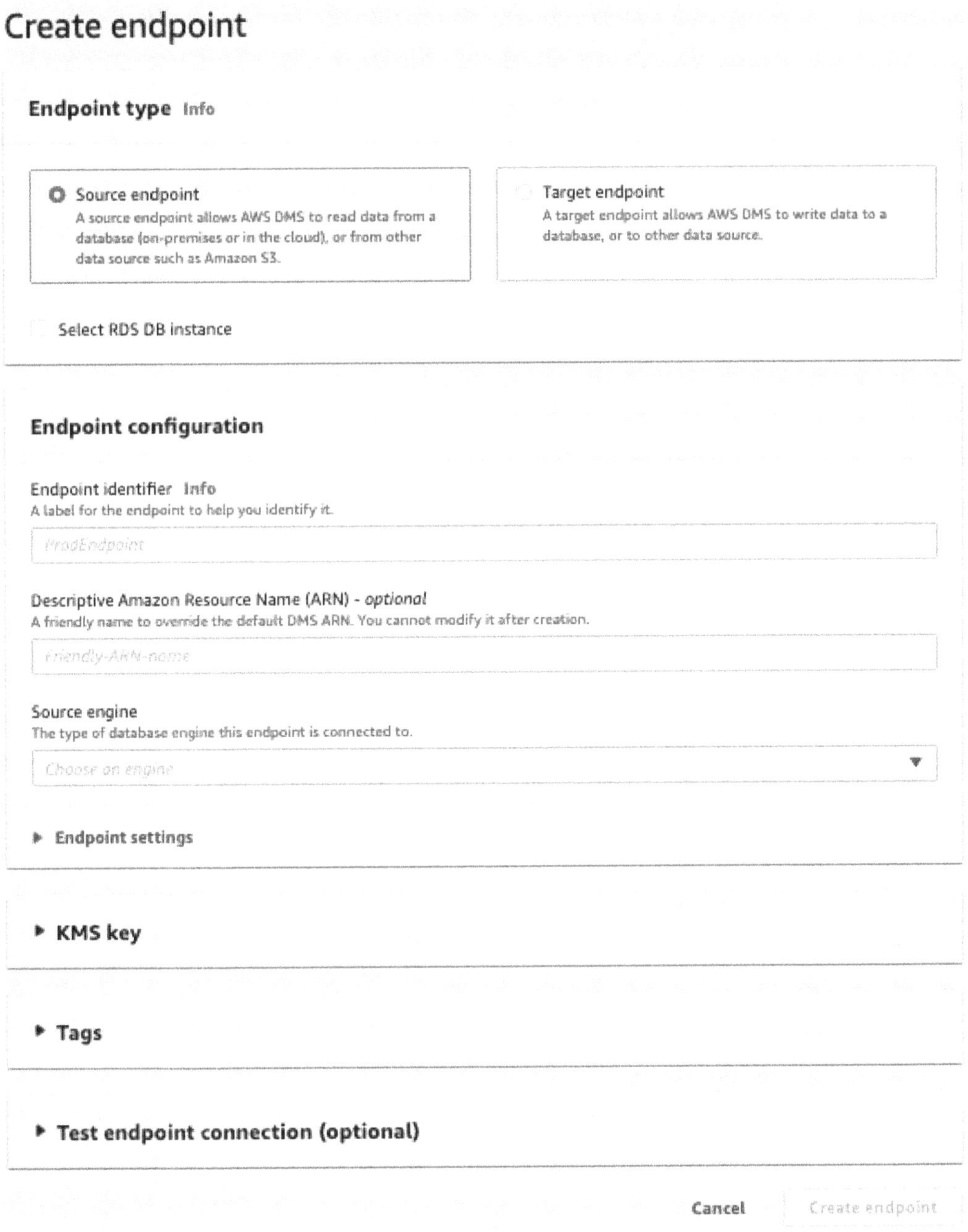

Create endpoint

Endpoint type Info

Source endpoint
A source endpoint allows AWS DMS to read data from a database (on-premises or in the cloud), or from other data source such as Amazon S3.

Target endpoint
A target endpoint allows AWS DMS to write data to a database, or to other data source.

Select RDS DB instance

Endpoint configuration

Endpoint identifier Info
A label for the endpoint to help you identify it.

ProdEndpoint

Descriptive Amazon Resource Name (ARN) - *optional*
A friendly name to override the default DMS ARN. You cannot modify it after creation.

Friendly-ARN-name

Source engine
The type of database engine this endpoint is connected to.

Choose an engine

▸ **Endpoint settings**

▸ **KMS key**

▸ **Tags**

▸ **Test endpoint connection (optional)**

Cancel Create endpoint

Figure 10.5 – DMS endpoint creation

Once created, you must validate the endpoints' connections before they can be used. The validation step checks whether the endpoints can be reached from your replication instance. If they cannot be reached, you will need to check the VPC configuration to ensure no security group or NACLs are restricting the connections and double-check that the database configuration information is correct. Once the endpoints for both the source and targets have been validated, you can create a DMS task to start migrating and replicating data from your source database to the target.

DMS tasks

The final step of setting up DMS for migration is to create the task. You must define the source and target endpoints, the replication instance you wish to use, and the rules that you want to control the conversion and migration. You must also set the logging you wish to have on the task. Enabling logging to CloudWatch lets you diagnose issues with a DMS task and is always recommended.

There are three types of DMS tasks you can run:

- **Full Only**: This option takes a full load of all in-scope data from the source database and migrates it to the target database.
- **CDC Only**: This option sets up synchronization between the source and target databases. DMS will track and apply any changes to the source database in the scope data and schema (with some restrictions, which we will cover later in this section) to the target database.
- **Full Load and CDC**: This option does an initial data load, and then runs in CDC mode to maintain the sync between the source and target databases.

For all these task types, DMS offers a high level of control for how tasks run. Some settings only apply to certain task types:

- **The Number of Tables Being Migrated in Parallel**: This can be used to both speed up a job and also stop a production database from being overloaded with too many tables being accessed at once.

- **The Transaction Consistency in Seconds**: This controls how long DMS will store the table's state from the time the table started to being loaded. If you are running against a live database, the underlying data will likely change, but to ensure transaction consistency, DMS needs to store the state of all the tables in the task at a fixed point in time. The higher this value is, the more data will need to be stored and the greater the impact on memory usage for the replication instance.
- **The Commit Rate**: This controls how regularly DMS commits rows to the target database. A higher number is typically faster, but uncommitted data needs to be stored on the replication instance, putting more strain on memory and CPU. This is only used in full-load tasks.
- **Batch Apply Mode**: This controls whether changes are written one by one or in a batch. Running in batch apply mode can greatly increase the performance of a CDC task, but applying in batch can cause issues with data integrity rules if a child row is added before its parent is created. This is only used during CDC tasks.
- **The Start Point Timestamp or Change Record Number**: When you're running a CDC-only task, you can define a specific start point for when you want synchronization to begin. This allows you to give the exact timestamp or database change record number from your source database that matches the latest timestamp on the data that has been migrated to the target. For example, if you took a backup at 05:13:56 and restored this to the target database outside of DMS, you would want your DMS CDC-only task to start at this exact timestamp to ensure all the changes after the backup has been made are applied.

You can also configure specific rules for how DMS handles **large objects** (**LOBs**). DMS handles LOBs by creating the target table and then migrating the LOB data. Due to their size and complexity, LOBs require a higher level of DMS processing than other database objects and take significantly more time.

A DMS task has two data control mechanisms:

- Selection rules
- Transformation rules

To control the data to be migrated, you can set up rules to only pull data from certain schemas or tables. You can use both include and exclude rules to give a high level of granularity to your selections. DMS also allows you to use `where` clauses to control the rows that are selected. This can be very useful for large tables that contain old, historic data that does not need to be migrated. You can also use a where clause on a date field to restrict only the recent records. The following screenshot shows an example of the selection rules you can create:

Table mappings
Editing mode Info
Wizard
You can enter only a subset of the available table mappings.
JSON editor
You can enter all available table mappings directly in JSON format.
Specify at least one selection rule with an include action. After you do this, you can add one or more transformation rules.
Selection rules
Choose the schema and/or tables you want to include with, or exclude from, your migration task. Info
Add new selection rule
where schema name is like 'dbcert-schema' and table name is like '%', include
Schema
Enter a schema
Schema name
Use the % character as a wildcard
dbcert-schema
Table name
Use the % character as a wildcard
%
Action
Choose "Include" to migrate your selected objects, or "Exclude" to ignore them during the migration.
Include

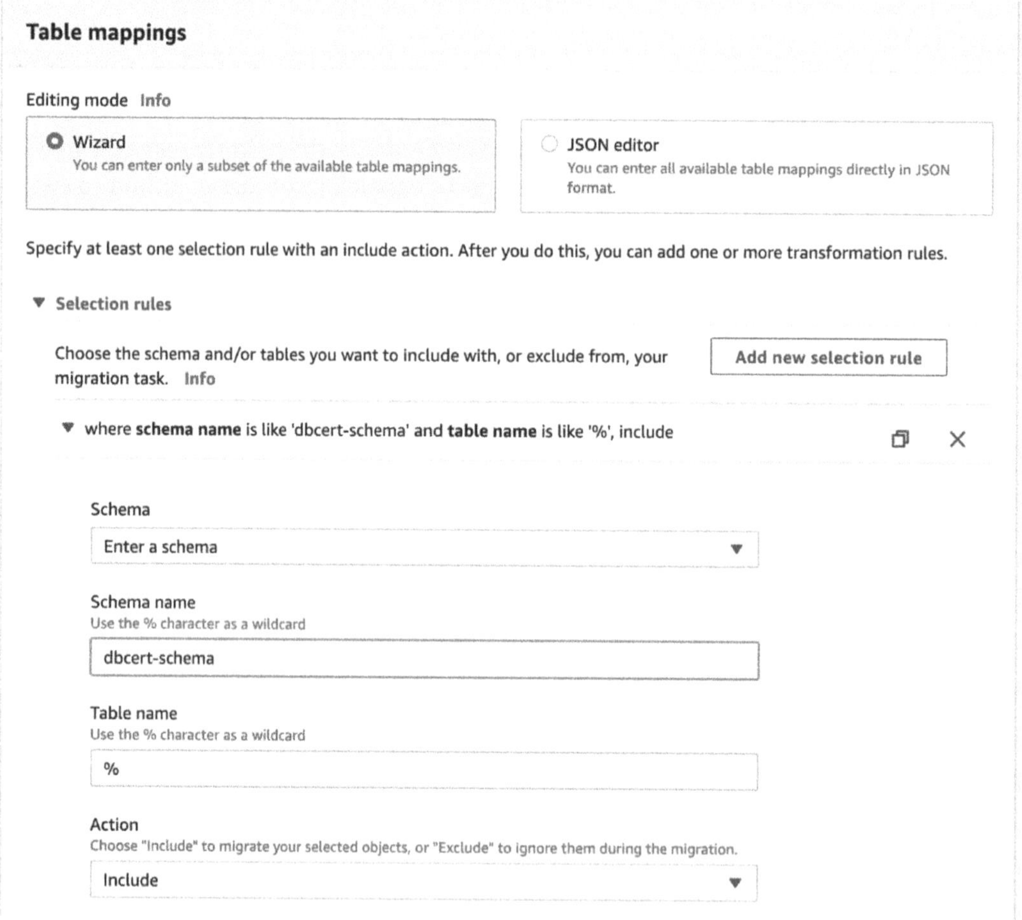

Figure 10.6 – DMS selection rules

These selection rules can be created using the wizard, as shown in the preceding screenshot, or you can write them in JSON. Here is the same rule that we had previously written in JSON:

```
{
  "rules": [
    {
      "rule-type": "selection",
      "rule-id": "1",
      "rule-name": "dccert-schema-include",
      "object-locator": {
        "schema-name": "dbcert-schema",
        "table-name": "%"
      },
      "rule-action": "include",
      "filters": []
    }
  ]
}
```

Using JSON is much faster than the wizard when you have a large number of rules and can be useful if you want to create similar rules for a different task as you can copy the JSON code across.

Transformation rules can be used to drastically change the target database schemas. The following screenshot shows that we are making two changes:

- Changing the data type of a column called `years` in `dbcert-tables-years`
- Renaming `dbcert-schema to dbcert-schema-1`

The following screenshot shows some of the transformation rules you can apply:

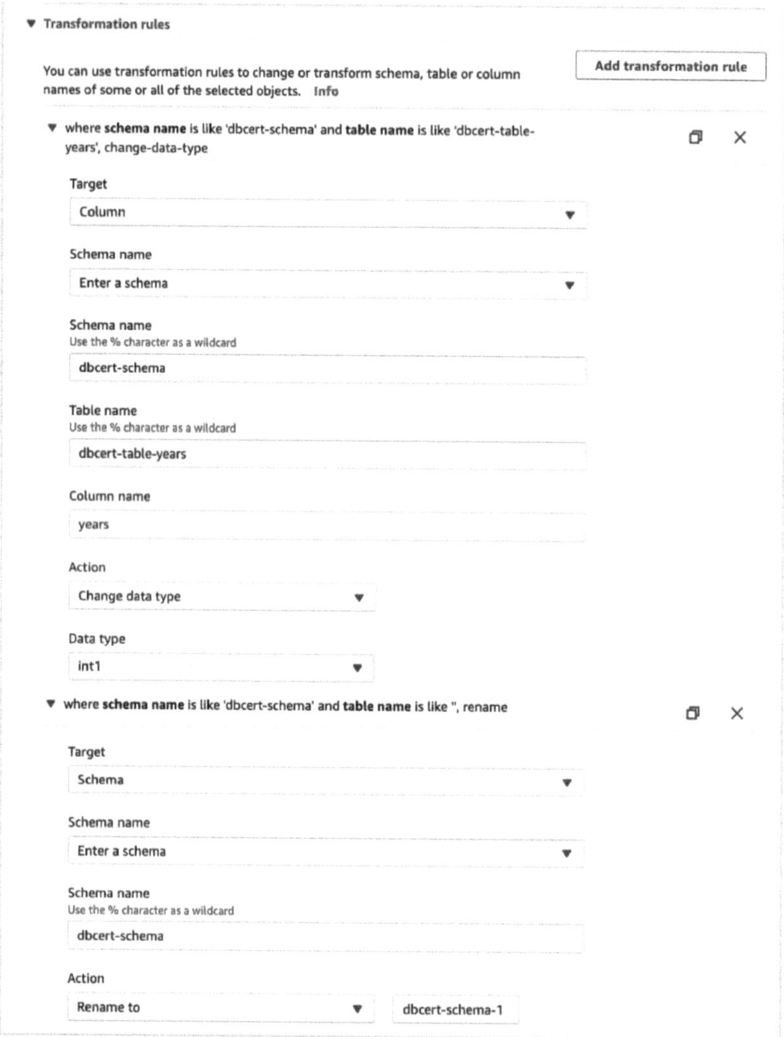

Figure 10.7 – DMS transformation rules

You can have multiple transformation rules per task, but you are restricted to a single rule at the schema or table level. This means that if you want to change a table or schema name from upper to lowercase, you cannot then also add a prefix. You can have multiple rules that run at the column level, allowing for highly complex transformations. There are two important things to note:

- All schema, table, and column names are case-sensitive
- DMS does not check the schema's or object's name before creating the task by default

Once you have defined all your rules, you can run a pre-assessment to check that the rules you have created work correctly. The premigration assessment can check for source table configuration issues with LOBs and any unsupported data types. If you are running in CDC mode, it can also check for primary keys on both the source and the target, which are needed for performance reasons.

Premigration assessment Info
A premigration assessment warns you of potential migration issues before starting your migration task. Premigration assessments generally have minimal impact on your databases and take minimal time to run.
Enable premigration assessment run
Premigration assessment run name
Use a friendly name to help you find your assessment run.
Assessment-run-2022-01-15-11-33-54
The assessment run name can only have valid characters: a-z, A-Z, 0-9, space, and - (hyphen).
Assessments to run
Large objects (LOBs) are used but target LOB columns are not nullable
Checks for nullability of a LOB column in the target when full LOB mode or inline LOB mode is used. AWS DMS requires a target LOB column to be nullable when using these LOB modes.
Source table with LOBs but without primary keys or unique constraints
Checks for the presence of source tables with LOBs but without a primary key or unique key. For AWS DMS to migrate LOBs, a source table must have a primary key or unique key.
Unsupported data types
Checks for data types unsupported by AWS DMS in the source endpoint. Not all data types can be migrated between endpoint types.
Source table without primary key for CDC or full load and CDC tasks only
Checks for the presence of a primary key or a unique key in source tables. The lack of a primary key or a unique key during change data capture (CDC) can cause performance issues during replication.
Target table without primary keys for CDC tasks only
Checks for the presence of a primary key or a unique key in already created target tables for a database migration task performing a change data capture (CDC) replication. Lack of a primary key or unique key in a target table can cause full table scans on the target when AWS DMS applies updates or deletes. This can result in performance issues during replication.
Unsupported source primary key types - composite primary keys
Checks for the presence of composite primary keys in source tables. This option is for migrating to either Amazon DynamoDB (applies to all DMS replication instance versions) or Amazon Elasticsearch Service (applies only to DMS replication instances before 3.3.3). The source table's primary key must be a single column.
Assessment report storage
Amazon S3 bucket or bucket folder path to store the assessment result report.
s3://bucket-name/bucket-folder/
View
Browse S3
IAM role
IAM role that can access the S3 bucket.
Choose an IAM role
Additional settings

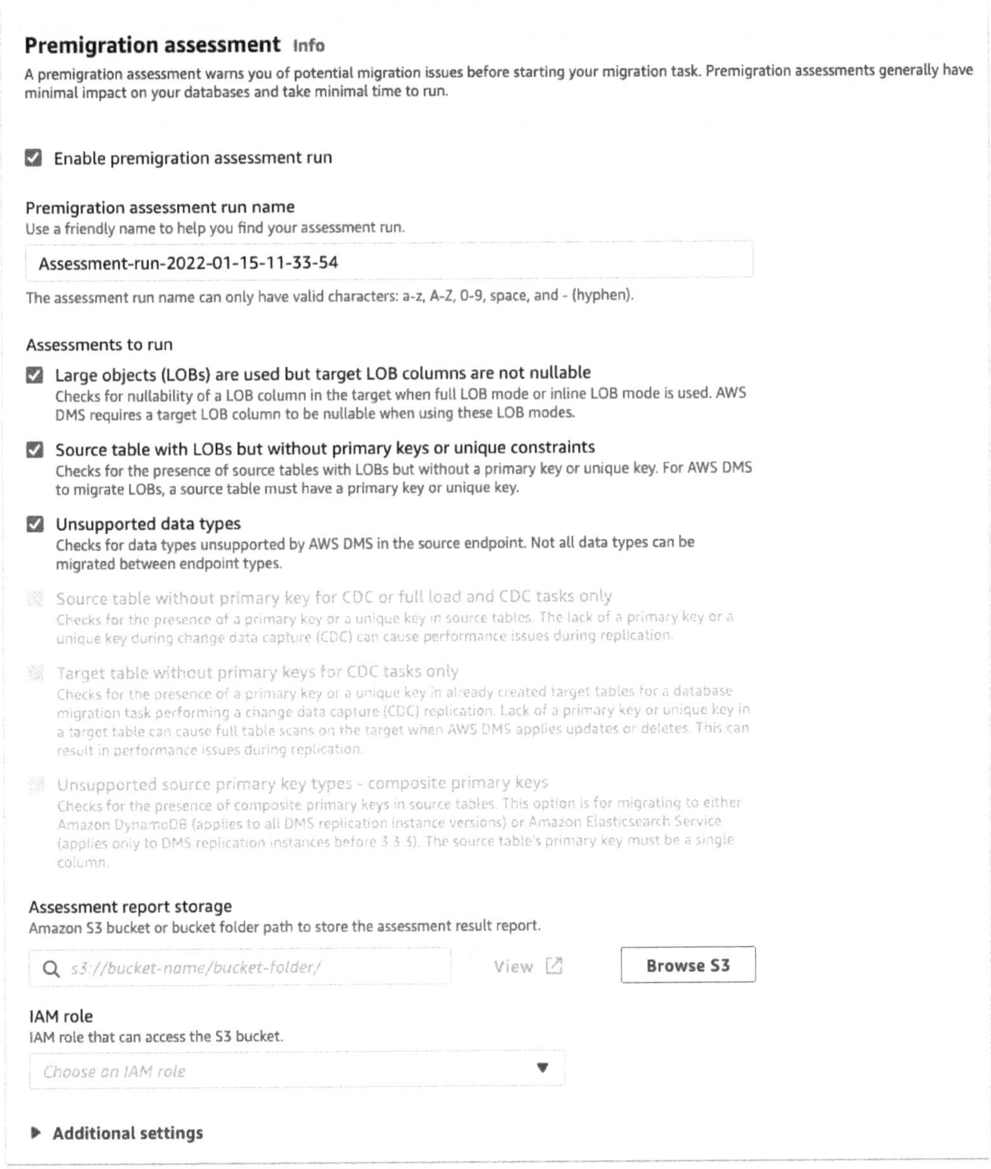

Figure 10.8 – DMS premigration assessment

The premigration assessment saves the report to an S3 bucket, so you can only use this if you have an S3 bucket ready and an IAM role with permissions to write to the bucket.

Finally, you can set up data validation for your DMS task. This helps DMS ensure that all the data has been migrated correctly by comparing the primary keys and columns on both the source and the target.

Once the premigration assessment has been completed, you can create the task. It will take a few minutes to be created before it can be run. Now, let's learn how to run a DMS task.

Running a DMS task via SCT

You can start a DMS task once the task has been successfully created and is showing a status of *Ready*. To start it, you can either click the checkbox next to it and then go to the **Actions** dropdown and select **Restart/Resume** (the naming here is ambiguous) or you can click on the task's name and go to the **Actions** dropdown and select **Restart/Resume**.

Once the job is running, you can monitor its progress on the **Table statistics** tab.

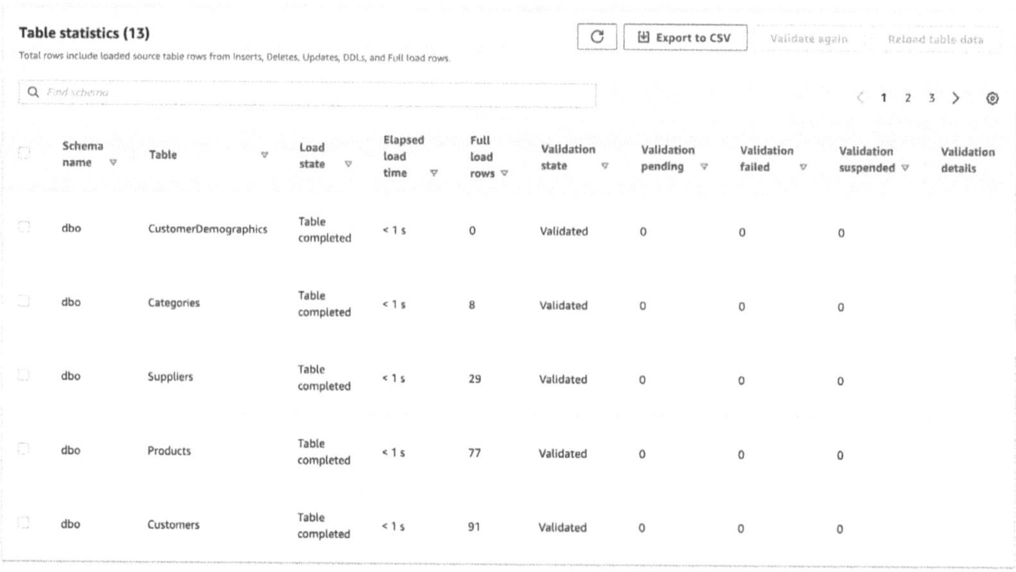

Table statistics (13)

Total rows include loaded source table rows from Inserts, Deletes, Updates, DDLs, and Full load rows.

Export to CSV | Validate again | Reload table data

Find schema

1 2 3

Schema name	Table	Load state	Elapsed load time	Full load rows	Validation state	Validation pending	Validation failed	Validation suspended	Validation details
dbo	CustomerDemographics	Table completed	< 1 s	0	Validated	0	0	0	
dbo	Categories	Table completed	< 1 s	8	Validated	0	0	0	
dbo	Suppliers	Table completed	< 1 s	29	Validated	0	0	0	
dbo	Products	Table completed	< 1 s	77	Validated	0	0	0	
dbo	Customers	Table completed	< 1 s	91	Validated	0	0	0	

Figure 10.9 – DMS table statistics

In the preceding screenshot, the table did not migrate successfully, with DMS reporting a mismatch between the source and the target after migration. To investigate this mismatch, you will need to inspect any CloudWatch logs that were created by DMS, as well as the source and target database logs. We will learn more about monitoring DMS in the next section. If you run a large DMS job with multiple tables, you will see that multiple tables are converted and migrated simultaneously. For larger tables, you will also be able to see that the number of rows increases in multiples of the commit rate that was configured in the job settings. Once all the rows have been migrated, DMS will perform data validation if you selected it in the job settings. The job's status will not change to *Success* until all the tables have been migrated and the validation has been completed. If the job fails for any reason, its current status will be stored, allowing you to resume it once the error has been fixed. You can also reload the data from any table while the job is running. This can be useful if a single table fails to migrate or suffers an error as you can fix the error and then restart that single table rather than the whole job.

Now, let's look more closely at monitoring a DMS job and some tuning options to make your migrations more reliable and faster.

Monitoring and tuning DMS

DMS offers a large number of options for logging and monitoring, depending on your needs. In general, for any new job or one that has not been tested, you should enable full debugging monitoring so that you can trace any errors. Once a job has been completed successfully, you can reduce monitoring on subsequent runs to minimize costs as all monitoring logs are charged for.

The following monitoring and logging tools are available to you:

- **DMS Console**: You can use the DMS GUI to check the status of the current tasks.
- **AWS CLI**: You can run `awscli` commands to obtain the current task's status.
- **AWS Simple Notification Service (SNS)**: You can configure SNS events to notify you via email of any changes to your tasks.
- **CloudWatch**: DMS can be configured to send enhanced logs to CloudWatch, allowing you to trace errors.
- **Time Travel Logs**: DMS Time Travel stores information about CDC changes that have been made, allowing you to see the exact state of your data historically. Time Travel logs only work for PostgreSQL sources.
- **Database Logs**: As data is retrieved from the source DB and loaded into the target DB, the database logs will provide updates as to any failed data inserts or updates, which can be used for advanced troubleshooting.

As well as monitoring the progress of the DMS tasks themselves, you should also monitor the DMS replication instance. For optimal performance and cost-efficiency, you want to ensure that the CPU and memory of the instance are not over- or under-utilized. The following screenshot shows some of the metrics that are monitored:

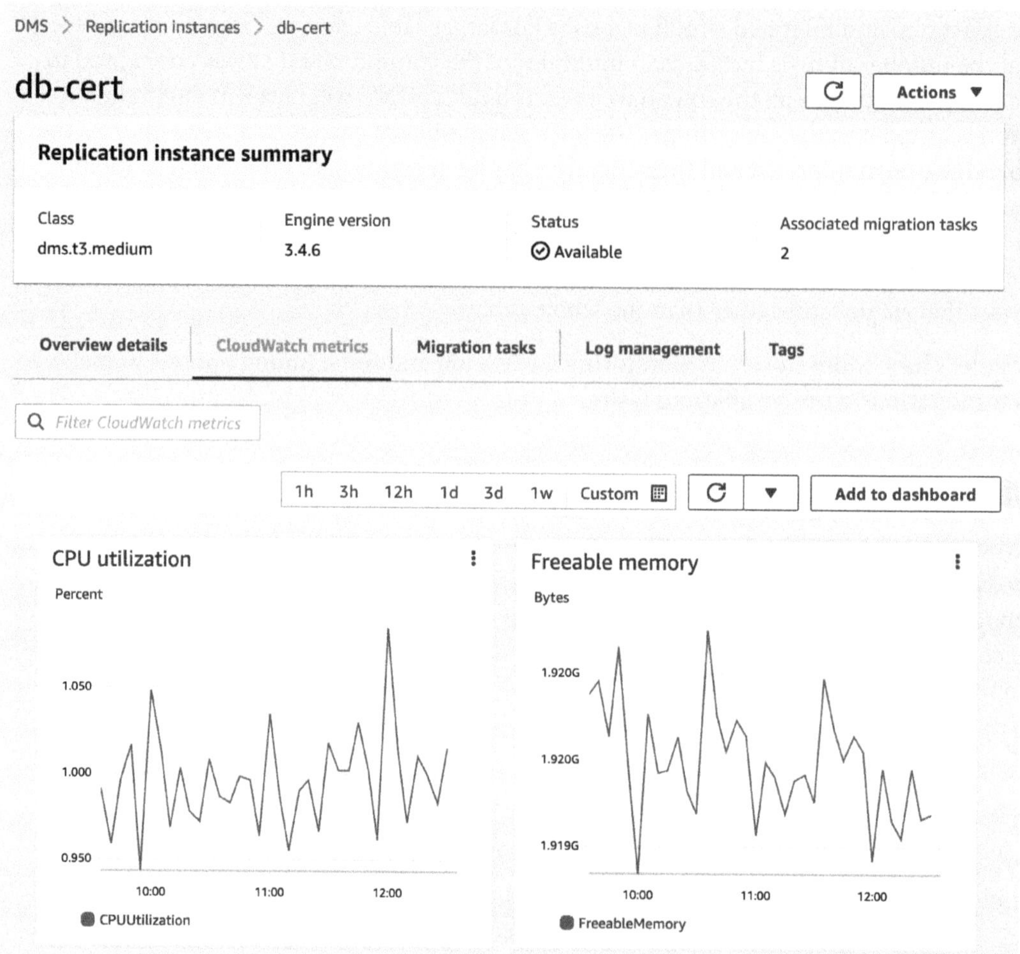

Figure 10.10 – DMS replication instance metrics

These metrics are also logged in Cloudwatch, which offers more filtering and customization. If the resources are being over- or under-utilized, you can modify the instance class of the replication instance. As changing the instance class will require a reboot, you cannot modify it while any tasks are running.

Now, let's look at some options for tuning your DMS jobs to make them more efficient.

Performance tuning

DMS tasks are highly customizable, with many parameters and settings to aid performance. There are six main areas to consider when you're tuning any DMS task:

- The replication instance class
- Task settings
- LOB settings
- Task splitting
- Database settings

The replication instance is one main bottleneck for any DMS task as it controls all of the data flows and converts the source DB into the target DB. During any task, closely monitor the resource usage of the replication instance and consider changing the instance class if CPU and memory are above 80% utilized for a sustained period; spikes can be ignored. DMS is typically memory-intensive and DMS replication instances can support the r5 and c5 instance classes, which have higher memory per core than other instance classes.

The next thing to tune is the task settings themselves. The main items that can improve performance are as follows:

- The commit rate
- The number of tables to load in parallel
- Creating primary key indexes after the full load

The commit rate controls the number of rows that are applied to the target DB in a single transaction. Setting this to a higher value can speed up the migration as there are fewer transactions. However, a higher commit rate requires a higher amount of memory for the replication instance, so you need to carefully control this value to ensure you do not over-utilize the memory.

The number of tables that are loaded in parallel is controlled by a value called *MaxFullLoadSubTasks*. The default setting is for eight tables to be loaded at once, but if you have a large number of smaller tables and a well-sized replication instance, you can increase the speed of the migration by setting this to a higher number.

The final task setting that can improve performance involves deferring the creation of primary key indexes. Primary keys are used as unique identifiers for each row and they typically have an index on them to speed up SELECT queries. However, indexes slow down INSERT and UPDATE queries as they need to be updated as well as the table. DMS allows you to defer the creation of these indexes until after the full load has been completed.

The next area that can cause poor migration performance is LOBs. Due to how DMS processes LOBs in two stages, as well as the need to hold LOBs in memory during conversion, the correct settings for LOB migrations can offer significant throughput improvement. The best way to optimize LOBs migrations is to identify whether any tables in scope contain LOBs. If they don't, then you can select **Don't include LOB columns** in the DMS task. If they do contain LOBs, then the best way to handle those is to split them into a task that's away from the other tables. This allows you to tune that task specifically for LOBs. The next step is to find the largest LOB in the tables in scope (you will need to refer to the documentation for your source DB to find out how to do that). Set the task to **Limited LOB mode** and set the maximum size to the size of the largest LOB you found. By doing this, DMS can more accurately size memory chunks to hold the LOB data, which means more LOB data can be migrated simultaneously, thereby speeding up the data transfer process.

> **Data Consistency**
>
> It is worth noting that DMS enforces data consistency across a single task, but if you split out the LOBs into a different task, that guarantee is lost. As a result, if you are trying to migrate a database that is still being used during the migration window, you may see data inconsistencies or referential integrity errors, which need to be resolved manually.

As well as splitting out LOBs into tasks, you can use a similar method for the other tables in the database. You can even split a large table into smaller tasks by using column filtering. For example, if you have a table that contains 500,000 rows and a sequence number in one column, you can create five tasks that take 100,000 rows each by using a `where` clause. This will allow DMS to process the table in parallel, which it is unable to do if the entire table is within a single task. Be aware of the previous callout regarding data integrity on a source database that is still open for transactions.

The final main area that needs to be tuned is the databases themselves. If possible, DMS recommends that all the indexes and foreign keys are dropped during the migration. Any indexes or foreign keys will add a large overhead to the migration and it is faster to recreate them once the data is migrated. However, this isn't possible on a system that is still being used. A major benefit of cloud technologies is the ability to scale both up and down as required rapidly and this technology can be used here. Before you start the migration, you can increase the sizing of your target DB instance to give it more compute resources. Them, once the migration has finished, you can size it back to the previous instance class to minimize additional costs. You should also ensure that the storage that's been allocated to the target DB is sufficient. While RDS can autoscale your storage as it fills, this takes a few minutes each time the storage needs to increase, which will slow down the migration. Be careful not to oversize as storage cannot be downsized without you moving the DB to a new instance.

Following these basic tuning steps will allow the majority of DMS tasks to run without issue.

DMS can be started and controlled within SCT. This can allow you to handle a full conversion and migration using just one interface, which can make the process simpler. Let's now learn how to configure DMS tasks via SCT.

Running a DMS task via SCT

SCT and DMS can work together to handle both schema conversion and data migration. Using a data extraction agent, SCT allows you to monitor and control DMS jobs via the SCT interface. To do this, you must configure an AWS service profile to use, which requires an AWS Access Key and an AWS Secret Key for a user who has permissions to create DMS tasks. Once that profile has been added, SCT will be able to create DMS tasks for you. The SCT DMS interface can only work with tasks and cannot create endpoints or replication instances, so these will need to be configured before you try to migrate. The following screenshot shows the **Global settings** view, which appears when you have correctly configured an AWS Access Key and profile:

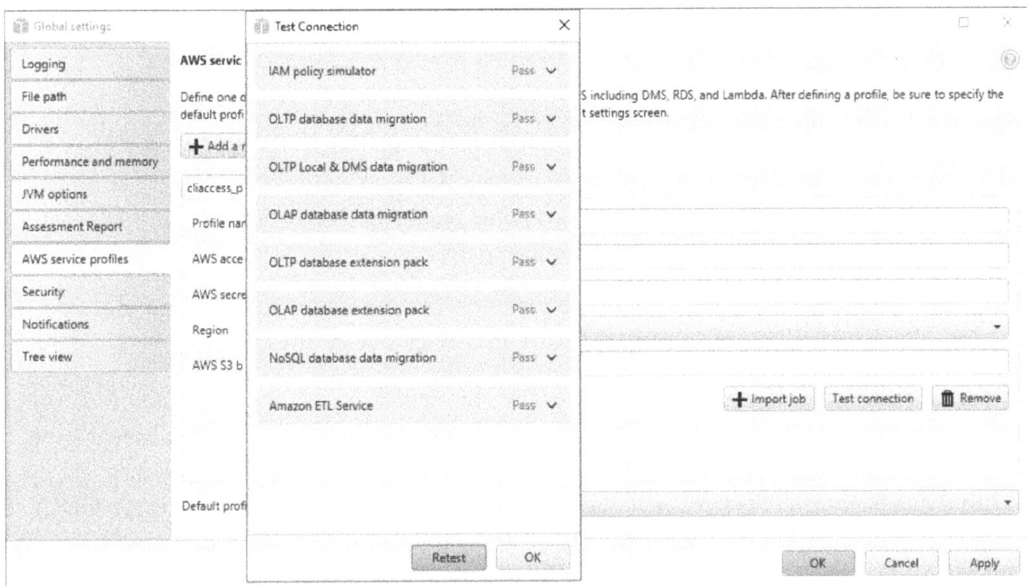

Figure 10.11 – AWS Global settings for AWS service profiles

To use DMS within SCT, you need to install a data extraction agent. This agent can also be used for complex SCT migrations, such as from Apache Cassandra to AWS DynamoDB. Let's learn more about the SCT data extraction agent.

The SCT data extraction agent

The data extraction agent is an SCT tool that allows you to transfer the data from your database to the AWS cloud for further processing. The following are some use cases when you can use the agent:

- To process large (multi-terabyte) on-premises databases by migrating the data to storage in S3 or via a device called Snowball Edge
- Migrating from Apache Cassandra to Amazon DynamoDB

In some cases, the source DB might be too large to migrate across the network in this way and all the tuning options may have been exhausted. For such scenarios, AWS offers a storage device called AWS Snowball that can assist you. Let's learn about it now and how it integrates with DMS.

Using AWS Snowball

AWS Snowball is a storage and compute device that's used to move large amounts of data from on-premises systems to AWS S3. A Snowball is a physical device that is sent to you via a courier. When you receive the device, you load it with data and simply ship it back to AWS. AWS loads the data into a predefined S3 bucket where you can move it to your target system – in our case, a database.

There are two different types of Snowball devices, depending on your use case and the size of your source data:

- **AWS Snowball**: 50 TB storage capacity (with an 80 TB device, which is only available in the US). Used for basic data transfers.
- **AWS Snowball Edge**: 100 TB storage capacity. The device includes a compute module, which allows data processing to be carried out on the device.

Two options are available when you're using AWS Snowball to migrate your data, depending on your target and source DB. If you are migrating to the same database engine as your source, you can use AWS Snowball to migrate the database backup files into S3 and run a database-level restore for the initial data load. If required, you must run a CDC DMS task to sync any missing data from the source database that was not captured in Snowball. You can do this by running a DMS CDC task with a timestamp start point.

The second option is to use AWS Snowball Edge to migrate the data. The compute resource within Snowball Edge is used to help convert the data on the device rather than your local computer, which can be considerably faster due to the higher computing power on the Snowball Edge device. To do this, follow these high-level steps:

1. Order your Snowball Edge from AWS via the AWS Snowball console.
2. Download any software you need, such as the SCT application and Snowball client.
3. When it arrives, configure Snowball Edge with the database drivers that are required to connect to your source database.
4. Install the DMS data extraction agent on a client machine that has connectivity to the source DB.
5. Create a new project in SCT and configure the project settings to use the Snowball Edge device by setting up the AWS service profile and importing the jobs.
6. Register the DMS agent with SCT and create local and remote DMS tasks.

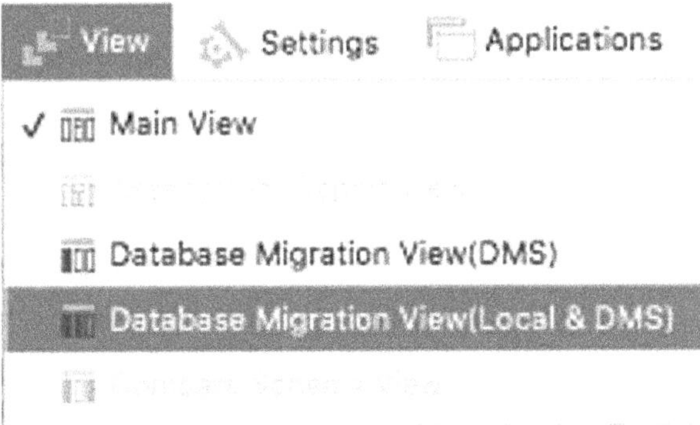

Figure 10.12 – Creating local and remote DMS tasks

7. Run and monitor the DMS tasks. The local task will complete first, which will convert the schema as required and then migrate the data to the Snowball Edge device. The second stage will only complete once the Snowball Edge device is sent back to AWS. The migration will restart automatically once AWS has the device.

Now that we've learned the theory of converting and migrating a database to AWS, let's practice our new skills in a hands-on lab.

Converting and migrating a database to AWS

Now that we've learned the theory behind how SCT and DMS work to assess, convert, and migrate a database, let's practice our knowledge in a hands-on lab. In this lab, we are going to create an RDS Microsoft SQL Server database as our source and convert and migrate it to an RDS MySQL database.

> **AWS Account Costs**
>
> RDS SQL Server and DMS are chargeable by AWS and are not covered by the free tier. This lab aims to let you learn about these tools, which are major areas within the DB Specialty exam, while keeping costs as low as possible.

Setting up

Before we can start any conversion and migration, we need a source and target database. To give us a schema to work with, we will use the Microsoft SQL Server Northwinds sample data, which is available here: `https://github.com/microsoft/sql-server-samples/blob/master/samples/databases/northwind-pubs/instnwnd.sql`.

First, we will create an RDS SQL Server database and restore the Northwinds database to it. If you have completed each chapter in this book so far, you should be able to complete this with only high-level steps:

1. Create an RDS SQL Server express edition instance using the smallest class available to minimize costs. The fee that's quoted at the end is the monthly cost and we will only have the database available for a few hours. Fill in all the required fields based on the VPC and subnets you have. You can turn off backups and all additional monitoring to save costs. Set the database instance to **publicly available**, and ensure your security groups are set to only allow your IP address to access the database.
2. Once the DB has been created, use a DB connection tool such as SQL Server Management Studio to connect to the database from your local machine. If you cannot reach the target database, double-check your security group configuration.

3. Run the Northwinds sample data SQL file you downloaded in the new database to create your schema and table. You can either copy and paste the commands from the file or you can open the file in the SQL management tool that you are using. First, you will need to edit the file by removing lines 15-17 and editing the new line 15 so that it states `EXECUTE (N'CREATE DATABASE Northwind')`. These changes allow the code to work on an RDS database.
4. Create an RDS MySQL database. RDS MySQL is available on the free tier on a `t2.micro` instance when configured with the *Free Tier* template. Fill in all the required fields based on the VPC and subnets you have. You can turn off backups and all additional monitoring to save costs. Set the database instance to publicly available, and ensure your security groups are set to only allow your IP address to access the database.

Next, you must download the necessary drivers to allow SCT to connect to your databases. The latest driver for SQL Server can be found at `https://docs.microsoft.com/en-us/sql/connect/jdbc/download-microsoft-jdbc-driver-for-sql-server?view=sql-server-ver15`, while the latest driver for MySQL can be found at `https://dev.mysql.com/downloads/`.

You will need to ensure you download the right driver for your environment while paying close attention to the x86 versus x64 bit versions. For MySQL, I recommend that you download the entire MySQL Workbench tool so that you can connect to the database at the end of the lab and verify that the data exists, as well as to run queries, but this is optional and you can download only the driver if you prefer.

Now that our environment has been set up, we can start to convert the schema.

Converting the database schema

We will use SCT to convert the schema from the source SQL Server database and apply it to the MySQL target. We will begin by running an assessment against our source to ensure we can convert it successfully. Let's get started:

1. Download and install the latest version of the AWS SCT program from `https://docs.aws.amazon.com/SchemaConversionTool/latest/userguide/CHAP_Installing.html#CHAP_Installing.Procedure`.
2. Select **New Project Wizard** from the **File** menu.

3. Fill in the form that appears by selecting **Microsoft SQL Server** from the dropdown:

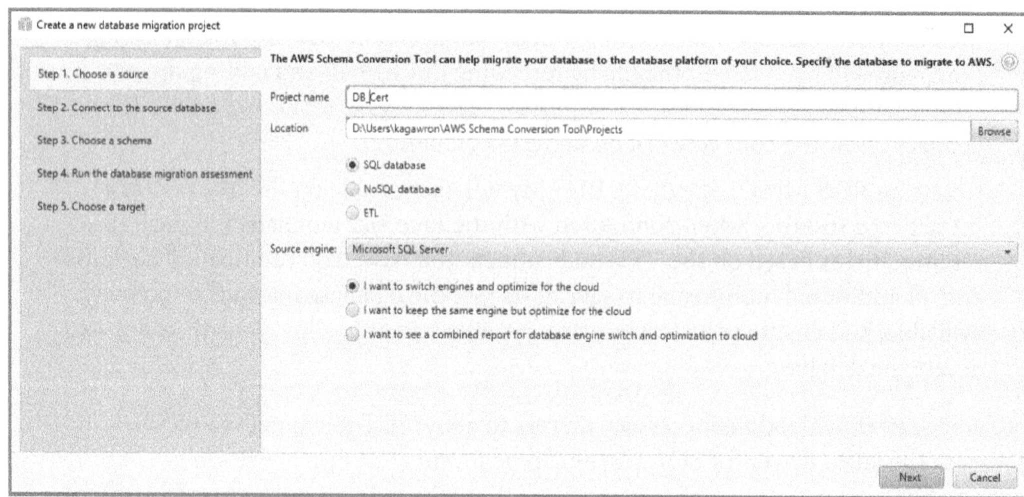

Figure 10.13 – SCT project wizard

4. Fill in the connection details for the RDS SQL Server database you created, including the path to the driver you downloaded, and click **Next**. A warning about SSL will appear. This is encouraging you to use an encrypted connection. Even though this is a best practice for production systems, we will not be using it during this lab. Click **Accept the risk and continue**.
5. On the next page, select only the **Northwind** database we created and click **Next**:

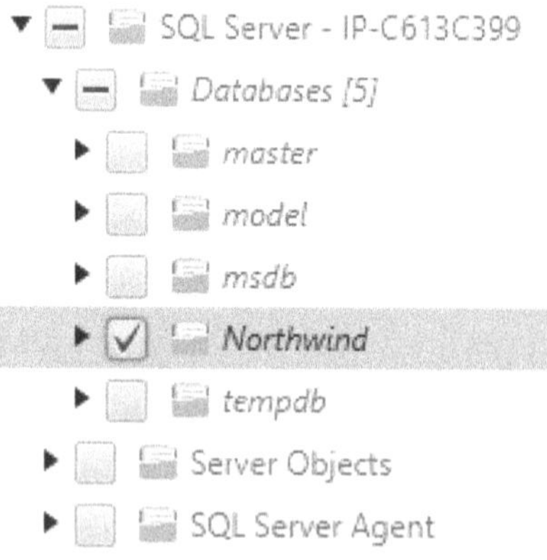

Figure 10.14 – Selecting the database

6. On the next screen, you will be shown the **Database migration assessment report** area. Here, you can see that the best fit for our database (the target database engine with the least manual conversion work) is **Amazon RDS MySQL**.

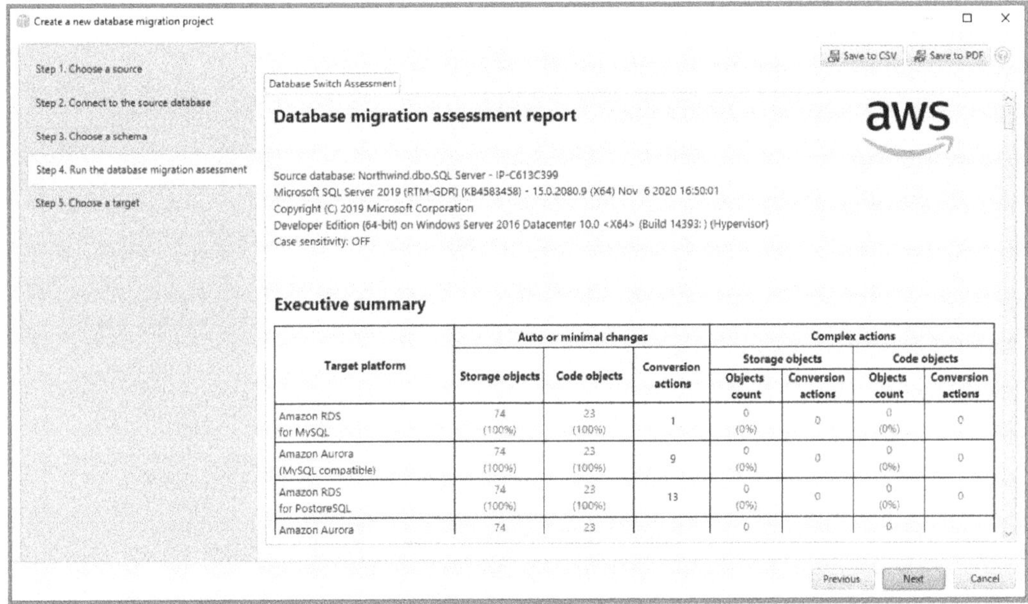

Target platform	Auto or minimal changes		Conversion actions	Complex actions			
	Storage objects	Code objects		Storage objects		Code objects	
				Objects count	Conversion actions	Objects count	Conversion actions
Amazon RDS for MySQL	74 (100%)	23 (100%)	1	0 (0%)	0	0 (0%)	0
Amazon Aurora (MySQL compatible)	74 (100%)	23 (100%)	9	0 (0%)	0	0 (0%)	0
Amazon RDS for PostgreSQL	74 (100%)	23 (100%)	13	0 (0%)	0	0 (0%)	0
Amazon Aurora	74	23		0		0	

Figure 10.15 – SCT assessment report

7. Feel free to read the report to understand its content. You can also **Save to CSV** or **Save to PDF** for future reference if you wish. Once you have finished reading the report, click **Next**.
8. Fill in the database connection details for the RDS MySQL target database, including the path to the driver you downloaded, and click **Finish**.

9. The project screen will open, with the source on the left and the target on the right. Ignore the other server types as we won't be using them here. **target** is the name of the connection; yours may have a different alias.

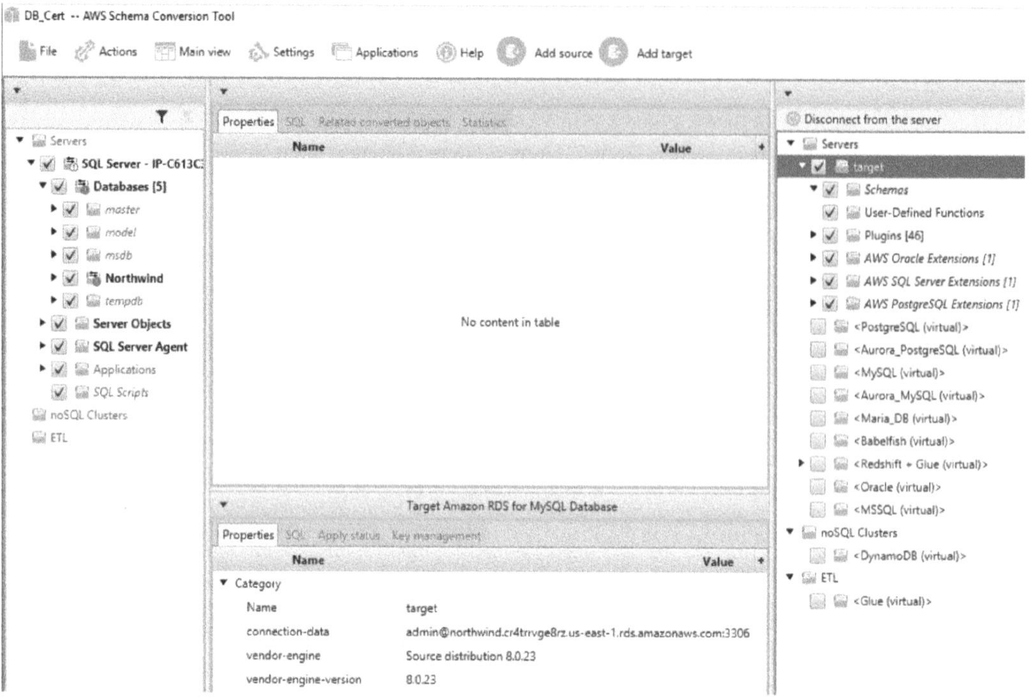

Figure 10.16 – Project main view

10. You'll notice that the **Northwind** database is the only one in bold and that it has a red warning logo next to it. This indicates that, currently, some action needs to be taken for the conversion to take place. If you read the full assessment report, you should know what the issue is that we need to deal with. If you didn't read the report, you can find the problem by expanding the **Northwind** database by clicking on the arrow next to it. Keep expanding the levels until you find the object(s) that has/have been flagged with the red warning symbol.

11. Once you've drilled down far enough, you will see that we have a procedure that cannot be converted automatically called **Ten Most Expensive Products**. There is no information about the problem at this point, though (although the assessment report does explain the problem if you read it!). Let's see what happens if we try to apply the schema to the target database while we have this issue with this procedure. Right-click on the name of the Northwind database and select **Convert Schema**. You will receive a warning about target objects, which we can ignore for now.

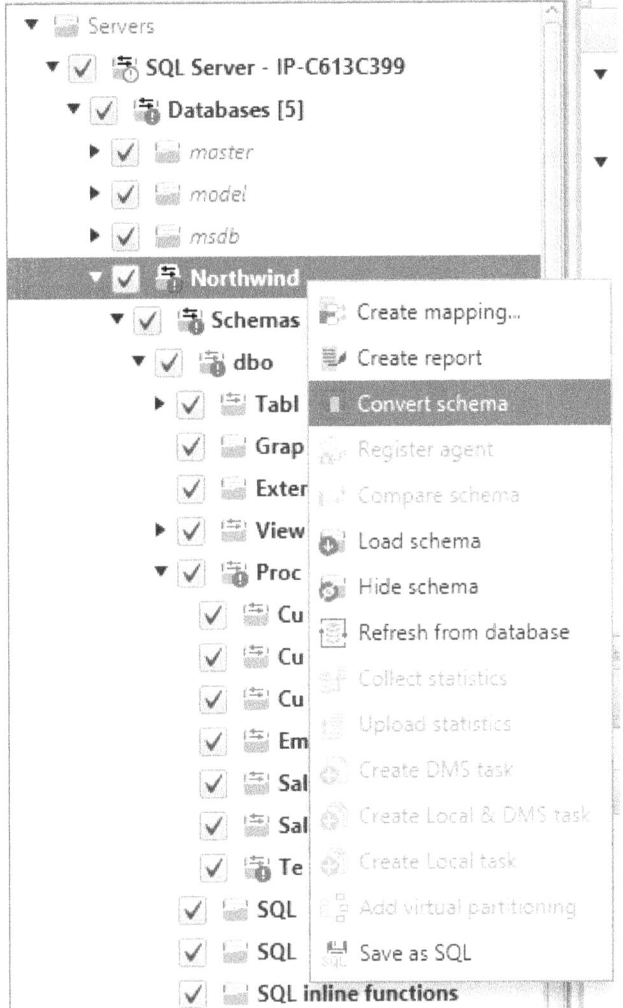

Figure 10.17 – The Convert schema option

12. Now, go back to the procedure with the warning flag. Notice that there is now some code in the bottom panel. This is the code we have applied to the target. However, there is a problem. In the middle of the procedure, we have the following code comment:

```
 [673 - Severity CRITICAL - Automatic conversion of
SETROWCOUNT statement is not supported. Perform a manual
conversion.]
    SET ROWCOUNT 10
```

This tells us that SCT does not know how to modify this procedure so that it matches MySQL syntax. Given that the procedure is called **Ten Most Expensive Products,** this `ROWCOUNT` of 10 is important to retain. I recommend that you try to resolve this error yourself to find an equivalent MySQL syntax, but if you are stuck, the solution can be found in this book's GitHub repository at `https://github.com/PacktPublishing/AWS-Certified-Database---Specialty-DBS-C01-Certification/blob/main/ch10/DMS_solution.sql`:

1. Once you have found the solution, you can modify the code in the lower panel, which will be written to the target database when we are ready. Make the required changes to the code and then, on the right-hand side of the window, right-click the **Ten Most Expensive Products** procedure and select **Apply to database**.

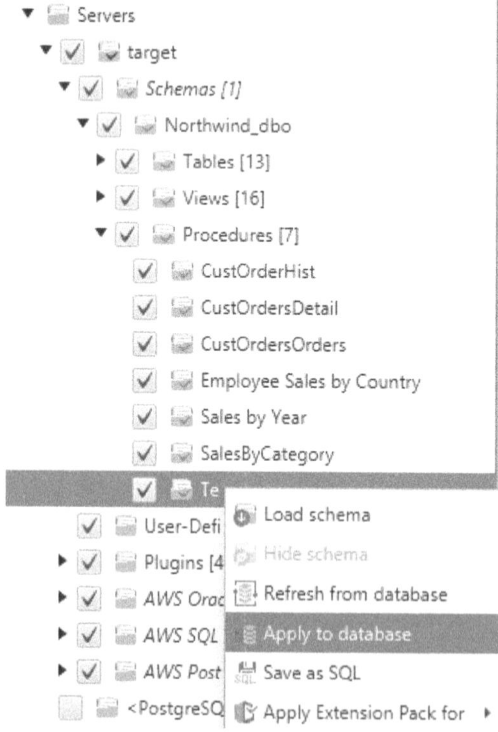

Figure 10.18 – Applying the code to the database

2. You will notice that the symbol next to the procedure changes and now looks different from the other schema items. This is because this is the only object we have written to the target database at this point. Right-click the **Schemas** object on the right-hand side and select **Apply to database** again to commit the objects to the target database. We could have done this instead of doing the procedure separately, but it's useful to know how to apply objects individually if needed.

3. Note that the schema's name is **Northwind_dbo** in my example. We will need this when we run DMS in the next section.
4. At this point, it is worth taking a look at the table columns on the target database and comparing them with the source. Look for any data types that have been changed. If you select the **Employees** table, you will be able to see that the **Photos** and **Notes** columns have been converted from `image` and `ntext` into `LONGTEXT` and `LONGBLOG` so that they match the MySQL data types.

With that, we've converted our database schema from SQL Server into MySQL and committed the schema to the target database. If you open your MySQL management tool and connect to the target database, you will be able to see all the tables and code objects, but the tables will be empty. Now, we need to create a DMS task to move the data.

Migrating the data

In this section, we are going to set up a DMS task to migrate the data from source to target. We'll need to create a replication instance and endpoints and then configure the task rules. Let's get started:

1. Log in to the AWS console and navigate to **Database Migration Service**.
2. Select **Replication instances** from the left-hand menu and select **Create replication instance** at the top right.

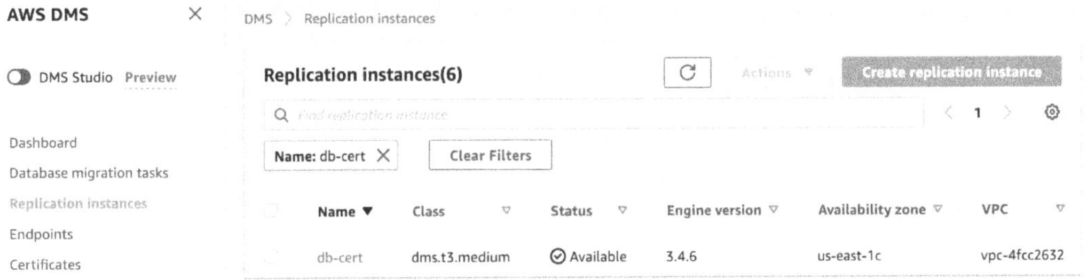

Figure 10.19 – Creating a replication instance

3. Fill in the form that appears. Provide a name for the replication instance and select the VPC that your databases have been created in. Leave all the other settings as-is and click **Create**.
4. Once the instance's status shows as **Available**, we can create our **Endpoints**. From the left-hand menu, select **Endpoints** and then **Create endpoint** from the top right.

5. Ensure that **Source endpoint** is highlighted and then tick the **Select RDS database instance** box so that you can select the database from a list. This only works for RDS databases within the same VPC as the replication instance, so it won't work for source databases that are on-premises or in a different account. Choose your source instance.
6. Select **Provide access information manually** (you can store the details within AWS Secrets Manager, but we won't cover that in this lab) and fill in the **Password** and **Database name** areas for your database.
7. Leave everything else as the defaults and open the **Test endpoint connection** section. Choose your **VPC** and **Replication instance** from the drop-down lists and then click **Run test**. After a few minutes, you may get an error about connectivity. Before continuing, think about what you may have missed.
8. If you created the databases while following best practices and created new security groups for them, then the replication instance cannot access our RDS databases. Navigate to the **VPC** service from the main AWS menu, and then select **Security groups**. Locate the ones that are being used by your RDS databases and click **Edit inbound rules**. Add a rule for your replication instance security group so that you can access the databases. It should look similar to this:

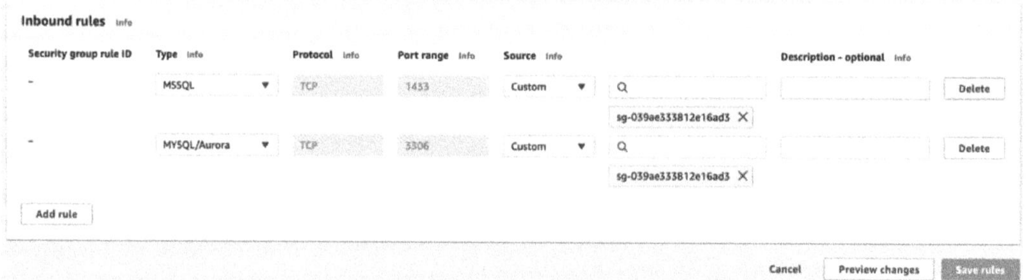

Figure 10.20 – Security group rules

Click **Save rules.**

9. If you had connectivity problems in the previous two steps, then you need to retest the endpoints before you can use them. Select **Endpoints** from the left-hand menu and click the name of one of your endpoints. Click on the **Connections** tab and select **Test connections**, and then **Run test**. Once the test shows as **Successful**, repeat these steps for the target endpoint.
10. Next, click **Database migration tasks** from the left-hand menu. Click **Create task** at the top right.
11. Fill in the **Task configuration** section with the details of your databases and replication instance. Leave **Migration type** set to **Migrate existing data**.

12. In the **Task settings** section, change **Target table preparation mode** to **Truncate**. If you leave this as the default (**Drop tables on target**), DMS will delete the tables and recreate them, which we don't want it to do. You can do nothing, but **Truncate** deletes any of the rows in the tables, ensuring we don't have data integrity issues. Change **Include LOB columns in replication** to **Full LOB mode**.

Task settings
Editing mode Info
Wizard
You can enter only a subset of the available task settings.
JSON editor
You can enter all available task settings directly in JSON format.
Target table preparation mode Info
Do nothing
Drop tables on target
Truncate
Possible data loss on target database
Truncate is the table preparation mode that you chose. Before migrating your source data, DMS leaves existing target tables and their metadata in place, but deletes all existing data from these tables before starting the migration.
Include LOB columns in replication Info
Don't include LOB columns
Full LOB mode
Limited LOB mode
Maximum LOB size (KB) Info
32
Enable validation
Choose this setting if you want AWS DMS to compare the data at the source and the target, immediately after it performs a full data load. Validation ensures that your data was migrated accurately, but it requires additional time to complete.
Enable CloudWatch logs Info
DMS task logging uses Amazon CloudWatch to log information during the migration process. You can change the component activities logged and the amount of information logged for each one.
Advanced task settings

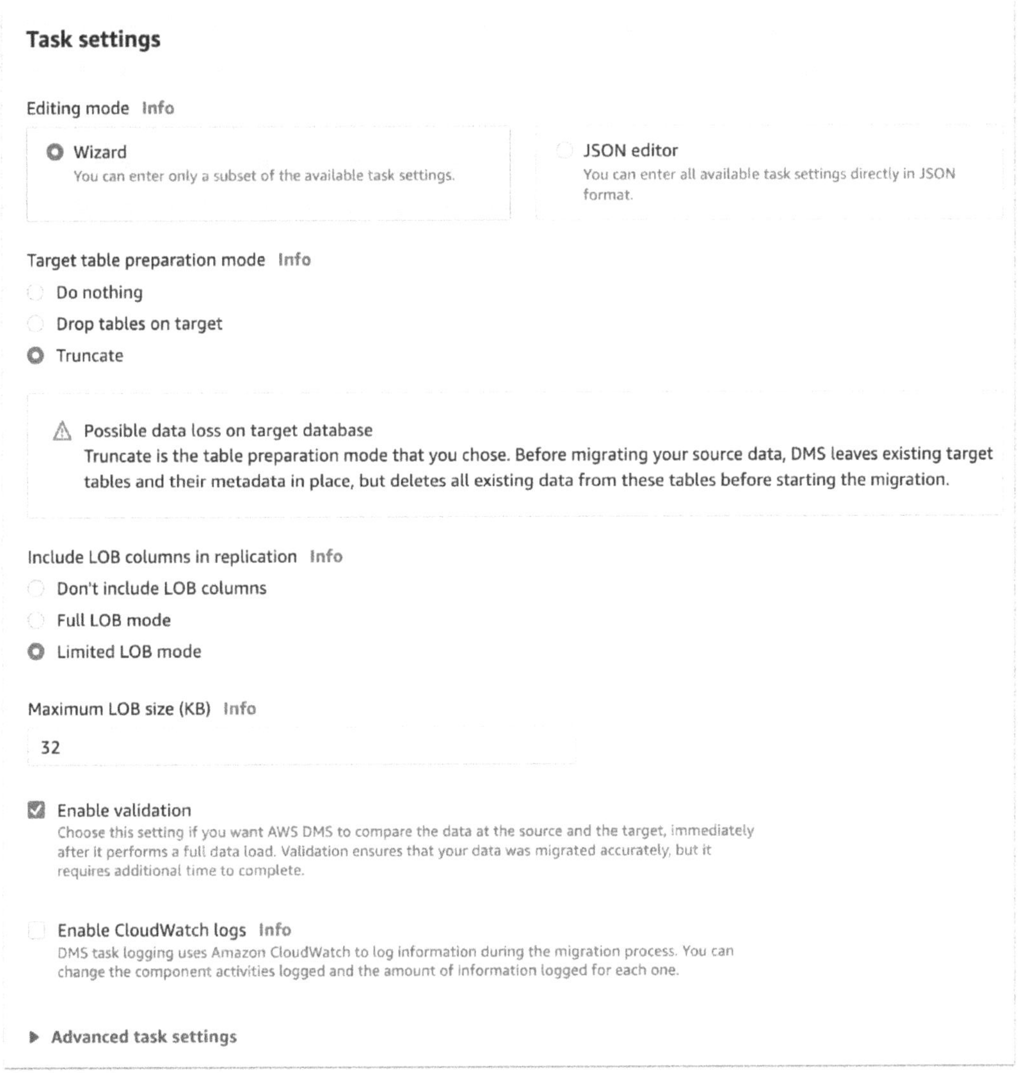

Figure 10.21 – Task settings

In the **Selection rules** section, use a **%** sign for both the schema and table names to pull all the data from our chosen database.

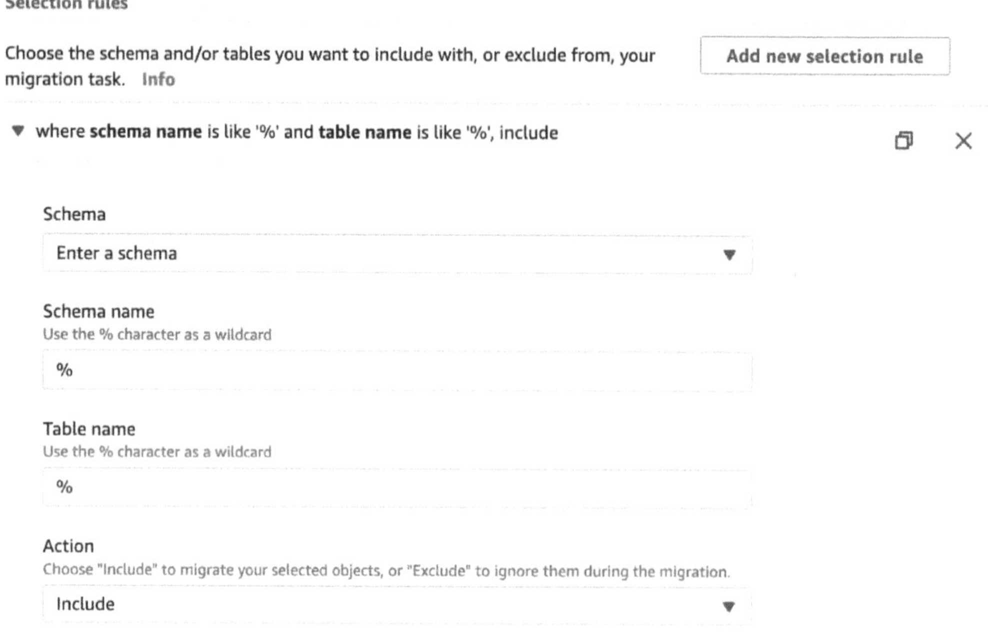
Selection rules
Choose the schema and/or tables you want to include with, or exclude from, your migration task. Info
Add new selection rule
where schema name is like '%' and table name is like '%', include
Schema
Enter a schema
Schema name
Use the % character as a wildcard
%
Table name
Use the % character as a wildcard
%
Action
Choose "Include" to migrate your selected objects, or "Exclude" to ignore them during the migration.
Include

Figure 10.22 – Selection rules

13. Now, we need to add a **Transformation task** to change the schema name from **dbo** to **Northwind_dbo** (or the name of your schema from SCT if it's different). Once you've done this, leave everything else as-is and click **Create task** at the bottom of the screen.
14. It will take a few minutes for the task to start. You can monitor its progress through the different tabs on the task's page.

Table statistics (13)

Total rows include loaded source table rows from Inserts, Deletes, Updates, DDLs, and Full load rows.

Schema name	Table	Load state	Elapsed load time	Inserts	Deletes	Updates	DDLs	Full load rows	Total rows	Validation state
dbo	CustomerDemographics	Table completed	< 1 s	0	0	0	0	0	0	Validated
dbo	Categories	Table completed	< 1 s	0	0	0	0	8	8	Validated
dbo	Suppliers	Table completed	1 s	0	0	0	0	29	29	Validated
dbo	Products	Table completed	1 s	0	0	0	0	77	77	Validated
dbo	Customers	Table completed	< 1 s	0	0	0	0	91	91	Validated
dbo	Employees	Table completed	< 1 s	0	0	0	0	9	9	Validated
dbo	EmployeeTerritories	Table completed	< 1 s	0	0	0	0	49	49	Validated
dbo	Order Details	Table completed	1 s	0	0	0	0	2,155	2,155	Validated
dbo	Orders	Table completed	1 s	0	0	0	0	830	830	Validated
dbo	Shippers	Table completed	1 s	0	0	0	0	3	3	Validated
dbo	Territories	Table completed	1 s	0	0	0	0	53	53	Validated
dbo	Region	Table completed	1 s	0	0	0	0	4	4	Validated
dbo	CustomerCustomerDemo	Table completed	< 1 s	0	0	0	0	0	0	Validated

Figure 10.23 – Table status view

When the task has been completed, you can review the data that's been migrated via the MySQL tool that you are using. This completes the hands-on lab and shows how a simple database conversion and migration can be managed in a few steps. SCT and DMS are major topics in the DB Specialty exam, so I strongly recommend practicing with different migrations so that you have a strong understanding of how everything works and can then apply that to scenario-based exam questions.

Summary

In this chapter, we learned how to use AWS Schema Conversion Tool and AWS Database Migration Service to migrate databases to AWS. We learned how to use SCT to assess whether a database needs to be converted into a different database engine, as well as how to assess it for migration to RDS. After that, we learned how to use DMS to migrate the data to our target database using full load and CDC tasks.

We also learned about AWS Snowball and how it works with the SCT data extraction agent. This allows you to migrate large or complex databases using a storage device to reduce network bandwidth and speed up a migration.

SCT, DMS, and migration strategies are major topics within the DB Specialty exam, so covering these tools and techniques in depth will have greatly enhanced your skills going into the exam.

In the next chapter, we are going to learn how to use automation techniques, including two data handling and querying tools that are offered by AWS: **AWS Athena** and **AWS Glue**.

Now, let's review the key points of this chapter.

Cheat sheet

This cheat sheet summarizes the main key points from this chapter:

- SCT is used to assess and convert a database from one engine into another for a heterogeneous migration.
- SCT can also be used to assess a homogenous migration in RDS to highlight features that are not supported in your source database.
- Once you have converted a schema using SCT, you can use DMS to migrate the data into the empty schema and tables.
- DMS can also be used to create a schema in your target database, but you have no control over the data types that are created in the table.
- DMS can be used in both full load and CDC mode.
- To run a DMS task, you need a replication instance, a source endpoint, and a target endpoint.
- You can run multiple tasks to migrate a single source database to improve performance.
- For very large databases or complex conversions, you can use AWS Snowball Edge with SCT and DMS to assist with the migration.

Review

Let's test our knowledge of the contents of this chapter with some example exam questions:

1. You have been hired to migrate an Amazon EC2 instance that's running Oracle Database Standard Edition to an RDS for Oracle DB instance. The database is used for critical production services and the business can only provide a 5-minute outage window. How can you achieve this?

    A. Configure Oracle Real Application Clusters on the EC2 instance with the RDS DB instance as one of the nodes. Once the EC2 and RDS DB instances are in sync, switch over from Amazon EC2 to Amazon RDS and update the application connection string.

    B. Export the Oracle database from the EC2 instance using Oracle Data Pump to an S3 bucket and import it into Amazon RDS. Shut down the application until the restore is complete. Change the database connection string and then restart the application.

   C. Create an AWS DMS task with the EC2 instance as the source and the RDS DB instance as the destination. Stop the application when the replication is in sync and change the database connection string.

   D. Create an AWS SCT project with the EC2 instance as the source and the RDS DB instance as the destination. Convert the database schemas. Stop the application when the replication is in sync and change the database connection string.

2. You are a database specialist that's transferring a database from one AWS region to another using an RDS SQL Server DB instance. Your company wishes to keep database downtime and costs to a minimum throughout the transfer.

   Which migration strategy would you recommend?

   A. Back up the source database using SQL Server backup to an Amazon S3 bucket in the same region. Create a target RDS SQL Server in the target region. Restore the backup to the target database.

   B. Back up the source database using SQL Server backup to an Amazon S3 bucket in the same region. Use S3 Cross-Region Replication to copy the backup to an S3 bucket in the target region. Create a target RDS SQL Server in the target region. Restore the backup to the target database.

   C. Create an AWS DMS task to replicate data from the source to the target database. Once the database replication is in sync, stop the DMS task.

   D. Provision an RDS SQL Server cross-region read replica in the target region. Once the replication is in sync, promote the read replica to master.

3. A large multination organization has provisioned a large storage capacity RDS MariaDB database as a target for migration. After the migration, the organization carried out housekeeping, which reduced the data that was stored within the database. The organization now wants to reduce the storage capacity to save money.

   Which solution would satisfy these criteria while minimizing downtime and maintaining the performance of the database?

   A. Create a snapshot of the current database and restore the snapshot to a new RDS instance that's been provisioned with the reduced storage allocation.

   B. Provision a new RDS DB instance with the reduced storage and migrate the databases from the old instances to the new instance using AWS DMS in CDC mode.

   C. Provision a new RDS DB instance and migrate the data using a native MariaDB backup and restore.

   D. Create a read replica and promote it to master by terminating the existing primary.

4. You are planning to migrate a 500 GB Oracle database to Amazon Aurora PostgreSQL while utilizing AWS SCT and AWS DMS. The database does not have any stored procedures or complex code, but it does contain several partitioned tables that are more than 100 GB in size each. The database supports a critical production application, so you must migrate with minimal downtime.

   Which process should you choose to speed up the migration? (Choose three)

   A. Install and configure the AWS SCT data extraction agent to migrate the database from Oracle to Aurora PostgreSQL.

   B. For the large partitioned tables, increase the setting for the maximum number of tables to load in parallel and perform a full load using DMS.

   C. For the large partitioned tables, create a table settings rule with a parallel load option in AWS DMS and then perform a full load using DMS.

   D. Use AWS DMS to set up **change data capture** (**CDC**) for continuous replication until the cutover date.

   E. Use AWS SCT to convert the schema from Oracle to Aurora PostgreSQL.

   F. Use AWS DMS to convert the schema from Oracle to Aurora PostgreSQL and set up a CDC task.

5. You are a senior database consultant working with a large business that is transferring its on-premises database workloads to AWS. The database engineer that's responsible for migrating an Oracle database with huge tables to Amazon RDS has picked AWS DMS. The database engineer notes that AWS DMS is consuming considerable time while migrating the data.

   Which activities would increase the pace of data migration? (Choose three)

   A. Create multiple AWS DMS tasks to migrate the large table using a column filter.

   B. Configure the AWS DMS replication instance with Multi-AZ.

   C. Increase the compute of the AWS DMS replication server.

   D. Establish an AWS Direct Connect connection between the on-premises data center and AWS.

   E. Enable an Amazon RDS Multi-AZ configuration.

   F. Enable full **large object** (**LOB**) mode to migrate all LOB data for all large tables.

Further reading

AWS DMS Studio – Getting Started: `https://docs.aws.amazon.com/dms/latest/userguide/CHAP_DMSStudio_GettingStarted.html`.

11
Database Task Automation

Automation is the practice of creating scripts, code, or programs to allow operational and development activities to be carried out automatically with minimal user involvement. Automation can be as simple as creating a script you can schedule to run at fixed time intervals to inspect a database, or it can be an entire package that deploys and configures an entire application stack within AWS. There is an IT field called **Development Operations** (**DevOps**) that specializes in using automation techniques to reduce failure, improve deployment speed and accuracy, and create systems that can fix themselves if something goes wrong. For the Database Specialty exam, we won't need to know advanced DevOps skills and tools, but questions on automation techniques that are specific to databases will be asked, so it's important to understand AWS automation techniques at a high level. By the end of this chapter you will be confidently able to use CloudFormation, AWS Glue and Athena to help automate your processes.

In this chapter, we're going to cover the following main topics:

- Overview of automation techniques
- Understanding AWS automation
- Creating infrastructure using CloudFormation

- AWS Glue
- Amazon Athena
- Querying data within an S3 bucket using AWS Glue and Amazon Athena

Technical requirements

For this chapter, you will require an AWS account with root access. Not everything we will do in this chapter will be available in the free tier, which means it may cost you a small amount to follow the hands-on sections. You will also require **Command-line Interface** (**CLI**) AWS access. The AWS guide at `https://docs.aws.amazon.com/cli/latest/userguide/cli-chap-configure.html` explains the steps you must follow, but I will summarize them here:

1. Create an AWS account if you have not already done so.
2. Download the latest version of the AWS CLI from `https://docs.aws.amazon.com/cli/latest/userguide/welcome-versions.html#welcome-versions-v2`.
3. Create an admin user at `https://docs.aws.amazon.com/IAM/latest/UserGuide/id_credentials_access-keys.html`.
4. Create an access key for your administration user: `https://docs.aws.amazon.com/IAM/latest/UserGuide/getting-started_create-admin-group.html#getting-started_create-admin-group-cli`.
5. Run the `aws configure` command to set up a profile for your user: `https://docs.aws.amazon.com/cli/latest/userguide/cli-configure-quickstart.html#cli-configure-quickstart-creds`.

You will also require a VPC that meets the minimum requirements for an RDS instance, as specified here: `https://docs.aws.amazon.com/AmazonRDS/latest/UserGuide/USER_VPC.WorkingWithRDSInstanceinaVPC.html`. If you followed the steps in *Chapter 3, Understanding AWS Infrastructure*, you will already have a VPC that meets these requirements.

Overview of automation techniques

One of the fundamental benefits of cloud technologies is the ability to use code to describe and build your infrastructure. This is called **Infrastructure as Code** (**IaC**). You can use IaC techniques on-premises as well but often, you will be limited by physical restrictions such as running out of storage within your storage arrays or running out of physical CPU cores on your virtual machine coordinators (hypervisors, for example). While the same physical restrictions can impact a cloud deployment, a capacity outage on a cloud platform is extremely rare. Using IaC on-premises is also often complex due to a wide variety of technologies that do not use a command interface, programming language, or **application programming interfaces** (**APIs**).

IaC allows you to create code that can be run multiple times to create exact copies of the same infrastructure, which is extremely useful when you're creating test and development environments. You can use code versioning to ensure that all the changes that are made to the code are logged, audited, and controlled. This helps improve the consistency of builds, removes manual errors, and speeds up the provisioning process.

IaC can be used to deploy multiple services at the same time. For example, you may have an application that runs on an EC2 server that requires an RDS MySQL database and uses AWS Secrets Manager to store the database's credentials. You can create IaC to create all these elements at the same time and link them together to meet the requirements of the application team.

An additional benefit of using IaC is that you can create tools that allow users to create services. For example, you can build a service catalog where an authorized user can fill in a form with their database requirements, and then click a button to automatically deploy a database within AWS that adheres to all of your company's rules and regulations, without having to grant users access directly to the AWS Console. This can reduce the workload on the database administration team.

Let's take a closer look at some of the different automation tools within AWS.

Understanding AWS automation

AWS offers a wide range of automation tools that you can use to achieve different things. Some of the tools specialize in working with application functionality, while some are used with containers. Containers are self-contained modules in which an application can be deployed, along with all the dependencies needed to run it, such as a Java runtime environment. Containers are not covered within the Database Specialty exam, but there is a link about this in the *Further reading* section if you'd like to know more.

First, let's look at a tool we have used previously in this book – the **AWS command-line interface** (AWS CLI).

AWS command-line interface (AWS CLI)

The AWS CLI is a command-line tool you can download from AWS. It runs on Windows, macOS, and most Linux distributions. Once downloaded, installed, and configured, the AWS CLI allows you to interact with AWS services using text-based commands. The CLI is very powerful and can be used to create and administer a wide range of AWS services, including RDS, EC2, and VPC services such as security groups.

The CLI can be used for automation by creating simple scripts that call the CLI the same way each time. You can do this to carry out simple tasks, such as checking the statuses of databases that have been deployed in an account or taking database snapshot backups at a scheduled time. However, for complex deployment tasks or where some parameters may need to change in the command, the AWS CLI can become limited and difficult to maintain. You also need to keep and share versions of your scripts with anyone who needs them. Unless handled carefully, this can result in different people running different versions of the script and a lack of consistency.

Another issue with relying on the AWS CLI for deployment is that it doesn't have any state management. The following steps show why this can cause problems:

1. You create an AWS CLI script to create a new RDS instance in a default VPC that also configures Cloudwatch monitoring and alerting within the script.
2. The script creates a custom parameter group for the RDS instance before creating the RDS instance.
3. You create an error in the parameter group code that stops the parameter group from being deployed.
4. The AWS CLI doesn't know that the parameter group failed to be created, so it tries to create the RDS instance.
5. This fails due to the missing parameter group.
6. The AWS CLI doesn't know that the database has failed to be created, so it tries to create the Cloudwatch monitoring rules, which will fail.

As you can see, you will end up wasting a lot of time and generating a lot of errors due to a failure in the early part of the script. If you are planning to automate deployments, then note that two AWS tools will do the job much more effectively. These are AWS CloudFormation and AWS Code Development Kit. Let's look at AWS CloudFormation first.

AWS CloudFormation

AWS CloudFormation is a tool that's designed for automatically deploying AWS services. CloudFormation is based on IaC concepts and uses templates and code to describe your AWS architecture. CloudFormation can use templates written in JSON and YAML and can understand dependencies, ensuring that the aforementioned situation cannot occur. This is because CloudFormation will understand that the parameter group needs to exist before it tries to create the RDS instance using it. It will also understand that the parameter group cannot be deleted while the RDS is using it, so if a future update to the infrastructure tries to remove the parameter group, CloudFormation will provide an error. CloudFormation calls these connected services Stacks. You can provision, update, alter, and delete in one operation, ensuring that you cannot deploy only a partially working solution.

CloudFormation allows you to create StackSets, which allow you to use the same templates to deploy a stack in multiple regions or multiple accounts. This can rapidly deploy cross-region applications using a standard build.

CloudFormation also allows you to create ChangeSets, which let you test run your proposed changes before you deploy them. This ensures everything works as expected before you modify your live systems. CloudFormation also allows you to add or delete protection to your stacks, which stops others from deleting objects it creates from outside of CloudFormation. This can be very useful for locking down the ability to delete objects to only a small number of authorized accounts.

As you can see, CloudFormation is extremely powerful for deployments, but it does not support ad hoc scripts or individual object-level queries like the AWS CLI does. It also only supports JSON and YAML documents, which do not support code logic statements such as `if`, `else`, or `while`.

The final automation tool you will need to know for the Database Specialty exam is the **AWS Cloud Development Kit** (**AWS CDK**).

AWS Cloud Development Kit (AWS CDK)

The AWS CDK allows you to use a traditional programming language such as Python, Java, or C# to create and interact with AWS services. The AWS CDK works closely with CloudFormation to monitor the state of AWS services and objects to ensure stack integrity is maintained.

The main benefit of using the CDK is that it allows your infrastructure deployments to be written in the same code as the rest of your application. This allows developers to write complex infrastructure creation statements within a language framework they already know and work with, reducing their need to retrain.

CDK also allows you to deploy all your infrastructure along with your application code. You can integrate CDK into the application deployment cycle, which can deploy, upgrade, and configure any required databases while updating the application code. In this way, your developers start to own and control the database deployments for what they need rather than relying on other teams to do this for them. This can increase the speed at which they can test and develop solutions.

Creating infrastructure using CloudFormation

Now, let's create a CloudFormation template that will create a full database stack for us. The template we are going to make and then launch will create and configure the following:

- An RDS MySQL instance
- A parameter group for the database
- Security group rules to let anyone access the database on port 3306

To do this, we are going to use a template from within this book's GitHub repository that can be modified if required. This template contains variables called parameters, which allow us to pass values to the CloudFormation service at runtime. This allows us to reuse the same template and create multiple databases.

Before you begin, download the `Chapter11.yaml` file from GitHub. You will also need to know which VPC to deploy in and which subnets to use. If you have more than one VPC, you will need to ensure you chose the correct ones when creating the stack. If you have do not have a VPC with at least two subnets in different AZs, you will need to create one now manually. You can refer to *Chapter 3, Understanding AWS Infrastructure*, to assist you if needed.

We are going to use both the AWS Console and the AWS CLI to create our database stack to learn how to use them. First, we are going to use the console and look at the graphic designer, which can help us create CloudFormation templates.

Using the CloudFormation console

Follow these steps:

1. Log in to the AWS Console with an account with permissions to create databases and security groups and one that can use CloudFormation.
2. Navigate to the **CloudFormation** service using the main menu.

3. Select **Create stack** from the top right and choose **With new resources (standard)**.

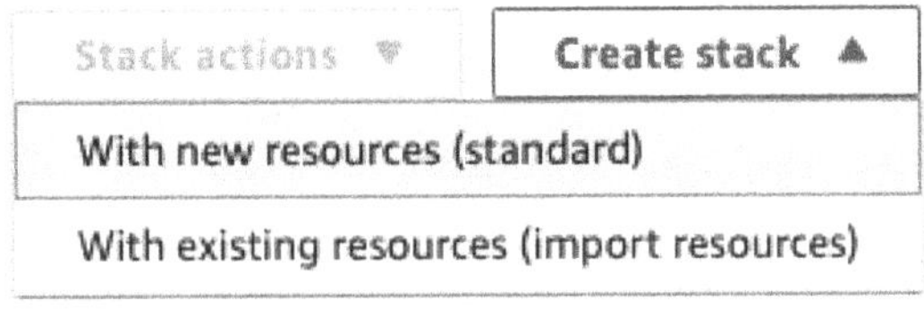

Figure 11.1 – Create stack – part I

4. Select **Template is ready**, and then **Upload a template file**. Click **Choose file** and locate the `Chapter11.yaml` file you downloaded from this book's GitHub repository (`https://github.com/PacktPublishing/AWS-Certified-Database---Specialty-DBS-C01-Certification`).

Create stack

Prerequisite - Prepare template

Prepare template
Every stack is based on a template. A template is a JSON or YAML file that contains configuration information about the AWS resources you want to include in the stack.

Template is ready | Use a sample template | Create template in Designer

Specify template
A template is a JSON or YAML file that describes your stack's resources and properties.

Template source
Selecting a template generates an Amazon S3 URL where it will be stored.

Amazon S3 URL | Upload a template file

Upload a template file
Choose file | No file chosen
JSON or YAML formatted file

View in Designer

Cancel | Next

Figure 11.2 – Create stack – part II

5. Once you have opened the template file, click **View in Designer**. This will open a page that looks similar to the following:

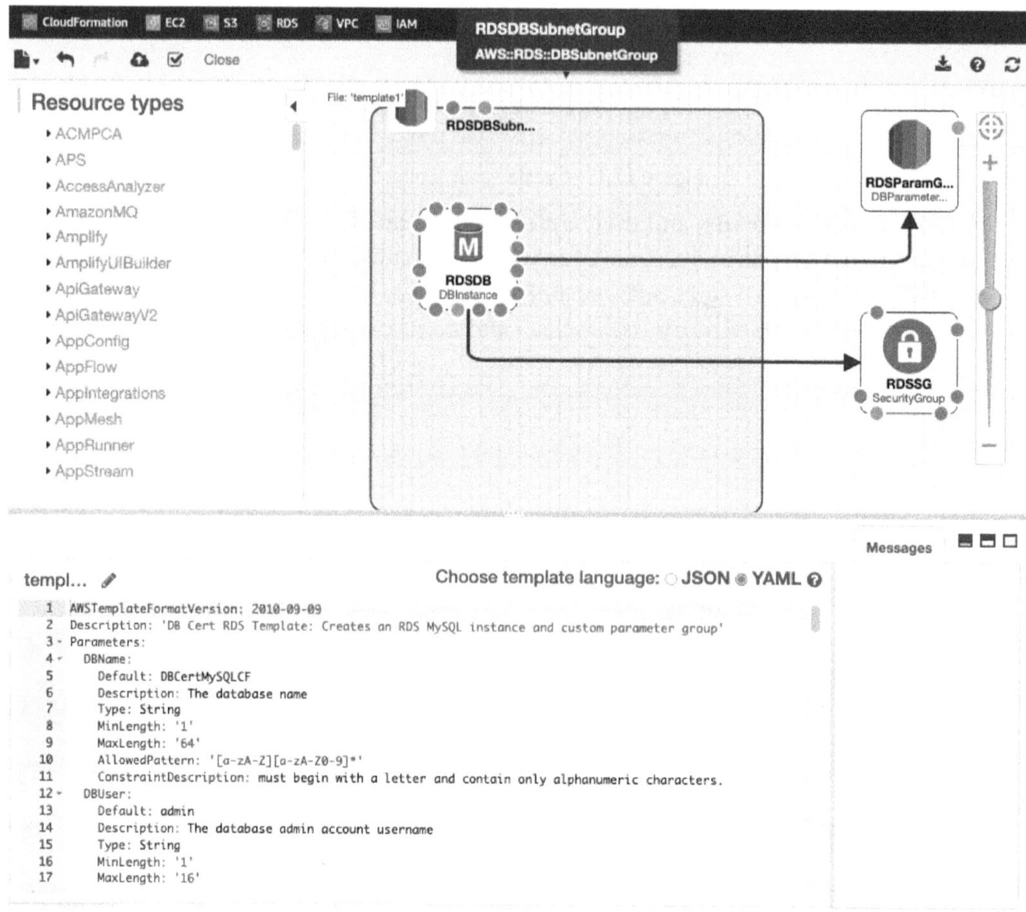

Figure 11.3 – CloudFormation Designer

6. The **Designer** view provides a graphical representation of the stack you are going to create. You can click on each element to view the specific code for each part. You can also simply scroll through the code and try to understand it. See whether you can understand the `!Ref` variables within the code.

7. When you are ready to create the stack, click the cloud logo on the top menu bar and click **Next** on the page that appears.

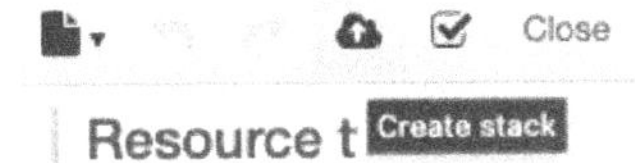

Figure 11.4 – The Create stack logo

8. Fill in the form by selecting the VPC and subnets you need. CloudFormation will show all the available subnets across all VPCs. It does not filter them based on the VPC you select, so ensure that you choose the correct ones.
9. Click **Next** on the next screen to leave all the settings as-is. Then, click **Create stack** to deploy the resources.
10. You will return to a dashboard showing the correct status of your stack. You can watch the stack being deployed by clicking the **Events** tab.

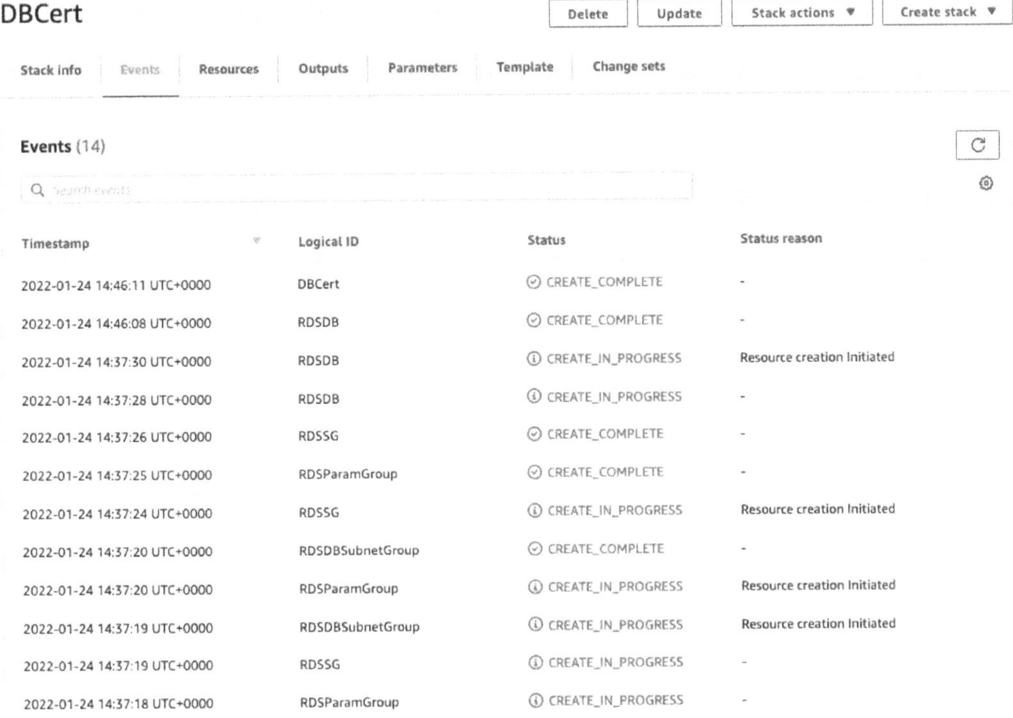

Timestamp	Logical ID	Status	Status reason
2022-01-24 14:46:11 UTC+0000	DBCert	CREATE_COMPLETE	-
2022-01-24 14:46:08 UTC+0000	RDSDB	CREATE_COMPLETE	-
2022-01-24 14:37:30 UTC+0000	RDSDB	CREATE_IN_PROGRESS	Resource creation Initiated
2022-01-24 14:37:28 UTC+0000	RDSDB	CREATE_IN_PROGRESS	-
2022-01-24 14:37:26 UTC+0000	RDSSG	CREATE_COMPLETE	-
2022-01-24 14:37:25 UTC+0000	RDSParamGroup	CREATE_COMPLETE	-
2022-01-24 14:37:24 UTC+0000	RDSSG	CREATE_IN_PROGRESS	Resource creation Initiated
2022-01-24 14:37:20 UTC+0000	RDSDBSubnetGroup	CREATE_COMPLETE	-
2022-01-24 14:37:20 UTC+0000	RDSParamGroup	CREATE_IN_PROGRESS	Resource creation Initiated
2022-01-24 14:37:19 UTC+0000	RDSDBSubnetGroup	CREATE_IN_PROGRESS	Resource creation Initiated
2022-01-24 14:37:19 UTC+0000	RDSSG	CREATE_IN_PROGRESS	-
2022-01-24 14:37:18 UTC+0000	RDSParamGroup	CREATE_IN_PROGRESS	-

Figure 11.5 – Stack events

11. When complete, the stack's status will change to **CREATE_COMPLETE**. If you navigate to the **Output** tab, it will show you the connection string for the database. We created this as an output for the script.
12. You can check the RDS dashboard to see that the new database has been created.
13. Once you have finished reviewing the outputs from the CloudFormation script, you need to delete everything. To do this, navigate to CloudFormation and select the stack you created. Then, click **Delete** at the top right. This will remove all the resources you created in one go.

With that, we've learned how to use the AWS Console to deploy a CloudFormation stack, but for true automation, we need to use the command line to avoid having to use a graphical interface. Let's learn how to deploy the same CloudFormation template via the AWS CLI.

Using the CloudFormation AWS CLI

For this lab, you will need to have downloaded and configured the AWS CLI with your account's access keys and secret key. If you have not done so, please refer to the *Technical requirements* section. We are going to use the AWS CLI to create the same CloudFormation stack we created using the AWS Console. Let's get started:

1. Let's try to create the stack in the same way we did previously and let CloudFormation prompt us for the necessary parameters, such as `DBName`, `Password`, and `VPC`, when we run the code. Open your command-line tool (Command Prompt on Windows or Terminal on Mac/Linux), navigate to the folder that contains the YAML file you downloaded, and enter the following code:

```
aws cloudformation create-stack --stack-name DBCertCLI
--template-body file://./Chapter11.yaml
```

   You will receive an error similar to the following:

```
An error occurred (ValidationError) when calling
the CreateStack operation: Parameters: [DBPassword,
PrivateSubnet02, VPCID, PrivateSubnet01] must have values
```

2. Unlike the Console, when we use the AWS CLI to run CloudFormation commands, we must pass all the values within the initial command. Obtain the VPC and Subnet IDs that you want to use. Modify the code by adding the required parameters. Note that you won't be prompted for the `DBUserName` parameter. This is because this parameter has a default of *admin*, which will be used if we don't provide a value to override it. You will need to change the `DBName` parameter so that we do not clash with the existing database that was created via the Console.

3. Your command should now look as follows (your values will be different for the VPC and Subnet IDs):

```
aws cloudformation create-stack --stack-name DBCertCLI
--template-body file://./Chapter11.yaml --parameters
ParameterKey=DBName,ParameterValue=DBCertCLI
ParameterKey=DBPassword,ParameterValue=Password1 Paramete
rKey=VPCID,ParameterValue=vpc-4fcc2634 ParameterKey=Priva
teSubnet01,ParameterValue=subnet-b9876d88 ParameterKey=Pr
ivateSubnet02,ParameterValue=subnet-68bca225
```

You will receive `StackId` as output to let you know that the stack is being created:

```
{
    "StackId": "arn:aws:cloudformation:us-east-
1:254711704212:stack/DBCertCLI/052b5c40-7d31-11ec-aa90-
0e68693b1117"
}
```

4. You can monitor the stack creation process by using the following command and entering your `--stack-name`:

```
aws cloudformation describe-stacks --stack-name DBCertCLI
```

You will see an output similar to the following:

```
{
    "Stacks": [
        {
            "StackId": "arn:aws:cloudformation:us-east-
1:254711704212:stack/DBCertCLI/052b5c40-7d31-11ec-aa90-
0e68693b1117",
            "StackName": "DBCertCLI",
            ...
            "StackStatus": "CREATE_COMPLETE",
            ...
}
```

When `StackStatus` is `CREATE_COMPLETE`, the database will be deployed.

5. To delete the stack, you can run a `delete` command from the CLI:

```
aws cloudformation delete-stack --stack-name DBCertCLI
```

   With that, you can see how easy it would be to accidentally delete the wrong stack. CloudFormation has two protection mechanisms you can set. The first is the *termination protection* mechanism, which stops anyone from deleting a stack. To delete a stack, you will need to switch this off. This is strongly recommended for any production system. Then, there's the *deletion policy*, which allows you to add a flag to your resources so that if the stack is deleted, the resources are not.

So far, we've learned how to use both the AWS Console and the AWS CLI to create and delete CloudFormation stacks. We've also learned how to enable termination protection to stop stacks from being accidentally deleted. Now, let's learn about two AWS services that are used to process data and can help automate database-level tasks, starting with AWS Glue.

AWS Glue

AWS Glue is a fully managed, serverless data integration and ETL service. It can extract, manipulate, and transform data from a wide range of sources, allowing you to create accurate data models that can be imported into a database, loaded into an analytics platform, or used for machine learning models.

AWS Glue can be controlled using both the Console and CLI commands to allow you to configure automated data handling and data loading into your databases.

There are three components that AWS Glue uses:

- **AWS Glue Data Catalog**: This is a central repository that holds information about your data. It acts as an index to your schema and data stores, which helps control your ETL jobs.
- **Job Scheduling System**: This is a highly customizable scheduler. It can handle not only time-based scheduling but also contains options to allow it to watch for new files or new data to be processed, as well as event-driven scheduling.

- **ETL Engine**: AWS Glue's ETL engine is the component that handles the actual data extraction, transformation, and loading. This is where you write the ETL code. AWS Glue supports the Python and Scala languages. You can use a GUI tool to write code for you that you can then manually customize.

AWS Glue offers a lot of benefits compared to trying to use external tools or manually creating ETL scripts, but it also has some restrictions that you'll need to know for the Database Specialty exam. Let's look at some of the benefits and limitations of using AWS Glue:

- The following are the benefits:
  - **Pay-as-you-go**: You only need to pay for what you use. There are no long-term contracts and costs are only occurred while AWS Glue is running.
  - **Scheduling**: AWS Glue lets you create complex custom schedules with multiple rules and event handling.
  - **GUI**: Using a GUI to assist with the creation of ETL code can allow non-developers to create powerful ETL jobs and functionality.
  - **Fully managed**: AWS Glue is a serverless and fully managed service. AWS takes responsibility for the infrastructure that's running the service, allowing you to focus directly on the ETL code.
- The following are the limitations:
  - **Complex**: AWS Glue offers so many customizations that new users may struggle to fully understand the platform and options that are available.
  - **Language support**: You are only able to use either Python or Scala to write ETL jobs.
  - **AWS only**: AWS Glue is only able to integrate with other AWS services; it cannot integrate with on-premises or non-AWS systems.

A common use case for AWS Glue is to retrieve data from an RDS database and a group of CSV files within S3. AWS Glue then processes the data to remove "bad records" and merge all the data into a combined dataset that is then pushed to an analytics platform such as Amazon Athena or Amazon EMR (a big data analytics tool). The data flow may look like this:

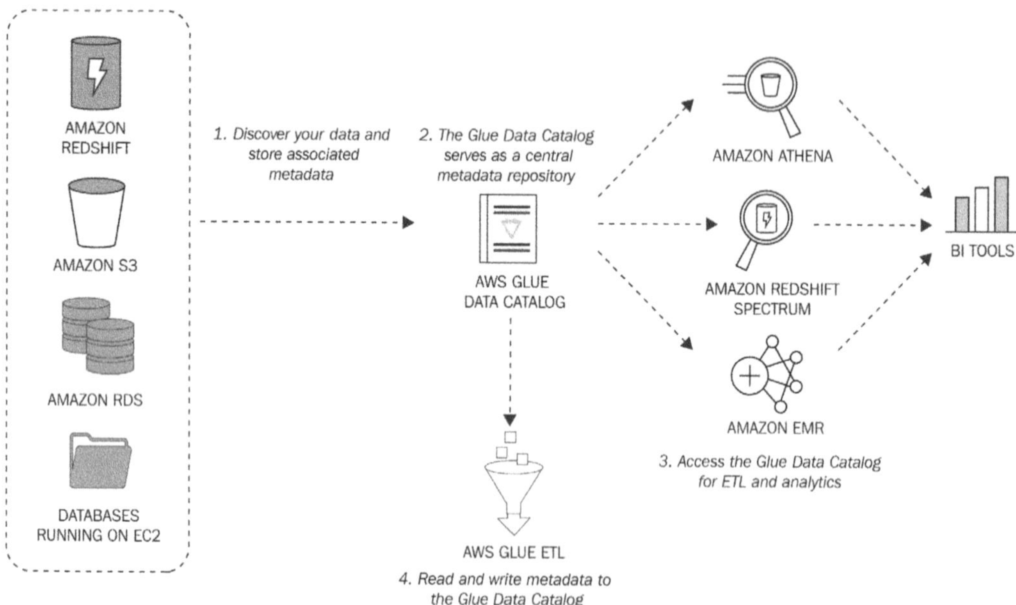

Figure 11.6 – AWS Glue data flow

To set up an AWS Glue job, you must create a crawler. This will be the ETL job itself and will be responsible for locating, extracting, and analyzing the data while following the rules you have defined. The crawler creates the necessary metadata, which can be consumed by other services such as Amazon Athena to allow them to view and process the data. The metadata that is created makes the data appear as if it is a database table and it can be queried using standard SQL. The following screenshot shows an AWS Glue table based on a sample dataset of flight details:

Schema

Showing: 1 - 65 of 65

	Column name	Data type	Partition key	Comment
1	year	bigint		
2	quarter	bigint		
3	month	bigint		
4	day_of_month	bigint		
5	day_of_week	bigint		
6	fl_date	string		
7	unique_carrier	string		
8	airline_id	bigint		
9	carrier	string		
10	tail_num	string		
11	fl_num	bigint		
12	origin_airport_id	bigint		
13	origin_airport_seq_id	bigint		
14	origin_city_market_id	bigint		
15	origin	string		
16	origin_city_name	string		
17	origin_state_abr	string		
18	origin_state_fips	bigint		
19	origin_state_nm	string		
20	origin_wac	bigint		

Figure 11.7 – AWS Glue schema

Note that the crawler has only created a metadata view; no actual data is stored at this time. AWS Glue is an interface that allows you to query data from other sources but it does not move or migrate any data – the data stays in its original location unless you use another tool such as Amazon Athena to move it.

You can use AWS Glue to partition and index your data. This can greatly speed up the performance of queries against it. AWS Glue will automatically find partitions within the data. For example, if you load data in monthly files, it will create a monthly partition. Indexes can also be created on the columns you will use for querying to improve the performance.

AWS Glue only supports datasets within the same region. To use cross-region data, you need to create a NAT gateway to allow AWS Glue to access the internet, which can be considered a security risk. However, AWS Glue does support cross-account access via the usage of resource policies, which are IAM-based.

With that, we've learned how AWS Glue works to create a view of our data that can be used by other services to query data in a wide range of locations as if they were database tables. Now, let's look at one of the tools that ingests AWS Glue metadata and allows us to query the actual data: Amazon Athena.

Amazon Athena

Amazon Athena is a serverless, data querying service. It is designed to allow you to run queries against data stored within an AWS S3 bucket without needing to import it into a database first. Athena uses a SQL programming language called Presto, which supports common SQL syntax such as `joins` and `where` clauses. Athena can connect to data within an S3 bucket on its own, or it can use a schema that's been created by AWS Glue. If you do not use AWS Glue, then Athena cannot use indexes or partitions to help speed up your queries, so Athena without Glue is only suitable for smaller datasets.

Athena offers a lot of benefits around querying data without you having to import it into a database first, but it also has some restrictions that you'll need to know for the Database Specialty exam. Let's look at some of the benefits and limitations of using Amazon Athena:

- The following are the benefits:
  - **Uses SQL**: You can use SQL syntax to run the queries. This is a commonly used language by database developers, so they will not need to learn a new language.
  - **Serverless and fully managed**: The infrastructure is fully managed by AWS, allowing you to focus on your data querying rather than worrying about patching or server provisioning.
  - **Performance**: The Presto SQL language offers parallelism for larger datasets.
  - **Pay-as-you-go**: You are only charged for what you use, based on the amount of data you query.

- The following are the limitations:
  - **Few data controls**: Athena cannot create indexes, which can cause larger queries to perform poorly.
  - **Code objects**: Athena cannot use stored procedures, functions, or triggers.
  - **Table names**: You cannot read data from a table whose name starts with an underscore.
  - **No S3 Glacier**: Athena cannot query data stored within S3 Glacier or S3 Deep Glacier Archive.

Athena supports both structured and unstructured data types. It can query files stored in CSV, JSON, **Optimized Row Columnar** (**ORC**), Apache Parquet, and Apache Avro format. It can also read files that are zipped using GZIP, LZO, Zlib, or Snappy without having to extract them first.

Due to some of the limitations around indexing and partitioning data, Amazon Athena is commonly used in conjunction with AWS Glue to form a complete ETL and querying tool.

Now, let's learn how to create an AWS Glue crawler of some sample data files in S3 before using Amazon Athena to run some queries against it.

Querying data within an S3 bucket using AWS Glue and Amazon Athena

In this hands-on lab, we are going to use some public sample flight data that is stored within a public S3 bucket to create an AWS Glue table. Then, we are going to run queries against that AWS Glue table to find out some flight information. Let's get started:

1. Log in to the AWS Console and navigate to **AWS Glue**.
2. Click on **Crawlers** from the main left-hand menu and then click **Add crawler**.
3. Enter `DBCertCrawler` for **Crawler name** and click **Next**.

4. Leave all the defaults on the **Specify crawler source** `type` page as-is:

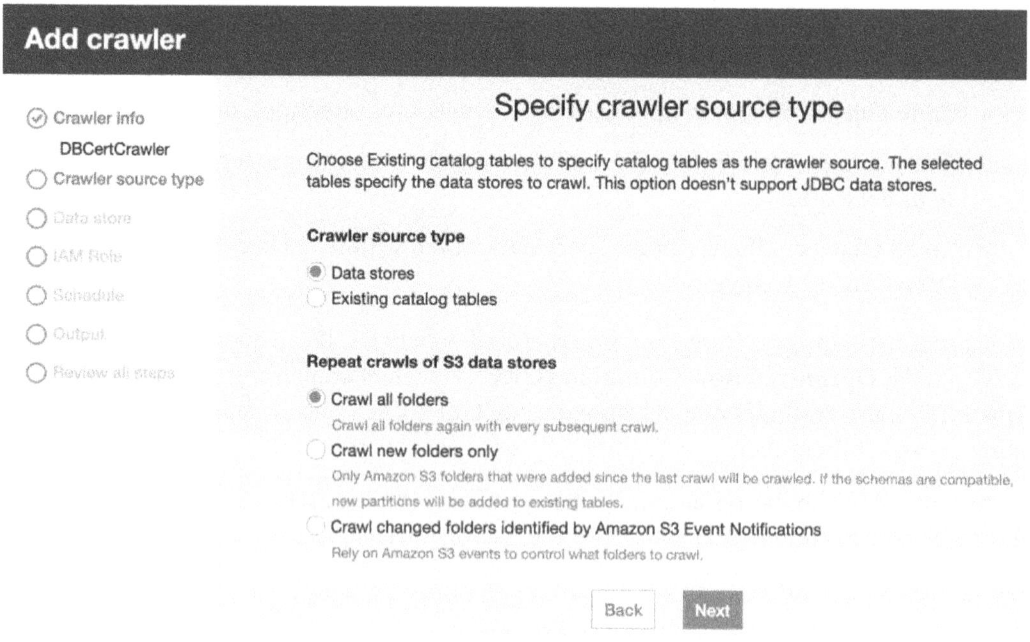

Figure 11.8 – Specify crawler source type

5. On the next page, leave the data source as **S3** and click **Add connection**. Complete the popup by using the following details:

    A. **Name**: `DBCertFlight`

    B. **Include path**: `s3://athena-examples/flight/`

    The following screenshot shows how the form should be completed:

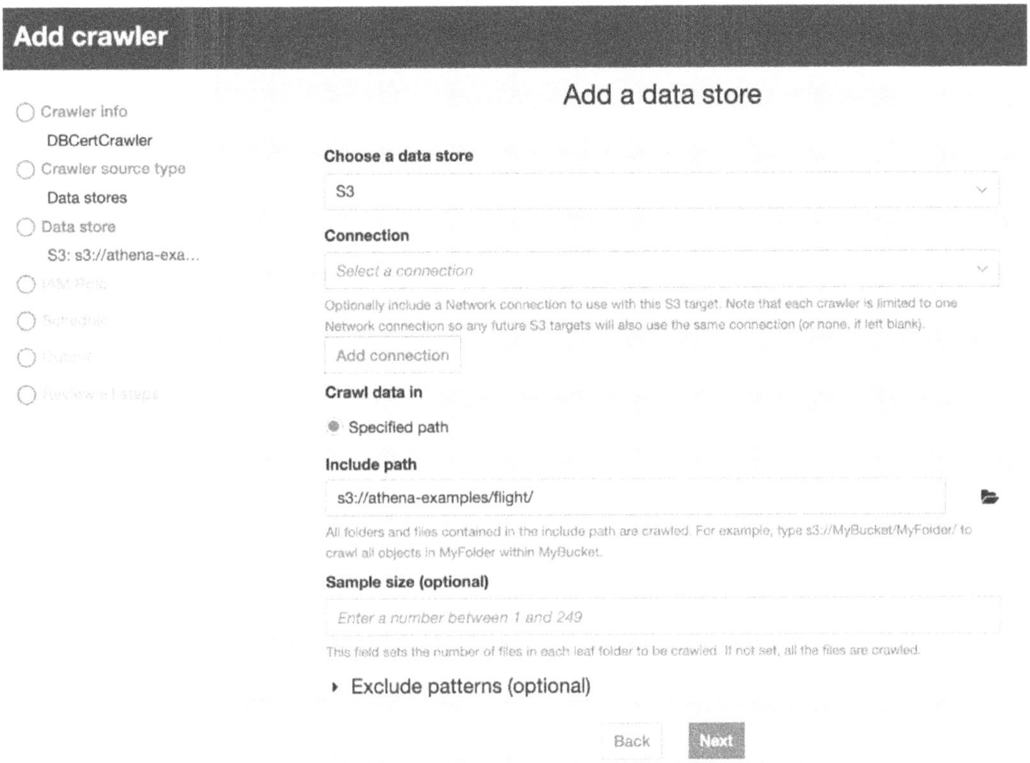

Figure 11.9 – Add a data store

Click **Next**.

6. Select **No** and click **Next** on the **Add another data store** page.
7. Enter `DBCertGlue` for **IAM role** and click **Next**.
8. Leave **Frequency** set to **Run on demand** and click **Next**.

   Click **Add database** and set **Database name** to `dbcertflight`. Then, click **Create**.

   Click **Next**.
9. Click **Finish** to create the table.
10. You will be taken back to the **Crawlers** dashboard. At the top of the screen, you will see the following message:

Crawler **DBCertCrawler** was created to run on demand. Run it now?

Figure 11.10 – Run it now?

Click **Run it now?**.

11. Let the crawler run. It will take around 1 minute to complete. When its status is **Ready**, click **Tables** from the left-hand menu. You will see that four new tables have been created. Click **avro**.
12. You will be able to see the schema that AWS Glue has created for us based on the **avro** file in S3. We can now use Athena to query it.
13. Navigate to **Amazon Athena** from the main menu.
14. Click on **Data sources** from the left-hand menu. You should see a data source called **AwsDataCatalog**. Upon clicking this, you will see the `dbcertflight` database we created in AWS Glue.
15. Click **Query editor** in the left-hand menu. Check that `AwsDataCatalog` has been selected for **Data Source** and choose `dbcertflight` from the **Database** dropdown.

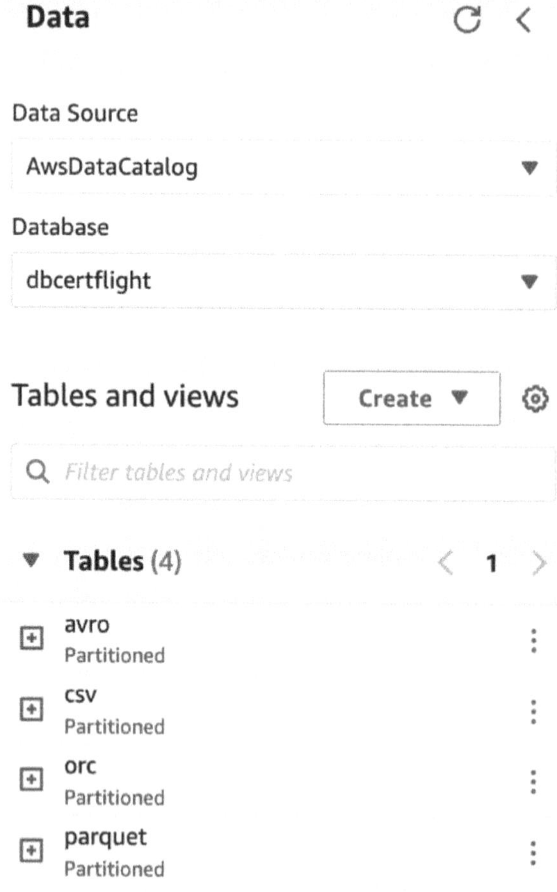

Figure 11.11 – Amazon Athena Query editor setup

16. Before we can run a query, we need to set up an S3 bucket for our query results. Click the **Settings** tab and then click **Manage**.
17. Enter an S3 bucket path in the box. You can also **Browse S3** to find a suitable bucket if needed. Once you have chosen your S3 bucket, click **Save**.
18. Go back to the **Editor** tab so that we can run our SQL queries. If you expand the `avro` table by clicking the (+) symbol next to it, you will see all the columns that you can query. Enter the following query into the box to find all the flights that were delayed by more than 15 minutes:

```
SELECT *
FROM avro
WHERE depdelay > 15;
```

This query will take around 90 seconds to complete as it's running a query against a GB dataset. When complete, you will see an output similar to the following:

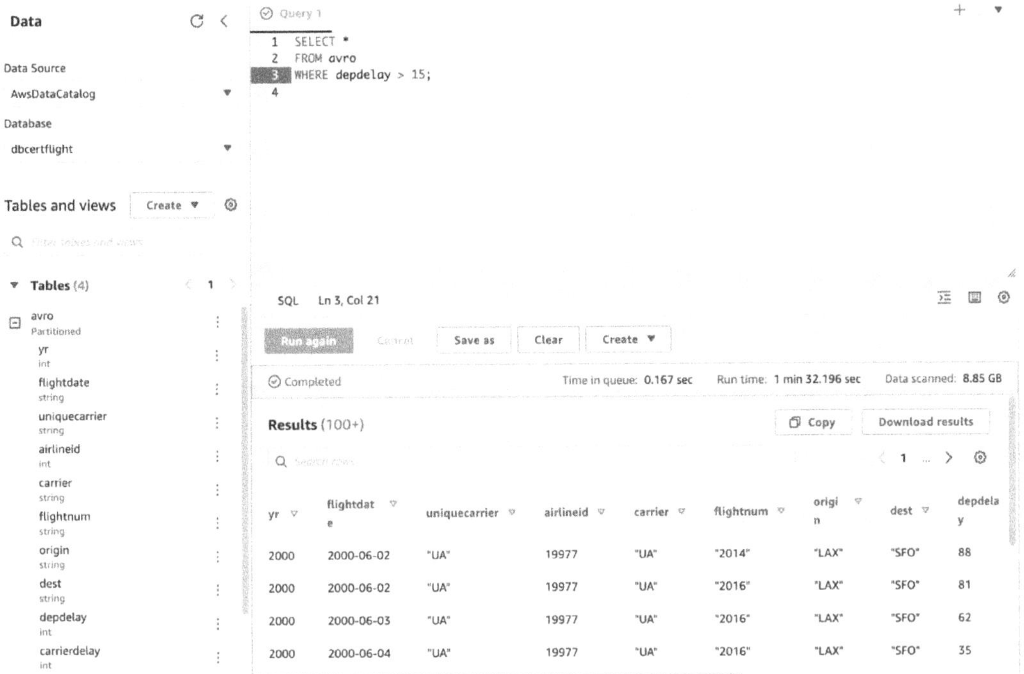

Figure 11.12 – Athena query output

Now, you can run other queries to learn more about querying with Athena and any SQL limitations.

19. Athena saves all the query output to the S3 bucket you specified earlier. If you wish, you can navigate to S3 to find the output files. The output files can now be used by another service if you wish, such as a graphical tool such as AWS Quicksight, but that is beyond the scope of this lab.

That completes the hands-on lab for AWS Glue and Amazon Athena. First, we created an AWS Glue table based on flight data stored in an S3 bucket and then we connected Athena to this Glue table to allow us to run SQL queries against it.

Now, let's summarize what we've learned in this chapter.

Summary

In this chapter, we learned about three different tools that are commonly used with AWS to automate infrastructure creation and administration – that is, the AWS CLI, CloudFormation, and CDK. Then, we learned how to automate how to load and handle data from S3 using AWS Glue and Amazon Athena.

Regarding automation, we learned how to create a CloudFormation stack using YAML or JSON templates and how to launch those stacks using both the AWS Console and the AWS CLI. We learned how we can use parameters within our stacks to allow the same code to be reused to create a controlled and automated method to create databases.

We finished this chapter by learning how to create an ETL job using AWS Glue and how to use Amazon Athena to query the data that's held within S3 without having to import it into a database first.

In the next chapter, we are going to learn about database security. We came across a few different database security tools and features earlier in this book, but now, we are going to look at the best practices for deploying secure and well-architected databases within AWS Cloud in more depth.

Cheat sheet

This cheat sheet summarizes the key points from this chapter:

- You can use a variety of tools to automate your AWS processes by using the AWS CLI, CloudFormation, and the CDK, depending on the use case.
- The AWS CLI is well suited for running creation tasks or for obtaining the status and information about your AWS infrastructure and services.

- CloudFormation is used to create stacks. Stacks are groups of AWS components that should be deployed together. They can be used to create a full application stack containing a VPC, security groups, EC2 servers, RDS databases, and almost all other AWS services.
- CloudFormation can offer deletion protection to stop someone from accidentally deleting a stack and its components.
- AWS Glue is used to create a metadata schema of a wide variety of data sources, such as CSV files within S3 or Amazon Redshift tables. It can also be used to create more complex ETL jobs by adding data transformation rules.
- AWS Glue supports both partitioned data and indexes.
- AWS Glue uses either Python or Scala to write ETL jobs.
- Amazon Athena is used to query data within an S3 bucket without you having to import it first.
- Amazon Athena uses the Presto language for querying, which is a SQL-compliant language.
- Amazon Athena saves all output to an S3 bucket that can be used by other tools, including graphical analytics tools such as AWS Quicksight.
- Amazon Athena supports cross-region querying.

Review

Now, let's practice a few exam-style questions:

1. Amazon Athena is being used by a large company to query data that's being held in S3 buckets in the `eu-central-1` and `eu-west-1` regions. The company wants to use Athena in `eu-west-1` to query data from Amazon S3 in both regions. The solution must be as low-cost as possible.

   What is the best solution?

   A. Enable S3 cross-region replication from `eu-central-1` to `eu-west-1`. Run the AWS Glue crawler in `eu-west-1` to create the AWS Glue Data Catalog and run Athena queries.

   B. Use AWS DMS to migrate the AWS Glue Data Catalog from `eu-central-1` to `eu-west-1`. Run Athena queries in `eu-west-1`.

C. Update the AWS Glue resource policy's IAM permissions to provide the `eu-central-1` AWS Glue Data Catalog with access to `eu-west-1`. Once the catalog in `eu-west-1` has access to the catalog in `eu-central-1`, run Athena queries in `eu-west-1`.

D. Run the AWS Glue crawler in `eu-west-1` to catalog the datasets in all regions. Once the data has been crawled, run Athena queries in `eu-west-1`.

2. You are working with a company to help analyze a large amount of data held in JSON format logs. These logs are uploaded hourly to an S3 bucket.

   Which is the most cost-effective and efficient way to analyze this data?

   A. Import the data into an RDS MySQL database and run SQL queries against it.

   B. Import the data into Redshift and run SQL queries against it.

   C. Use Amazon Athena to query the data directly from S3.

   D. Create an EC2 instance to hold the data and use Bash scripting to retrieve the data you require.

3. A company uploads multiple 110 GB `.gzip` files to S3 Glacier each month that contain financial records. The company needs to query the data in the file for an audit request. Which is the most cost-effective method you can use?

   A. Query the data using Amazon Athena directly from S3 Glacier.

   B. Temporarily move the data into S3 and use Amazon Athena to query it.

   C. Load the data into DynamoDB to run the queries.

   D. Move the data into S3 and use Amazon Redshift Spectrum to query it.

4. Your company uses CloudFormation to create AWS resources. One morning when you arrive at work, you discover that a production RDS database has been deleted when someone accidentally deleted a CloudFormation stack.

   What sensible steps can you take to stop this from happening again? (Choose 2)

   A. Revoke permissions to CloudFormation from all users.

   B. Enable deletion protection on all production CloudFormation stacks.

   C. Enable termination protection on all production CloudFormation stacks.

   D. Revoke permissions to delete any RDS instances from all users.

   E. Enable deletion protection on the production RDS resources within the stack.

5. A company wants to create a method to quickly create and then delete test environments to support their development teams. Which is the best solution?

    A. Use CloudFormation templates to provision the entire stack.

    B. Use IAM policies to create templates that can be used to provision the required resources.

    C. Use AutoScaling groups to allow the infrastructure to grow when required.

    D. Create custom scripts using the AWS CLI to create and delete resources when required.

Further reading

For more information on the topics that were covered in this chapter, please refer to the following resources:

- *Complete 2020 AWS DevOps Bootcamp for Beginners*: `https://subscription.packtpub.com/video/cloud_and_networking/9781800566132/p1/video1_1/introduction`
- *Actionable Insights with Amazon Quicksight*: `https://subscription.packtpub.com/book/data/9781801079297/1`
- *Mastering AWS CloudFormation*: `https://subscription.packtpub.com/book/cloud_&_networking/9781789130935/12/ch12lvl1sec82/introducing-aws-cdk`

12
AWS Database Security

Database security is a critical part of both the AWS Database Specialty exam and the work that an AWS DBA carries out daily. Database security focuses on how to restrict access to your databases and how to audit it efficiently, how to encrypt your data both in transit and at rest to stop unauthorized access to the data, and how to use other AWS services, such as Key Management Service and Secrets Manager, to protect passwords and login credentials. There will be several questions about database security in the AWS Database Specialty exam, so this is an important chapter if you wish to apply database security to a wide range of case studies.

In this chapter, we're going to cover the following main topics:

- Database encryption
- Working with RDS encryption
- Implementing database and VPC access controls
- Auditing databases
- Configuring AWS Key Management Service and Secrets Manager

Let's start by looking at database encryption, a topic we have already covered briefly in this book.

Technical requirements

For this chapter, you will need an AWS account with root access. Not everything we will do in this chapter may be available in the free tier, which means it may cost you a small amount to follow the hands-on sections. You will also require **command-line interface** (**CLI**) AWS access. The AWS guide at `https://docs.aws.amazon.com/cli/latest/userguide/cli-chap-configure.html` explains the steps you must follow, but I will summarize them here:

1. Create an AWS account if you have not already done so.
2. Download the latest version of the AWS CLI from `https://docs.aws.amazon.com/cli/latest/userguide/welcome-versions.html#welcome-versions-v2`.
3. Create an admin user at `https://docs.aws.amazon.com/IAM/latest/UserGuide/id_credentials_access-keys.html`.
4. Create an access key for your administration user: `https://docs.aws.amazon.com/IAM/latest/UserGuide/getting-started_create-admin-group.html#getting-started_create-admin-group-cli`.
5. Run the `aws configure` command to set up a profile for your user: `https://docs.aws.amazon.com/cli/latest/userguide/cli-configure-quickstart.html#cli-configure-quickstart-creds`.

You will also need a VPC that meets the minimum requirements for an RDS instance: `https://docs.aws.amazon.com/AmazonRDS/latest/UserGuide/USER_VPC.WorkingWithRDSInstanceinaVPC.html`. If you followed the steps in *Chapter 3, Understanding AWS Infrastructure*, you will already have a VPC that meets these requirements.

Database encryption

Encryption is when the data that's stored or transmitted is encoded. Encoded means that it is changed from its original values into something meaningless without the means to decode it again. The decoding tool is called a key. An encryption key is a long string of alphanumeric characters that, when used alongside a mathematical function called an algorithm, allows your data to be encrypted and decrypted. Only applications or users with access to the decryption key will be able to read the data.

Data that's stored on disks is called **data at rest**. Data at rest within a managed AWS database, such as RDS, DynamoDB, DocumentDB, Neptune, and Timestream, can be encrypted using AES-256 encryption. Data that passes from the client or application to the database is called **data in transit**. Data in transit can be encrypted using SSL/TLS cryptography. Data at rest needs to be protected from someone gaining access to the instance or server your database is running on. If someone gains access to this server, they can retrieve the data that's stored there and if that isn't encrypted, it can be read without using any special tools. For data in transit, you must use encryption to stop someone from reading the data as it is sent from the database to the application. For the exam, you will not need to know about the different encryption standards, but you may need to know about the types that are commonly used.

Now, let's look at the different key options within AWS and how those keys are stored.

AWS Key Management Service (KMS)

Key Management Service (**KMS**) is a tool that's used to securely store any encryption keys that are being used in your AWS account. Two types of keys can be used within AWS databases:

- **AWS managed keys**: These keys are created by AWS when needed by a customer and stored within the AWS KMS service.
- **Customer-managed keys**: These keys are provided by the customer and created externally to AWS. This offers you a way to follow any cryptographic standards that are required by your organization. These keys are loaded into KMS to allow them to be used by AWS services.

AWS KMS creates and uses symmetric keys. This means that the same key is used to encrypt and decrypt your data. Anyone with access to the key can decrypt the information, so keeping the key safe and secure is critical.

AWS KMS keys are regional, which means a key can only be used in the same region where it was created. This can have an impact on cross-region databases or read replicas, as we will discuss in the next section.

Managing RDS encryption

Encryption in RDS is enabled by default when you create an instance, but you can opt to turn it off at instance creation time. Once the instance has been created, you can no longer change the encryption settings or change the encryption key. If you create an RDS instance without encryption and wish to add it at a later stage, you need to migrate to a new instance. Additionally, you cannot restore an unencrypted database snapshot or back it up in an encrypted RDS instance. If you want to encrypt an unencrypted RDS instance, then you need to create an encrypted snapshot of your source instance and restore this to the encrypted target. You must use the same key for encrypting the snapshot that you used for the encryption key of the target RDS instance.

If you ever lose the key or access to the key is revoked from an RDS instance, the RDS instance is immediately terminated. Even if you relocate the key or restore the correct privileges to the RDS instance, the only way to recover the data is to restore it from a backup. Therefore, it is critical to always back up any encrypted databases because otherwise, they can become entirely unrecoverable.

Finally, a read replica must use the same encryption key as the primary node if they are running in the same region. You cannot have unencrypted read replicas if the primary is encrypted, or encrypted read replicas if the primary is unencrypted. If you are using cross-region replicas, then the target replica must use a key from within its region, even though this will differ from the primary. When you copy the snapshot to the new region to restore it as the read replica, you can specify the key from the target region for encryption.

Encrypting data in transit

So far, we've looked at how to encrypt data stored on disks, but what about how to secure and encrypt data that's moving between an application and the database? RDS supports the usage of SSL/TLS-based encryption to secure data in transit. Each RDS instance that is provisioned will be configured with an RDS SSL certificate. You need to download, install, and configure the certificate within your application so that this is used to encrypt and decrypt database data. For RDS Oracle, you need to enable Oracle SSL via an **Options** group, which creates a new port for encryption connections.

Now, let's practice some of these encryption techniques in a lab.

Working with RDS encryption

In this lab, we are going to create an RDS instance without encryption and then create an encrypted snapshot to restore in a new instance to enable encryption. Then, we are going to migrate our encrypted database to a different region to learn how to use different keys to encrypt and share snapshots.

Encrypting an existing RDS instance

Let's begin by creating an RDS MySQL instance using the Dev/Test options. We cannot use the free tier here as there is no option to disable encryption. As you should have created several RDS instances by now in this book, these steps will be kept at a high level:

1. Log in to the AWS console or use the AWS CLI to create a free tier RDS MySQL database but disable encryption before creating it. If you use a t3.micro, your costs will be very low.
2. You can also disable **Performance Insights** and **Monitoring** if you wish.

Encryption
Enable encryption
Choose to encrypt the given instance. Master key IDs and aliases appear in the list after they have been created using the AWS Key Management Service console. Info
Performance Insights Info
Enable Performance Insights
Monitoring
Enable Enhanced monitoring
Enabling Enhanced monitoring metrics are useful when you want to see how different processes or threads use the CPU.

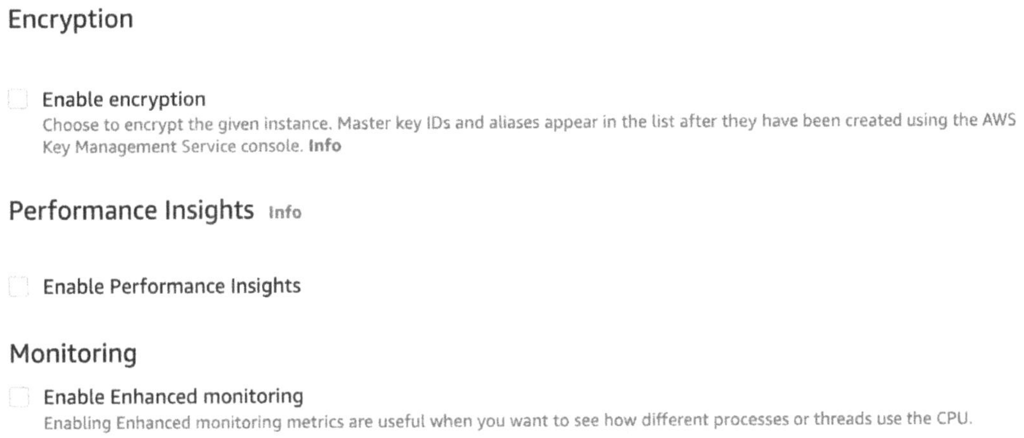

Figure 12.1 – RDS encryption disabled

3. When the database has a status of **Available**, we can take a snapshot. Click the selection circle next to the database you just created and then select **Take a snapshot** from the **Actions** dropdown. Fill in the form and click **Take snapshot**.

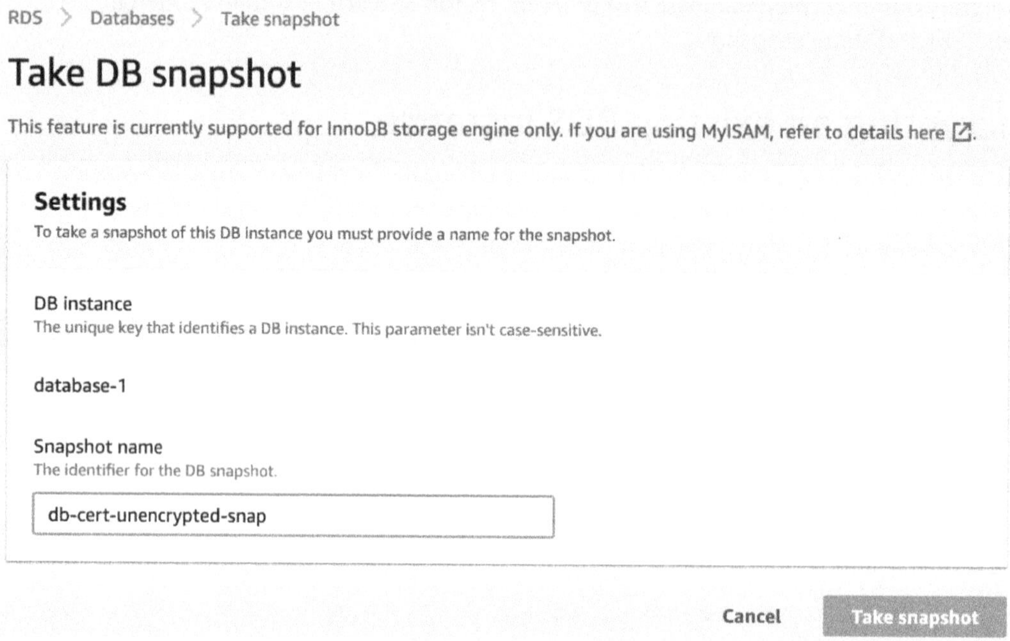

RDS > Databases > Take snapshot

Take DB snapshot

This feature is currently supported for InnoDB storage engine only. If you are using MyISAM, refer to details here.

Settings

To take a snapshot of this DB instance you must provide a name for the snapshot.

DB instance

The unique key that identifies a DB instance. This parameter isn't case-sensitive.

database-1

Snapshot name

The identifier for the DB snapshot.

db-cert-unencrypted-snap

Cancel Take snapshot

Figure 12.2 – Take DB snapshot

4. This will take a few minutes to complete, but if you click the snapshot's name, you can look at its details. Toward the bottom of the page, you will see that **KMS key ID** is set to **None**, confirming that it isn't encrypted.

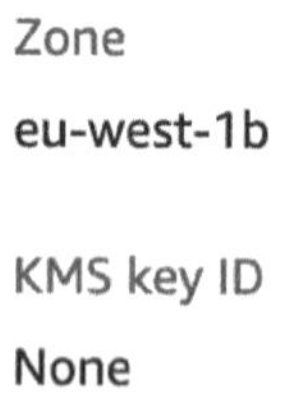

Zone

eu-west-1b

KMS key ID

None

Figure 12.3 – KMS key ID

5. When the snapshot's status is **Available**, we can create an encrypted version of it. Go to the **Snapshots** dashboard and click the checkbox next to the snapshot you created. Expand the **Actions** dropdown and select **Copy snapshot**.
6. Fill in the form while leaving the destination region as the default (we will learn how to use this to create a cross-region database in the next stage of this lab). Tick the **Enable encryption** checkbox and leave the key as the default. Click **Copy snapshot**.
7. It will take a couple of minutes to create the new snapshot. Wait until **Status** is set to **Available**. Then, click the **Actions** dropdown and select **Restore snapshot**.
8. Fill in the RDS creation form with the same details you used previously to minimize costs. You will need to change the database's name to avoid any conflicts. At the bottom of the form, you will see that all the **Encryption** options are grayed out.

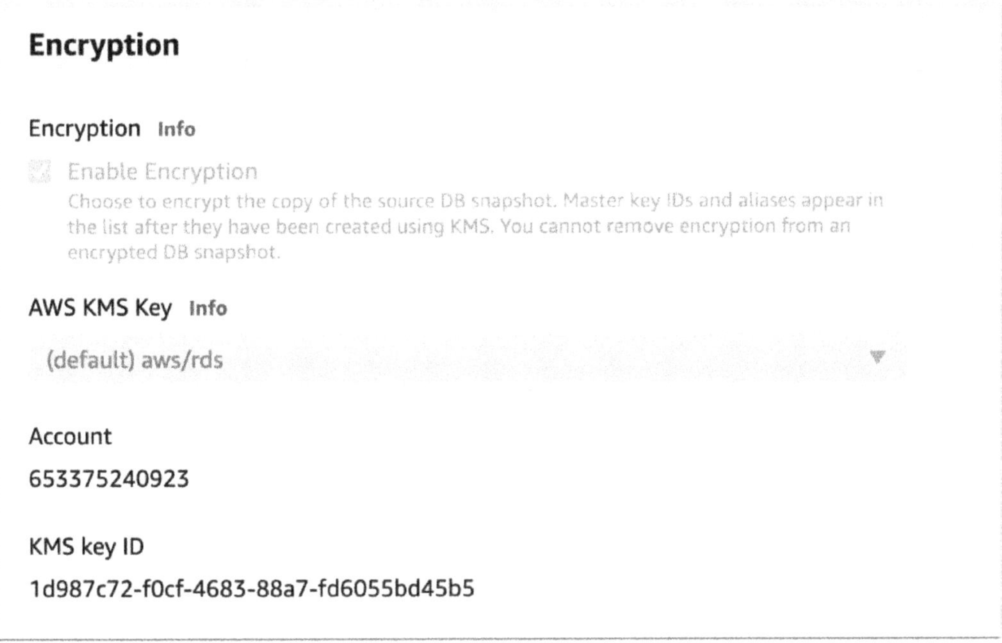

Figure 12.4 – Grayed out encryption options

Click **Restore DB instance**.

9. When the instance has been restored and **Status** is set to **Available**, click the database name you just created and look at the **Configuration** tab.

Instance

Configuration	Instance class	Storage
DB instance ID dbcert-encrypted	Instance class db.t3.micro	Encryption Enabled
Engine version 8.0.23	vCPU 2	AWS KMS key aws/rds
DB name -	RAM 1 GB	Storage type General Purpose SSD (gp2)
License model General Public License	Availability	Storage 20 GiB

Figure 12.5 – The Configuration tab

You'll see that **AWS KMS key** now shows **aws/rds**, meaning that this is now an encrypted instance.

10. Now, you can delete the instances, but do not delete the unencrypted snapshot we created as we will use it in the next section.

With that, you've learned how to encrypt an RDS instance using a snapshot restore. Now, let's learn how to migrate our database to a different region using a snapshot.

Migrating an encrypted database to a different region

Now, let's use a customer-managed key to encrypt and migrate our database to a different region using an encrypted snapshot. Follow these steps:

1. First, we need to create a new customer-managed key with AWS KMS. Navigate to **Key Management Service** and change **Region** to your target destination by using the dropdown at the top right of the screen.
2. Click **Create a key**.
3. Choose **Symmetric** and leave the other options as-is. Click **Next**.

4. Give the key an alias.

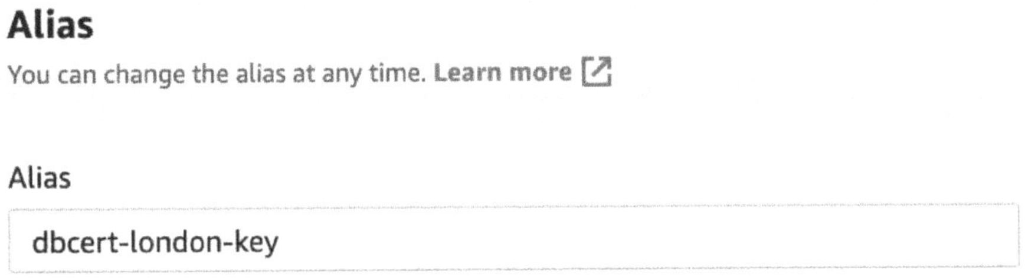

Alias

You can change the alias at any time. **Learn more**

Alias

dbcert-london-key

Figure 12.6 – Alias

5. Change back to your source region.
6. Navigate to the **Snapshot** section under **Amazon RDS** and locate the encrypted snapshot you took earlier.
7. Check the box next to that snapshot and select **Copy snapshot** from the **Action** dropdown.
8. Choose a different region from your current one. On the **Encryption** page, select the **AWS KMS Key** property you created in the target region. If you choose the wrong region, it will not appear.

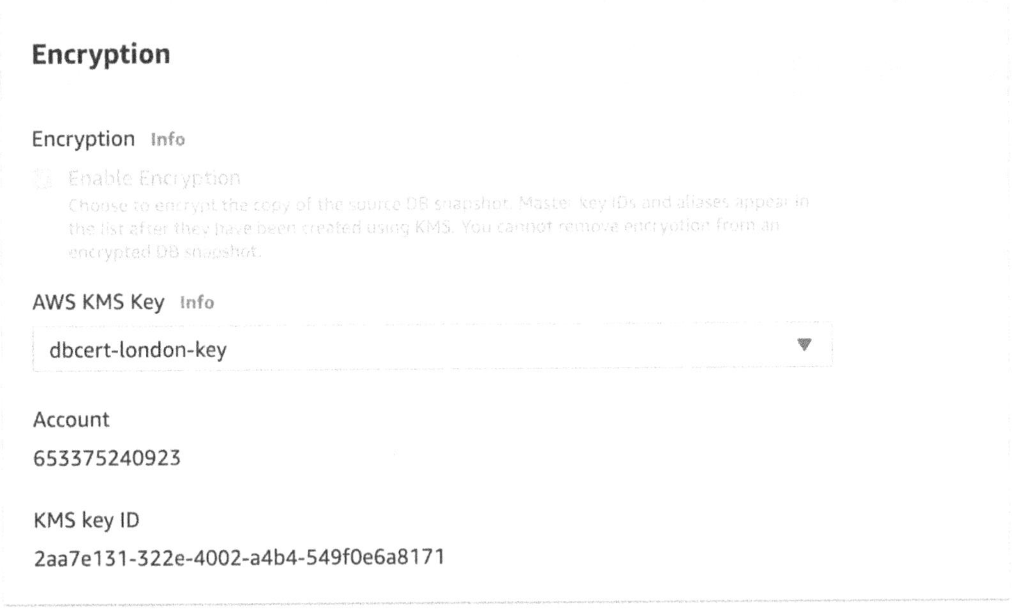

Encryption

Encryption Info

Enable Encryption

Choose to encrypt the copy of the source DB snapshot. Master key IDs and aliases appear in the list after they have been created using KMS. You cannot remove encryption from an encrypted DB snapshot.

AWS KMS Key Info

dbcert-london-key

Account

653375240923

KMS key ID

2aa7e131-322e-4002-a4b4-549f0e6a8171

Figure 12.7 – Encryption options for the snapshot

Click **Copy snapshot**.

You will notice that our **Snapshot** does not appear in this dashboard. This is because snapshots are region-based. Change **Region** to your target to see the snapshot.

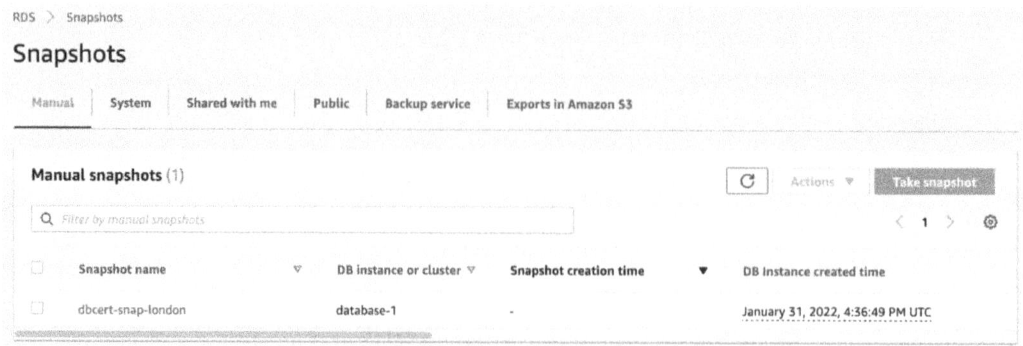

Figure 12.8 – Snapshot dashboard in the target region

9. The snapshot will take a few minutes to create and the **Snapshot creation time** area will update when it is ready. Once the snapshot is ready, you can create a new database by using it in this region.
10. Select **Restore snapshot** from the **Actions** dropdown and create the new database by filling in the form as required. As you are using a new region, you may not have created a VPC there. If that is the case, select **Create a new VPC** from the **Virtual Private Cloud (VPC)** dropdown.
11. Click **Restore DB instance**.

With that, we've learned how to work with KMS and encryption options to encrypt and copy snapshots between regions while maintaining the encryption throughout. The exam will likely feature questions asking you how to encrypt an existing RDS instance or how to move an encrypted snapshot to a new region, so knowing these steps will help you answer correctly.

You can delete the instances in both regions and delete all the snapshots when you're ready to reduce your costs.

Now, let's learn how to use database and VPC access controls to limit who can access our databases.

Implementing database and VPC access controls

All RDS and Aurora databases run within a VPC. As you may recall, a VPC is a section of the AWS Cloud that is secured for your use only. A VPC operates similarly to a data center and can be secured using a variety of security measures, from user accounts to security groups. Databases that do not run within a VPC such as DynamoDB, Timestream, and QLDB use different security controls, such as AWS **Identity and Access Management (IAM)** roles and users, which we will discuss later in this section.

Let's start by learning how to use VPC subnets to keep your databases hidden from the internet.

Subnets and bastion hosts

Subnets are a range of IP addresses that form logical groups within a VPC. There are two types of subnets you can create: public and private. A public subnet is one where the servers and databases within it can reach the public internet and be reached from the internet via an internet gateway. A private subnet is one where the servers and databases within it cannot reach the public internet, nor can they be reached from the internet via an internet gateway.

Most databases are used to support an application, so any connections to the database will come from the application directly and will not come from an external internet connection. Therefore, you are advised to place your databases in a private subnet unless there is a requirement for it to be able to communicate with the public internet. Applications are typically accessed directly from the internet, so they would normally sit within a public subnet. The following diagram shows how you would typically provision an RDS instance and a web server:

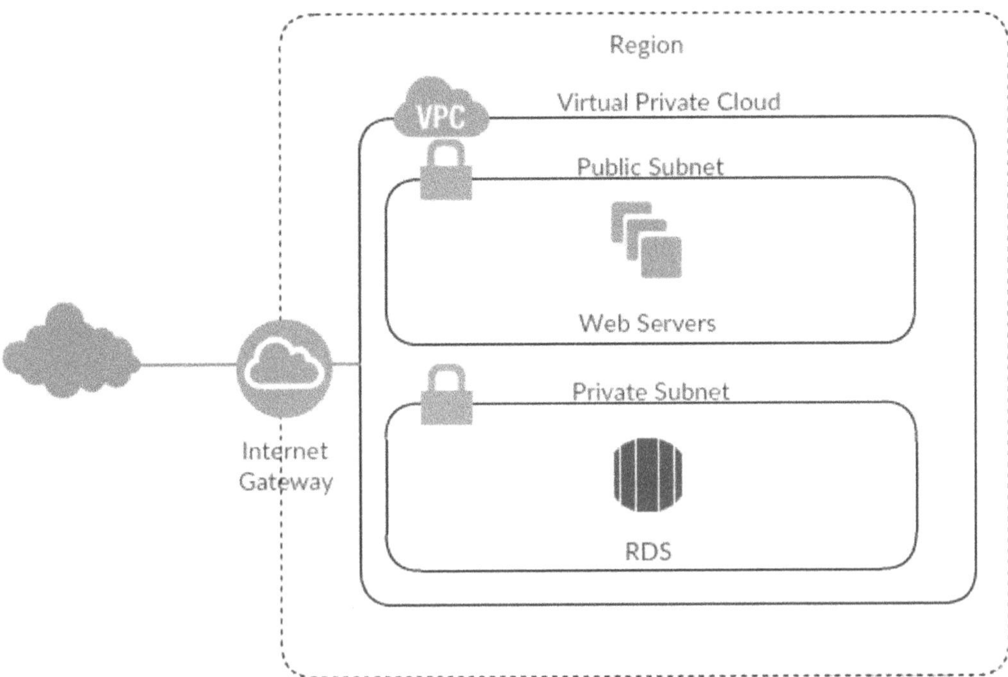

Figure 12.9 – Private and public subnets

This configuration can make it difficult for developers or database administrators to access a database as there will be no route from their laptop that they can use. To solve this problem, many companies use what is called a bastion host or a jump box. A bastion host is an EC2 server that sits in a public subnet that has your company's operational and database access tools installed on it. This server can be accessed from the public internet using secured credentials and is granted access to the database that is within the private VPC. As such, you can create an administrative route to the database that is still highly secured and requires someone with access to the bastion host to be able to use it. This technique is known as reducing the attack surface. By offering only one route or attack vector to the database, you only need to focus on keeping the bastion host secured to ensure the database is protected. You can also rapidly revoke access to the database from the bastion host if this is attacked without having to take your database offline or stop legitimate connections from the application servers. The following diagram shows how to use a bastion host:

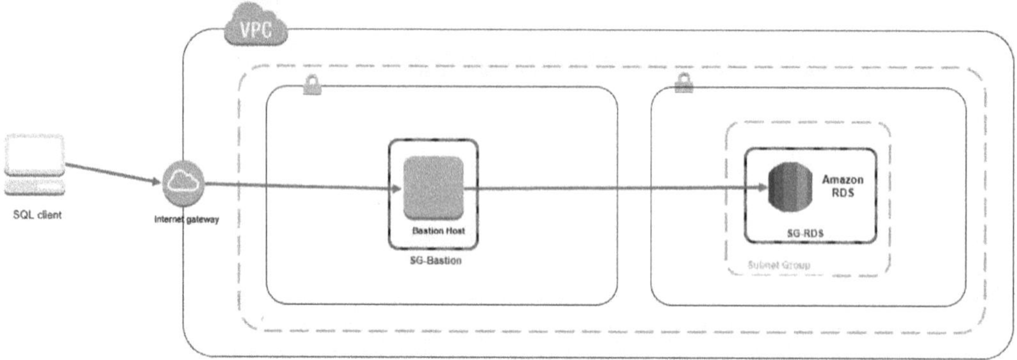

Figure 12.10 – Bastion host

To allow the bastion host to communicate with the database, it must be granted permission through security group rules and **network access control lists (NACLs)**. Let's learn more about how these are used for database security.

Security groups and NACLs

Security groups and NACLs are used to control the ingress and egress of network traffic. They can both be used to restrict access on certain ports, to certain IP addresses, and even to other security groups, allowing for highly customizable controls. We learned about security groups and NACLs in *Chapter 3, Understanding AWS Infrastructure*, so in this chapter, we'll focus on specific configurations for databases.

By default, security groups and NACLs contain no rules for access, which means that everything is blocked. To manage access to your database from only trusted hosts such as the application servers and your bastion host, you need to modify the rules to allow ingress into the RDS security group. A best practice is to always create a new security group for each database and application so that any rule changes only affect that single database.

You can set up security groups and rules to only allow specific routes and ports to be accessible. Your setup should look similar to the following:

Host/DB	Subnet	Security Group	Allows access from	Ports
Bastion	Public	bastion_sg	0.0.0.0/0	22 - SSH, 3389 - RDP
Application	Public	application_sg	bastion_sg	22 - SSH, 3389 - RDP
Application	Public	application_sg	0.0.0.0/0	52255 - custom app port
RDS - PostgreSQL	Private	database_sg	bastion_sg	5432 - PostgreSQL
RDS - PostgreSQL	Private	database_sg	application_sg	5432 - PostgreSQL

Figure 12.11 – Security group configuration

Here, you can see that only your bastion server is publicly accessible (**0.0.0.0/0** means all IPs) and SSH/RDP access to the application server is restricted only to connections coming from the bastion server. However, anyone can connect to the application port, allowing users to connect from the internet. The RDS PostgreSQL database can be reached from the bastion server and the application server on the PostgreSQL port. If possible, you should further restrict bastion and application access to only known IP ranges, such as ones offered by a company or a VPN connection, to remove the requirement to open a bastion up to everyone. However, this can cause management overhead if your IP ranges regularly require access changes.

Security groups can only have *allow* rules; you cannot explicitly *deny* any IP addresses or ports. NACLs can be used to finely control access by explicitly denying access to certain IPs or ports. This can be useful if you become aware of an IP address that is trying to hack into your bastion server. Changing the rules to remove this one IP from the security group would be difficult, but you can add the IP to a *deny* rule within the NACL to resolve this problem. NACLs can also be used to ensure that someone changing a security group by mistake doesn't open your network to attack. Remember that NACLs work at the subnet level and that security groups work at the instance level, so NACLs can be used to secure the entire subnet, regardless of the security group settings.

The exam will likely contain questions focusing on a database being hacked or someone gaining unauthorized access and what steps you should take to secure it in the future, as well as questions about problems with accessing a database after someone has changed a corporation's IP address range or NACL settings.

Security groups, NACLs, and subnets can only be used for databases that reside within a VPC, so they cannot be used for DynamoDB, Timestream, or QLDB. To secure these databases, you must rely on IAM authentication.

IAM authentication

IAM authentication is where you use the AWS Identity and Access Management service to control access to your databases. An IAM user can be mapped to a database-level user to allow you to log in without using a password and simply rely on the IAM user to grant access. Access for the user is still controlled at the database level and only the login is handled by IAM. This means that if you create an IAM user with login privileges in your databases that map to an account called `test` but do not grant the required privileges to log into the `test` database user, then the login will still fail. Equally, if you grant the login privileges, this does not grant full database access to the IAM user as this is still controlled by internal database permissions. Using IAM authentication can be useful if you wish to avoid using passwords that are being stored or sent in plain text, which can be breached. It also allows easier administration of database accounts. For example, you can create a single database account for all DBAs to use, and then grant each DBA access to that account through their own personal IAM user. If a new DBA joins or leaves the team, you can create and remove the new accounts through IAM without needing to change the logins at the database layer. You can grant access to multiple databases to each IAM user as well, and IAM supports the use of wildcards so that you can grant access to all databases (or a subset) within an account in a single statement. This allows you to grant DBAs the correct access to all the databases within your account with minimal manual effort.

Using IAM authentication also offers benefits in terms of auditing. If you rely on database-level accounts, you will need to use database-level auditing to track logins, but if you use IAM authentication, then every login is tracked by Cloudtrail. Let's learn more about this.

Auditing databases

Database auditing can be configured to help you identify unauthorized access to the databases, as well as closely monitor highly sensitive tables to stop them from being tampered with. In AWS, you can use four different tools to comprehensively monitor your database estate:

- **CloudWatch**: You can configure your databases to send their logs to CloudWatch, which acts as a centralized repository.
- **CloudTrail**: This can be used to monitor actions that have been taken by a user or another AWS service that affects your RDS instance. Creating, deleting, or modifying an RDS would be recorded. This also tracks user logins using IAM authentication.
- **Database Activity Stream**: This is only used for RDS Oracle. It sends a record of all audited database changes to an external stream that the DBAs have no access to, thereby improving compliance.
- **Database logs**: As well as the other monitoring tools, RDS gives you access to the standard logs for each database, such as the alert log, monitoring log, and errors logs. You can access them via the console or via an AWS CLI call.

RDS offers a wide range of auditing and monitoring tools by default with minimal additional configuration, but if you need fine-grained auditing where only certain tables or queries are logged, then you will need to install audit plugins via the RDS option groups for your target database. Let's set auditing up for a sample RDS MySQL database.

Enabling auditing for an RDS MySQL database

For this lab, we are going to create (or reuse) an RDS MySQL database. We are going to create some sample tables and then enable auditing before running some test queries to make sure it's all working. As you should have created several RDS instances by now, these steps will be more high-level than in the previous chapters. Let's get started:

1. Log in to the AWS console or gain access via the AWS CLI and create a single-AZ RDS MySQL on the smallest instance class available. Leave all the settings as-is.
2. While you wait for the instance to become available, create a new option group that we can attach to the MySQL instance. Navigate to **RDS Dashboard** and select **Option groups** from the left-hand menu. Click **Create group** at the top right.

3. Fill in the form as follows, ensuring that you match your **Major Engine Version** with the one you used to deploy the RDS MySQL instance. It should be **8.0**.

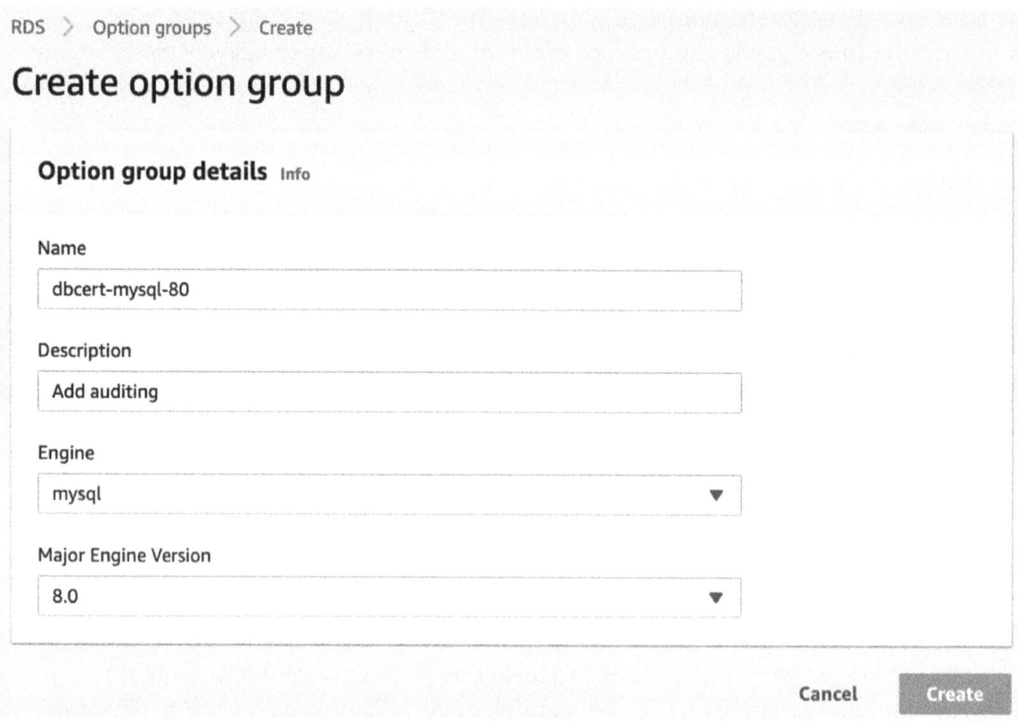

Figure 12.12 – Create option group

Click **Create**.

4. Select your **Option group** by clicking its name. Scroll down until you see the **Options** section. Click **Add option**:

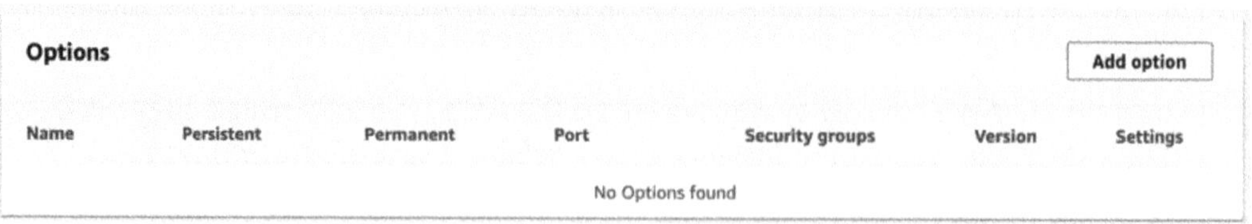

Figure 12.13 – Add option

5. Select **MARIADB_AUDIT_PLUGIN** from the **Option name** dropdown and leave all the other values as-is.

Option details

Option group name

dbcert-mysql-80

Option name Info

Choose the option that you want to add to this group.

MARIADB_AUDIT_PLUGIN

Option settings (9)

Filter by option settings

1 2

Option setting	Value	Allowed values
SERVER_AUDIT	FORCE_P	FORCE_PLUS_PERMANENT
SERVER_AUDIT_EVENTS*	CONNECT	CONNECT, QUERY, QUERY_DDL, QUERY_DML, QU
SERVER_AUDIT_EXCL_USERS		
SERVER_AUDIT_FILE_PATH	/rdsdbda	
SERVER_AUDIT_FILE_ROTATE_SIZE		1-1000000000

* Indicates multiple, comma-separated values are allowed, e.g. AES256,RC4_128. (Note that spaces after commas are not accepted.) Otherwise, only a single value is allowed.

Apply immediately Info

Yes

No

Cancel Add option

Figure 12.14 – Adding an audit option

Click **Add option**.

6. With that, our RDS MySQL instance should have been created and be **Available**. Return to the **Databases** page and find the instance. Obtain its **Endpoint** settings and try to connect to it using a MySQL querying tool such as MySQL Workbench. If you hit any connectivity errors, try to resolve them by checking whether your database is publicly available and that the security groups allow you IP access.
7. Download the World Database Sample schema from the MySQL website: `https://downloads.mysql.com/docs/world-db.zip`. This will download a ZIP file containing a single `world.sql` file. Open this file in your MySQL query tool and run it to create our sample schema.
8. Now, let's enable auditing by attaching our **Option group** to our MySQL instance. Return to the AWS console's **RDS Dashboard** and click the checkbox next to the MySQL instance. Select **Modify** at the top right.
9. Locate the **Additional configuration** section, click the **Option group** dropdown, and select our **Option group**.

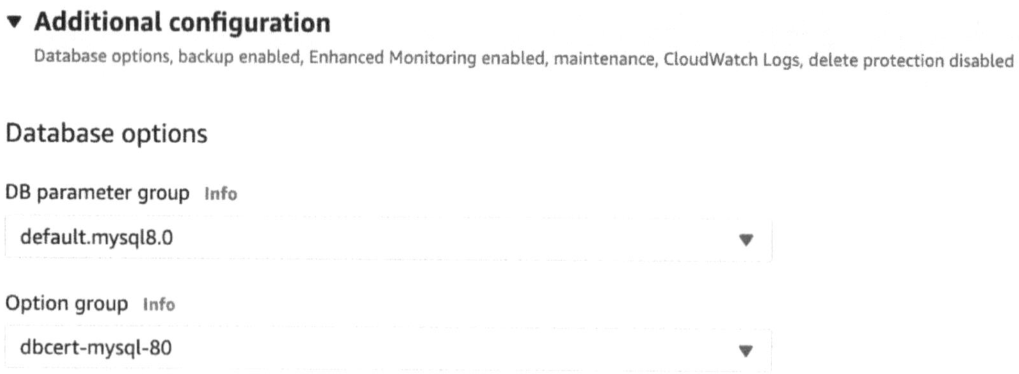

▾ **Additional configuration**

Database options, backup enabled, Enhanced Monitoring enabled, maintenance, CloudWatch Logs, delete protection disabled

Database options

DB parameter group Info

default.mysql8.0 ▾

Option group Info

dbcert-mysql-80 ▾

Figure 12.15 – Option group

Leave all the other options as-is and click **Continue**.

10. Select **Apply immediately** and then click **Modify DB instance**. Wait for the instance's status to change to **Available** from **Modifying**.

    Now, let's generate some SQL statements to see how they get logged.

11. Return to your MySQL query tool and run the following queries:

```
select * from world.city;
delete from world.city where ID=3;
```

Open the AWS console, navigate to **RDS Dashboard**, and click the name of the MySQL instance to view its details. Open the **Logs & events** tab and locate **Logs**.

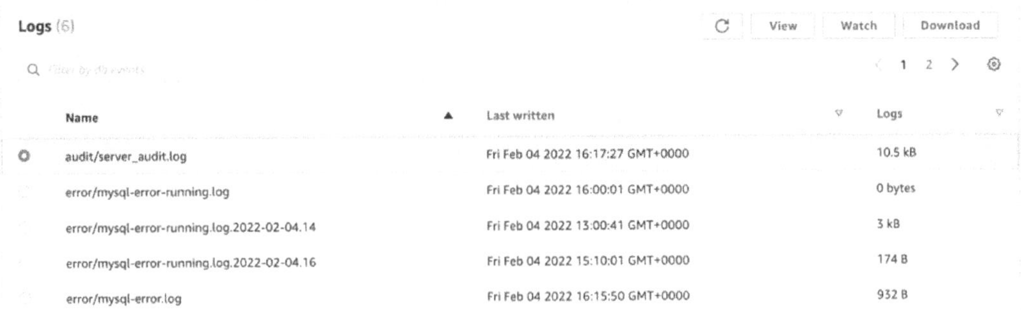

Figure 12.16 – Audit logs

12. Select the `audit/server_audit.log` file and click **View** to open it. You will see some entries, as shown in the following screenshot:

```
20220204 16:17:00,ip-10-22-1-94,rdsadmin,localhost,15,68,QUERY,,'SELECT 1',0,,
20220204 16:17:00,ip-10-22-1-94,rdsadmin,localhost,15,69,QUERY,,'SELECT count(*) from mysql.rds_history WHERE action = \'disable set master\' GROUP BY
action_timestamp,called_by_user,action,mysql_version,master_host,master_port,master_user,master_log_file ,master_log_pos,master_ssl ORDER BY
action_timestamp LIMIT 1',0,,
20220204 16:17:00,ip-10-22-1-94,rdsadmin,localhost,15,70,QUERY,,'SELECT 1',0,,
20220204 16:17:00,ip-10-22-1-94,rdsadmin,localhost,15,71,QUERY,,'SELECT count(*) from mysql.rds_replication_status WHERE master_host IS NOT NULL and
master_port IS NOT NULL GROUP BY action_timestamp,called_by_user,action,mysql_version,master_host,master_port ORDER BY action_timestamp LIMIT 1',0,,
20220204 16:17:09,ip-10-22-1-94,admin,82.18.28.101,58,72,QUERY,,'select * from world.city\nLIMIT 0, 1000',0,,
20220204 16:17:09,ip-10-22-1-94,admin,82.18.28.101,57,73,QUERY,,'SELECT st.* FROM performance_schema.events_statements_current st JOIN
performance_schema.threads thr ON thr.thread_id = st.thread_id WHERE thr.processlist_id = 58',0,,
20220204 16:17:09,ip-10-22-1-94,admin,82.18.28.101,57,74,QUERY,,'SELECT st.* FROM performance_schema.events_stages_history_long st WHERE
st.nesting_event_id = 0',0,,
20220204 16:17:09,ip-10-22-1-94,admin,82.18.28.101,57,75,QUERY,,'SELECT st.* FROM performance_schema.events_waits_history_long st WHERE
st.nesting_event_id = 0',0,,
20220204 16:17:09,ip-10-22-1-94,admin,82.18.28.101,57,76,QUERY,,'SHOW INDEX FROM `world`.`city`',0,,
20220204 16:17:12,ip-10-22-1-94,rdsadmin,localhost,15,77,QUERY,,'SELECT 1',0,,
20220204 16:17:12,ip-10-22-1-94,rdsadmin,localhost,15,78,QUERY,,'SELECT 1',0,,
20220204 16:17:12,ip-10-22-1-94,rdsadmin,localhost,15,79,QUERY,,'SELECT 1',0,,
20220204 16:17:12,ip-10-22-1-94,rdsadmin,localhost,15,80,QUERY,,'SELECT count(*) from information_schema.TABLES WHERE TABLE_SCHEMA = \'mysql\' AND
TABLE_NAME = \'rds_heartbeat2\'',0,,
20220204 16:17:12,ip-10-22-1-94,rdsadmin,localhost,15,81,QUERY,,'SELECT 1',0,,
20220204 16:17:12,ip-10-22-1-94,rdsadmin,localhost,15,82,QUERY,,'SELECT value FROM mysql.rds_heartbeat2',0,,
20220204 16:17:12,ip-10-22-1-94,rdsadmin,localhost,15,83,QUERY,,'SELECT 1',0,,
20220204 16:17:12,ip-10-22-1-94,rdsadmin,localhost,15,84,QUERY,,'SELECT @@GLOBAL.read_only',0,,
20220204 16:17:27,ip-10-22-1-94,rdsadmin,localhost,15,85,QUERY,,'SELECT 1',0,,
20220204 16:17:27,ip-10-22-1-94,rdsadmin,localhost,15,86,QUERY,,'SELECT 1',0,,
```

Figure 12.17 – Output of the audit file

If you are using a GUI tool to query the MySQL instance, you will likely see a lot of strange queries that you didn't run, such as `SELECT 1',0,,`. These are queries that have been generated by the tool and can be ignored. To make it easier to find the queries, you can download the log and view it in a text editor.

This completes this lab for database auditing. You can now delete or terminate your RDS instances if you wish.

So far, we've discussed using IAM authentication to access RDS and other database instances such as DynamoDB, but in some situations, IAM authentication cannot be deployed or isn't suitable or there is still a need for some users to use a password. In those cases, you should consider securing your passwords in Secrets Manager, as we'll see next.

Configuring AWS Key Management Service and Secrets Manager

Secrets Manager is an encrypted and secure key-value store where you can save any information you would like to keep secret. It integrates natively into a wide range of AWS services, including most of their database platforms, such as RDS and DocumentDB. It can automate password rotation and sync the changes to your databases to ensure your application is disrupted.

A common problem that is resolved using AWS Secrets Manager is storing database passwords within the application or in text files that can easily be accessed by unauthorized users. You can store the database passwords in AWS Secrets Manager and use the AWS CLI to retrieve them. These passwords can be changed on an automatic schedule and will update both the passwords stored with AWS Secrets Manager, as well as within the RDS databases. To allow your application to obtain these passwords from Secrets Manager, you will need to modify the code to allow your application to query AWS Secrets Manager. Users can obtain the passwords in plain text by using an API call that's similar to the following:

```
aws secretsmanager get-secret-value --secret-id databases/
dbcert-mysql-admin
```

This will return a JSON output with the secret's details:

```
{
    "ARN": "arn:aws:secretsmanager:eu-west-
1:46035369564:secret:databases/ dbcert-mysql-admin",
    "Name": " databases/dbcert-mysql-admin",
    ...
    "SecretString": "dbcert_p@55word",
    ...
}
```

As well as storing passwords and usernames, you can store entire database connection strings. This can be useful if you want to change your database details without having to change any hardcoded values within the application.

Some databases, such as DynamoDB, do not have native syncing with AWS Secrets Manager, so you will need to create some code to do the database password rotation for you when AWS Secrets Manager rotates it. For these databases, you can use AWS Lambda code to do this for you. You will not need to know the Lambda code to do this for the exam, but there is a guide in the *Further reading* section at the end of this chapter.

Now, let's summarize what we've learned in this chapter.

Summary

In this chapter, we explored the key database security features that are offered by AWS. This included encryption, audit controls and monitoring, VPC security, and secure password storage.

We learned how to configure a VPC securely for our database and learned how to set a database in a private subnet that's protected by security groups that only allow access to authorized hosts. In addition, we learned how bastion hosts are used to provide administrative access to a database without exposing the database to the public internet.

Then, we looked at database encryption techniques and how to work with encrypted snapshots, including how to copy an encrypted snapshot between regions using customer-managed keys stored in AWS KMS.

Finally, we learned how to store secret database connection details and passwords using AWS Secrets Manager.

Database security is a major topic within the AWS Certified Database Specialty exam and there will be several questions about it. You may also see questions that ask for the most secure option out of the available answers. In the next chapter we will be learning CloudWatch and Logging which we use to identify and help us resolve database issues and problems.

Cheat sheet

This cheat sheet summarizes the key points from this chapter:

- AWS databases such as RDS and DynamoDB can be encrypted at rest and in transit.
- RDS uses SSL/TLS to encrypt data in transit, so you will need to download and install the right certificate in your application to allow it to connect.
- Databases should be placed in a private subnet within your VPC.
- You should use security groups to tightly control which source IPs are allowed to connect to the database. They should not be left as 0.0.0.0/0 (everywhere).
- Bastion hosts or jump boxes can be used to allow administrative traffic to the databases while maintaining a private subnet for the database.
- AWS Secrets Manager can store database credentials securely and rotate them on a schedule.
- Your applications can be written to request the password from AWS Secrets Manager rather than requiring the database password to be hardcoded within the application configuration files.

- Database auditing can be turned on via Option groups, allowing you to see specific queries being run within the databases.
- CloudTrail will log all the actions that have been taken to modify databases within your account. This includes creation, deletion, or modification.

Review

Now, let's practice a few exam-style questions:

1. You are advising a large financial company on the best strategy to migrate its on-premises MySQL database, application, and web servers. RDS MySQL is being considered as the target database engine. Access to the database should be limited to only the application servers and a bastion host.

   Which solution meets these security requirements?

   A. Provision the RDS MySQL database in a private subnet. Modify the `login.cnf` file on the RDS host to allow connections from only the application servers and bastion host.

   B. Provision the RDS MySQL database in a public subnet. Create a new security group with inbound rules to allow connections from only the security groups of the application servers and bastion host. Attach the new security group to the DB instance.

   C. Provision the RDS MySQL database in a private subnet. Create a new security group with inbound rules to allow connections from only the security groups of the application servers and bastion host. Attach the new security group to the DB instance.

   D. Provision the RDS MySQL database in a private subnet. Create an NACL with inbound and outbound rules to allow connections to and from the application servers and bastion host.

2. An audit has highlighted the need to encrypt all databases at rest. You need to enable encryption at rest for all the existing RDS PostgreSQL DBs urgently. The business is prepared to take an outage during key hours if required.

   What actions will complete the task in the simplest and fastest way?

   A. Export the database to an Amazon S3 bucket with encryption enabled. Create a new database and import the export file.

   B. Create a snapshot of the database. Create an encrypted copy of the snapshot. Restore a new database from the encrypted snapshot.

C. Modify the database to enable encryption. Apply this setting immediately without waiting for the next scheduled maintenance window.

D. Create a snapshot of the database. Restore the snapshot in a new database with encryption enabled.

3. A new compliance rule has come into effect, which means you may no longer use shared passwords for database administration and each DBA must have its own named account. Your company has a large estate of Aurora instances that they need to modify to stop password sharing and to improve auditing of admin accounts.

   What is the best way to configure this?

   A. Use the AWS CLI to retrieve the AWS usernames and passwords of all team members. For each username, create an Aurora user with the same password as the IAM account.

   B. Enable IAM database authentication on the Aurora cluster. Create a passwordless database user for DBA. Attach an IAM policy to each IAM user account that grants the connect privilege using their database user account.

   C. Create a database user for each team member. Email each user their new password. Set up a password policy to expire each user's password every 30 days.

   D. Create an IAM role and associate an IAM policy that grants the connect privilege using the shared account. Configure a trust policy that allows the administrator's IAM user account to use the role.

4. An application was migrated over the weekend to a new EC2 instance. Users are complaining that they are seeing database timeout error messages when they try to run any queries through the application. The database is an RDS SQL Server instance.

   What is the most likely problem, and what is the solution?

   A. The IP address has changed on the RDS instance. Modify the application to use the new IP address.

   B. The new application server has not been added to a security group with permissions to access the database. Add the EC2 instance to the correct security groups.

   C. The application is sending too many requests to the databases, causing timeouts. Review the application settings.

   D. The application server has been placed in a different VPC to the database. Set up VPC peering to resolve the connectivity issue.

5. A company is using RDS PostgreSQL. The compliance team wants all database connection requests to be logged and retained for 180 days. The RDS PostgreSQL DB instance is currently using the default parameter group. You have identified that setting the `log_connections` parameter to `1` will enable connection logging.

   Which steps should you take to meet these requirements? (Choose 2)

   A. Allow database engine logs to be published to an Amazon S3 bucket and set the life cycle policy to 180 days.

   B. Update the `log_connections` parameter in the default parameter group.

   C. Create a custom parameter group, update the `log_connections` parameter, and associate the parameter with the DB instance.

   D. Connect to the RDS PostgreSQL host and update the `log_connections` parameter in the `postgresql.conf` file.

   E. Allow database engine logs to be published to CloudWatch and set the expiration to 180 days.

Further reading

To learn more about the topics that were covered in this chapter, take a look at the following resources:

- *Using AWS Lambda with AWS Secrets Manager*: `https://aws.amazon.com/premiumsupport/knowledge-center/lambda-function-secrets-manager/`
- *AWS Security Cookbook*: `https://www.packtpub.com/product/aws-security-cookbook/9781838826253`

Part 4: Monitoring and Optimization

You've learned how to evaluate your use case and to pick the right database, you've converted and migrated your database, so now you need to monitor and optimize it.

This section includes the following chapters:

- *Chapter 13, CloudWatch and Logging*
- *Chapter 14, Backup and Restore*
- *Chapter 15, Troubleshooting Tools and Techniques*

13
CloudWatch and Logging

Monitoring and logging your databases using CloudWatch is a key topic in the exam, and also a technique required by all database administrators. We have previously learned about CloudWatch and logging at a high level, but in this chapter, we are going to learn some more advanced features and options within CloudWatch. We will end the chapter with a hands-on lab, where we will customize our monitoring and alerts, and generate some heavy load on an **Relational Database Service** (**RDS**) instance to ensure we receive an alert. We will also look at a tool called **Application Insights** that allows you to monitor your databases as part of a wider application stack to help identify the root cause of any incident or outage.

In this chapter, we're going to cover the following main topics:

- Overview of CloudWatch and logging
- Working with CloudWatch
- Understanding Performance Insights
- Understanding RDS Enhanced Monitoring
- Configuring CloudWatch monitoring and alerts

First, let's remind ourselves what CloudWatch is and how it can be used to help monitor your database.

Technical requirements

You will require an AWS account with root access; not everything we will do in this chapter will be available in the Free Tier, which means you may incur a small cost to follow the hands-on sections. You will also require AWS **command-line interface** (**CLI**) access. This AWS guide (`https://docs.aws.amazon.com/cli/latest/userguide/cli-chap-configure.html`) explains the steps required, but I will summarize them here:

1. Open an AWS account, if you have not already done so.
2. Download the AWS CLI latest version from here: `https://docs.aws.amazon.com/cli/latest/userguide/welcome-versions.html#welcome-versions-v2`.
3. Create an admin user: `https://docs.aws.amazon.com/IAM/latest/UserGuide/id_credentials_access-keys.html`
4. Create an access key for your administration user: `https://docs.aws.amazon.com/IAM/latest/UserGuide/getting-started_create-admin-group.html#getting-started_create-admin-group-cli`.
5. Run the `aws configure` command to set up a profile for your user: `https://docs.aws.amazon.com/cli/latest/userguide/cli-configure-quickstart.html#cli-configure-quickstart-creds`.

You will also require a **Virtual Private Cloud** (**VPC**) that meets the minimum requirements for an RDS instance: `https://docs.aws.amazon.com/AmazonRDS/latest/UserGuide/USER_VPC.WorkingWithRDSInstanceinaVPC.html`. If you completed the steps in *Chapter 3, Understanding AWS Infrastructure*, you will already have a VPC that meets the requirements.

Overview of CloudWatch and logging

CloudWatch is the primary monitoring and logging service offered by AWS. It acts as a data and metrics repository storing all of your RDS monitoring metrics in near real time. CloudWatch can generate graphs, allow you to download raw values into several different formats, trigger alarms and alerts, call AWS Lambda functions, and allow you to read log files from multiple databases at once.

CloudWatch metrics can be viewed graphically, both via the RDS and CloudWatch dashboards. It also offers full **Application Programming Interface** (**API**) and AWS CLI integration, allowing you to use other tools, such as Amazon QuickSight, to view and analyze the data as required. The metrics you can view from the RDS dashboard are more limited but offer a clear and quick overview of your database health. The following figure shows some of the metrics available via the RDS dashboard:

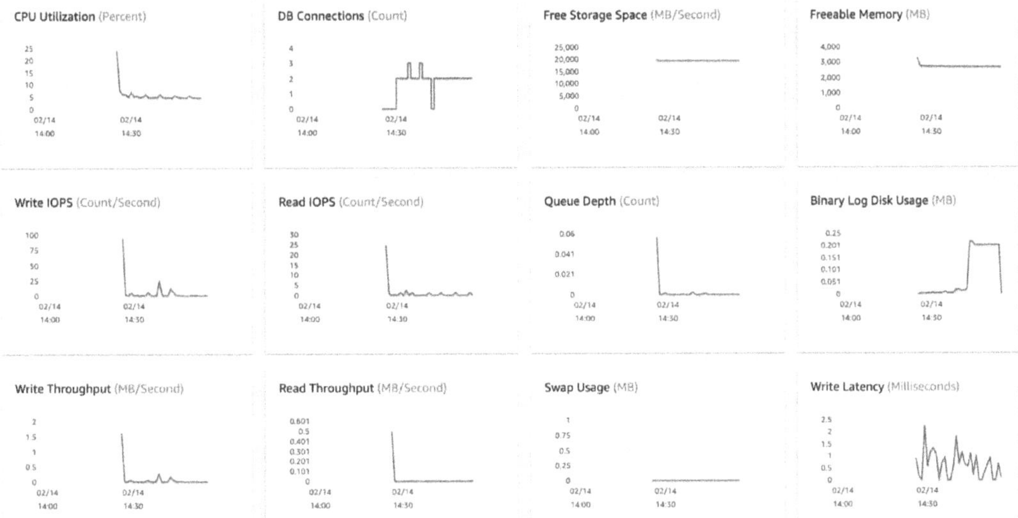

Figure 13.1 – RDS dashboard CloudWatch metrics

You can also access three monitoring sections via the RDS dashboard if you enabled them at instance creation time:

- **Enhanced Monitoring** – This allows you to monitor the underlying resource usage of the instance your RDS database is running on.
- **Peformance Insights** – This offers a graphical and text-based view of all database loads and queries running, allowing you to drill down into the root cause of a performance problem.
- **Operating System (OS) Process List** – This allows you to trace individual OS processes to help identify queries or commands causing performance problems.

All of these metrics are also sent to the CloudWatch dashboard, where you can use text filters, generate graphs with multiple metrics to identify trends, and create alarms to alert you to problems.

Let's take a closer look at the CloudWatch dashboard now to learn how to use some of its advanced features for database monitoring.

Working with CloudWatch

CloudWatch is the central monitoring and alerting repository for all AWS services. As such, it is extremely powerful and features many advanced tools and processes, which we do not need to know for the Database Specialty exam. However, given the usefulness of many of these additional features, there is a recommended book in the *Further reading* section for anyone wanting to know more beyond the scope of this chapter.

CloudWatch can be used to monitor any of your databases running within AWS, not just RDS. It can also be used to monitor databases running on-premises by installing the CloudWatch agent within your data center.

The main page of CloudWatch is **Dashboards**. You can create your own dashboards to show the metrics that are the most useful to you across all AWS services. For example, if you had an application running on EC2 with a load balancer and an RDS instance, you could create a dashboard that monitored the CPU and memory of the EC2 instances, the latency of the load balancer and the CPU, the memory, and the top five query runtimes of the RDS instance to give you a good view of the entire application stack. As a database administrator, you might want a view showing the highest CPU and memory utilization across all instances that you manage. This is an example dashboard, showing an application running in a container and an RDS database:

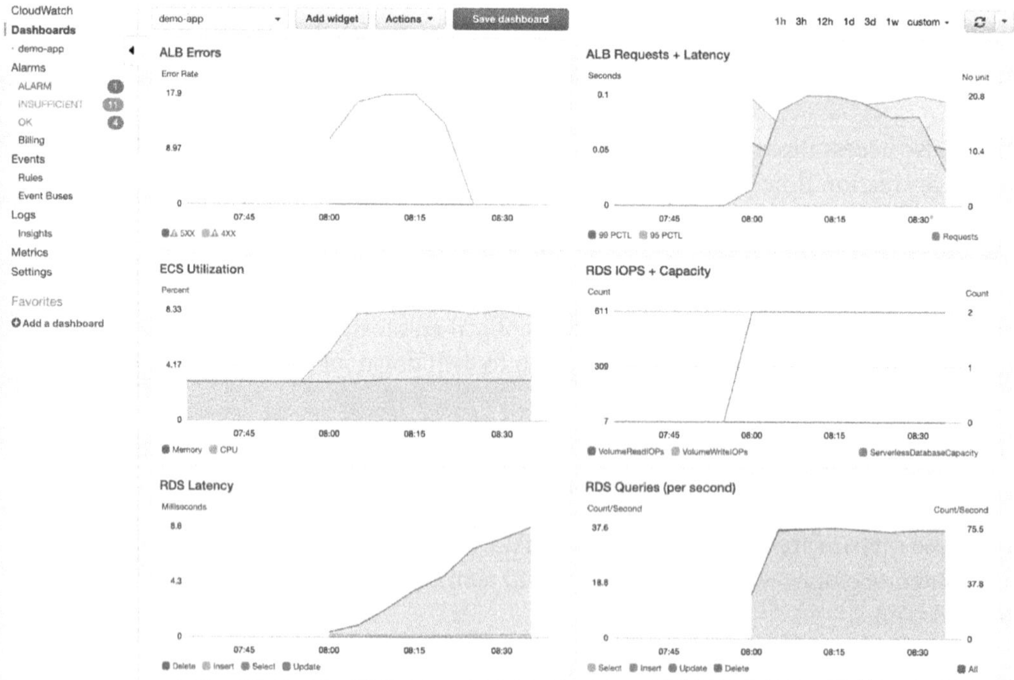

Figure 13.2 – CloudWatch application dashboard

The next area is **Alarms**. You can create an alarm against any metric that is collected. Alarms will cause a warning to appear within CloudWatch and can also be set up to send an alert, such as an email or SMS, using **Amazon Simple Notification Service** (**Amazon SNS**).

Alarms can be configured with highly customizable rules that include both **static** values and moving values, known as **anomaly detection**.

Anomaly detection allows you to create an acceptable tolerance band, and any values outside of this will trigger an alarm. This is an adaptive alarm, as the tolerance band and values that will trigger an alarm will change depending on the database load. This type of alarm is useful to identify when your database usage has changed unexpectedly, allowing you to analyze and resolve the error before any performance issue or downtime occurs.

Static values are used when you have known specific limits that you need to be notified of if they are breached. These could be a failed database task, errors in a database log, or running out of I/O credits for RDS instances using burst credits (typically these are the `db.t3` instance classes). You can also use static alerts for known limits when performance starts to drop. You may have been running your application for a while and noticed that if the number of database connections is higher than a specific number, the performance of the application drops to an unacceptable level. You could create a static alarm to warn you that you are approaching this level.

You can create alarms based on specific text within a database log. To do this, you can create a **metric filter** against the log file required. A metric filter is a pattern match query that can contain static text or regular expressions. Once the metric filter is created, you can then create an alarm that will alert when anything matches the filter. You can use this to be alerted on specific error values, such as ORA alerts, custom text that your database jobs write to the database error, or alert logs.

As CloudWatch collects so many metrics, it can quickly become difficult to find the ones you want. When you go to the **Metrics** view, you can see **AWS namespaces**. A namespace is a collection of similar metrics. In the following figure, you can see that there are **144** metrics for RDS:

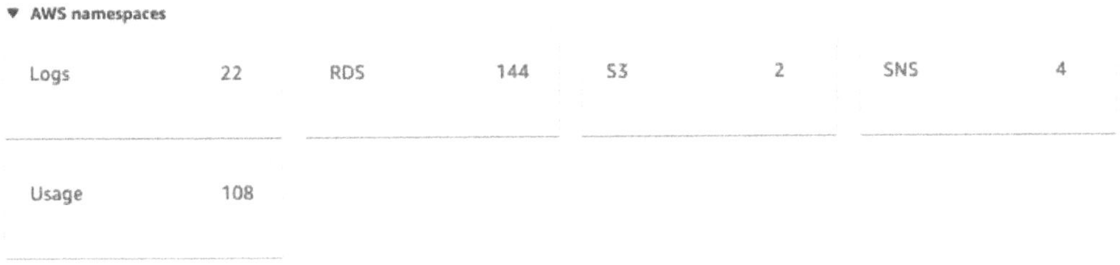

Figure 13.3 – AWS namespace metrics

You can view multiple metrics from multiple namespaces at the same time to see an overlaid graph, which can allow you to see a root cause. For example, if you are suffering a database performance problem, it might also be useful to see if the load on the application also increased at the same time, which might point to an application configuration error.

Let's now look at some of the other database monitoring tools available through CloudWatch, starting with Performance Insights.

Understanding Performance Insights

Performance Insights allows you to view queries and database load in real time through a graphical interface. It is available for all RDS database engines, but is not available on the `t3.small` and lower instance classes.

Performance Insights is accessed directly from the RDS dashboard rather than via CloudWatch. It is not a standard feature and it must be enabled for each instance that you need. This can be done at instance provisioning or later, by modifying the instance and enabling Performance Insights, which will not incur any outage. Performance Insights is free for data stored for a maximum of 7 days, and it is chargeable if you need to keep data for a longer period.

The Performance Insights dashboard offers an overview graph that you can customize with any metrics you wish, and further down the page, you can see details for specific queries and database load. The following figure shows how you can add multiple metrics to the graph to help identify any trends:

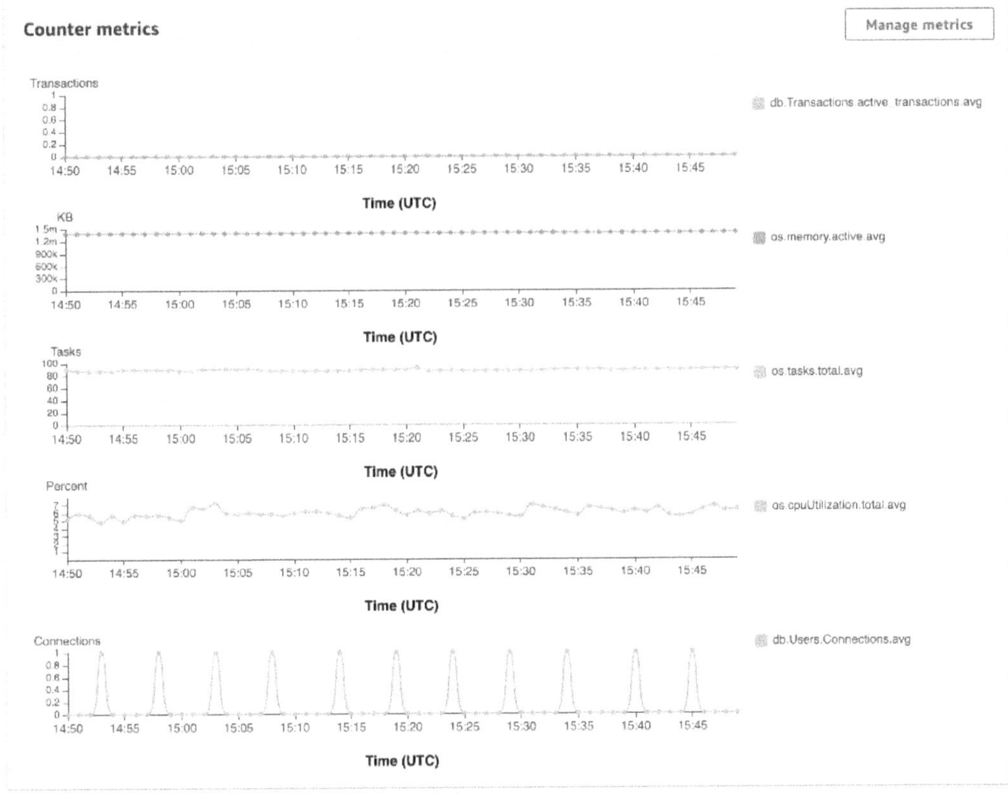

Figure 13.4 – Performance Insights overview graph

You can also view several different categories with different data to try to locate the problem. The options are as follows:

- **Top waits** – This shows the highest wait categories.
- **Top SQL** – This shows the SQL queries using the highest database load.
- **Top hosts** – This shows the application hosts consuming the highest database load.
- **Top users** – This shows the database users using the highest database load.
- **Top databases** – This shows the most utilized databases.

The following figure shows the top SQL queries running along with the specific waits they are suffering and the CPU load:

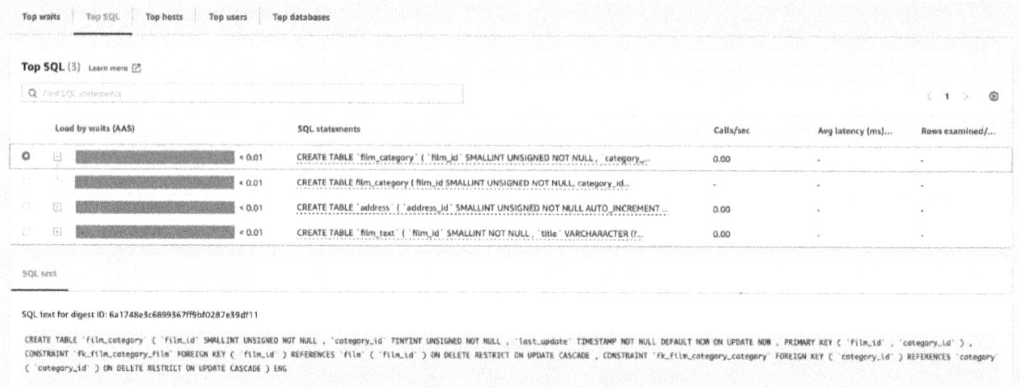

Figure 13.5 – Performance Insights metrics

Performance Insights offers a very useful interface for identifying specific performance issues, both with your database and on the RDS host; however, for more detailed performance metrics of the underlying **Operating System** (**OS**) host, you should use RDS Enhanced Monitoring, which we will learn about now.

Understanding RDS Enhanced Monitoring

CloudWatch offers limited monitoring of the virtual machine or host that your RDS instances run on. To get a deeper and more accurate view, you need to enable RDS Enhanced Monitoring. This installs a small agent onto the RDS host that obtains and sends OS metrics back to CloudWatch up to every 1 second.

You can use these metrics in conjunction with database-level monitoring to get a highly accurate view of the real-time workload of your database. This can be very useful if you need to decide to increase an instance class to overcome a performance issue. By using Enhanced Monitoring, you can more accurately see whether the bottleneck is at the host level and, therefore, you would benefit from increasing the instance class or not.

Enabling Enhanced Monitoring also allows you to view OS metrics from within the RDS dashboard, which reduces the need for your databases to have access to CloudWatch. The following figure shows some of the metrics available under Enhanced Monitoring:

Figure 13.6 – Enhanced Monitoring metrics

Enhanced Monitoring also allows you to view individual OS processes, which can help you identify whether a certain process is using larger than expected amounts of resources. There are RDS background processes that run on the OS, and occasionally these can use high amounts of CPU or memory, which can cause performance problems. Enhanced Monitoring would give a view of these.

Let's now complete a hands-on lab to create a CloudWatch dashboard, set up some custom metrics, and enable alarms.

Configuring CloudWatch monitoring and alerts

We are now going to practice a hands-on session where we will set up some CloudWatch metrics, create a dashboard so we can view all the critical metrics in one place, and finally, configure some alarms to send us emails about database issues.

If you do not have any RDS MySQL databases, then please create one. Make sure you configure the security groups to allow you to log in to it, as we will be connecting and generating traffic to trigger alarms. Make sure you request it to send all logs to CloudWatch.

Let's start by creating a CloudWatch dashboard.

Creating a CloudWatch dashboard

Let's create a CloudWatch dashboard that will allow us to monitor all our key metrics in one place. If you have more than one database, you can monitor them all from one dashboard, but in this lab, we only use one database:

1. Log in to the AWS console and navigate to **CloudWatch**.
2. Click **Dashboard**, and then click **Create dashboard**. Give it a relevant name.

3. Select **Line** from the options that appear:

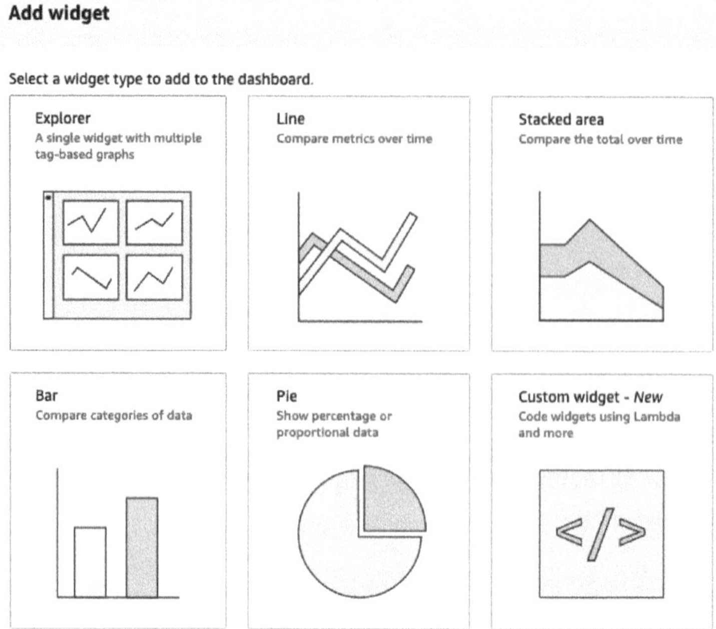

Figure 13.7 – CloudWatch graph options

4. Then, select **Metrics**. A new panel will appear showing an empty graph with some categories at the bottom. Click **RDS**, and then **By Database Engine**:

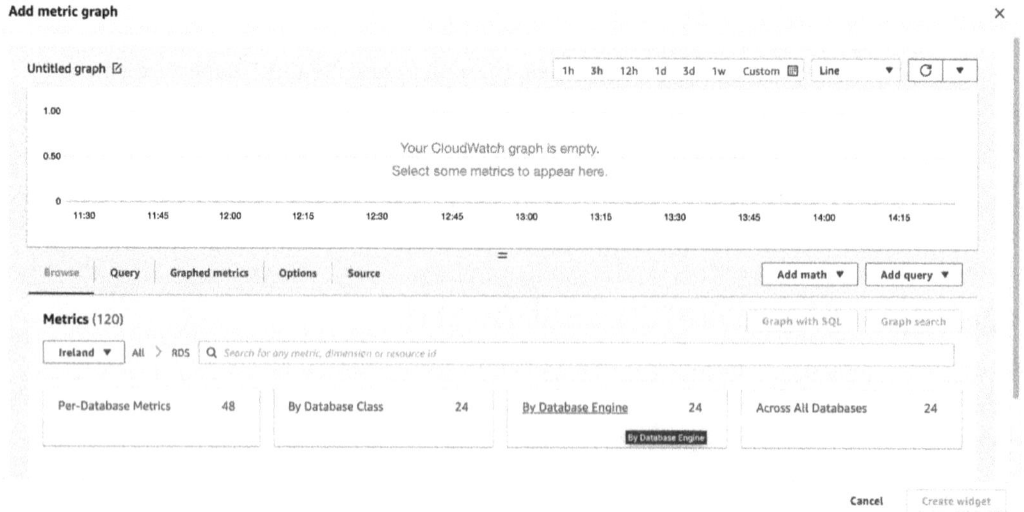

Figure 13.8 – Add dashboard widget

5. Choose a metric you'd like to monitor. This demonstration will use the **CPU utilization**, **Database connections**, and **Freeable memory** metrics. Create a single widget for each metric individually.
6. We will also add a number widget to see instantly if we are using any of the CPU credits we are allocated for a `t3` instance class. Using them might indicate performance problems. Click **Add widget**, select **Number**, then find **CPUSurplusCreditsCharged**. Click **Create widget**.
7. Finally, we will add a logs table that will let us view the latest errors from the database logs within the Dashboard to save us having to go to the RDS page to get them. Click **Add widget**, then choose **Logs table**. In the dropdown at the top, select your log group for your RDS instance:

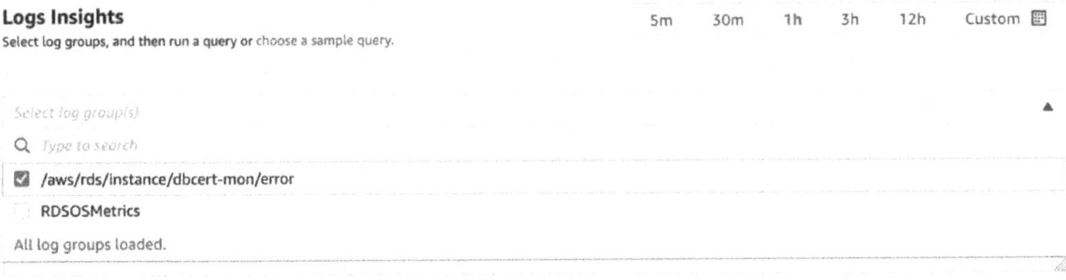

Figure 13.9 – Log groups

8. Click **Create widget** in the top right; it will test the query, but at the moment, it is unlikely we will have any errors in the logs.
9. Click **Save dashboard**.
10. If you wish, you can log in to your MySQL database and run some queries to generate traffic, which you'll be able to monitor here. Feel free to explore other metrics, graphs, and options you can add to your dashboards.

We are now going to create some alarms to alert us if our databases suffer an issue, such as high CPU utilization:

1. Select **All alarms** from the left-hand menu, and then, select **Create alarm**.
2. Click **Select metric** and find the `DatabaseConnections` metric under **RDS**.

   We are going to create a very simple alarm to ensure we can trigger it on a test database. We are going to want an alarm if the number of database connections (logins) is higher than one, so it should trigger as soon as we connect to the database. In the real world, you'd use much better metrics than this.
3. The **Specify metrics and conditions** page will open. Review the page to make sure you understand the options, in particular, **Anomaly Detection**, which allows you to define a metric that will alert if the values are very different from usual.

   We are going to set a static value of **Greater than** `1`:

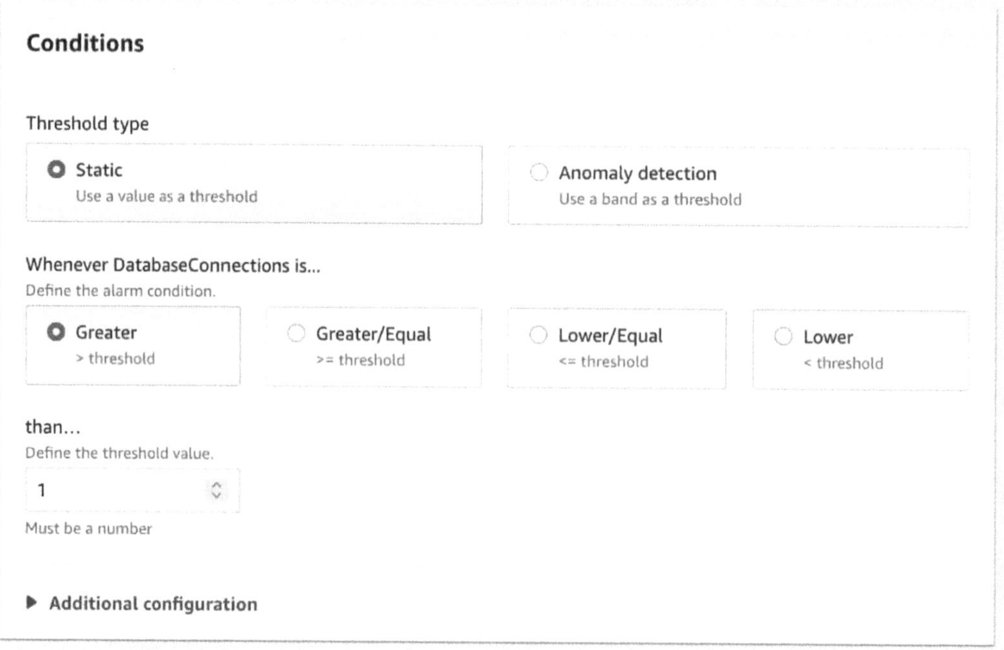

Figure 13.10 – Static metric alarm value

You can see the value set in the preceding graph to show the alarm value compared to recent values of that same metric. This is useful to ensure you don't set an alarm incorrectly:

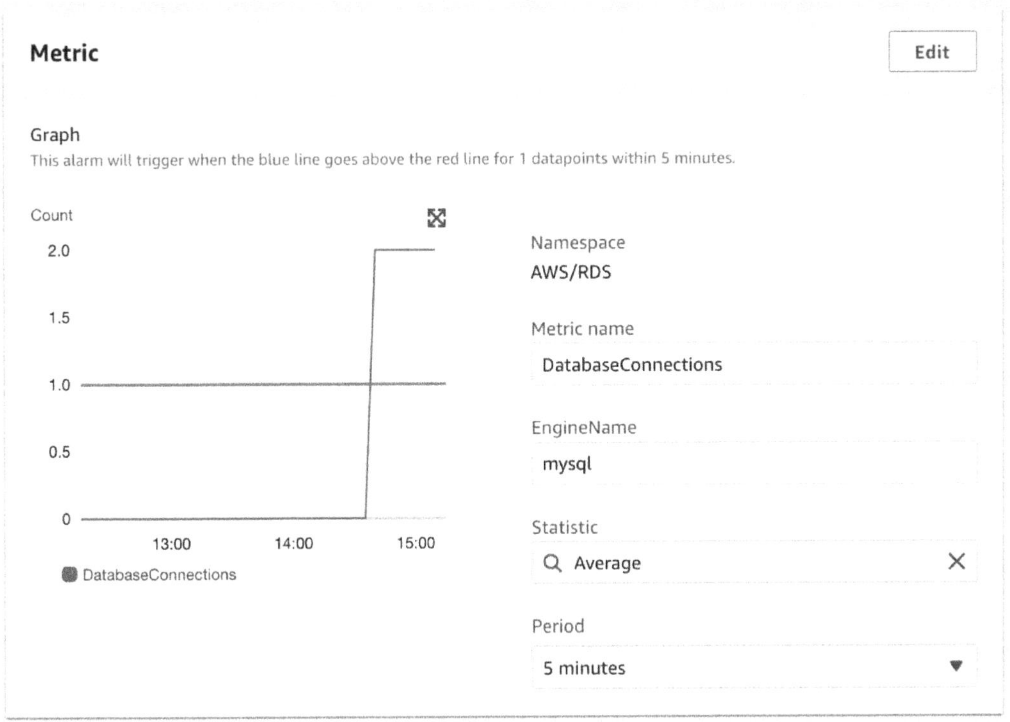

Figure 13.11 – Metric alarm graph

4. Click **Next**.

5. Leave **Alarm state trigger** as **In alarm**, but select **Create new topic** under **Select an SNS topic**. Give the topic a name, and then enter your own email address in the **Email endpoints that will receive the notification…** textbox:

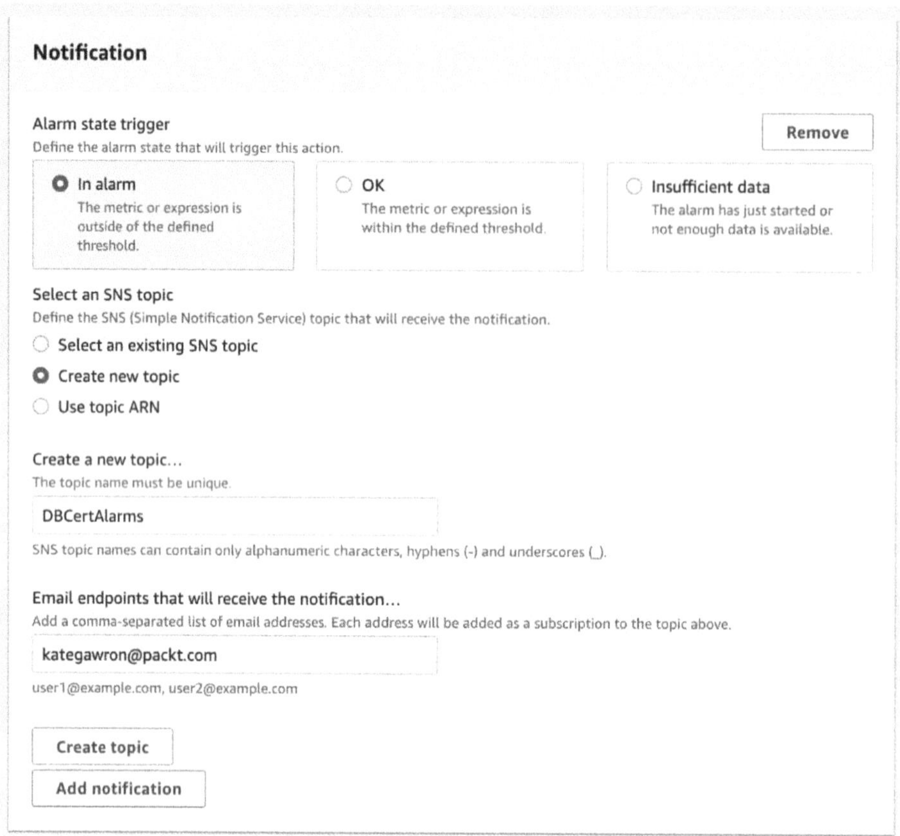

Figure 13.12 – Create SNS alarm topic

6. Click **Create topic**.
7. Leave everything else as default, and then click **Next** at the bottom of the page.
8. Give the alarm a name and click **Next**, then review on the next page, and click **Create alarm**.
9. Before the alarm will email you, you need to accept the SNS notification. In a new browser window, navigate to **SNS** from the AWS menu, and then select **Subscriptions** from the left-hand menu.
10. You will see the subscription you created in the window with a **Pending confirmation** status. Select it, and click **Confirm subscription** to enable it:

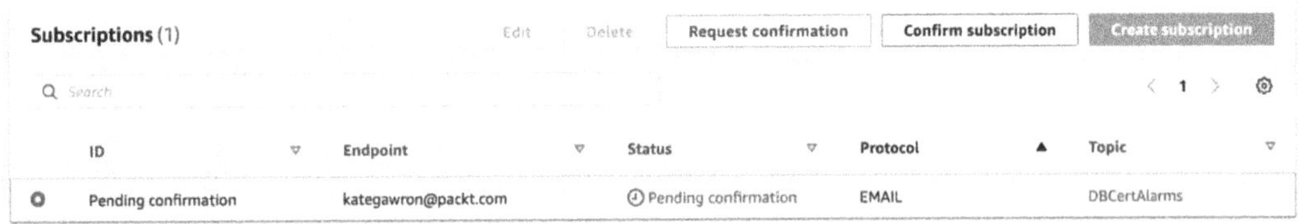

Figure 13.13 – SNS subscriptions

11. The alarm will need to collect data first, which can take around 1 minute. You can log in to your RDS database and run some queries while you wait. As soon as the alarm detects that someone has logged into the database and and there is now more than one connection, you should receive an email, and the dashboard will update to show the alarm:

Figure 13.14 – CloudWatch alarm

We've now set up a CloudWatch dashboard to allow us to see various database metrics in one location, and then created an alarm to notify us of any potential database problems that might be occurring.

Let's now recap what we've learned in this chapter.

Summary

In this chapter, we learned about how to use CloudWatch to monitor your databases running in AWS. CloudWatch offers a powerful and highly customizable setup of tools, such as dashboards, alarms, and anomaly detection, to finely tune your alerts and monitoring across your database estate.

We learned how to use Enhanced Monitoring to be able to closely monitor the health and performance of the virtual machines that run our RDS databases to help diagnose performance issues more accurately.

Finally, we learned how to use Performance Insights to graphically see ongoing and real-time performance metrics at the query level to help identify the root cause of any database performance issues and areas that could be tuned.

Accurate and comprehensive monitoring of your databases is critical to ensure there are no outages and that performance is maintained, and CloudWatch is one of the best tools to do so. In the exam, there will be a large number of questions about performance problems or errors with databases, and you will need to know where to look within CloudWatch to find the information you need to resolve the issue and answer the questions.

In the next chapter, we are going to learn about backup and restore techniques within RDS and other database engines supported by AWS.

Cheat sheet

The cheat sheet summarizes the main key points from this chapter:

- CloudWatch is the central monitoring tool for all AWS services.
- RDS, EC2, and other AWS databases all natively send metrics to CloudWatch, and they can also be configured to send their log files to CloudWatch.
- CloudWatch offers Enhanced Monitoring, which lets you accurately monitor the virtual machine the RDS database is running on.
- You can use Performance Insights to get a visual representation of the real-time workload running on your database and its performance to help diagnose performance issues and to find queries that could be tuned.
- CloudWatch allows the creation of dashboards to let you monitor all of your services and key metrics in one place, reducing the need for application teams to have access to the RDS console, which can help improve your database security.
- You can create custom alarms within CloudWatch that can be configured to send emails or text messages if there is a problem.

Review

Let's now practice a few exam-style questions:

1. You are a database consultant for a small local company. The company needs to monitor the read and write **Input/output Operations Per Second (IOPS)** metrics for their AWS MySQL RDS instance and send real-time alerts to their database team. Which AWS services can accomplish this as simply and at as low cost as possible? Choose two answers:

   A. Amazon **Simple Email Service (SES)**

   B. Amazon CloudWatch

C. Amazon **Simple Queue Service (SQS)**

D. Amazon SNS

E. AWS Lambda

2. You are a database administrator for an online shopping company. Over the weekend, their critical production database went down due to a larger than expected number of orders. What type of alarms could you create to get a warning of abnormal database load?

   A. Create a CloudWatch alarm based on a static metric, such as database connections or CPU.

   B. Use Performance Insights to observe database load statistics in real time.

   C. Create a custom AWS Lambda function to run a script against the database at regular intervals to obtain usage information.

   D. Create a CloudWatch alarm based on an anomaly detection metric to get alerted if things deviate from a standard behavior.

3. What is the simplest and most efficient method to be notified by email when an RDS database exceeds certain metric thresholds?

   A. Create a CloudTrail alarm and configure a notification event to send an SMS.

   B. Create a CloudWatch alarm and associate an SNS topic with it that sends an email notification.

   C. Create an Amazon CloudWatch Logs rule that triggers an AWS Lambda function to send emails using AWS SES.

   D. Configure a database job to check for the current status of the database, which calls database mail to send alerts.

Further reading

Infrastructure Monitoring with Amazon CloudWatch: `https://www.packtpub.com/product/infrastructure-monitoring-with-amazon-cloudwatch/9781800566057`

14
Backup and Restore

We covered a high-level view of how backups work in AWS in earlier chapters, covering the different database technologies, but in this chapter, we will assess backup and recovery techniques and the use of specific AWS tools, such as AWS Backup. The aim of this chapter is to learn how you gather backup and restore requirements for your applications and then how to create appropriate recovery plans to meet those needs. We will then learn how to create those plans using AWS Backup and finish with a hands-on lab to use those skills in practice.

In this chapter, we're going to cover the following main topics:

- Understanding **Recovery Time Objective** (RTO) and **Recovery Point Objective** (RPO)
- Working with maintenance windows
- Creating backup plans with AWS Backup

Technical requirements

You will require an AWS account with root access; not everything we will do in this chapter may be available in Free Tier, which means it may cost you a small amount to follow the hands-on sections. You will also require access to the AWS **Command-Line Interface** (**CLI**). The AWS guide at `https://docs.aws.amazon.com/cli/latest/userguide/cli-chap-configure.html` explains the steps required, but I will summarize them here:

1. Create an AWS account if you have not already done so.
2. Download the latest version of the AWS CLI from here: `https://docs.aws.amazon.com/cli/latest/userguide/welcome-versions.html#welcome-versions-v2`.
3. Create an admin user: `https://docs.aws.amazon.com/IAM/latest/UserGuide/id_credentials_access-keys.html`.
4. Create an access key for your administration user: `https://docs.aws.amazon.com/IAM/latest/UserGuide/getting-started_create-admin-group.html#getting-started_create-admin-group-cli`.
5. Run the `aws configure` command to set up a profile for your user: `https://docs.aws.amazon.com/cli/latest/userguide/cli-configure-quickstart.html#cli-configure-quickstart-creds`.

You will also require a **Virtual Private Cloud** (**VPC**) that meets the minimum requirements for a **Relational Database Service** (**RDS**) instance: `https://docs.aws.amazon.com/AmazonRDS/latest/UserGuide/USER_VPC.WorkingWithRDSInstanceinaVPC.html`. If you completed the steps in *Chapter 3*, *Understanding AWS Infrastructure*, you will already have a VPC that meets the requirements.

Understanding RTO and RPO

There are two critical terms we need to understand when it comes to backup and recovery, RTO and RPO. These two terms are used to help understand the requirements for a business in terms of the speed of recovery required in case of a failure and how much data could be lost in a worst-case scenario. Correct use of these two values will allow you to ensure your backup and recovery strategy meets these requirements.

Let's first look at RTO.

RTO

RTO is the maximum amount of time a system can be unavailable before the impact to the business becomes too severe and a large amount of damage is done. The damage could be financial, legal, or reputational. With RTO, we are focusing on how quickly the database will be returned to a usable state, and depending on the type of failure, we may end up with different RTO values. For example, imagine that you have a Multi-AZ RDS instance. Your primary database suffers a failure due to an underlying network issue within AWS. RDS will automatically failover the instance typically within 60–120 seconds. This would mean your RTO is 120 seconds in a worst-case scenario using a Multi-AZ deployment. But let's now consider that a developer accidentally runs a `delete` statement without a `where` clause and deletes all the rows in a critical table. This is called a logical failure. You cannot failover to your standby database, as the same command will have been run there already due to the sync between the two AZs. The only way to recover is to either recreate the table manually or restore it from a backup. Restoring from a backup will take considerably longer than the 120 seconds it would take to failover. Your RTO would need to be established by practicing a restore of an RDS snapshot or automated backup to confirm how long it takes. To speed up your RTO, it is quicker to use manual snapshots of an RDS instance than to run a point-in-time restore from an automated RDS backup, as a snapshot is a restore of a full backup, whereas a point-in-time restore also requires all changes since the last backup to be applied as well. The downside of using a snapshot is that you are likely to be restoring a version of the database that is much older than the restore you could get using a point-in-time recovery. This leads us to RPO, and acceptable data loss.

RPO

RPO is the maximum amount of data specified in minutes or hours that a business could lose during a disaster before the impact to the business becomes too severe and a large amount of damage is done. Again, the damage could be financial, legal, or reputational. This metric focuses on how to protect data within the database as opposed to the speed at which it can be restored. In simple terms, RPO typically points to the amount of time between backups, either of the entire database or the transaction log, that will allow the system to be recovered. In the case of RDS, the automated backups that are available will take a full backup of the entire instance once per day and then transaction log backups every 5 minutes. Therefore, RDS offers an RPO of 5 minutes. For DynamoDB, you can enable continuous backups that offer an RPO of less than 5 minutes. However, as pointed out in the *RTO* section, a point-in-time recovery takes longer than restoring a full backup or snapshot, so there will always be a trade-off between RPO and RTO. In general, the smaller the RPO, the longer the RTO, and vice versa. It is almost impossible to create an RPO of zero in the real world. Consider the developer from earlier who ran a `delete` statement without a `where` clause. To offer a zero RPO, all changes to your primary database need to be sent in sync to your standby site. If this doesn't happen and there is a delay, you could end up failing over to a standby that has not yet written all the changes that were committed to your primary site, and therefore, you have data loss. However, if the changes are synced, then the incorrect `delete` statement will also be written at the same time to the standby site, which also introduces data loss.

Using RTO and RPO together

As you can see, you will need to use both RTO and RPO together to allow you to create the best recovery plan for your database. There will almost always be a trade-off between the two policies, and therefore, as a database administrator or consultant, it is important that the application understands the compromise that needs to be made between the speed of recovery and any potential data loss in doing so. It is also important to consider all technologies and services available to help build your recovery plan. You should understand how the following technologies work with regard to recovery:

- **Automated backups** – allow for point-in-time recovery for short RPO during a logical failure.
- **Snapshots** – offer rapid recovery for short RTO during a logical failure.
- **Multi-AZ deployments** – offer rapid RTO and zero RPO for a physical failure.

- **Read replicas** – offer potentially low RTO and low RPO for a physical failure, including cross-Region. Read replicas, however, use asynchronous replication, which means that if there is a sync lag caused by heavy usage on the primary database or a network issue, then your RPO could be higher than expected. Read replicas do not typically have automated failover capabilities, meaning the RTO may be longer while you manually promote the read replica.

Using a combination of technologies will often be required to meet the RTO and RPO needs of the application, and there will likely be several questions in the exam asking you to give the best solution to meet a certain RTO/RPO for a database.

Let's now look at how we can use maintenance windows to control any required outages for patching, general maintenance, and to control the time that our full daily backups run.

Working with maintenance windows

All of the AWS-managed database services offer a maintenance window that can be defined by the customer. A maintenance window is a weekly timeslot when AWS is authorized to carry out patching work or other tasks that may cause an outage of your database. These outages will always be communicated in advance, but they cannot always be avoided. There is another window that will be created for a daily backup on RDS. AWS will assign a random maintenance window when you create a managed database. As a result, it is critical that the maintenance and backup windows are set for the quietest time for your application to avoid an unexpected outage or performance issue due to a backup running during peak hours.

You can modify the windows during and after the creation of a managed database.

You can also control the backup times and patterns using AWS Backup, which we will learn next.

Creating backup plans with AWS Backup

AWS Backup is a backup scheduling and storage tool for a wide range of AWS services, including RDS, DocumentDB, Neptune, and DynamoDB. AWS Backup allows you to create centralized and standardized backup policies to ensure compliance with an organization's RTO and RPO requirements and to simplify the control of backups and recoveries across an entire AWS account. AWS Backup can also be configured to back up on-premises resources by using a gateway, but this can only be used to back up virtual machines and servers rather than initializing a database-level backup. AWS backups are stored in a backup vault to protect them from unauthorized access.

AWS Backup allows you to define a large number of policies to meet your needs; these include the following:

- **Backup intervals** – how often do you want a backup to be taken and what type? For databases, this could be a full backup or a continuous backup.
- **Data retention** – you can define how long AWS Backup will store the backups it takes.
- **Archival** – AWS Backup lets you define policies to move data to S3 Glacier after a certain number of days to reduce storage costs.

Let's create an AWS Backup policy and attach it to an RDS instance. If you do not have an RDS instance running, please create one before continuing. You can refer to the steps in *Chapter 4, Relational Database Service*, for assistance if required. We are going to create a backup plan that ensures our databases are backed up every hour to reduce our RTO. We will also store our backups for 90 days before moving them to cold storage, and we want all backups to be deleted after 1 year:

1. Log in to the AWS Management Console.
2. Navigate to **AWS Backup** from the main menu.
3. Click **Create Backup plan** from **Dashboard**:

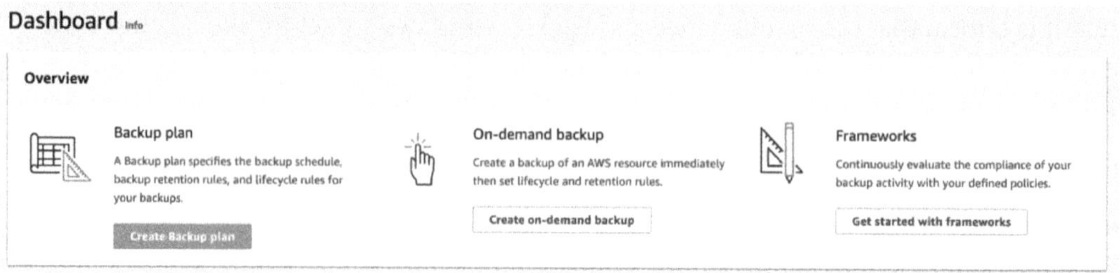

Figure 14.1 – AWS Backup – Create Backup plan

4. Select **Build a new plan** and enter a name:

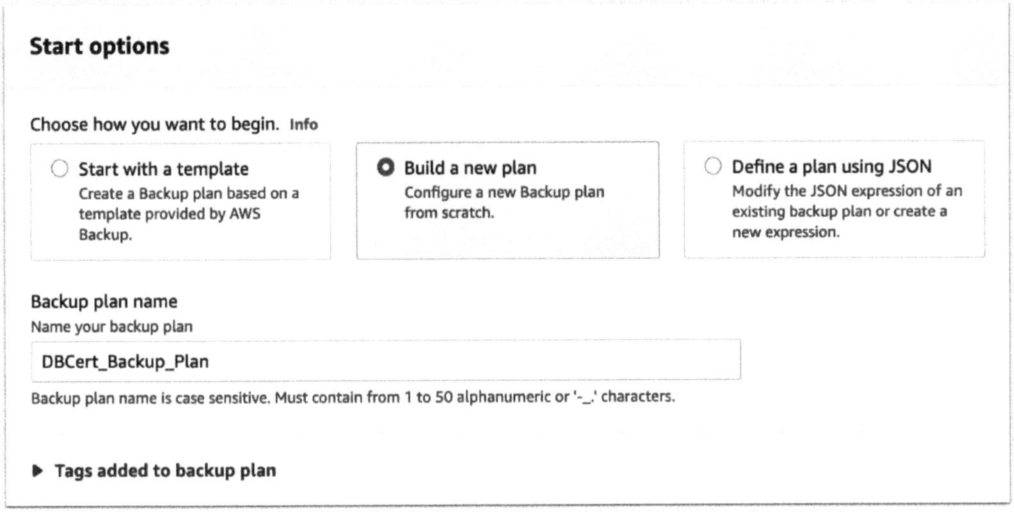

Start options

Choose how you want to begin. Info

Start with a template
Create a Backup plan based on a template provided by AWS Backup.

Build a new plan
Configure a new Backup plan from scratch.

Define a plan using JSON
Modify the JSON expression of an existing backup plan or create a new expression.

Backup plan name
Name your backup plan
DBCert_Backup_Plan
Backup plan name is case sensitive. Must contain from 1 to 50 alphanumeric or '-_.' characters.

▶ Tags added to backup plan

Figure 14.2 – Build a new plan

5. First, let's add our hourly backup rule:

    - Give the rule a name.
    - Set **Backup frequency** to **Hourly**.
    - Set **Backup window** to **03:00 AM**.
    - Set **Transition to cold storage** to **90** days.

- Set **Retention period** to **1** year.
- Leave all other settings as default:

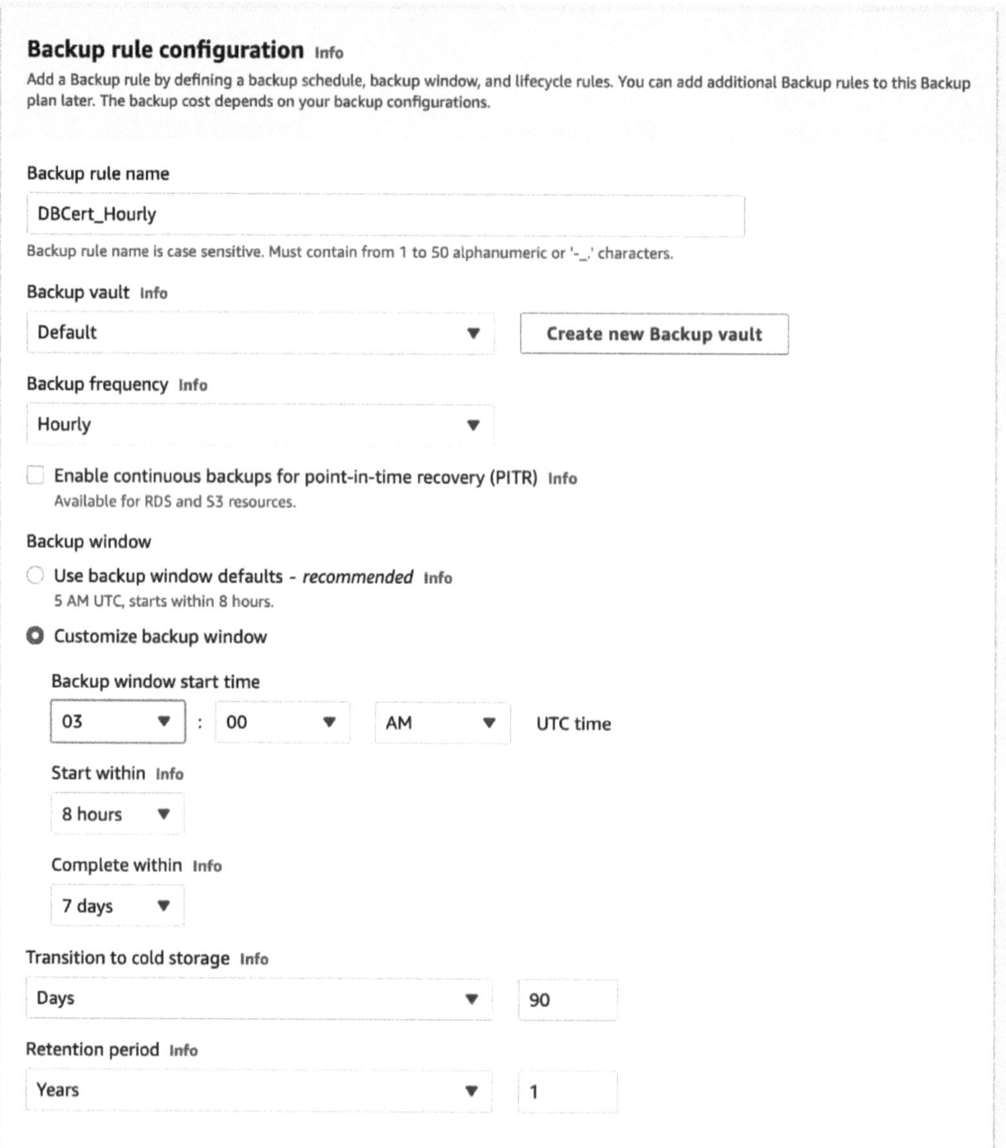

Figure 14.3 – The hourly backup settings

6. Click **Create plan** at the bottom of the page.

   We now need to attach this policy to our RDS instance before it can be used.

7. Navigate to **Backup plans** on the left-hand menu and select the plan you just created.
8. Under the **Resource assignments** section, select **Assign resources**:

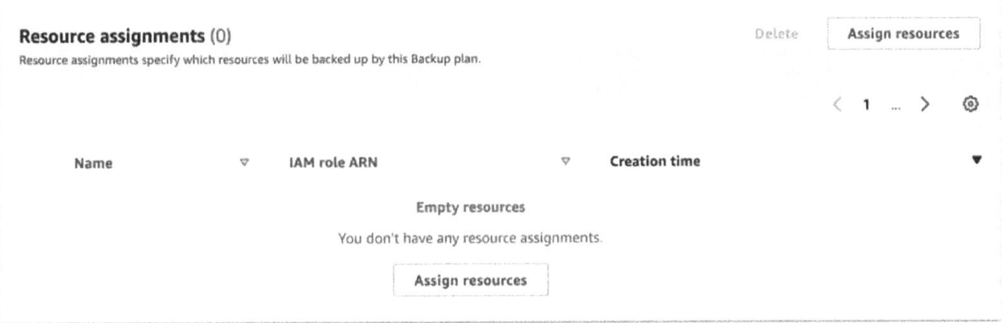

Figure 14.4 – Assign a resource to the backup plan

9. Give the resource assignment a name and leave the IAM role as default.

   We want to assign all of our RDS instances to this backup plan. This will affect both existing RDS instances and all new ones that are created too, ensuring that our backups always meet our policies.

Under **Define resource selection**, select **Include specific resource types.** Select **RDS** from the **Resource type** dropdown and leave **Database names** as **All databases (*)**:

Assign resources Info

Assign resources to this Backup plan using tags and resource IDs.

1. Define resource selection Info

Protect all resources or specify resources by type or ID.

○ Include all resource types
Protect all resource types that are enabled in your account.

◉ Include specific resource types
Choose resources by type or specify individual resources by ID.

2. Select specific resource types Info

Choose specific resource types that you want to protect with this backup plan. You can also exclude specific resource IDs from the selection.

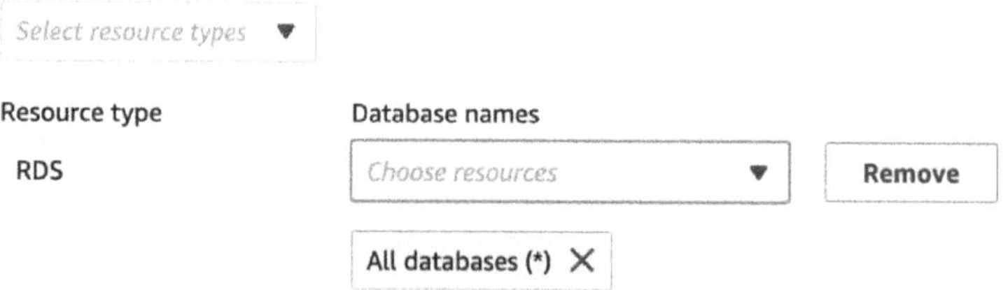

Figure 14.5 – Assign a resource to the backup plan

10. Click **Assign resources** at the bottom and accept the warning about backing up a large number of resources.
11. Navigate to the dashboard. You will see that all the values are still showing as zero. This is because we scheduled our backup to take place at 3 A.M. Let the backups run overnight and check the dashboard tomorrow to see the reports.

Once you have confirmed that the backups ran successfully, you can delete the backup plan and any RDS instances you are no longer using.

Let's now review the chapter, starting with the summary.

Summary

In this chapter, we have explored several backup and recovery technologies and philosophies, such as RTO and RPO, the use of maintenance windows. We learned how we can use AWS Backup to create backup policies and rules that can be applied across all of our databases to ensure consistency and adherence to required data retention policies.

The AWS Certified Database – Specialty exam will ask questions about the required configuration to meet a specific RTO/RPO need, and you will need to know the recovery times offered for different databases, specifically RDS and DynamoDB. In the next chapter, we will learn about troubleshooting tools and techniques you can use to resolve issues on your AWS database.

Cheat sheet

This cheat sheet summarizes the key points from this chapter:

- RPO is the maximum amount of data a company can lose without sustaining major damage.
- RTO is the maximum amount of time a system can be unavailable without sustaining major damage.
- RPO and RTO need to be considered together to define a backup and recovery strategy.
- A recovery strategy can include backups, standby databases, read replicas, and manual scripts.
- AWS Backup allows you to create centralized backup policies and plans to ensure that all your databases will meet your RTOs and RPOs.
- AWS-managed databases offer maintenance windows that can be configured by the user to control the times that patching or other tasks that may cause a service disruption can run.
- RDS daily backups run during a backup window, which should be set during the least busy times for the application to avoid performance impact.

Review

Let's now practice a few exam-style questions:

1. End users of an application are complaining that they are experiencing intermittent performance issues with RDS for MySQL. After investigation, a database specialist determines that the performance issues occur during the automated backup window. What actions can the specialist perform to improve backup performance? (Select two.)

   A. Schedule an automated backup window to occur outside of peak hours.

   B. Increase the instance class.

   C. Create backups from a read replica.

   D. Increase the number of shards.

   E. Increase the storage on the RDS instance.

   F. Change the storage to provisioned **Input/Output Operations per Second** (**IOPS**).

2. Your company has a policy that requires all RDS backups to occur automatically on a specified schedule and be stored for 90 days. What is the optimal solution to meet this requirement?

   A. Create an AWS Backup policy for all RDS databases to include automated backups on RDS. Configure the data retention period to 90 days.

   B. Modify each RDS database to turn on automated backups. Configure backup retention to 90 days.

   C. Create a Lambda function to create an RDS database snapshot. Create a CloudWatch Events rule to run the Lambda function according to the required schedule.

   D. Configure an RDS backup life cycle policy to archive data in Amazon S3 Glacier.

3. Your company's recovery policy requires that all database backups are stored in a different AWS Region. What is the most cost-effective and optimal solution to meet this requirement?

   A. Configure an RDS read-replica instance in the secondary Region. Enable RDS automated backups on the read-replica instance.

   B. Create an AWS Backup policy to store the backups in a different Region.

   C. Manually copy the RDS database snapshots to an S3 bucket. Enable Cross-Region Replication on the S3 bucket.

   D. Manually copy the RDS database snapshot to the secondary Region.

Further reading

To understand the concepts of this chapter in further detail, refer to the AWS Backup guide: `https://aws.amazon.com/backup/`.

15
Troubleshooting Tools and Techniques

Being able to quickly identify and resolve common errors on your **Amazon Web Services (AWS)** database is important both in the workplace to avoid prolonged outages and also during the *AWS Certified Database – Specialty* exam. The exam will often ask questions about the most likely root cause of a problem or the simplest way to resolve an issue. Understanding the basic troubleshooting steps and knowing some advanced tools that AWS offers to help diagnose faults will help you in the exam.

In this chapter, we're going to cover the following main topics:

- Using Trusted Advisor
- Troubleshooting techniques
- Resolving common errors

Let's start by learning about Trusted Advisor, including how to use it to assist with troubleshooting scenarios and how it can be used to help you correctly configure and use your AWS databases.

Technical requirements

You will require an AWS account with root access; not everything we will do in this chapter may be available in **Free Tier**, which means it may cost you a small amount to follow the hands-on sections. You will also require **AWS Command Line Interface** (**CLI**) access. The AWS guide found at `https://docs.aws.amazon.com/cli/latest/userguide/cli-chap-configure.html` will explain the steps required, but I will summarize these here:

1. Open an AWS account if you have not already done so.
2. Download the AWS CLI latest version from here: `https://docs.aws.amazon.com/cli/latest/userguide/welcome-versions.html#welcome-versions-v2`.
3. Create an admin user by going to the following link: `https://docs.aws.amazon.com/IAM/latest/UserGuide/getting-started_create-admin-group.html#getting-started_create-admin-group-cli`.

   Create an access key for your admin user by going to the following link: `https://docs.aws.amazon.com/IAM/latest/UserGuide/id_credentials_access-keys.html`.
4. Run the `aws configure` command to set up a profile for your user. The following link shows you how to do this: `https://docs.aws.amazon.com/cli/latest/userguide/cli-configure-quickstart.html#cli-configure-quickstart-creds`.

You will also require a **virtual private cloud** (**VPC**) that meets the minimum requirements for a **Relational Database Service** (**RDS**) instance. Go to the following link for assistance with this: `https://docs.aws.amazon.com/AmazonRDS/latest/UserGuide/USER_VPC.WorkingWithRDSInstanceinaVPC.html`. If you completed the steps in *Chapter 3*, *Understanding AWS Infrastructure*, you will already have a VPC that meets the requirements.

Using Trusted Advisor

AWS Trusted Advisor is a tool you can use to get real-time reports on all of your AWS services. Trusted Advisor will by default highlight the following areas:

- **Cost optimization**—You will be given recommendations that can save you money. Typically, this will be downsizing an instance or changing a storage type if it isn't being used.
- **Performance**—You will be advised on how to improve the performance of your applications or databases. For example, this may show when an RDS instance is running at a high **central processing unit** (**CPU**) or is suffering from high disk **input/output** (**I/O**).
- **Security**—You will be able to see recommendations about security for your application and database, including security group configuration and patches that need to be applied.
- **Fault tolerance**—Typically, Trusted Advisor will notify you if you are not using a **Multi-Availability Zone** (**Multi-AZ**) configuration for production workloads or if you have any databases that are not being backed up.
- **Service limits**—Most AWS services have limits applied. For example, you cannot have more than five VPCs in a single region by default. Trusted Advisor will notify you when you are using more than 80% of any limit.

The following screenshot shows a typical Trusted Advisor dashboard with critical (**Action recommended**) and advisory (**Investigation recommended**) checks. You can see the different headings we just learned about and the number of recommendations in each area.

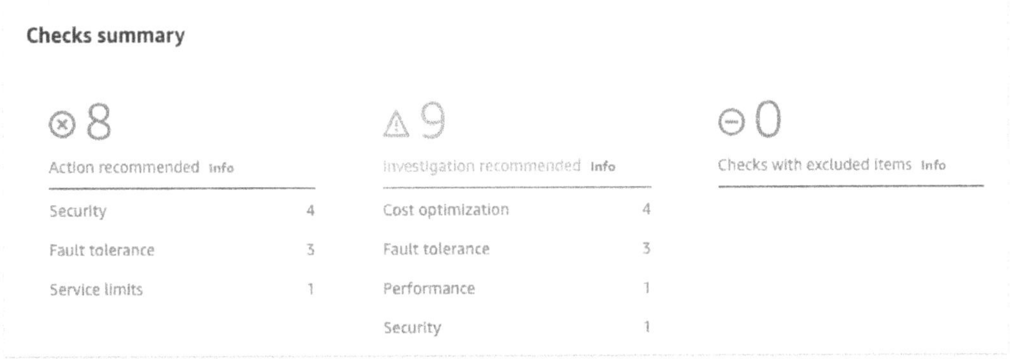

Figure 15.1 – Trusted Advisor dashboard

Once you have seen the **Dashboard** view, you can drill down into the specific headings to find out exactly what Trusted Advisor is recommending. The following screenshot provides an example of an issue with security groups that have been set to **Allow All IPs.** This would be considered a potential major security issue as anyone could theoretically log in to your **Elastic Compute Cloud** (**EC2**) or RDS instance:

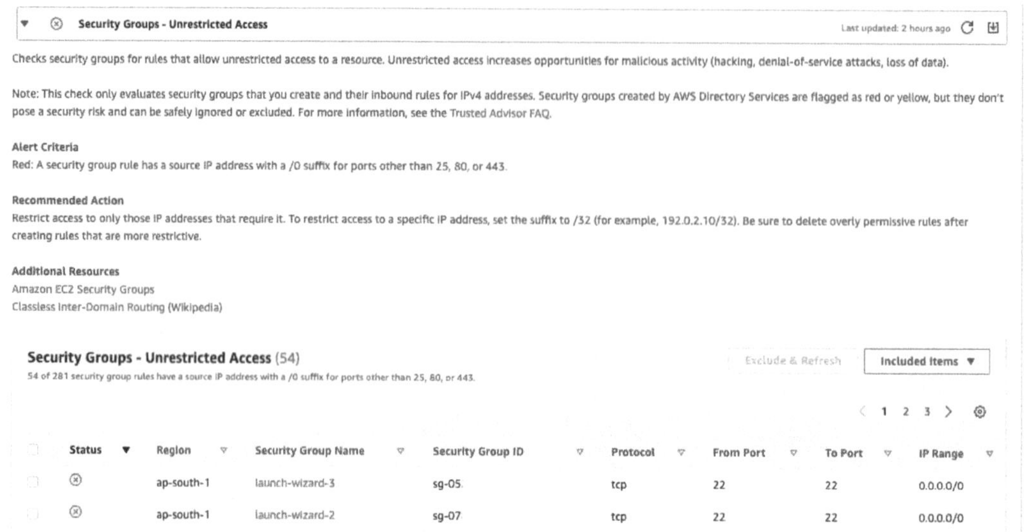

Figure 15.2 – Security group recommendations

Trusted Advisor will also show you the potential savings available if you follow the recommended actions as well as highlighting security and configuration concerns. AWS will advise you to downgrade instance classes if they are not being used efficiently, as well as change storage instance types for RDS if appropriate. The amount you could potentially save per month is highlighted on the **Dashboard**, as illustrated in the following screenshot:

Potential monthly savings

$10,206.02

Trusted Advisor has identified 5 cost optimization checks that can save you money. For example, you might have unused resources in your AWS account that can be deleted. Choose a cost optimization check to view the recommendations.

Figure 15.3 – Potential monthly savings

Trusted Advisor is not region-specific, which means you can see a report for all services across all regions. This makes it a very useful centralized reporting tool for larger companies or businesses running a multi-region AWS estate.

Trusted Advisor can be configured to email contacts with a weekly status report. You can create a different contact for different areas such as **Billing**, **Operations**, and **Security** so that the right teams are notified, as illustrated in the following screenshot:

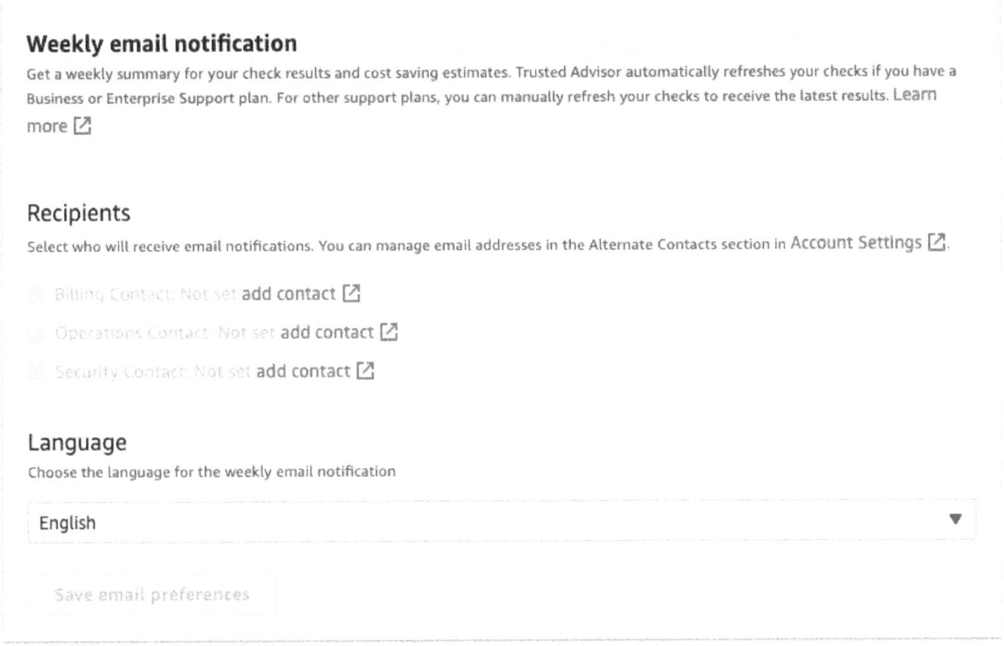

Weekly email notification

Get a weekly summary for your check results and cost saving estimates. Trusted Advisor automatically refreshes your checks if you have a Business or Enterprise Support plan. For other support plans, you can manually refresh your checks to receive the latest results. Learn more

Recipients

Select who will receive email notifications. You can manage email addresses in the Alternate Contacts section in Account Settings.

Billing Contact: Not set add contact

Operations Contact: Not set add contact

Security Contact: Not set add contact

Language

Choose the language for the weekly email notification

English

Save email preferences

Figure 15.4 – Weekly email notification

Trusted Advisor connects with the **AWS Health Dashboard** to monitor any pending patching or maintenance windows. You can use the **AWS Health Dashboard** to find out if any of your RDS or EC2 instances are due maintenance and, if so, you can look to schedule the outage at a time convenient for the application and business. Don't forget that if you ignore a maintenance request or patching notification for too long, AWS will force the change during the scheduled maintenance window.

Trusted Advisor is a useful high-level view of your global AWS estate and looks at your services through the five headings of **Security**, **Fault tolerance**, **Cost optimization**, **Performance**, and **Service limits**. These headings directly align with the AWS Well-Architected Framework. The AWS Well-Architected Framework offers guidance and advice on how to best design, provision, operate, and maintain your workloads with the AWS cloud.

The AWS Well-Architected Framework helps a business to understand the trade-offs and compromises needed to meet its needs; for example, running a Multi-AZ deployment for all workloads will improve fault tolerance but it will cost more. For some workloads, the associated recovery time from a backup for a Single-AZ instance is sufficient, and therefore they can achieve the **Recovery Time Objective** (**RTO**) and **Recovery Point Objective** (**RPO**) without the additional costs of Multi-AZ. While Trusted Advisor cannot offer specific guidance for those use cases, using it in combination with the Well-Architected Framework will help optimize your AWS estate in the most appropriate way for each application. You can also use the AWS Well-Architected Framework to generate reports to help in those decisions. The difference between the two tools is that Trusted Advisor watches workloads you already have running in AWS, whereas **Web Application Firewall** (**WAF**) is used to plan those workloads before you migrate them by answering questions about the workload, its data patterns, compliance rules, RPO and RTO, and operational questions. You will receive a customized report with full recommendations of how to deploy that workload or how to optimize it if it is already running within AWS. The following screenshot shows a sample of an AWS Well-Architected Framework report once completed:

Security

Question	Status	Your Answers	Fixes
How are you protecting access to and use of the AWS root account credentials?	☑	- MFA and Minimal Use of Root	ADDITIONAL BEST PRACTICES: - No Use of Root

Question	Status	Your Answers	Fixes
How are you defining roles and responsibilities of system users to control human access to the AWS Management Console and API?	☑	- Employee Life-Cycle Managed - Minimum Privileges	

Question	Status	Your Answers	Fixes
How are you limiting automated access to AWS resources? (e.g., applications, scripts, and/or third-party tool or service)	☑	- Dynamic Authentication for Automated Access	

Question	Status	Your Answers	Fixes
How are you capturing and analyzing logs?	⚠	- AWS Cloud Trail Enabled - Monitored OS or Application Logs	ADDITIONAL BEST PRACTICES: - Activity Monitored Appropriately

Figure 15.5 – AWS Well-Architected Framework sample report

We've learned how to find configuration and operational recommendations for workloads already running in AWS using Trusted Advisor. We then discovered how we can use the AWS Well-Architected Framework to help us design and plan our workloads and migrations into AWS. Both of these tools offer a high-level view at the service level, but what can we use if we are suffering a problem with a specific query or we are receiving a database error? Let's now take a look at some troubleshooting techniques to try to identify where an error is coming from.

Troubleshooting techniques

With any of the AWS managed services such as RDS, it can be difficult to work out if any error you are seeing or performance issue is being caused by the database itself or if there is a problem with the RDS service or the VPC. For example, users are complaining of not being able to log into the database; this could be a database-level issue where perhaps a password has changed or user permissions have been modified, or perhaps they are hitting connection limits, or this could be an issue with the RDS service itself—the RDS instance may be down or the underlying **virtual machine** (**VM**) may have a fault, or the issue could be linked to security groups or **network access control lists** (**NACLs**) not allowing the end user's connection through. As you can see, without further information, you might need to check in multiple different locations. The first troubleshooting technique is to always gather as much information as required before you start to debug, and don't make any changes until you are sure of the resolution as this can make things worse or open up a security problem. The error message itself will often give a lot of information and guidance as to where the problem is. For a connection issue, you would get a different type of error if the database cannot be contacted at all from one where the user has the wrong password or locked account. Firstly, you can quickly check the status of an RDS instance to ensure there are no RDS-level errors or outages that might be causing your problem. This can be useful even for a performance problem, as a running backup can cause slowness. The following code will return all events and status changes of your RDS instance for the time period specified:

```
aws rds describe-events --source-identifier dbcert-mon
--source-type db-instance --start-time 2022-03-20T16:00Z --end-
time 2022-03-20T17:00Z
```

To get full error messages, you can use the RDS console or the AWS CLI to view the database logs. Using the CLI is often the quickest way if you have access keys configured. You can use a similar command to this to download the latest `error.log` log for MySQL into a file called `errorlog.txt`:

```
aws rds download-db-log-file-portion --db-instance-identifier
dbcert-mon --starting-token 0 --output text --log-file-name
log/ERROR.1 > errorlog.txt
```

You can use similar code for any RDS instance, changing the log filename as appropriate.

If you cannot find any errors in the logs, this would indicate a problem with the RDS instance or the VPC itself.

Another useful tool you can use to help diagnose errors reported by your applications is Application Insights. Applications Insights is an advanced feature of CloudWatch that uses **machine learning** (**ML**) (through SageMaker) to model failure patterns of similarly configured applications from around the world. It can then offer guidance as to the best course of action to take to resolve them. This can be really useful in situations where you are seeing an application issue but the real fault is with the database. For example, if you are running a web application that starts giving **HyperText Transfer Protocol** (**HTTP**) `500` errors (internal server error), your operations team might start looking at the application first, which would be a logical troubleshooting step, but using Application Insights to look at the entire stack from the web frontend right to the database storage would inform them that the database is currently experiencing high memory utilization, which means it is performing poorly and the application is timing out. By using Application Insights, you can identify the root cause much faster and reduce your RTO for major incidents. The following screenshot shows an example dashboard for a .NET web-based application running SQL Server on EC2 where the database did not have backups running, which caused the database log to fill up; this was the root cause of the application problems:

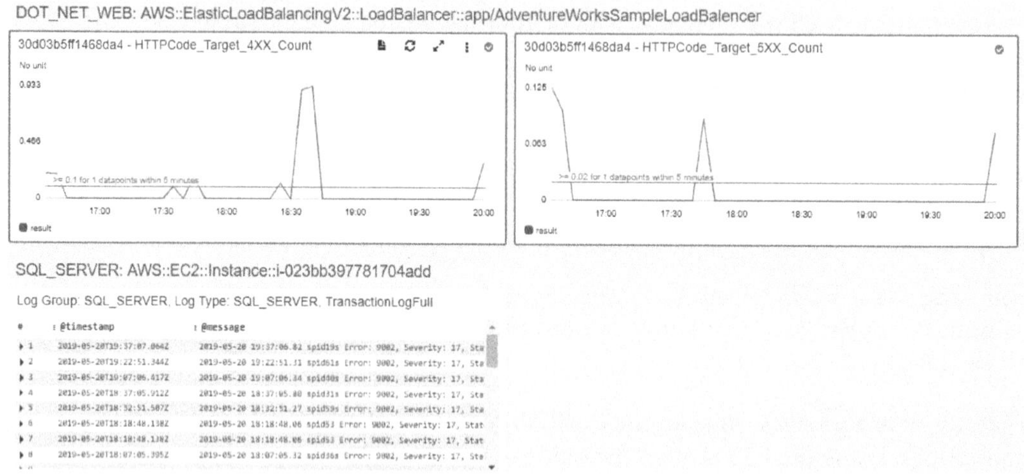

Figure 15.6 – Application Insights dashboard

Now we've learned some troubleshooting techniques and tools we can use to help quickly identify the problems we are seeing, let's go on to learn some of the most common errors you are likely to encounter on RDS.

Resolving common errors

Some issues on RDS are seen more frequently than others. We are going to learn some of the most common errors and how to resolve them. Firstly, we will learn how to deal with connectivity issues with an RDS instance.

RDS connection issues

Typically, connection errors are caused by one of five areas, as outlined here:

- **Security group rules**—Review your security groups to make sure the inbound rules allow connections from the source on the port the database is running on.
- **NACL rules**—Review your NACLs to ensure that inbound or outbound traffic to/from the database has not been set to `DENY`.
- **Publicly available not set**—To access the RDS instance from outside of your VPC, you need to have made it publicly available and given it a public **Internet Protocol (IP)** address. You can change this by modifying the instance.
- **Internet gateway**—To access the RDS instance, you need an internet gateway within the public subnets of your VPC to allow traffic to flow over the internet to the user.
- **Local network configuration issues**—If none of the preceding areas is causing the issue, then you may have an internal firewall blocking your connection.

During the exam, you will often be asked what is the most likely problem that has caused a connection problem. Look closely at the question to see if it refers to work being done or any changes made to the VPC or security groups, as often, changes can be made to security groups by a team that doesn't understand the impact on the databases using those security groups.

RDS security issues

When using **Identity and Access Management (IAM)** authentication, you may receive the following error: `"ERROR 1045 (28000): Access denied for user 'root'@'10.0.4.201' (using password: YES)"`.

To resolve this error, you need to go through the following steps:

1. Check IAM authentication is enabled on the instance.
2. Ensure the user has been granted the correct IAM role permissions.
3. Check that the database user mapped to the IAM user has been properly configured.

Remember that an IAM user is only used for authentication and that permissions are granted at the database layer. If you do not have a mapped user within the database or they do not have permissions to log in, then you will receive errors.

Resetting the DB instance owner password

Only the account owner using the root account can reset the master password on an RDS instance. You can reset the password using either the AWS CLI or the console.

RDS DB instance outage or reboot

Certain changes or modifications to an RDS instance will cause it to reboot instantly if you choose to do so. Some other changes will cause it to reboot during the next maintenance window.

A DB instance reboot occurs immediately when one of the following occurs:

- The backup retention period is changed from `0` to a nonzero value or from a nonzero value to 0 and **Apply Immediately** is set to `true`
- The instance class is changed and **Apply Immediately** is set to `true`
- You change the storage type and **Apply Immediately** is set to `true`

A DB instance reboot occurs during the maintenance window when one of the following occurs:

- The backup retention period is changed from 0 to a nonzero value or from a nonzero value to 0 and **Apply Immediately** is set to `false`
- The instance class is changed and **Apply Immediately** is set to `false`

With most RDS changes, you can specify if you want the change to be applied immediately or during the maintenance window. You will need to decide the right option depending on the situation and acceptable downtime for the application.

RDS DB parameter changes not taking effect

Some parameters require the instance to be rebooted before they take effect. You can check the current status of the parameter group via the RDS console configuration tab for the instance. If the instance needs a reboot, you will see the following indication:

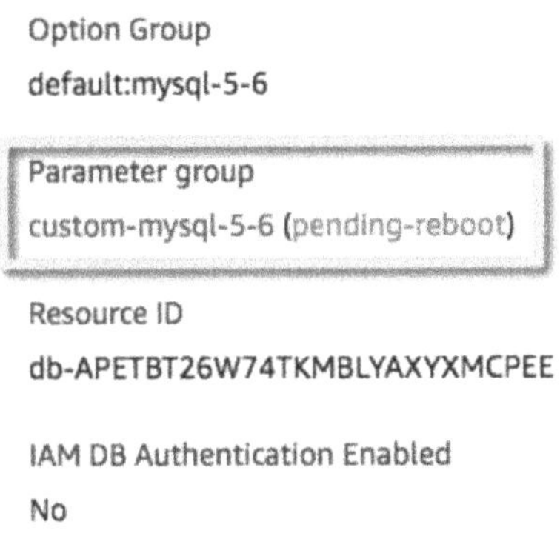

Option Group
default:mysql-5-6

Parameter group
custom-mysql-5-6 (pending-reboot)

Resource ID
db-APETBT26W74TKMBLYAXYXMCPEE

IAM DB Authentication Enabled
No

Figure 15.7 – Parameter (pending-reboot)

Once you reboot the instance, the parameter change will be applied.

RDS DB instance running out of storage

An RDS DB instance can run out of storage even when storage autoscaling is turned on as you define the maximum storage limit the instance can auto-extend into. You are recommended to use CloudWatch alerts to be notified if the free space on your RDS DB instance falls below an acceptable limit. To increase the storage, you can modify the RDS instance via the AWS console, or you can use the AWS CLI as demonstrated here, where the `allocated-storage` size is in **gigabytes** (**GB**):

```
aws rds modify-db-instance --db-instance-identifier dbcert-mon
--allocated-storage 60 --apply-immediately
```

Using the `--apply-immediately` flag means that the storage will be added as soon as the RDS instance can do so. Adding storage does not cause an outage, but it can cause performance issues as the storage is rebalanced or moved around to spread it more equally over the available disks.

RDS insufficient DB instance capacity

An `InsufficientDBInstanceCapacity` error can be seen when you try to start, modify, or provision a new RDS instance. It means that there are no available RDS VMs to run your workload at the time. You are more likely to see the error if you pick a specific AZ to deploy in rather than letting AWS decide, as this limits the number of available VMs that you could use. To work around this error, you can do one of the following:

- Use a different instance class
- Use a different AZ

- Don't specify an AZ to deploy in
- Wait a few minutes and try again

We've now learned some of the most common errors seen for RDS instances and the steps you should follow to resolve them. In the exam, you will be asked troubleshooting-based questions about the easiest or simplest way to resolve an error or the most likely root cause. Learning these common errors and resolutions will help you in answering such questions. Let's now look at how you identify when changes are made to your AWS databases and by whom they were done.

Auditing changes

A common situation database administrators and engineers are often faced with is a database being altered or shut down unexpectedly. You will need to review who has made the change so that your security controls and procedures can be updated as quickly as possible. You may also need to know exactly what was accessed or modified for compliance reporting reasons. Database-level changes will be stored in the database logs, but if a shared account was used, it can be hard to determine who actually made the changes. CloudTrail might be able to help as it keeps an audit of any changes that have been made to a service in an AWS account, along with a record of who made the change. If someone shut down or modified an RDS instance, you would be able to find the account that did it. CloudTrail can also audit all **application programming interface** (**API**) calls made to a DynamoDB instance, allowing you to audit all modifications to records.

Learning how to troubleshoot common problems and resolve them as efficiently as possible is a useful skill both for the exam and for daily database administration tasks. Auditing of changes made to your databases is also another very useful skill and can be a requirement for compliance and regulatory frameworks.

Let's now remind ourselves of the key learning points in this chapter.

Summary

In this chapter, we have learned about Trusted Advisor and used it to help identify security configuration problems, wrongly sized RDS instances, and RDS servers that need to be patched. We then looked at some best practices for troubleshooting RDS, DynamoDB, and other AWS-managed databases, including how to use the database logs, CloudWatch, CloudTrail, and AWS Health Dashboard to identify problems. Finally, we looked at how you can resolve some common problems and error messages from AWS-managed databases.

The *AWS Certified Database – Specialty* exam will have many questions about troubleshooting errors with connectivity, storage issues, performance bottlenecks, and excessive costs, so being able to understand best-practice methods to diagnose and resolve them will greatly improve your chances of success in the exam.

In the next chapter, we will be completing a practice exam so that you can learn the style of the AWS exam questions. You will also be able to note which answers you got wrong as key points for revision and further practice before you schedule your actual exam date.

Let's now review the chapter in the *Cheat sheet* section and then answer a few questions about the topics from this chapter.

Cheat sheet

This cheat sheet summarizes the main key points from this chapter, as follows:

- Trusted Advisor will offer recommendations about your AWS services.
- Trusted Advisor follows the same pillars as the Well-Architected Framework:
  - **Security**
  - **Cost optimization**
  - **Fault tolerance**
  - **Performance**
  - **Service limits**
- You can use Trusted Advisor to view all AWS services in all regions.
- The AWS Health Dashboard gives an overview of any current operational issues that may be affecting your AWS services.
- The AWS Health Dashboard also shows any outstanding patches or maintenance operations that need to be carried out on your services.
- You can use Application Insights to get the power of ML analytics to help quickly identify the root causes of application failures or errors.

Review

Let's now practice a few exam-style questions, as follows:

1. A company has a critical system that runs on RDS SQL Server and is accessed through an in-house web application. The web application has recently been improved with additional reporting capabilities. The program has been slow to reply to certain reporting requests after the upgrade. How can you find the root cause of the issue?

   A. Install and configure Amazon CloudWatch Application Insights for Microsoft .NET and Microsoft SQL Server. Use a CloudWatch dashboard to identify the root cause of application issues.

   B. Enable RDS Performance Insights and determine which query is creating the problem. Request changes to the query to address the problem.

   C. Use AWS X-Ray deployed with Amazon RDS to track query system traces.

   D. Create a support request and work with AWS Support to identify the source of the issue.

2. You are a database administrator for a small company. Over the weekend, some security modifications were made to your AWS accounts after an audit failed. End users have been complaining that they cannot access the RDS Oracle database since the changes were made. What is the most likely reason?

   A. The RDS instance has been shut down

   B. The RDS instance has failed over to the secondary AZ and the connection strings have not been updated

   C. The security groups have been altered, which now blocks access to the RDS instances

   D. There is an issue with the VPC being used for access

3. You have received a CloudWatch notification that your RDS MySQL instance has less than 100 **megabytes (MB)** of storage space left. Which is the correct command to immediately increase the storage to 10 GB using the AWS CLI?

   A. `aws rds modify-db --db-instance-identifier dbcert-mon --allocated-storage 10`

   B. `aws rds alter-database --db-instance-identifier dbcert-mon --allocated-storage 10 --apply-immediately`

C. `aws rds modify-db-instance --db-instance-identifier dbcert-mon --allocated-storage 10 --apply-immediately`

D. `aws rds alter-db-instance --db-instance-identifier dbcert-mon --allocated-storage 10240 --apply-immediately`

Answers can be found in *Chapter 17, Answers*.

Further reading

To understand the concepts of this chapter in further detail, you can refer to the following sources:

- AWS service limits:

  `https://docs.aws.amazon.com/awssupport/latest/user/service-limits.html`

- AWS Trusted Advisor documentation:

  `https://docs.aws.amazon.com/awssupport/latest/user/trusted-advisor.html`

Part 5: Assessment

Now it's time to put the learning into practice through a practice exam complete with full explanations of the answers with context and tools to improve learning.

This section includes the following chapters:

- *Chapter 16, Exam Practice*
- *Chapter 17, Answers*

16
Exam Practice

This chapter contains a practice exam with 60 questions. Some of these questions have been asked before and some have not. These are very close to the feel and style of the **Amazon Web Services** (**AWS**) exam. Remember the tips in *Chapter 1, AWS Certified Database - Specialty Exam Overview*—remove obviously wrong answers first and then re-read the question to see if there are clues to help work out the right answer. You may not know the right answer to each question, but you should be able to work out the wrong answers and obtain the correct answer in that way. It is likely when you come to take the AWS exam that you will not know every answer as the subject is very broad, but being able to remove clearly wrong answers will greatly improve your chances of being able to work out the correct answer. If you wish to time your exam attempt, then allocate 170 minutes to complete this.

The 60 questions are presented here:

1. A small company is developing an **Internet of Things** (**IoT**) application using **DynamoDB** as the data store for device event data. The application requires us to purge all event data older than 30 days. What is the best solution to implement this requirement?

    A. Enable **Time to Live** (**TTL**) on the DynamoDB table and store the expiration timestamp in the TTL attribute in the epoch format.

    B. Implement a Lambda function to perform a query and delete on the table for items with a timestamp greater than 30 days. Use CloudWatch Events to trigger the Lambda function.

C. Create a new DynamoDB table every 30 days. Delete the old DynamoDB table.

D. Enable DynamoDB Streams on the table. Implement a Lambda function to read events from the stream and delete expired items.

2. A company based in Asia wishes to expand its operation to the North American regions. They wish to perform some performance testing and **User Acceptance Testing** (**UAT**) on the production-like data of their DynamoDB-based backend system in the North American regions. What is the optimal solution for achieving data migration to enable the team to perform their testing tasks?

   A. Perform **Point-in-time Recovery** (**PITR**) of the current DynamoDB table into the new region.

   B. Enable DynamoDB Streams on the current DynamoDB table. Create a new DynamoDB table in the new region. Create a Lambda function to pull the current DynamoDB table stream and deliver batch records from the streams to the new DynamoDB table.

   C. Create a new DynamoDB table in the new region. Create an AWS Glue job to perform data export from the current DynamoDB table and data import into the new DynamoDB table.

   D. Enable DynamoDB Streams. Add a North American region to the current DynamoDB table **Global Tables** settings.

3. An Amazon **Relational Database Service** (**RDS**) MySQL database instance is failing to reboot. Event logs show the following error: `MySQL could not be started due to incompatible parameters`. Which actions must be performed to resolve this issue?

   A. Use a **Structured Query Language** (**SQL**) statement to identify system variables that have custom values. Use a `SET` statement to set any modified system variables to their values.

   B. Select the default database parameter group in the RDS console. Choose a reset parameter group action to revert the parameters to their default values.

   C. Modify the RDS database instance to use the default DB parameter group. Reboot the instance.

   D. Compare the RDS database instance parameter group to the default parameter group. Roll back any custom parameters that have been changed since the last instance restart to their default values. Reboot the instance.

4. An organization is looking to migrate from their RDS MySQL database instance to an Aurora MySQL database cluster to improve performance. What is the optimal solution for performing data migration in this scenario?

    A. Use AWS **Database Migration Service** (**DMS**) to migrate the data.

    B. Use the `mysqldump` utility to copy the data.

    C. Create an Aurora read replica of the source database. After the migration is complete, promote the Aurora read replica to a standalone DB cluster.

    D. Copy the backup files from the source database to an Amazon **Simple Storage Service** (**S3**) bucket. Restore the Aurora MySQL DB cluster from those files.

5. An application uses a `GetItem` operation to read data from a DynamoDB table. Which strategy can be used to reduce the size of the read operations and increase read efficiency?

    A. Use a filter expression

    B. Use pagination

    C. Use a parallel scan

    D. Use a projection expression

6. An application development team complains that they are experiencing performance issues with ElastiCache. After investigation, a database specialist determines that the performance issues occur during the automated backup window. Which actions can the specialist perform to improve backup performance? (Select two)

    A. Schedule the automated backup window to occur at midnight

    B. Set the `reserved-memory-percent` parameter

    C. Create backups from a read replica

    D. Increase the number of shards

7. An application team complains that a DocumentDB cluster is taking a long time to return query results. What can a database specialist use to investigate the query execution plan and analyze the query performance?

    A. CloudWatch Logs

    B. CloudTrail events

    C. AWS X-Ray

    D. The MongoDB `explain()` method

8. An application stores its data in a DynamoDB table. The application team finds that they have a new access pattern where the application has to perform strongly consistent queries on an attribute that's not the partition key. How can the team solve this problem?

   A. Create a new DynamoDB table

   B. Create a new **global secondary index** (**GSI**)

   C. Create a new **local SI** (**LSI**)

   D. Create a **DynamoDB Accelerator** (**DAX**) cluster

9. A solution architect would like to implement a caching solution for an application. The application is read-heavy, performing frequent read operations. The application load is very unpredictable, so the solution architect would like to be able to horizontally scale the caching system up and down as required while keeping infrastructure costs minimal. What is the optimal solution to this problem?

   A. Deploy an Amazon ElastiCache for Redis (cluster mode disabled) cluster

   B. Deploy an Amazon ElastiCache for Redis (cluster mode enabled) cluster

   C. Deploy an Amazon DAX cluster

   D. Implement a write-through caching strategy

10. A company has a **Linux, Apache, MySQL, PHP** (**LAMP**) stack application deployed to AWS. The availability requirements for their backend database specify automatic failover in case of **disaster recovery** (**DR**). What is the optimal solution that meets this requirement?

    A. RDS with **Multi-AZ** deployment.

    B. RDS with read-replica deployment.

    C. DynamoDB with Global Tables deployment.

    D. Deploy multiple RDS instances. Use Route53 with **Health-Check** and **Domain Name System** (**DNS**) failover configured.

11. A company DR policy requires that all RDS backups are retained in a secondary AWS region. What is the optimal solution to meet this requirement?

    A. Configure an RDS read-replica instance in the secondary region. Enable RDS automated backups on the read-replica instance.

    B. Configure an AWS backup policy to enforce RDS automated backups, target region to the secondary region.

C. Copy a manual RDS DB snapshot to an S3 bucket. Enable **Cross-Region Replication** (**CRR**) on the S3 bucket.

D. Copy a manual RDS DB snapshot to the secondary region.

12. A developer is implementing an AWS Lambda function that will read data from an Amazon DynamoDB table. What is the most secure method of providing the Lambda function access permissions to the DynamoDB table?

    A. Create an **Identity and Access Management** (**IAM**) role. Create an IAM policy granting necessary access permissions from AWS Lambda. Assign the IAM policy to the IAM role. Assign the IAM role to the DynamoDB table.

    B. Create an IAM user and access key. Create an IAM policy granting necessary access permissions to the DynamoDB table. Assign the IAM policy to the IAM user. Provide the access key **identifier** (**ID**) and the access key to the developer.

    C. Create a DynamoDB username and password. Provide the username and password to the developer.

    D. Create an IAM role. Create an IAM policy granting necessary access permissions to the DynamoDB table. Assign the IAM policy to the IAM role. Assign the IAM role to the Lambda execution role.

13. A retail organization is developing a data lake solution utilizing Amazon S3 to store a large amount of data. The solution must be accessible via SQL queries. The organization wants to minimize infrastructure costs. Which AWS service should be part of their solution?

    A. Amazon DynamoDB

    B. Amazon Redshift Spectrum

    C. Amazon Aurora

    D. Amazon Athena

14. An application uses Amazon RDS for MySQL deployed in a Multi-AZ configuration as the backend database. Users have started raising complaints regarding the performance of the application. It has been identified that the performance issues are caused by increased repeated read activity on the database. What is the most performance-optimized resolution to this problem?

    A. Configure the application to read from the Multi-AZ standby instance

    B. Deploy an RDS read replica in the same AZ as the master DB instance

    C. Deploy an RDS read replica in a different AZ from the master DB instance

    D. Deploy an Amazon ElastiCache cluster in front of the RDS DB instance

15. To enforce compliance and auditing requirements, the TTL feature is enabled on a DynamoDB table. Which approach can be used to ensure unauthorized updates to the TTL attribute are prevented?

    A. Use IAM policies to deny update actions to the TTL attribute or feature configuration. Create an IAM role policy that allows `dynamodb:updateTimeToLive`. Assign the policy to the authorized users.

    B. When configuring DynamoDB table TTL, specify authorized users' **Amazon Resource Names** (**ARNs**).

    C. TTL is a DynamoDB compliance and audit feature and cannot be altered once enabled.

    D. Create an inline resource-based policy that allows `dynamodb:ConfigureTimeToLive` and denies other update actions. Attach the policy to the DynamoDB table.

16. A DynamoDB table has TTL enabled. A solution for processing items deleted by TTL needs to be implemented. What is the optimal solution to this requirement?

    A. Enable continuous backups with PITR for the table.

    B. Enable DynamoDB Streams on the table.

    C. Use CloudWatch Events to collect TTL delete events. Create a Lambda function to process the event. Configure the Lambda function as the target for CloudWatch Events.

    D. Use CloudTrail to collect TTL delete events. Create a Lambda function to process the event. Create a **Simple Notification Service** (**SNS**) topic and trigger a Lambda function to process the event.

17. A company testing team created an Aurora read replica for an RDS MySQL database to evaluate the performance behavior of an Aurora instance under production loads. After completing the evaluation, the team is unable to delete this read-replica instance. What is the cause and solution to this problem?

    A. Read replicas must be deleted using the **command-line interface** (**CLI**) with the `-enable-delete` flag.

    B. Deletion protection is enabled on the RDS MySQL primary database. Disable this.

    C. It is impossible to delete an active read-replica instance. Turn off the read-replica instance in order to delete it.

    D. It is impossible to delete the last instance of a read-replica DB cluster. It must be promoted to a standalone DB cluster.

18. When deleting an RDS instance using the AWS CLI, the following error is encountered: `An error occurred (InvalidParameterCombination) when calling the DeleteDBInstance operation: FinalDBSnapshotIdentifier cannot be specified when deleting a cluster instance`. How can you resolve this?

    A. Deletion protection is enabled. Use the `aws rds modify-db-instance` command with the `-no-deletion-protection` flag.

    B. In the `cli delete` command, specify the S3 bucket ARN where the final database snapshot must be stored.

    C. You cannot take a cluster-level snapshot. Use the `-skip-final-snapshot` flag in the `cli delete` command.

    D. There is not enough allocated storage for the final database snapshot. Use the `aws rds modify-db-instance` command to allocate additional storage for the snapshot.

19. An organization has a hybrid cloud architecture consisting of their on-premises data center and AWS cloud-connected service using AWS Direct Connect. The organization is looking to migrate from an on-premises PostgreSQL database to an Amazon Aurora PostgreSQL database cluster. What is the optimal solution for performing data migration in this scenario? The organization is particularly concerned about performing the migration as fast as possible and they are willing to take downtime to achieve this.

    A. Use AWS DMS to migrate the data.

    B. Use the PostgreSQL `pg_dump` utility to copy the data to S3 and restore it from there.

    C. Create an Aurora read replica of the source database. After the migration is complete, promote the Aurora read replica to a standalone DB cluster.

    D. Use the Percona `XtraBackup` utility to create backup files from the sourced database to an Amazon S3 bucket. Restore the Aurora PostgreSQL DB cluster from those files.

20. A company is developing a business-critical application. Their **Recovery Time Objective** (**RTO**) and **Recovery Point Objective** (**RPO**) requirements call for a relational database in an active-active configuration, with zero downtime for all database operations. What is the optimal database choice for these requirements?

    A. Amazon Aurora Global Database

    B. Amazon DynamoDB with global tables

C. Amazon Aurora multi-master cluster

D. Amazon RDS with Multi-AZ

21. A solution architect is designing a migration strategy from on-premises MySQL to Amazon Aurora. An assessment of feature compatibility must be performed. Which engine is used by Amazon Aurora and must be taken into consideration during this analysis?

    A. InnoDB

    B. MyISAM

    C. MySQL 5.4

    D. XtraDB

22. An application uses DynamoDB tables for its data store. The application requires performing a write operation on a sequence of items and rolling back and reversing all operations in case of any one faulty operation. What is the best method to accomplish this requirement?

    A. DynamoDB does not support atomic transactions. Use a relational database (such as RDS) that supports atomic transactions.

    B. Use a `TransactWriteItems` operation.

    C. Use a `BatchWriteItem` operation.

    D. Update the application to manage and perform rollback operations.

23. A company security team wants to implement a solution for securely storing database credentials. The solution should provide automatic rotation of database credentials. Which AWS service can the team use to meet these requirements?

    A. AWS **Key Management Service (KMS)**

    B. AWS Systems Manager Parameter Store

    C. AWS **Resource Access Manager (RAM)**

    D. AWS Secrets Manager

24. Which graph query languages are supported by Amazon Neptune? (Select two)

    A. Gremlin

    B. Cypher

    C. **SPARQL Protocol and RDF Query Language (SPARQL)**

    D. **Property Graph Query Language (PGQL)**

25. Which AWS service can be used to generate a database migration assessment report with recommendations regarding schema conversion, database object compatibility, and conversion effort estimates?

    A. AWS DMS

    B. AWS **Schema Conversion Tool** (**SCT**)

    C. AWS Migration Hub

    D. AWS **Server Migration Service** (**SMS**)

26. A solutions architect is planning a database conversion and migration from an on-premises database cluster to AWS. A database migration assessment report needs to be created to assess the migration compatibility, task, effort, and recommendations. Which steps are required to configure AWS SCT?

    A. Configure Direct Connect between the on-premises data center and the Amazon **Virtual Private Cloud** (**VPC**)

    B. Install the AWS SCT tool

    C. Assign an IAM role to the AWS SCT service

    D. Create an S3 bucket for assessment report storage

27. A solutions architect is migrating an enterprise 1-**terabyte** (**TB**) Oracle database to RDS instances requiring 10,000 **input/output operations per second** (**IOPS**). Which **Elastic Block Store** (**EBS**) volume type would be appropriate for this scenario?

    A. `gp2`

    B. `io1`

    C. `st1`

    D. `sc1`

28. A company is migrating its on-premises Teradata data warehouse system to AWS. Which AWS service offers a columnar data store suitable for data warehousing?

    A. Amazon Athena

    B. Amazon Aurora

    C. AWS Lake Formation

    D. Amazon Redshift

29. A database specialist wishes to save costs on Amazon RDS instances by stopping them. Which of the following statements accurately describes stopping Amazon RDS instances?

    A. You can stop a DB instance for up to 7 days when it is in a Single- or Multi-AZ configuration.

    B. You cannot stop a DB instance. It must be deleted instead.

    C. You can stop a DB instance for any duration when it is in a Single-AZ configuration.

    D. You can stop a DB instance for any duration when it is in a Multi-AZ configuration.

30. A database administrator needs to move an Oracle database deployed on EC2 from one region to another. Which steps must the administrator perform to accomplish this?

    A. It is not possible to move an EC2 instance from one region to another.

    B. Create a read replica of the RDS database in another region and promote the replica to a primary database.

    C. Shut down the EC2 instance, then take the **Amazon Machine Image** (**AMI**) and copy it into another region. Launch a new EC2 instance from the AMI.

    D. Configure a Multi-AZ for the database. Promote a Multi-AZ node to a primary database.

31. Which statement best describes partition key and sort key designs of DynamoDB indexes?

    A. GSI should have the same partition keys as the base table

    B. GSI can have a different partition key and sort key from the base table

    C. LSI can have a different partition key and sort key from the base table

    D. LSI must have the same sort key as the base table

32. Which of the following is an example of a good DynamoDB hash key?

    A. Book title

    B. **International Standard Book Number** (**ISBN**)

    C. Book author

    D. Book language

33. Which of the following data replication methods is utilized by Amazon RDS Multi-AZ?

    A. Multi-active replication
    B. Lazy replication
    C. Synchronous replication
    D. Asynchronous replication

34. A testing team is experiencing performance issues with their Amazon RDS instance. They wish to measure database load and identify SQL commands with a high **central processing unit** (**CPU**) load. Which service can the team use to help them solve this issue?

    A. CloudTrail Insights events
    B. CloudWatch Enhanced Monitoring
    C. Inspector assessment report
    D. RDS Performance Insights

35. You are advising a large financial company on the best strategy to migrate its on-premises MySQL database, application, and web servers. RDS MySQL is being considered as the target database engine. Access to the database should be limited to only the application servers and a bastion host.

    Which solution meets the security requirements?

    A. Provision the RDS MySQL database in a private subnet. Modify the `login.cnf` file on the RDS host to allow connections from only the application servers and bastion host.
    B. Provision the RDS MySQL database in a public subnet. Create a new security group with inbound rules to allow connections from only the security groups of the application servers and bastion host. Attach the new security group to the DB instance.
    C. Provision the RDS MySQL database in a private subnet. Create a new security group with inbound rules to allow connections from only the security groups of the application servers and bastion host. Attach the new security group to the DB instance.
    D. Provision the RDS MySQL database in a private subnet. Create a **network access control list** (**NACL**) with inbound and outbound rules to allow connections to and from the application servers and bastion host.

36. A database specialist needs to truncate a DynamoDB table. How can this operation be performed?

    A. Use the `aws dynamodb delete-from` CLI command.

    B. Use the `aws dynamodb truncate-table` CLI command.

    C. Use the `aws dynamodb scan` CLI command to scan the table. Iterate through all keys and use the `aws dynamodb delete-item` CLI command to delete each item.

    D. Use the `aws dynamodb batch-delete-item` CLI command.

37. A game development company is developing a new online multiplayer game. Game user profile data will contain the user's match history. Match history data is expected to be in size on the order of 500 **kilobytes** (**KB**) and can be stored as a **JavaScript Object Notation** (**JSON**) or text file. Additionally, the user profile data schema is expected to go through revisions as new game features are implemented. How should the team store the user profile data?

    A. Use Amazon DynamoDB to store user profile data.

    B. Use Amazon RDS to store user profile data.

    C. Use Amazon DynamoDB to store user profile data. Use Amazon RDS to store user match history.

    D. Use Amazon DynamoDB to store user profile data. Use S3 to store match history. Store a link to the S3 object as an attribute in DynamoDB.

38. An application development team is looking to implement a caching solution with cross-region read-replica capability. Which solution meets this requirement?

    A. ElastiCache for Redis with cluster mode enabled

    B. ElastiCache for Redis with `--automatic-failover -enabled` flag

    C. ElastiCache for Redis with Global Datastore feature

    D. Amazon DAX cluster

39. To optimize the cost and performance of a DynamoDB table, a database specialist would like to identify frequently accessed keys. Which service can the specialist use to achieve this most optimally?

    A. Performance Insights

    B. CloudWatch Contributor Insights

    C. CloudTrail events

    D. AWS X-Ray

40. A DocumentDB database specialist wants to examine the execution time of operations that are being performed on a cluster to investigate slow operations. What can the specialist use to perform this analysis?

    A. DocumentDB profiler

    B. AWS X-Ray

    C. Performance Insights

    D. Amazon Inspector

41. You are planning a migration from MySQL to DynamoDB using DMS. What is the first step you should take in planning the table design in the DynamoDB database?

    A. Map SQL tables to DynamoDB

    B. Generate **data definition language** (**DDL**) statements to recreate the SQL tables in DynamoDB

    C. Plan and detail all data access patterns

    D. Identify data capacity amount

42. The security team wants to maintain a record of all `GetItem` and `PutItem` operations performed on a DynamoDB table for audit purposes. Which solution can they use to meet this requirement?

    A. CloudWatch.

    B. CloudTrail.

    C. Enable DynamoDB Streams. Use AWS Lambda to read and record stream records.

    D. AWS Config.

43. A game company is developing a mobile multiplayer game. As the game's popularity increases with many concurrent users, the company wants to implement a leaderboard feature. Which database would provide an optimal solution for this use case?

    A. DynamoDB

    B. AWS RDS

    C. ElastiCache for Memcached

    D. ElastiCache for Redis

44. A solution architect is planning a deployment of Amazon ElastiCache for Redis with cluster mode disabled. What is the maximum number of shards and read replicas that the cluster can have?

    A. 1 shard and 5 read replicas

    B. 5 shards and 0 read replicas

    C. 1 shard and 90 read replicas

    D. 83 shards and 5 read replicas

45. A solution architect is planning a deployment of Amazon ElastiCache for Redis with cluster mode enabled. Each shard is planned to have 5 read replicas. What is the maximum number of shards that can be deployed?

    A. 5

    B. 15

    C. 83

    D. 500

46. A solution architect is planning a database migration from an Oracle database to Amazon Aurora with PostgreSQL. During the planning phase, the solution architect would like to perform an assessment of migration complexity and size and identify any proprietary technology that would require database and application modifications. Which service can help the solution architect with developing this assessment report and provide recommendations on migration strategies and tools?

    A. AWS DMS

    B. AWS SCT

    C. AWS **Workload Qualification Framework (WQF)**

    D. AWS DataSync

47. A database specialist would like to manually promote a read-replica node in an ElastiCache (cluster mode disabled) cluster to a primary node. Which step must the specialist perform before they can promote the node to a primary?

    A. Enable Multi-AZ with automatic failover

    B. Disable Multi-AZ with automatic failover

    C. Create a manual backup

    D. Stop the cluster

48. A database specialist wants to resolve some performance problems with their application by using a cache in front of an RDS database. The cache will store a small amount of **application programming interface** (**API**) data and some user query results and needs to be able to scale up the processor count when required. Which is the best solution?

    A. ElastiCache for Redis (cluster mode disabled)

    B. ElastiCache for Memcached

    C. Elasticsearch

    D. Amazon DAX

49. A developer is doing some testing on an application using an Amazon Aurora database. During the testing activities, the developer accidentally executes a `DELETE` statement without a `WHERE` clause. They wish to undo this action. What is the optimal solution to revert the database to the correct state with minimal effort?

    A. Use the Amazon Aurora backtracking feature

    B. Use the Amazon Aurora **Restore to point in time** feature

    C. Restore the Amazon Aurora database from a snapshot

    D. Restore the Amazon Aurora database from a read replica

50. A solution architect would like to integrate an Amazon RDS for SQL Server instance with an existing **Active Directory** (**AD**) domain. Which service would enable the solution architect to implement a solution?

    A. AWS Directory Service

    B. AWS **Single Sign-On** (**SSO**)

    C. Amazon Cognito

    D. Amazon WorkLink

51. A company that uses a MySQL database on-premises has encountered a damaging loss after a database corruption due to a disk failure. The incident has prompted the database team to build a **proof of concept** (**POC**) for their database operations using Amazon Aurora MySQL. The team needs to demonstrate the effect of a disk failure event on the application performance. Which of the following will help the team simulate such an event?

    A. Reboot the Aurora DB cluster and enable the **Reboot with Failover** option

    B. Use fault injection queries

C. Stop the Aurora DB cluster

D. Use the Aurora **Backtrack** feature

52. A company is running an application using DynamoDB in provisioned mode. The manager instructed you to gather and analyze the usage and cost of different AWS services for the past 3 months. You noticed that DynamoDB is responsible for almost half of the total cost of your account. How can you lower the operating cost of the DynamoDB database?

    A. Enable burst capacity

    B. Use spot capacity

    C. Modify the adaptive capacity

    D. Use reserved capacity

53. A company has an enterprise application hosted in an Amazon **Elastic Container Service** (**ECS**) cluster and uses an Amazon RDS for MySQL database with a read replica. The application uses the read replica to generate business reports and avoid performance issues on the primary DB instance. However, the users noticed that the queries to the read replica have a slow response time. Which of the following is the most likely root cause of this issue?

    A. The replica lag metric has reached a value of 0

    B. The replica DB instance class is higher than the primary DB instance

    C. The **Change Data Capture** (**CDC**) option is enabled on the primary DB instance for continuous data replication

    D. There are long-running queries on the primary DB instance

54. A database specialist currently manages Amazon Aurora with a PostgreSQL compatibility cluster. Every afternoon, performance is degraded due to huge spikes in read operations, maximizing the CPU utilization of the Aurora read replica. The product owner asked for a solution that could dynamically meet the application connectivity and workload requirements. What is the most cost-effective solution that can address the requirement?

    A. Enable Aurora Auto Scaling in the cluster

    B. Upgrade the instance class of the Aurora read replica

    C. Create a new Aurora cluster with at least one read replica and Aurora Auto Scaling enabled

    D. Migrate to Aurora Global Database

55. A multimedia company based in Japan wants to build a highly available database solution in AWS. It will be used for a content management application that expects high-volume requests and hence can scale depending on the read throughput. The fully managed database service will store data in JSON-like documents with attribute value sizes as large as 16 **megabytes** (**MB**). Which database service would best fit the company's needs?

    A. Amazon ElastiCache with Redis cluster
    B. Amazon DynamoDB
    C. Amazon DocumentDB
    D. Amazon RDS

56. A company based in São Paulo intends to migrate a company management system from an on-premises Oracle database to an Amazon Aurora PostgreSQL DB cluster. The manager asks the database specialist to review the license requirements and hardware configurations of both source and target database instances. The report should also include an estimate of the effort it will take to convert the code. What should the database specialist do to meet these criteria?

    A. Use an AWS SCT data extraction agent. By default, it will generate a report that lists down any migration issue.
    B. Enable AWS DMS data validation on the task to compare the source and target records and report any issues.
    C. Use AWS SCT and create a database migration assessment report.
    D. Enable and start an AWS DMS premigration assessment.

57. A small company utilizes Amazon DynamoDB to power a web-based survey program. A database specialist encounters a `ProvisionedThroughputExceededException` problem during peak use, while survey answers are being written. What is the database specialist's role in resolving this issue? (Select two answers)

    A. Change the table to use Amazon DynamoDB Streams
    B. Purchase DynamoDB reserved capacity in the affected region
    C. Increase the write capacity units for the specific table
    D. Add a GSI to help with the data patterns

58. A multinational company has a **customer relationship management** (**CRM**) system that is hosted on an Amazon RDS for PostgreSQL DB instance. According to new compliance rules, the database must be encrypted at rest. Which course of action will satisfy these criteria?

    A. Create an encrypted copy of a manual snapshot of the DB instance. Restore a new DB instance from the encrypted snapshot.

    B. Modify the DB instance and enable encryption.

    C. Restore a DB instance from the most recent automated snapshot and enable encryption.

    D. Create an encrypted read replica of the DB instance. Promote the read replica to a standalone instance.

59. Amazon Aurora MySQL is being used by a web-based retail business to migrate its main application database. The firm is now doing **online transaction processing** (**OLTP**) stress testing using concurrent database connections. A database professional detected sluggish performance for several particular write operations during the first round of testing. Examining the Amazon CloudWatch statistics for the Aurora DB cluster revealed a CPU usage of 90%. Which actions should the database professional take to determine the main cause of excessive CPU use and sluggish performance most effectively?

    A. Enable Enhanced Monitoring at less than 30 seconds of granularity to review the operating system metrics before the next round of tests.

    B. Review the `VolumeBytesUsed` metric in CloudWatch to see if there is a spike in write **input/output** (**I/O**).

    C. Review Amazon RDS Performance Insights to identify the top SQL statements and wait events.

    D. Review Amazon RDS API calls in AWS CloudTrail to identify long-running queries.

60. A database professional is required to evaluate and improve a performance-related Amazon DynamoDB table. The database professional determines that the partition key is generating hot partitions and hence creates a new partition key. The database professional must apply the new partition key to all current and new data in an efficient manner. How should they go about implementing this solution?

    A. Use Amazon **Elastic MapReduce** (**EMR**) to export the data from the current DynamoDB table to Amazon S3. Then, use Amazon EMR again to import the data from Amazon S3 into a new DynamoDB table with the new partition key.

    B. Use AWS DMS to copy the data from the current DynamoDB table to Amazon S3. Then, import the DynamoDB table to create a new DynamoDB table with the new partition key.

    C. Use the AWS CLI to update the DynamoDB table and modify the partition key.

    D. Use the AWS CLI to back up the DynamoDB table. Then, use the `restore-table-from-backup` command and modify the partition key.

17
Answers

Chapter 3

1. 4

   An internet gateway is not used with a private IP, so this answer is incorrect.

   Security groups have all outbound ports open by default, so there is no need to open port `80` specifically.

   A private subnet can connect to the internet with the correct configuration.

   A correctly configured route table is required for any internet connectivity, so answer *4* is correct.

2. 3

   A security group does not allow connections to other AWS services such as S3 and RDS by default, so this is incorrect.

   Security groups block all inbound traffic by default, so this answer is incorrect.

   Security groups *do* allow all outbound traffic by default, so *3* is the correct answer.

   A route table is required for an internet gateway to be used, so this is incorrect.

3. 1 and 4

   Each subnet can only be deployed in a single AZ, so *1* is a correct answer.

   The smallest CIDR block you can allow is `/28`, so this is incorrect.

   Private subnets connect to the internet using a NAT gateway, and they do not need an elastic IP allocated.

   All subnets in a VPC can communicate with each other by default, so *4* is a correct answer.

   Each subnet can only be deployed in a single AZ, so this answer is incorrect.

4. 1

   A route table can have multiple subnets associated with it, so *1* is the correct answer.

   A subnet can have just one route table, so this cannot be correct.

   You can associate multiple subnets with the same route table, so this is incorrect.

   Answer *1* was correct; therefore, *None of these* cannot be right.

5. 2

   An internet gateway doesn't have a security group, so this isn't correct.

   An instance does need a public IP to connect to the internet via an internet gateway in a public subnet, so *2* is the correct answer.

   A security group allows outbound traffic to return to the requester (remember it's stateful, in other words, if traffic is allowed out, it is allowed back) by default, so this isn't correct.

   Source/Destination check is only used for NAT gateways, so this is also incorrect.

Chapter 4

1. 3

   Moving from RDS to EC2 doesn't solve the storage problem. RDS also has autoscaling.

   Using S3 might reduce the incoming writes, but it is very complex, therefore, this isn't correct.

   Enabling autoscaling storage is the easiest solution, and is the correct answer.

   A read replica will not help with full storage, so this cannot be correct.

2. 2

   If you cannot connect, then the account details don't matter at this stage, so this isn't correct.

   The inbound rules are likely blocking any connections to the RDS instance from your EC2, so this is the correct answer.

   The outbound rules are set to allow all outbound traffic by default, so this is unlikely to be the cause.

   As you are connecting from within your VPC, you will not need a NAT to access it, so this is incorrect.

3. 1

   Primary is upgraded first, so this is the correct answer.

   There is no downtime during an upgrade, so this is not correct.

   The standby is not upgraded first and there is no downtime, so this is not correct.

   The standby is not upgraded first, so this is not correct.

4. 1

   You must use a CMS key for the share, so this answer is correct.

   You must use a CMS key for the share, so this answer is incorrect.

   Using FTP will not work, so this is incorrect.

   You must use a CMS key for the share, so this answer is incorrect.

5. 2

   The default retention is 30 days for the console and 7 days for the `aswcli`, so only answer *2* is correct.

Chapter 5

1. 3

   Creating a multi-AZ deployment with another read replica works, but it isn't the most cost-efficient.

   Moving to EC2 is not a valid solution.

   Creating a multi-AZ read replica is a cost-effective and highly-available solution, and is correct.

   Creating two single-AZ read replicas is not highly available.

2. 4

   RDS only supports multi-AZ in the same region.

   Aurora Global Tables will work, but this is the incorrect process, as you need read replicas.

   Deploying MySQL in two regions will not work as there is no replication.

   Global tables will work and it uses read replicas, so this is the correct answer.

3. 2

   Aurora does not fully meet the needs of this scenario.

   Aurora Serverless will meet the needs of the temporary nature of the application.

   RDS does not fully meet the needs of this scenario.

   MySQL on EC does not fully meet the needs of this scenario.

4. 1

   Creating read replicas in a different region will meet the needs in the most cost-effective way.

   Copying EBS volumes will not work.

   Enabling a global database for Aurora will work, but it is not the most cost-effective option.

   Copying a snapshot of EBS will not work.

5. 3

   Using AWS SCT is unnecessary for homogenous database migration.

   A manual script could work but is not the best solution.

   Creating a read replica and promoting it as an Aurora database cluster is the correct answer.

   You cannot create an Aurora replica from **PostgreSQL**. This option only exists for MySQL.

Chapter 6

1. 4

   TTL will only help if it can remove older records; therefore, this won't immediately help and is incorrect.

   DAX may improve performance but it is not the most cost-efficient option.

DynamoDB Streams will not help any performance issue.

Autoscaling is the correct answer, as the issue is a restriction of provisioned capacity units.

2. 1

   An item is 3 KB, so you need one RCU per two items in eventually consistent mode, and three WCUs per item as standard write. This gives you 50 RCUs and 30 WCUs.

3. 4

   25 GB is provided free for each account when using DynamoDB.

4. 2

   An LSI can only be provisioned when the table is created.

   A GSI can contain different keys to the base table.

5. 3

   This error is seen when using DAX and not when using DynamoDB, so autoscaling won't help.

   This error is seen when using DAX and not when using DynamoDB, so on-demand won't help.

   This is a DAX throttling error and is fixed by increasing the number of DAX nodes.

   Global tables will not help with the DAX error.

Chapter 7

1. 2

   Increasing the queue to the highest priority will improve the performance, but this will impact other queries.

   Increasing concurrency scaling will allow the queue to scale as required.

   A query monitoring rule will take too long to scale and will not fix the problem.

   Queue hopping only works for manually configured workload management.

2. 4

   The clue in the question is *least possible customization and coding*. All of these answers will work, but the simplest is using QuickSight directly, as it can query all of those sources. This was partially a trick question by putting in the RedShift option.

3. 4

   As the data can be easily recovered, there is no need to take backups. The other answers all still involve taking backups, so they are not correct.

4. 3

   DocumentDB is the only solution that supports JSON document querying.

5. 4

   DocumentDB has a document limit of 16 MB, so the 20 MB document is too large.

Chapter 8

1. 2 and 4

   The Neptune VPC endpoint won't be used to import from S3.

   You do need an S3 endpoint, so this is correct.

   The EC2 does need to access S3, so this isn't correct.

   Neptune will need an IAM role to access S3, so this is correct.

   S3 will not be reading from Neptune so it does not need an IAM role.

2. 3

   You cannot delete from Timestream, so that is the only correct answer.

3. 4

   QLDB only supports 20 tables, so you have hit the maximum allowed.

4. 1 and 5

   Gremlin and SPARQL are the only languages supported by Neptune.

5. 1

   The `_ql_committed` tables show all the history for any modifications, and this is the correct answer.

Chapter 9

1. 2 and 3

   You do not know when the peak hours for this application are, so setting backups to midnight might make things worse.

   Setting `reserved-memory-percent` stops backups from taking all the memory and is correct.

   Running a backup from the read replica will also reduce the load on the primary instance and is correct.

   Additional read replicas will not help as the load is on the primary instance.

   Increasing the number of shards will not help as the load will remain the same.

2. 1

   Write-through applies the changes to the cache first before writing to the database so the data is always current, and this is the correct answer.

   Lazy-loading is where the cache only loads data after it is requested and it doesn't maintain current data.

   Cache-aside is where the application can directly access both the database and the cache.

   Read-through is where the application can only access the cache directly.

3. 1

   Redis (cluster mode disabled) only allows a single shard, so answer 1 is the only correct option.

4. 2

   Redis (cluster mode enabled) can support up to 500 nodes (the total of all primary and read replicas). To have five read replicas per shard means each shard contains six nodes (five replicas and the primary node). Therefore, you can have a maximum of 83 shards before hitting the 500 node limit (6 * 83 = 498).

5. 2

   To ensure the cluster doesn't try to fail over while you promote an instance to a standalone primary, you must disable multi-AZ.

Chapter 10

1. 3

   Running a RAC cluster on EC2 doesn't meet the solution required.

   A Data Pump export would work, but it will not meet the 5 minutes outage allowed.

   Using DMS in CDC mode will allow the application to take only a minimal outage and is the correct answer.

   SCT is typically used for changing a database engine and is not required in this scenario.

2. 3

   You cannot restore from s3 cross-region, so this will not work.

   You can use S3 cross-region replication and restore, but there will be a long downtime, so this is not the best solution.

   Using DMS will allow a migration with minimal downtime, so this is the best solution.

   There is no cross-region replication for RDS SQL Server.

3. 2

   This is a method to reduce storage allocated but it will involve downtime.

   Using CDC will allow the storage to be reduced with minimal downtime and is the best solution.

   Using a backup and restore method may reduce storage needs but it will involve downtime.

   Switching over to a read replica will not resolve the storage issue.

4. 3, 4, and 5

   The three steps required are to use SCT to change the database engine, set up a DMS task to migrate the data in CDC to minimize any downtime, and split out the large LOB tables into their own task to allow them to import in parallel.

   You don't need to use the SCT data extraction agent for Oracle to PostgreSQL conversions.

   Setting an increase of tables in parallel for the larger tables will not improve the speed, as each table should be handled in parallel, not multiple tables at one time.

5. 1, 3, and 4

   Using a column filter will allow the table to be split into multiple jobs to run in parallel.

   Multi-AZ will not help speed up the jobs.

   Increasing the compute may help improve performance.

   Adding a DirectConnect VPN line will improve bandwidth between on-premises and AWS and will speed up the migration.

   Multi-AZ RDS will not improve performance.

   Full LOB mode will make the job run slower.

Chapter 11

1. 4

   Enabling cross-region replication to pull all the s3 data into one region would work, but it isn't cost-efficient.

   DMS cannot migrate a Glue catalog.

   You cannot give permission for Glue to read another catalog in this way.

   Glue can create a data catalog across all regions allowing Athena to query them, so this is the correct answer.

2. 3

   RDS will work but it is not cost-effective.

   Redshift will work but it is not cost-effective.

   Athena can directly query data from S3, so this is the most cost-effective solution.

   Using EC2 to do this is complex and unnecessary.

3. 2

   Athena cannot query directly from Glacier.

   Moving the data to standard S3 is the most cost-effective solution.

   DynamoDB and Redshift would work, but they are not as cost-effective.

4. 3 and 5

   Revoking permissions is not a good solution.

   Deletion protection does not exist for stacks.

   Termination protection is a good solution, so this is correct.

   Revoking permissions to delete RDS is not a good solution.

   Deletion protection against the RDS instances within the stack will protect them, so this is correct.

5. 1

   Using CloudFormation templates is the simplest solution.

   IAM policies will not provision any resources, so this is incorrect.

   Autoscaling doesn't provide the solution.

   Manual scripts would work, but using CloudFormation is simpler.

Chapter 12

1. 3

   You cannot modify the `login.cnf` file on RDS.

   Provisioning a database in a public subnet is not secure.

   Provisioning a database in a private subnet protected by security groups is the correct answer.

   Using NACLs can help further secure a VPC, but you also need security groups, so this is incorrect.

2. 2

   Exporting to S3 is not an option here.

   Creating a snapshot, encrypting a copy of it, and then creating a new snapshot is the best option.

   You cannot add encryption using **Modify**, so this is incorrect.

3. 3

   You cannot restore a snapshot into a database with encryption enabled.

   Using IAM authentication for each individual user will remove the reliance on shared passwords and will enforce the policy of each individual having their own account.

4. 2

   Applications use the RDS endpoint to access the database, so the IP change would not break the service.

   It is most likely the new EC2 is not in the security group for the database, so this is the correct answer.

   An application sending too many requests is unlikely to be the culprit.

   It is unlikely that the app server has been placed in a different VPC.

5. 3 and 5

   There is no option to publish database logs to S3.

   You cannot modify the default parameter group.

   Creating a new parameter group is a good solution here.

   You cannot manually edit the `postgres.conf` file on RDS.

   You can enable database logs to be published to CloudWatch, so this is a good solution.

Chapter 13

1. 2 and 4

   To do this, you need to enable CloudWatch alerts and use SNS to send the notifications to the specified recipients.

   SES only handles emailing and not notifications.

   SQS is used for application queues, not notifications.

   Lambda is a complicated solution.

2. 4

   Using anomaly-detection-based rules in CloudWatch is the best solution to quickly find workload changes and spikes.

3. 2

   The simplest solution is to use CloudWatch metrics and SNS to send the notification to the email address.

Chapter 14

1. 1 and 3

    Changing the times the backups run to outside peak hours is a good solution.

    Increasing the instance class may help but it will not be cost-effective.

    Using a read replica for backups will reduce the load on the primary node and is a good solution.

    Increasing the number of shards will not help.

    Increasing the storage will not help.

    Changing to provisioned IOPS will not help.

2. 1

    Creating an AWS Backup policy for 90 days and applying it to all RDS instances is the simplest solution.

    Modifying each RDS instance with 90-day backup retention will work but it is not the best solution, as new instances may get missed and it is a manual effort.

    Using Lambda is a very complicated solution.

    There is no such feature on RDS to push backups to Glacier.

3. 2

    A read replica in a secondary region is a very expensive solution.

    AWS Backups can store backups to another region, so this is the best solution.

    Manually copying the snapshots to S3 is time-consuming and is not a good solution.

    Manually copying the snapshots to a different region is time-consuming and is not a good solution.

Chapter 15

1. 1

    Using Application Insights will help identify the root cause quickly and is the correct answer.

    Performance Insights is useful if this is definitely a database problem, but it will not help find any potential application issue.

AWS X-Ray is used to diagnose issues with microservices and it does not meet the needs of this use case.

Contacting AWS support is not a good solution, as they will not understand your application.

2. 3

   All answers could be correct, but the most likely answer is that security groups have been altered, which will stop your application from connecting to the database.

3. 3

   This command misses the `-apply-immediately` flag.

   The wrong syntax is used `-alter-database` is wrong.

   `Modify-db-instance` is correct and this command has the `-apply-immediately` flag, so this is the correct answer.

   The wrong syntax is used `-alter-db-instance` is wrong.

Chapter 16

1. 1

   Using TTL will automatically remove data older than 30 days, and is the correct answer.

   A Lambda function will work but it is complex and not the best solution.

   Creating a new DynamoDB table is not a good solution.

   DynamoDB Streams won't remove the items from the source table.

2. 1

   Creating a separate UAT database is the best option and, therefore, a PITR recovery in a different region is the best solution.

   Using DynamoDB Streams and Lambda is a very complicated solution.

   Using Glue would likely not work for the migration.

   Adding Global Tables would mean that changes made by testing would be written to the production database and, therefore, this doesn't meet the needs of the business.

3. 4

   You cannot modify parameters at the RDS instance level using SET, so this isn't correct.

   You cannot modify the parameters in the default parameter group.

   Modifying the instance to use the default parameter group would work, but using the default parameter group isn't the best practice.

   Changing any custom parameters to their defaults is the best way to resolve this issue.

4. 3

   DMS would work but it is not the best solution for this scenario.

   The MySQL dump utility would not work on RDS.

   You can create an Aurora read replica of the MySQL RDS instance and promote it to migrate to Aurora.

   You cannot create an Aurora cluster using a backup in this way.

5. 4

   A filter expression is used with scans, not **GetItem**.

   Pagination is used to control the number of records returned in a block using a scan.

   A parallel scan can improve performance but does not improve read efficiency.

   Projection expression controls the attributes returned and will improve read efficiency.

6. 2 and 3

   The peak times are not specified, so they could be at midnight. Moving a backup window may not improve its performance.

   The `reserved-memory-percent` parameter controls the memory usage of background activities, and it can improve performance during backups.

   Using a read replica for backups will reduce the load on the read/write node and can improve performance.

   Increasing shards will not help in this situation.

7. 4

   CloudWatch does not show the database activity at the query level for DocumentDB.

   CloudTrail does not monitor database query events.

AWS X-Ray is used for application-level tracing and does not apply here.

MongoDB `explain` is the correct answer, as DocumentDB is MongoDB-compliant and the other answers are not correct.

8. 1

   Creating a new DynamoDB table is the only option here, as LSIs must contain the original partition key, and a GSI cannot support strongly consistent reads.

   DAX is an option to increase performance, not new access patterns.

9. 2

   Cluster mode disabled would not meet the horizontal scaling needs of the use case.

   Cluster mode enabled would allow the system to scale horizontally.

   DAX would help improve performance but only for DynamoDB, and there, it would not work for application-based caching.

   A write-through strategy will not improve performance or allow for scaling.

10. 1

    RDS with Multi-AZ is the only solution that meets the need to have a MySQL database with a fully automated DR.

11. 2

    Creating a read-replica in a different region would work but is not cost-efficient.

    AWS Backups allows you to store RDS backups in a secondary region, so this is the optimal solution.

    Manually copying backups to S3 is not an optimal solution.

    Manually copying RDS snapshots to the secondary region is not an optimal solution.

12. 4

    IAM roles only have access permissions *to* the service, not *from* them. You grant the role to the service requesting the permissions, so this is incorrect.

    Creating an IAM user is not the correct way to grant permissions and Lambda is a service and, therefore, uses roles.

    DynamoDB does not support usernames and passwords.

    Creating a role with permissions for the DynamoDB table and granting that role to the Lambda execution role is the correct way to grant the permissions.

13. 4

    DynamoDB would not be used in this scenario.

    Redshift Spectrum can query directly from S3, but only if they are using Redshift, which does not minimize infrastructure costs.

    Aurora would not be used in this scenario.

    Amazon Athena would be used to query the data directly from S3.

14. 4

    You cannot read from the standby instance.

    Deploying a read replica in the same AZ would work, but a cache would likely work better given the repeated reads.

    Deploying a read replica in a different AZ would work, but a cache would likely work better given the repeated reads.

    ElastiCache is the best solution here given the repeated reads.

15. 1

    The correct IAM policy is `updateTimeToLive`, so this is the correct answer.

    Specifying authorized users will not stop the editing of the TTL value.

    TTL can be altered once created, so this is incorrect.

    `configureTimeToLive` is not the correct IAM policy, so this is incorrect.

16. 2

    Continuous backups would not process the deleted items.

    DynamoDB Streams is the best and simplest solution, as the deleted items need further processing.

    CloudWatch does not monitor TTL events.

    CloudTrail can monitor TTL events, but using Lambda to process them is complicated and not the optimal solution.

17. 4

    The `-enable-delete-` flag does not exist.

    Deletion protection on the primary RDS instance would not affect the deletion of the read replica.

You can delete an active read replica so this is incorrect.

You cannot delete the final read replica of a cluster. It must first be promoted to a standalone cluster.

18. 3

Deletion protection would give a different error.

Snapshots are not stored in S3, so you do not give an S3 location.

You cannot take a cluster-level snapshot at deletion time, so you will need to give the flag to skip it.

Snapshots are not stored on the database instance, so storage allocation would not matter.

19. 2

DMS is often a slower and more expensive solution than using a backup, so this is incorrect here.

Taking a `pg_dump` file, copying it to S3, and restoring is the fastest and simplest solution.

You cannot create an Aurora read replica from an on-premises database.

Percona XtraBackup is only used for MySQL databases so it is required for MySQL.

20. 3

Aurora Global Database is **Active-Passive**, not **Active-Active**.

DynamoDB is not a relational database.

Aurora Multi-Master will offer **Active-Active** and so is correct.

RDS with Multi-AZ does not support **Active-Active**.

21. 1

InnoDB is the only MySQL engine supported by Aurora.

22. 2

DynamoDB does support atomic transactions in some scenarios, so this is incorrect.

`TransactWriteItems` supports transactional writes and is the correct answer.

`BatchWriteItems` does not support transactional writes.

Updating the application to manage this is not an optimal solution.

23. 4

    Key Management Service supports SSH keys, not credentials.

    Systems Manager Parameter Store does not rotate credentials.

    Resource Access Manager does not store credentials.

    Secrets Manager can store and automatically rotate database credentials, and so is the correct answer.

24. 1 and 3

    Gremlin and SPARQL are the two languages supported by Neptune.

25. 2

    DMS is used for migrating data.

    SCT is used to assess the migration feasibility of a database and is correct.

    Migration Hub is used for large-scale migrations.

    Server Migration Service is used to migrate servers and VMs.

26. 2

    The only step required for an on-premises database assessment is to install SCT. There is no need for any connection to AWS at this stage.

27. 2

    `gp2` would only give 3 IOPS per 1 GB, giving 3,000 IOPS for the 1 TB database.

    `io1` would allow you to provision 10,000 IOPS and is the correct answer.

    `st1` and `sc1` are hard disk drives for low IOPS but high throughput.

28. 4

    Redshift is a columnar database and is the correct answer.

29. 1

    You can stop an RDS database for up to 7 days before it is restarted.

    You can stop a database, so this is incorrect.

30. 3

    You can move an EC2 instance, so this is not correct.

    You cannot create a read replica from an EC2 Oracle database.

You can move an EC2 instance by creating an AMI of the instance and launching it in a new instance.

You cannot use multi-AZ with an EC2 database.

31. 2

    GSIs can have a different partition and sort key; LSIs must have the same partition key.

32. 2

    A `hash` key should have the widest spread of values available and be unique, if possible, to allow for efficient retrieval, so the ISBN is the best key here.

33. 3

    Multi-AZ uses synchronous replication.

34. 4

    CloudTrail does not monitor database-level events.

    CloudWatch enhanced monitoring shows the VM resource usage and not database queries.

    Inspector does not monitor database-level events.

    RDS Performance Insights will show the queries running on the database, and is the correct answer.

35. 3

    You cannot amend the `login.cnf` file on an RDS instance.

    You should not provision an RDS database in a public subnet unless you need to give the public access to it.

    You should provision the RDS database in a private subnet protected by security groups, only allowing the application server and bastion host to connect to it, so this is the correct answer.

    NACLs are an optional security feature that operates at the subnet level, but a security group is mandatory, therefore, a security group is still required.

36. 3

    There is no `truncate` method in DynamoDB so you would need to iterate through all items and delete them individually. A better method not offered in these answers would be to export the table structure to JSON, delete the table, and recreate it.

37. 4

    DynamoDB can only store up to 400 KB per item, so you need to store the match history somewhere else.

    RDS is not a suitable location for the user data as it needs to change, therefore, a fixed schema will not work.

    DynamoDB is a good location for the user data, but RDS is not a good home for the match history data as it does not appear to need a relational database.

    DynamoDB is a good location for the user data and stores the match history in S3 with a pointer from the DynamoDB record.

38. 3

    ElastiCache for Redis with cluster mode enabled only supports same-region replication.

    The `-automatic-failover-enabled` flag does not help with multi-region deployment.

    ElastiCache for Redis with a global datastore will allow a multi-region deployment, so this is the correct answer.

    An Amazon DAX cluster only supports DynamoDB and not application caching.

39. 2

    Performance Insights does not support DynamoDB.

    CloudWatch Contributor Insights, while not covered in this book, is the correct answer, because the others are incorrect.

    CloudTrail does not monitor database-level queries for DynamoDB.

    AWS X-Ray is used to trace full stacks from the application and is not correct.

40. 1

    DocumentDB profiler is a tool you can use to examine queries on your DocumentDB cluster.

    AWS X-Ray is used to trace full stacks from the application and is not correct.

    Performance Insights does not support DocumentDB.

    Amazon Inspector offers advice based on the five pillars of the Well-Architected Framework.

41. 3

    Mapping SQL databases directly to DynamoDB is not an optimal way to use DynamoDB.

    You cannot create DynamoDB using SQL statements.

    You should start by identifying the data access patterns before doing any other migration planning.

    Storage capacity is important but it should come later in the process.

42. 3

    CloudWatch does not monitor at the DynamoDB database level.

    CloudTrail will only monitor API calls and TTL events.

    DynamoDB Streams and Lambda can audit the events on a DynamoDB table, and this is the correct answer.

    AWS Config does not monitor database-level events.

43. 1

    DynamoDB is the best fit for a game leaderboard.

44. 1

    ElastiCache for Redis with cluster mode disabled only supports a single shard and five read replicas.

45. 3

    ElastiCache for Redis with cluster mode enabled supports a maximum total of 500 nodes. Each shard will contain size nodes (five read replicas and a read/write node) so you can have a maximum of 83 shards to remain below the 500-node limit.

46. 2

    DMS will likely be used for the data transfer but not for the assessment phase.

    SCT is the tool you would use to assess the complexity of the migration from Oracle to PostgreSQL.

    AWS WQF can help to correctly size the RDS instance but will not assess the ability for migration.

    DataSync is a data transfer service and is not used here.

47. 2

    You do not need to enable Multi-AZ to promote a read replica.

    You do need to disable Multi-AZ to promote a read replica to stop ElastiCache from trying to automatically fail over when the read replica is promoted.

    There is no need to create a manual backup.

    You do not need to stop the cluster.

48. 2

    Redis cannot scale up the instance and can only scale read replicas.

    Memcached can scale the instance and is the best solution.

    ElasticSearch will not help here.

    Amazon DAX is only available with DynamoDB.

49. 1

    Using the Aurora Backtracking feature will get the database recovered in the quickest time.

    You can use a **Restore to time** feature, but this is not the fastest solution.

    Restoring from a snapshot is likely to lose data and is not the best solution.

    Restoring from a read replica is not possible.

50. 1

    AWS Directory Service is needed to authenticate users against an Active Directory domain.

    AWS Single Sign-On allows users to authenticate with a third party.

    AWS Cognito handles session data for applications.

    Amazon WorkLink supports mobile phones to secure access to internal websites and applications.

51. 2

    You cannot simulate a disk failure by rebooting an Aurora cluster with a **Reboot with failover** option, so this is incorrect.

    Fault injection queries can be used to test hardware failures.

    Stopping the Aurora cluster would not initiate a failover.

    Aurora Backtrack is used to recover data that has been lost or accidentally modified.

52. 4

    DynamoDB does not have customizable burst capacity.

    Spot capacity can only be used with EC2 instances.

    Adaptive capacity is a default feature of DynamoDB and it cannot be turned on or off.

    Using reserved capacity will greatly reduce the cost of DynamoDB where you have a consistent workload, and is the correct answer.

53. 4

    A lag of zero would not cause slow responses.

    A read replica with a higher instance class would not cause slow response times.

    CDC running against the primary instance would not cause slow response times on the read replica.

    Long-running queries on the primary instance can cause the read replicas to hang while they wait for the transactions to finish, and this is the most likely cause.

54. 1

    Enabling Auto Scaling of the Aurora cluster will allow it to grow with load, so this is the best solution.

    Upgrading the instance class may solve the problem but it will cost more than using Auto Scaling.

    Creating a new Aurora cluster will be more complex than enabling Auto Scaling.

    Migrating to Aurora Global Tables will not help the performance issue.

55. 3

    DocumentDB is the best solution for storing JSON documents that can scale with load.

56. 3

    You do not need to use the data extraction agent for Oracle to PostgreSQL assessment.

    DMS data validation will not give you a migration report.

    Creating a database assessment report with SCT is the correct answer.

    A DMS pre-migration report will not give you the required information for migration.

57. 3

    DynamoDB Streams will not help increase the capacity of the table.

    Purchasing reserved capacity will optimize cost but it will not improve the performance.

    Increasing the write capacity of the table will improve performance.

    Adding a GSI will not help with the performance.

58. 1

    Creating a snapshot, encrypting a copy of it, and then creating a database from that snapshot is the best way to encrypt an RDS database.

    You cannot modify an instance to encrypt it without having to create a new database or use snapshots.

    You cannot restore a non-encrypted snapshot to an encrypted database.

    A read replica must match the primary instance encryption status, so you cannot do this.

59. 2 and 3

    Enhanced Monitoring will not help here.

    High I/O can cause performance issues including high CPU, as the database will be forced to wait for the disks to respond.

    RDS Performance Insights can be used to identify the SQL commands causing the slow performance.

    CloudTrail will not show performance data or database queries.

60. 4

    Amazon EMR is a complex solution that is not optimal.

    AWS DMS is a complex solution that is not optimal.

    You cannot update the partition key on an existing DynamoDB table.

    You cannot modify a partition key on a DynamoDB table, so your only option is to create a new table and migrate the data across.

Index

A

B

C

D

E

G

H

I

J

K

L

M

N

O

P

S

T

U

V

W

Packt.com

Subscribe to our online digital library for full access to over 7,000 books and videos, as well as industry leading tools to help you plan your personal development and advance your career. For more information, please visit our website.

Why subscribe?

- Spend less time learning and more time coding with practical eBooks and Videos from over 4,000 industry professionals
- Improve your learning with Skill Plans built especially for you
- Get a free eBook or video every month
- Fully searchable for easy access to vital information
- Copy and paste, print, and bookmark content

Did you know that Packt offers eBook versions of every book published, with PDF and ePub files available? You can upgrade to the eBook version at packt.com and as a print book customer, you are entitled to a discount on the eBook copy. Get in touch with us at customercare@packtpub.com for more details.

At www.packt.com, you can also read a collection of free technical articles, sign up for a range of free newsletters, and receive exclusive discounts and offers on Packt books and eBooks.

Other Books You May Enjoy

If you enjoyed this book, you may be interested in these other books by Packt:

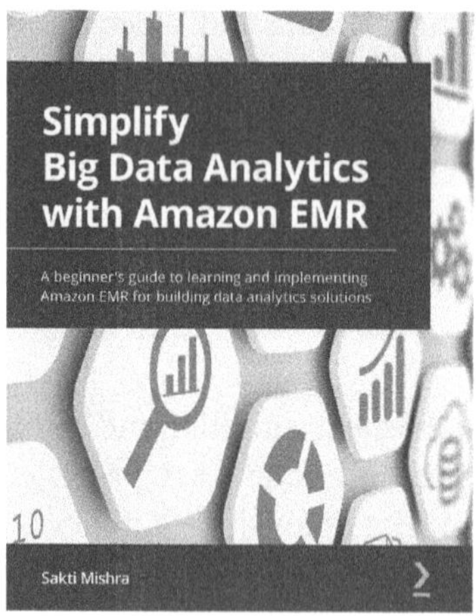

Simplify Big Data Analytics with Amazon EMR

Sakti Mishra

ISBN: 978-1-80107-107-9

- Explore Amazon EMR features, architecture, Hadoop interfaces, and EMR Studio
- Configure, deploy, and orchestrate Hadoop or Spark jobs in production
- Implement the security, data governance, and monitoring capabilities of EMR
- Build applications for batch and real-time streaming data analytics solutions
- Perform interactive development with a persistent EMR cluster and Notebook
- Orchestrate an EMR Spark job using AWS Step Functions and Apache Airflow

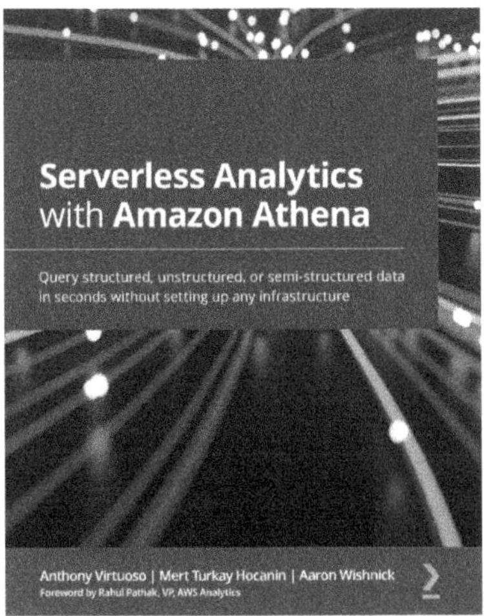

Serverless Analytics with Amazon Athena

Anthony Virtuoso, Mert Turkay Hocanin, Aaron Wishnick

ISBN: 978-1-80056-234-9

- Secure and manage the cost of querying your data
- Use Athena ML and User Defined Functions (UDFs) to add advanced features to your reports
- Write your own Athena Connector to integrate with a custom data source
- Discover your datasets on S3 using AWS Glue Crawlers
- Integrate Amazon Athena into your applications
- Setup Identity and Access Management (IAM) policies to limit access to tables and databases in Glue Data Catalog
- Add an Amazon SageMaker Notebook to your Athena queries
- Get to grips with using Athena for ETL pipelines

Packt is searching for authors like you

If you're interested in becoming an author for Packt, please visit `authors.packtpub.com` and apply today. We have worked with thousands of developers and tech professionals, just like you, to help them share their insight with the global tech community. You can make a general application, apply for a specific hot topic that we are recruiting an author for, or submit your own idea.

Share Your Thoughts

Now you've finished *AWS Certified Database - Specialty (DBS-C01) Certification Guide*, we'd love to hear your thoughts! Scan the QR code below to go straight to the Amazon review page for this book and share your feedback or leave a review on the site that you purchased it from.

`https://packt.link/r/1-803-24310-4`

Your review is important to us and the tech community and will help us make sure we're delivering excellent quality content.

Milton Keynes UK
Ingram Content Group UK Ltd.
UKHW032143070124
435550UK00007B/483